The Palgrave Macmillan Animal Ethics Series

In recent years, there has been a growing interest in the ethics of our treatment of animals. Philosophers have led the way, and now a range of other scholars have followed from historians to social scientists. From being a marginal issue, animals have become an emerging issue in ethics and in multidisciplinary inquiry. This series will explore the challenges that Animal Ethics poses, both conceptually and practically, to traditional understandings of human-animal relations. Specifically, the Series will:

- provide a range of key introductory and advanced texts that map out ethical positions on animals;
- publish pioneering work written by new, as well as accomplished, scholars;
- produce texts from a variety of disciplines that are multidisciplinary in character or have multidisciplinary relevance.

For further information or to submit a proposal for consideration, please contact Amy Invernizzi, amy.invernizzi@palgrave-usa.com.

Kimberly C. Moore

The Case for the Legal Protection of Animals

Humanity's Shared Destiny with the Animal Kingdom

palgrave
macmillan

Kimberly C. Moore
Pillsbury Winthrop Shaw Pittman LLP
Washington, DC, USA

ISSN 2634-6672 ISSN 2634-6680 (electronic)
The Palgrave Macmillan Animal Ethics Series
ISBN 978-3-031-46064-7 ISBN 978-3-031-46065-4 (eBook)
https://doi.org/10.1007/978-3-031-46065-4

Credit line: Buena Vista Images/Getty Images

This Palgrave Macmillan imprint is published by the registered company Springer Nature Switzerland AG.
The registered company address is: Gewerbestrasse 11, 6330 Cham, Switzerland

Paper in this product is recyclable.

Prologue

Legal systems have historically viewed animals through an anthropocentric lens, classifying animals as mere "property." Unlike people, who possess certain legal rights and protections, animals benefit from few (if any) legal rights or protections. It is against this backdrop that the case for legal protection of animals will be made.

Washington, DC — Kimberly C. Moore

Series Editors' Preface

This is a new book series for a new field of inquiry: Animal Ethics.

In recent years, there has been a growing interest in the ethics of our treatment of animals. Philosophers have led the way; and now a range of other scholars have followed, from historians to social scientists. From being a marginal issue, animals have become an emerging issue in ethics and in multidisciplinary inquiry.

In addition, a rethink of the status of animals has been fueled by a range of scientific investigations which have revealed the complexity of animal sentiency, cognition, and awareness. The ethical implications of this new knowledge have yet to be properly evaluated, but it is becoming clear that the old view that animals are mere things, tools, machines, or commodities cannot be sustained ethically.

But it is not only philosophy and science that are putting animals on the agenda. Increasingly, in Europe and in the United States, animals are becoming a political issue as political parties vie for the "green" and "animal" vote. In turn, political scientists are beginning to look again at the history of political thought in relation to animals, and historians are beginning to revisit the political history of animal protection.

As animals grow as an issue of importance, so there have been more collaborative academic ventures leading to conference volumes, special journal issues, indeed new academic animal journals as well. Moreover, we have witnessed the growth of academic courses as well as university posts in Animal Ethics, Animal Welfare, Animal Rights, Animal Law, Animals and Philosophy, Human-Animal Studies, Critical Animal Studies, Animals and Society, Animals in Literature, Animals and Religion—tangible signs that a new academic discipline is emerging.

"Animal Ethics" is the new term for the academic exploration of the moral status of the non-human—an exploration that explicitly involves a focus on what we owe animals morally, and which also helps us to understand the influences—social, legal, cultural, religious, and political—that legitimate animal abuse. This series explores the challenges that Animal Ethics poses, both conceptually and practically, to traditional understandings of human–animal relations.

The series is needed for three reasons: (i) to provide the texts that will service the new university courses on animals; (ii) to support the increasing number of students studying and doing academic research in animal related fields, and (iii) to fill a gap: there is currently no book series that is a focus for multidisciplinary research in the field.

Specifically, the series will

- provide a range of key introductory and advanced texts that map out ethical positions on animals
- publish pioneering work written by new, as well as accomplished scholars, and
- produce texts from a variety of disciplines that are multidisciplinary in character or have multidisciplinary relevance.

The new Palgrave Macmillan Series on Animal Ethics is the result of a unique partnership between Palgrave Macmillan and the Ferrater Mora Oxford Centre for Animal Ethics. The series is an integral part of the mission of the Centre to put animals on the intellectual agenda by facilitating academic research and publication. The series is also a natural complement to one of the Centre's other major projects, the *Journal of Animal Ethics*. The Centre is an independent "think tank" for the advancement of progressive thought about animals, and is the first Centre of its kind in the world. It aims to demonstrate rigorous intellectual enquiry and the highest standards of scholarship. It strives to be a world-class center of academic excellence in its field.

We invite academics to visit the Centre's website www.oxfordanimalethics.com and to contact us with new book proposals for the series.

Andrew Linzey
Clair Linzey

Acknowledgments

I would like to express my deepest gratitude to Palgrave Macmillan for their invaluable support and belief in this project. Their expertise and dedication to academic excellence has been instrumental in the development of this book. I would also like to acknowledge Revd. Professor Andrew Linsey, Director of the Oxford Centre for Animal Ethics, and Dr. Clair Linsey, Deputy Director of the Oxford Centre for Animal Ethics, whose unwavering dedication to the ethical treatment of animals inspired me to write this book. I would like to thank my colleague Craig A. de Ridder for his invaluable feedback on this work and for his support for the project. I have dedicated this book to animal law specialists who are making the world a more compassionate place for animals one law at a time.

Disclaimer

Some statements in this book rely, in part, on news accounts, press statements, and statements from governments and governmental officials, the accuracy of which I have assumed is correct for purposes of this book. Laws are also subject to change without notice.

Praise for *The Case for the Legal Protection of Animals*

"Kimberly Moore powerfully and persuasively makes the case for the legal protection of animals demonstrating the undeniable link between animal welfare, public health and the environment. A compelling read!"

—Joan Schaffner, Faculty Co-director, Animal Legal Education Initiative, The George Washington University Law School

"*The Case for the Legal Protection of Animals* is a thoroughly researched account of how we treat animals today and why far-reaching reforms are urgently needed, for the sake of the animals, the environment, and humans as well. The book is an excellent guide to the emerging field of animal law and to the challenges it faces."

—Peter Singer, author of *Animal Liberation* and *Animal Liberation Now*

"Nonhuman animals (animals) need all the help they can get. The Anthropocene, often referred to as 'the age of humanity,' has evolved into 'the rage of inhumanity,' and despite the fact that we now know far more about animal sentience and emotions than in the past, countless individuals are treated as if they are merely unfeeling objects and 'property' to be 'owned' rather than as deeply feeling beings. Why, for example, does the Federal Animal Welfare Act inanely exclude rats, mice, and other animals from its definition of 'animals,' and why can more industrially farmed and brutalized pigs be legally killed per hour now when compared to years past? In her clearly written and jargon-free book, Kimberly Moore makes a strong case for granting legal rights to animals for a wide variety of reasons, including our moral obligation to respect their highly evolved emotional lives. The book unequivocally establishes that what works for 'them'—to be treated with respect, dignity, kindness, and compassion – is also good for our own well-being, a win-win for all."

—Marc Bekoff, author of *The Animals' Agenda: Freedom, Compassion, and Coexistence in the Human Age* and *The Emotional Lives of Animals: A Leading Scientist Explores Animal Joy, Sorrow, and Empathy—and Why They Matter*

"As this book goes to print, activists are being incarcerated for rescuing animals from inhumane conditions and ag gag laws are being defended in court and introduced in national legislatures. At the same time animal abuse on factory farms, zoos and research facilities goes unpunished. Moore's timely book provides the social and legal context to understand and appreciate the myriad ways that the law makes animal suffering invisible, while also providing reasons for optimism and concrete proposals for legal reform that would make a tangible difference, such as a 'general legal right to rescue animals in distress.' The book is a rare blend of research, passion, and readability, and it is a call to action."

—Justin Marceau, Director of the Animal Law Program at the University of Denver and author of *Beyond Cages*

Contents

About the Author

Kimberly Moore is a senior attorney at Pillsbury Winthrop Shaw Pittman LLP in Washington, D.C., where she specializes in federal tax law and private equity investments. She is an expert on animal law and has represented and advised animal protection organizations on formation and operational matters. She has also worked on state legislation to ban the manufacture and sale of animal fur. Kimberly is a Fellow at the Oxford Centre for Animal Ethics in Oxford, England.

CHAPTER 1

Introduction

"The day may come when the non-human part of the animal creation will acquire the rights that never could have been withheld from them except by the hand of tyranny." (Bentham, Jeremy (1748–1832), An Introduction to the Principles of Morals and Legislation *(1789), 282-83n.)*
—Jeremy Bentham

We are living in an extraordinary legal era. The past three decades have witnessed a global movement for the protection and granting of rights to animals, and the past two decades have brought unprecedented legal reforms around the world. At the same time, humanity continues to inflict indescribable suffering and misery on animals. Most people agree that animals deserve some measure of protection under the law. They may disagree as to the extent of that protection, but very few believe that animals merit no legal protection whatsoever.[1] A Gallup poll revealed that nearly a third of Americans think that animals should be afforded the *same* rights

[1] According to the 2015 Gallup Poll, only 3% of Americans believed that animals should be afforded little protection from exploitation and harm because "they are just animals." *See*, Riffkin, Rebecca, "In U.S., More Say Animals Should Have Same Rights as People," *Gallup, Social & Policy Issues*, May 18, 2015.

K. C. Moore, *The Case for the Legal Protection of Animals*, The Palgrave Macmillan Animal Ethics Series,
https://doi.org/10.1007/978-3-031-46065-4_1

as people.[2] Society's values and attitudes are clearly changing when it comes to the treatment of animals.

This fundamental question of how animals should be treated has been raised throughout history. In 1789, English philosopher Jeremy Bentham (1748–1832) questioned why legal protection should be denied to any sensitive being.[3] An indisputable body of scientific evidence tells us today that animals are sentient beings, yet laws in the United States do not reflect evolving societal values when it comes to the proper treatment of animals. The fundamental purpose of any legal system is to protect the individuals in the society, to safeguard their rights, and to ensure that they are neither abused nor exploited. Sadly, our legal system affords little to no protection to animals. The laws that do exist set minimal standards for behavior and fall far below what many in society deem to be acceptable. The consequences for animals are profound. Animals are at the mercy of factory farms, fur farms, canned hunts, trophy hunters, trappers, live export, research labs, the entertainment industry, the fashion industry, and so many other industries that treat them with cruelty, callousness, and disregard.

Unfortunately, laws and morality are not always aligned. Federal and state laws are often shaped by politics and special interests, and too often, laws protect the most powerful in society at the expense of everyone else. In fact, at the federal level, there is very little, if any, legal protection for animals.[4] A legal system that affords little to no protection to the most vulnerable in society is fundamentally flawed.

Court systems in the United States also provide far too little legal protection for animals. Our common law legal system classifies animals as "property," but this classification is not appropriate in light of scientific advances and evolving standards and judges find it challenging. In one

[2] Ibid.

[3] Bentham, 282-83n.

[4] The Humane Methods of Livestock Slaughter Act of 1958, 7 U.S.C. 1901, *et seq.*, as amended by the Humane Methods of Slaughter Act of 1978, is one of just a few laws at the federal level. The law requires that animals be rendered insensible to pain (i.e., stunned into unconsciousness) before being slaughtered. The law does not, however, extend protection to chickens, turkeys or other birds in the U.S. despite being the largest number of animals slaughtered.

case, the judge stated that an animal is no different from a child.[5] This property classification allows humans to exploit animals to satisfy any need, want, or desire, even when it is at our detriment. For animals, the world is a chaotic, unpredictable, and brutal place. If laws are meant to reflect the morality and conscience of a society, then laws would change to protect these creatures.

Advances in technology have exposed many forms of animal cruelty, and with the growing awareness of animal suffering, the drumbeats for legal change have grown louder. There is also growing recognition that animals are sentient beings.[6] The private sector, with its finger on the pulse of consumers, is producing more and more non-animal based products. The public is increasingly demanding certain "freedoms" for animals (the "Five Freedoms"), including freedom from hunger and thirst, freedom from discomfort, freedom from pain, injury, or disease, freedom to engage in normal behaviors, and freedom from fear and distress.[7] A more enlightened legal classification would grant animals important rights such as the right to enjoy natural and protected habitats, the right to bodily integrity, and the right to be free.

This evolving view stands in stark contrast to laws that treat all non-human animals as "property." If laws are the embodiment of the moral sentiment of the people, as English jurist Sir William Blackstone (1723–1780) proclaimed,[8] then laws must not discriminate against animals. A change in the legal status of animals will require each of us to examine our relationship with animals, and more and more people are

[5] Hunt, Amber, "St. Clair Shores: Man Gets Jail for Leaving Dog to Die", *Detroit Free Press* (Michigan), July 19, 2007. *But see,* Kelly Thomas James Henderson v. Suzanne Dawn Henderson, *Queen's Bench for Saskatchewan (Family Law Division),* August 31, 2016, for a Canadian judge who refused to treat a family dog as having "familial rights."

[6] On the most basic level, sentience refers to the capacity for sensation or feeling. *See,* Merriam-Webster Dictionary, definition of sentience. For a deeper analysis of why animal suffering matters, *see* Andrew Linzey, *Why Animal Suffering Matters, Philosophy, Theology, and Practical Ethics.* Oxford: Oxford University Press (2009). ISBN: 9780199351848.

[7] The Five Freedoms, codified by the Farm Animal Welfare Council in 1979, have been adopted by many organizations and form the basis for some animal welfare standards in the private sector. For a history of the Five Freedoms, *see,* Elischer, Melissa, "The Five Freedoms: A history lesson in animal care and welfare", *Michigan State University Extension,* September 6, 2019 (updated from an original article written by Tina Conklin).

[8] Sir William Blackstone (1723–1780) was an English jurist and judge of the eighteenth century.

doing just that as we discover that humanity's destiny is tied to how we treat animals.

Informed citizens around the globe are getting involved in the political progress to effect positive change by lobbying public officials, forming political parties,[9] and running for office.[10] In France, 26 animal welfare organizations collaborated to produce a French Manifesto "Animal Politique" dedicated to the welfare of animals in advance of the 2017 presidential election.[11] Record-breaking numbers of activists have marched for the recognition of animal rights in major cities all over the world, including in New York, London, Berlin, Zurich, Prague, France, Tel-Aviv, Taiwan, Madrid, and elsewhere.[12] The result of this activism is that the case for animal legal protection has never been stronger.

The list of countries that have updated or overhauled their animal protection laws (to varying degrees) in recent years continues to grow and includes, inter alia, Australia,[13] Austria,[14] China,[15] Denmark,[16] France,[17] Germany,[18] India,[19] Italy,[20] Luxembourg,[21] Malaysia,[22] Mexico,[23]

[9] The Animal Justice Party in Australia is the country's only political party that is dedicated to the protection of animals. *See*, www.animaljusticeparty.org

[10] Emma Christine Hurst ran for election for the New South Wales Legislative Council in 2019 to represent the Animal Justice Party in Australia.

[11] *See*, "'Animal Politique' French Manifesto Dedicated to the Welfare of Animals," *Eurogroup For Animals Magazine*, January 2017, at 8.

[12] *See*, e.g., Chiorando, Maria, "Record-Breaking 40,000 Activists Attend Official Animal Rights March Globally," *Plant Based News*, September 30, 2019.

[13] *See*, World Animal Protection, "Animal Protection Index", Australia, n.d., at https://api.worldanimalprotection.org/

[14] World Animal Protection, Austria.

[15] World Animal Protection, China.

[16] World Animal Protection, Denmark.

[17] World Animal Protection, France.

[18] World Animal Protection, Germany.

[19] World Animal Protection, India.

[20] World Animal Protection, Italy.

[21] *See generally*, ADW, "Luxembourg adopts new animal welfare act", Luxembourg Times, July 6, 2018.

[22] World Animal Protection, Malaysia.

[23] World Animal Protection, Mexico.

Netherlands,[24] New Zealand,[25] Poland,[26] Spain,[27] Sweden,[28] Switzerland,[29] Turkey,[30] the UAE,[31] and the U.K.[32] Some countries, such as Russia,[33] Thailand[34] and Lebanon[35] have recognized animal welfare in legislation for the first time. In enacting updated animal protection laws, Luxembourg recognized that "[p]eople's attitudes towards animals have substantially changed," requiring a "fundamentally new approach, based on the legal recognition of the dignity of animals."[36] In countries where legal reform has proved challenging, animal welfare is being incorporated into educational curriculums.[37] In 2017, representatives from 180 member countries of the World Organisation for Animal Health (OIE) voted to adopt the first global strategy on animal welfare with international standards, aiming to achieve "[a] world where the welfare of animals is respected, promoted and advanced, in ways that complement the pursuit of animal heath, human well-being, socio-economic development and environmental sustainability."[38]

[24] World Animal Protection, Netherlands.

[25] World Animal Protection, New Zealand.

[26] World Animal Protection, Poland.

[27] World Animal Protection, Spain.

[28] World Animal Protection, Sweden.

[29] Switzerland enacted an Animal Welfare Act in 2005 and the Animal Welfare Ordinance in 2020. *See*, World Animal Protection, Switzerland.

[30] World Animal Protection, Turkey.

[31] *See*, United Arab Emirates Ministry of Climate Change & Environment, "Ministry of Climate Change and Environmental Issues Executive Regulations for Federal Law on Animal Welfare," December 12, 2018, at https://www.moccae.gov.ae/en/media-center/news/11/11/2018/ministry-of-climate-change-and-environment-issues-resolution-on-executive-regulation-of-federal-law-on-animal-care.aspx#page=1

[32] The U.K. was the first country to pass animal protection legislation and it has a long tradition of animal welfare. In recent years, laws have continued to improve conditions for animals. *See*, World Animal Protection, U.K.

[33] World Animal Protection, Russia.

[34] World Animal Protection, Thailand.

[35] "Lebanon gets first animal protection law," *Phys. Org.*, August 29, 2017, at https://phys.org/news/2017-08-lebanon-animal-law.html

[36] Luxembourg Government, "Animal protection in Luxembourg," Introduction, August 27, 2008, at http://gouvernement.lu/en/dossiers/2018/tierschutz.html

[37] *See,* e.g., Richards, Shauna, "A Long Awaited Return to Kenya," *Farmers Helping Farmers,* February 21, 2022.

[38] World Organisation for Animal Health (Founded as OIE), "Adoption of the first WOA global strategy on animal welfare," May 24, 2017. https://www.woah.org/en/what-we-do/animal-health-and-welfare/animal-welfare/development-of-animal-welfare-standards/

As more countries adopt higher standards of animal protection, other nations are following suit and new global precedents and standards are being established. This leads to the emergence of "customary international law," considered by some to be "international common law."[39] Under United States law, customary international laws are recognized as a source of international law.[40] Customary international law results from a general and consistent practice of nations and states adopted by them from a sense of legal obligation.[41] General principles common to the major legal systems, even if not incorporated or reflected in customary international law or international common law, may be invoked as supplementary rules of international law, where appropriate.[42] Some scholars and courts have considered customary international law to have the status of federal common law.[43] While evaluating the strength of that view is beyond the scope of this book, what is clear is that as norms change, industries that exploit animals will find it increasingly difficult to look to custom and past practice to justify their cruel practices. While there has been some encouraging legal reforms at the state level in the United States, this has not occurred at the federal level. In failing to keep pace with changing international standards, the United States risks becoming an outlier when it comes to legal protections and rights for animals. Without being engaged with its global partners on matters that impact animals, the United States could miss out on the opportunity to be a part of the creation of new international customs and norms for the treatment of animals and new "rights" that reflect the dignity and inherent worth of animals.

The purpose of this book is to present the case for meaningful legal protection for animals in the United States. To make this case, we explore laws that have been enacted around the world that are changing the legal

[39] *See*, e.g., Connie de la Vega, "The Right to Equal Education: Merely a Guiding Principle or Customary International Legal Right?" 11 Harv. Blackletter Law Journal, Vol. 11, No. 1, 1994, 8 (1994) ("Customary international law essentially is international common law."). https://ssrn.com/abstract=1149880

[40] A rule of international law is one that has been accepted by such by the international community of states (a) in the form of customary law; (b) by international agreement; or (c) by derivation from general principles common to the major legal systems of the world. *See*, Restatement (3d) of the Foreign Relations Law of the United States, §102(1) (1987).

[41] *Id.*, §102(2).

[42] *Id.*, §102(4).

[43] For a critique of this "modern position," *see* Bradley, Curtis A. and Goldsmith, Jack L., "Customary International Law as Federal Common Law: A Critique of the Modern Position," *Harvard Law Review* 110, no. 4 (1997).

landscape for animals. 'Chapter 2—Animals in Crisis' explains why legal reform is needed, detailing the abuse and exploitation inflicted on the animal kingdom and how legal reforms are developing to prevent this. 'Chapter 3—Media as a Driver of Change' examines how media exposure can raise awareness and lead to change, with stories of individual animals who have commanded worldwide attention. 'Chapter 4—The Link Between Human Rights and Animal Rights' explores how humanity's exploitation of animals has resulted in global threats that impact all life on the planet. In 'Chap. 5—Challenges to Legal Reform', we consider challenges to legal reform and how obstacles are being overcome to create positive legal change for animals. In 'Chap. 6—Animal Law as an Emerging Field' we explore the developing area of animal law and how it intersects with other areas of law to create a more equitable legal system for all. In 'Chap. 7—The Road to Personhood' we examine emerging areas of law that recognize animals as sentient beings. In the final chapter, 'Chap. 8—Concluding Remarks', we bring together concepts from the book to make the case for legal reform for animals in the United States.

One of my colleagues, a nationally recognized legal scholar, once asked me "who are these animals" and "what rights do they want"? This question underscores the reality that few people, even legal scholars, fully understand the extent to which humanity abuses and exploits animals. To achieve legal reform for animals, we must first understand the state of the world for animals.

CHAPTER 2

Animals in Crisis

The question is not, Can they reason?
Nor, can they talk? But can they suffer? (Bentham, 282-83n.)
—Jeremy Bentham

We live in a world where cruelty and violence against animals are normalized and hidden, and the cruelty inflicted by humanity on animals is unmatched by any violence on the planet. Animals are under sustained, brutal assaults by human activity, driven by greed and fueled by ignorance and indifference. There is a growing consensus today that animals are in crisis. Legal reforms show that some segments of the global community are committed to change, as witnessed by the increasing number of laws that are being passed to protect animals. The passage of new laws may not solve all issues. There may be loopholes, unintended consequences, compliance issues, and legal challenges that may require further action. Still, the growing body of laws is building a foundation that promises to bring transformative change for animals. Meaningful legal reform for animals first requires that we understand how our actions contribute to suffering.

K. C. Moore, *The Case for the Legal Protection of Animals*, The Palgrave Macmillan Animal Ethics Series,
https://doi.org/10.1007/978-3-031-46065-4_2

Animals in Entertainment

For our "entertainment", animals are forced to, amongst other things: race (e.g., horse racing; greyhound racing; pig racing; dog-sled racing; pigeon racing); run (e.g., rodeos; bull-running); fight each other (e.g., dogfighting; water buffalo fighting; camel wrestling; cockfighting; goose fighting; bulbul fights; finch fighting; duck fighting); fight with humans (e.g., kangaroo boxing; bear wrestling; pig wrestling; alligator wrestling); fight with other species (e.g., hog dog rodeos; badger-baiting); fight for their lives (e.g., bullfighting); and run or fly for their lives (e.g., wildlife killing contests; canned hunts; hare coursing; turkey and pigeon shoots). Animals are forced to carry people (e.g., horse carriages; elephant rides; camel rides; pony rides; elephant polo); drag rocks (e.g., Basque dragging games); live in barren concrete cages and enclosures (e.g., zoos; aquariums; wildlife parks); perform unnatural tricks (e.g., circuses; marine parks; carnivals; film and television productions); and engage in activities that result in injuries or death (e.g., horse diving; turkey drops from planes). Animals are muzzled, whipped, poked, prodded, shocked, beaten, drugged, deprived of food, put on display, and denied every biological need, all for commercial gain and our "entertainment." Some activities and events end in the immediate death of the animal, while others involve long-term cruelty and suffering, but they all have a few things in common—they are degrading, demeaning, and cruel.

The information age has given the public a glimpse into what animals in captivity endure, and with that knowledge, public opinion has shifted against the captivity of animals. We now know that animals held in captivity suffer both physically and mentally. Caged for most hours of the day, animals endure tiny, uncomfortable cages and miserable transportation to entertainment venues. It is estimated that circus animals live a staggering 96% of their lives in either chains or cages.[1] In one Indian court's view, "a zoo, no matter how well equipped, is no less than a concentration camp for living beings" that violates "the natural rights" of animals.[2]

[1] PAWS, "Enjoy the Circus? The Animals Don't.", April 6, 2016, at https://www.lcps.org/cms/lib/VA01000195/Centricity/Domain/16265/Enjoy%20the%20Circus_%20The%20Animals%20Dont%20PAWS.pdf

[2] Islamabad Wildlife Management Board Versus Metropolitan Corporation Islamabad, etc., In the Islamabad High Court, Islamabad (Judicial Dept.), W.P. No. 1155/2019, C.M. No. 3976/2020, December 14, 2020.

Perhaps more troubling than the physical abuse is the torment of isolation that animals in entertainment endure. Lolita, an orca once held at the Miami Seaquarium, lived in isolation, "in total absence of stimuli," in a barren concrete tank from 1980 until her death in 2023.[3] Despite the mountain of evidence presented at a trial that the captivity of Lolita was detrimental to both her physical and psychological well-being,[4] as well as evidence of violation of the federal Endangered Species Act, the 11th U.S. Court of Appeals ruled in 2018 that there was no "threat of serious harm" to Lolita.[5] The court did clarify that it did not intend to tie "the hands of future courts in cases involving younger, healthier animals who may be faced with different circumstances,"[6] but the idea that small barren tanks are not a violation of the Animal Welfare Act or the Endangered Species Act troubled many.[7] That animals like Lolita suffer in captivity is indisputable. Hugo, another killer whale captured from the Puget Sound and held in captivity at the Miami Seaquarium, was so traumatized in captivity that he died in 1980 after repeatedly ramming into the side of the tank.[8]

Animal racing involves tremendous suffering. Horse racing is steeped with cruelty, including the use of performance enhancing drugs, whips, and shock devices.[9] With every race, horses face the risk of a catastrophic injury or death. Horses are known to bleed from their lungs due to exer-

[3] Expert Report by Maddalena Bearzi, PhD, Ocean Conservation Society, President. Case 1:15-cv-22,692-UU, Document 117, Entered on FLSD Docket 03/11/2016, p. 28–30 of 97.

[4] *Id.* at 52. The expert explains that killer whales are "one of the most social mammals on earth" and that Lolita's captivity is "profoundly detrimental from a biological, ecological and psychological perspective."

[5] People For The Ethical Treatment of Animals, Inc., Animal Legal Defense Fund, Howard Garrett, Orca Network vs Miami Seaquarium, Festival Fun Parks, LLC, 879 F.3d 1142 (11th Cir. 2018); *see also*, Stempel, Jonathan, "Captive orca Lolita can stay at Miami aquarium: U.S. appeals court", *Reuters*, January 12, 2018.

[6] Ibid.

[7] *See generally*, Dunagan, Christopher, "Endangered Species Act can't help Lolita, judge says in legal ruling", *Kitsap Sun*, June 8, 2016; "Appeals court rules against groups that want to free orca", *Associated Press*, June 22, 2015.

[8] Sands, Cara, "One Dolphin's Story – Hugo," *Dolphin Project*, Blog, n.d., at http://www.dolphinproject.com/blog/one-dolphins-story-hugo/

[9] *See*, e.g., Drape, Joe, "Seamy Side of a Sport: Prodding Horses with Shocks," *New York Times*, March 27, 2014; *see also*, McKeever, Amy, "It's Triple Crown season: Here's what to know about horse doping", *National Geographic*, May 14, 2021.

cise-induced pulmonary hemorrhage, a direct result of racing. When horses are no longer profitable, they join thousands of other horses every year who are shipped to Mexico and Canada for slaughter.[10] Greyhound dogs in racing face similar risks of catastrophic injury or death and suffer from physical abuse, drugs, parasitic infestations, starvation, and lack of veterinary care.[11] Horses that pull carriages face their own miseries: long workdays in heavy traffic; loud noise and pollution; hard pavements; exposure to a wide range of temperatures and humidity; and lack of access to pastures.[12]

In the past, circuses have brought people into dangerous proximity with wild animals, with fatal consequences to animals, circus workers, and members of the public.[13] Circuses have permitted children to come in contact with wild animals, with tragic consequences.[14] The public is less familiar with the cruelty associated with zoo captivity.

Zoos are notoriously deadly for animals. The slogan "captivity kills" has become a public battle cry because animals suffer neglect, sustain injuries, and die while in captivity.[15] Habitats are compromised and zoo animals can disappear.[16] Animals deemed to be "surplus" are euthanized.[17] During financial crises, zoos slaughter animals to feed other zoo animals.[18] Dr. Marc Bekoff, former professor of Ecology and Evolutionary Biology at

[10] Peter, Josh, "Horses go from racetracks to slaughterhouses: 'It's just a job to me'", *USA Today*, November 1, 2019.

[11] *See*, ASPCA, "Greyhound Racing", n.d., at https://www.aspca.org/improving-laws-animals/public-policy/greyhound-racing

[12] *See*, 'Horse-Drawn Carriages", *Animal Welfare Institute*, n.d., at https://awionline.org/content/urban-carriage-horses-out-step-responsible-horse-welfare

[13] For specific incidents that have led to injuries and deaths by circus animals, *see*, "Federal Circus Bill, Public Health & Safety", *Animal Defenders International*, n.d., at https://www.federalcircusbill.org/briefings/public-health-safety/

[14] Wang, Amy B., "Startled camel tears through Pittsburgh circus, injuring 6 children", *Washington Post*, September 17, 2018.

[15] *See*, e.g., Jouvenal, Justin, "Mauling, escapes and abuse: 6 small zoos, 80 sick or dead animals", *Washington Post*. September 18, 2015.

[16] *See*, e.g., Babineau, Andi and Wolfe, Elizabeth, "Dallas Zoo believes 2 of its monkeys were stolen after their habitat was 'intentionally compromised.' It follows a strong of suspicious activity," *CNN*, January 31, 2023.

[17] Bekoff, Marc, "Zoothanasia: the cruel practice of killing healthy zoo animals", *Salon*, February 3, 2018.

[18] In 2020, a German zoo announced its contingency plan to slaughter zoo animals to feed other zoo animals as a result of financial strain caused by the COVID-19 pandemic. *See*, e.g., Schuetze, Christopher, "Zoo May Feed Animals to Animals as Funds Dry Up in Pandemic," *New York Times*, April 15, 2020.

the University of Colorado, Boulder, notes that healthy but "surplus" animals are often killed because they are no longer useful to the zoo.[19] The Copenhagen Zoo sparked international outcry when it announced that it would euthanize Marius, a young, healthy giraffe deemed genetically unsuitable for breeding, and feed his body to the zoo's lions.[20] Dr. Bekoff objects to the use of the term "euthanasia," intended to sanitize the killing for the public, preferring the term "zoothanasia."[21] Zoo animals are often abandoned and left to starve in war-torn areas like Yemen[22] and in countries facing economic hardship like Lebanon.[23] Mass euthanasia of animals also occurs when habitats are destroyed.[24] In countries that face food shortages, zoo animals are stolen to be eaten as food, as was the case in Venezuela[25] and more recently in war-torn Ukraine.[26] At a Mexican zoo, the director was accused of cooking pygmy goals for a New Year's dinner.[27] Organizations are sometimes able to rescue a small number of captive animals from zoos. In 2017, abandoned and starving tigers, bears, lions, and hyenas were rescued from a zoo in Aleppo, Syria,[28] but most abandoned animals perish.

[19] Bekoff, Zoothanasia.

[20] The Danish zoo claimed that the animal was killed due to European laws on inbreeding. *See*, Erikson, Lars, "Copenhagen zoo sparks outrage by killing healthy giraffe named Marius," *Guardian*, February 9, 2014; *see also*, Naik, Bharati and Gumuchian, Marie-Louise, "Danish zoo kills healthy giraffe, feeds body to lions," *CNN*, February 10, 2014.

[21] Bekoff, Marc, "'Zoothanasia' is Not Euthanasia: Words Matter", *Psychology Today*, August 9, 2012.

[22] Browning, Noah, "Zoo animals starve in Yemen city shattered by war," *Reuters*, February 25, 2016.

[23] Abdallah, Issam, "Animals starve in Lebanon's zoos as economy crumbles," *Reuters*, June 29, 2021.

[24] Mayer, Chloe, "Ukraine Zoo to Euthanize All Animals After Russia Destroys Enclosures," *Newsweek*, April 5, 2022.

[25] Danieri, Lenin and Urrutia, Isaac, "Police believe thieves steal Venezuela zoo animals to eat them," *Reuters*, August 16, 2017.

[26] Husselbee, Rebecca, "Vlad's Sick Besieged Russian troops 'eat zoo animals including a bison, a kangaroo & ostriches to stay alive in Ukraine frontline'", *The U.S. Sun*, November 4, 2022.

[27] Suarez, Karol and Humayun, Hira, "Former zoo director accused of serving pygmy goats for dinner in Mexico," *CNN*, February 2, 2023.

[28] Specia, Megan, "Animals, Abandoned and Starving, are Evacuated from Zoo in Syria", *New York Times*, July 27, 2017.

Zoos are dangerous places for people, but they are especially dangerous for children. In 2016, Harambe, a critically endangered western lowland gorilla at the Cincinnati Zoo, was shot and killed when a toddler was able to enter the zoo's enclosure.[29] The toddler was safely rescued, but another toddler was mauled to death at the Pittsburgh Zoo in 2012 when he fell into the enclosure for African painted dogs from an observation deck.[30] In 2014, another young child survived a fall into the jaguar exhibit at an Arkansas zoo.[31] Tragedy also struck the San Francisco Zoo in 2007 when Tatiana, a critically endangered Siberian tiger, was shot and killed after escaping from her enclosure and attacking a group of men who had been taunting the tiger.[32] Two polar bears at the Prospect Park Zoo in Brooklyn and a child were also killed in 1987 when the child climbed into the polar bear exhibit.[33] Despite the public awareness triggered by these tragedies, zoos remain dangerous places. In 2021, Eko, a rare Malaysian tiger at the Naples Zoo in Florida, was shot and killed after it latched onto the arm of a cleaning crew member who had entered an unauthorized area to pet or feed the tiger. [34] Animals who escape from zoos suffer similar fates.[35]

As far back as 1892 and as recently as 2021, captive animals have been escaping from zoos,[36] often with deadly consequences. Tyke, a female African bush elephant, was captured in Mozambique in 1973 when she was a baby.[37] Elephants separated from their social group cry, scream,

[29] Brulliard, Karin, "What Harambe's death means for a critically endangered species of gorilla," *Washington Post*, June 2, 2016.

[30] Kearney, Laila, "Pittsburgh Zoo, parents settle over toddler's mauling death," *Reuters*, June 2, 2014.

[31] Ansari, Azadeh and Berlinger, Joshua, "Child who fell into jaguar exhibit at Arkansas Zoo is in stable condition", *CNN*, October 12, 2014.

[32] Derbeken, Jaxon, "Police: Zoo survivor told of standing on railing and yelling at tiger", *San Francisco Chronicle*, January 18, 2008. One man died from his injuries.

[33] Barron, James, "Polar Bear Kills a Child at Prospect Park Zoo", *New York Times*, May 20, 1987.

[34] Naples Zoo statement on killing of Ego, n.d., at https://www.napleszoo.org/eko

[35] *See*, e.g., Kelly, John, "Great escapes: Remembering other zoo animals that have made a run for it", *Washington Post*, September 19, 2021; *see also*, Mohamed, Edna, "Two bears shot at Whipsnade Zoo after escaping from enclosure", *Guardian*, May 21, 2021; *see also*, "Two tigers show dead after killing zookeeper at Central China's Henan", *Global Times*, May 25, 2021.

[36] Kelly, John, "Great escapes: Remembering other zoo animals that have made a run for it", *Washington Post*, September 19, 2021.

[37] Margaritoff, Marco, "The Tragic Story of Tyke, The 'Elephant Outlaw' Who Was Killed by Police", *ATI*, May 4, 2021.

grieve, and can suffer "gripping fear", "broken-heart syndrome" and "sudden-death syndrome."[38] This becomes more heartbreaking when we understand that her natural instinct as a baby was to trust humans.[39]

Tyke was sent to the United States to perform in circuses, the last one of which was Circus International of Honolulu, Hawaii. Based on U.S. Department of Agriculture (USDA) and Canadian law enforcement documentation, Tyke was physically and mentally abused.[40] According to the documentation, "[t]he elephant handler was observed beating the single-tusk African elephant in public to the point [where] the elephant was screaming and bending down on three legs to avoid being hit. When the handler walked by [Tyke] after this, the elephant screamed and veered away, demonstrating fear from his presence."[41] Since that time, bull hooks have been banned in several countries and jurisdictions in the United States because of the intense pain that they inflict on an elephant's delicate skin, but Tyke lacked legal protection to protect her from the beatings, captivity, and exploitation.[42] In Mozambique, Tyke would have enjoyed long walks, exploration, and complex social relationships with other elephants. As a captive of a circus, she was isolated from her family, bound by chains for 22 hours a day, and routinely beaten during trainings.[43]

Tyke was unquestionably a traumatized animal, and on August 20, 1994, that trauma was unleashed when she trampled on her groomer and killed her trainer. Tyke charged out of the arena, and for 30 minutes, she was chased by Honolulu law enforcement. Perhaps one of the most haunting images of an abused, captive animal ever taken was the photograph showing the sheer terror and disbelief in Tyke's eyes as she was repeatedly shot a total of 87 times. Tyke eventually collapsed from the onslaught of gunshots and died.[44] It was reported that she had tear stains at her death, not surprising given that elephants are capable of deep feelings and

[38] Masson J. Moussaieff, and Susan McCarthy, *When Elephants Weep, The Emotional Lives of Animals*. New York, Delacorte Press, 1995, at 52.

[39] Id. at 59–60.

[40] PETA, "Factsheet: Hawthorne Corporation (John Cuneo)", n.d., at https://www.peta.org/wp-content/uploads/2021/06/Hawthorn-Corporation-pdf.pdf

[41] PETA, Factsheet: Hawthorne.

[42] For more on Tyke's life, *see*, *Tyke Elephant Outlaw*, a 2015 documentary co-directed and co-produced by Susan Lambert and Stefan Moore.

[43] Margaritoff, Tragic Story of Tyke.

[44] Vorsino, Mary "Steve Hirano obituary", *Honolulu Star-Bulletin*, December 21, 2003.

complex thoughts.[45] This tragic killing deeply impacted the community in Hawaii and no elephants have performed in Honolulu since. Tyke's story was a pivotal moment in the history of animal rights, when the cruelty and suffering inflicted on circus animals was exposed.

In 2013, the documentary film "Blackfish"[46] told the story of Tilikum, an orca captured from the wild in 1983 at the age of two off the coast of Iceland and forced to perform in captivity. During his captivity, Tilikum killed three people, including trainer Dawn Brancheau in February 2010 at SeaWorld Orlando, thought to be the result of the confinement of the emotionally tormented animal in a small barren tank. As Marine neurologist, Dr. Lori Marino, explained, "All whales in captivity have a bad life. They're all emotionally destroyed. They're all psychologically traumatized. So they are ticking time bombs."[47] In the aftermath of the release of Blackfish, SeaWorld faced severe financial losses, with its stock dropping 50%[48] and its second-quarter income in 2015 plunging 84%.[49] Legislative action was spurred in New York and California, and an amendment to the Agricultural Appropriations Act was passed requiring the USDA to update its regulations under the Animal Welfare Act of 1966 with respect to captivity of marine mammals. SeaWorld criticized the film, calling it inaccurate and misleading, but the company later paid more than $5 million for misleading its investors about the impact of Blackfish.[50]

Emma Marris, an environmental writer, notes that zoos have attempted to portray themselves as critical to conservation, but even zoos that are accredited by the Association of Zoos and Aquariums spend relatively little

[45] Moussaieff and McCarthy, *When Elephants Weep,* at 107–108; *see also*, "Echo: An Elephant to Remember (S29 Ep1), Elephant Emotions", *PBS*, October 11, 2010.

[46] Blackfish (2013), Magnolia Pictures, directed and produced by Gabriela Cowperthwaite.

[47] Blackfish, 1:14, cited in Waller, Randall L. and Iluzada, Christina L., "Blackfish and SeaWorld: A Case Study in the Framing of a Crisis", *International Journal of Business Communication*, 57(2), 2020, at 227–243. https://doi.org/10.1177/2329488419884139

[48] Stock, Kyle, "SeaWorld's Slump Raises a Question: Is Shamu Too Sad, or Too Expensive?", *Bloomberg Business Week*, August 29, 2013; *see also*, Kosman, Josh, "SeaWorld stock sinks 50% in 2014", *New York Post,* November 16, 2014.

[49] Rhodan, Maya, "Seaworld's Profits Drop 84% After Blackfish Documentary", *Time*, August 6, 2015.

[50] Gibson, Kate, "SeaWorld, former CEO to pay $5 million fine to settle SEC fraud charge", *U.S. Securities and Exchange Commission,* September 18, 2018.

on conservation efforts.[51] Marris acknowledges that while some modern zoos provide good care for animals, many animals exhibit stress in captivity, such as pacing back and forth and other compulsive behaviors, self-biting, mutilation, infanticide and extreme aggressiveness, so much so that many zoos use pharmaceutical drugs, including Prozac, Haldol, and Valium, to help animals deal with life in captivity.[52]

We now know that animals held in captivity and forced to perform suffer in ways no different from Tyke or Tilikum. In a report commissioned by the Welsh Government, 658 experts and organizations around the world were contacted for their opinions on the welfare of wild animals in traveling circuses and mobile zoos. The report concluded that conservation efforts by traveling circuses and mobile zoos are "at best likely to be marginal."[53] The experts agreed that there were welfare concerns, including inadequate space, stressful noise, the use of force for training, isolation of social species of animals, maladaptive behaviors, and species inappropriate food.[54] For these reasons, the use of wild animals for public entertainment is no longer considered to be ethically acceptable by many in the global community.

Many public authorities, animal behavior experts, and veterinarians worldwide agree that the use of wild animals for entertainment presents a serious public safety concern[55] and have acknowledged that the welfare of animals will always be compromised in circuses.[56] In 2015, 28 scientists with expertise in wildlife biology, ecology, and ethology agreed that there are five primary welfare concerns with using wild animals in circuses, including limited space availability, maternal separation, restricted social

[51] Marris, Emma, "Modern Zoos Are Not Worth the Moral Cost", *New York Times*, June 11, 2021. Marris notes that zoos accredited by the Association of Zoos and Aquariums spend approximately $231 million annually on conservation efforts, compared to the $4.9 billion they spent on operations and construction in 2018.

[52] Ibid.

[53] *See*, Jo Dorning, Stephen Harris, and Heather Pickett, *The welfare of wild animals in traveling circuses*, April 2016, at 42. https://doi.org/10.13140/RG.2.1.2404.2483

[54] *Id.* at 43–45.

[55] *See*, "FVE position on the use of animals in traveling circuses", FVE/013/pos/007, Federation of Veterinarians of Europe, adopted June 6, 2015, at https://fve.org/cms/wp-content/uploads/FVE-position-on-the-travelling-circuses_adopted.pdf

[56] *See*, Eurogroup for Animals, *Wild Animals in EU Circuses, Problems, Risks and Solutions* (updated edition), March 2021, at 7, at https://www.eurogroupforanimals.org/files/eurogroupforanimals/2021-08/E4A-Circus_Report-09-08-2021.pdf

interactions, frequent traveling, and training and performance.[57] Over 100 Italian psychologists have also declared that the use of wild animals in circuses lacks any educational benefit and can actually have an adverse effect on the public's perception of wild animals, especially for children who see animals deprived of their freedom, confined in unnatural conditions, and forced to perform unnatural behaviors.[58] Scientists believe that such experience can hinder a child's development of empathy, promote a lack of respect for living beings, and "may solicit an incongruous response—that is, amusement and joy—to punishment, discomfort and injustice."[59] The Committee of Psychology of the Polish Academy of Sciences has also expressed concerns about the "brutal training methods", the "highly distressing" performances, the "constant stress of isolation and confinement in cramped spaces" and lack of socialization, all of which are "particularly cruel and an outrage to the moral standards of today" and can be "detrimental to children's upbringing."[60]

Where there is exploitation, there is abuse and neglect, but amidst the tragedy of captivity, there are seeds of hope. A recent wave of new laws has been passed in a number of countries to protect animals in entertainment venues.

Recent Developments for Animals in Entertainment

The list of countries that have prohibited or limited the use of wild animals in circuses continues to grow and includes Armenia, Austria, Belgium, Bolivia, Bulgaria, Columbia, Costa Rica, Croatia, Czech Republic, Denmark, [61] Ecuador, El Salvador, England, Estonia, France (effective

[57] Eurogroup for Animals, *Wild Animals*, at Annex 2 (Statement on ethological needs and welfare of wild animals in circuses).

[58] *See*, "Psychologists' Statement on the anti-pedagogical value of the abuse of animals in circuses and performances", *Dolphinaria-Free Europe*, n.d., at www.dfe.ngo/psychologists-statement/

[59] Ibid.

[60] Eurogroup for Animals, *Wild Animals*, at Annex 4 (Resolution of the Committee of Psychology of the Polish Academy of Sciences on Endorsing the Activities Aimed at Limiting the Use of Animals for Circus Entertainment).

[61] In 2019 Denmark spent 11 million kroner ($1.6 million) to purchase and retire the last four circus elephants in Denmark so that they could be properly retired. *See*, "Denmark buys country's last remaining circus elephants to let them retire", *PBS News Hour*, September 2, 2019.

2028), Guatemala, Honduras, India, Iran, Ireland, Israel, Italy, Latvia, Lebanon, Lithuania, Luxembourg, North Macedonia, Mexico, Netherlands, Norway, Panama, Paraguay, Peru, Poland, Portugal (effective 2024), Romania, Scotland, Serbia, Singapore, Slovakia, Slovenia, Spain (regional bans), Taiwan and Wales.[62] Some countries, including Bosnia-Herzegovina, Cyprus, Greece, Italy, and Malta, have enacted laws that ban the use of *any* animals in circuses.[63] As more countries ban the use of wild animals in circuses, it forms the foundation of new international norms and standards for nations.

The laws of other countries prohibit the use of *specific* animals in circuses. In Sweden, circuses are prohibited from using certain animals, including elephants, rhinoceroses, hippopotami, seals, apes, predators, sea lions, giraffes, kangaroos, fallow deer, crocodiles, predatory birds, and ostriches. In Finland, the use of elephants, rhinoceroses, hippopotami, seals, apes, predators, crocodiles, predatory birds, ostriches, and wild forms of ruminant or equine animals in circuses is prohibited.[64] Hungary prohibits the use of elephants, rhinoceroses, primates, newly captured animals from the wild, and species listed in Appendix I of the CITES Convention.[65] The European Commission is currently discussing a potential ban on wild animals in circuses after 1 million citizens demanded action.[66]

While some countries have not banned wild animal circus acts, various states, cities and local municipalities within them have done so. In Germany, more than 90 towns and cities have enacted a ban on the use of wild animals in circuses and in 2020 a draft ordinance was introduced that would ban elephants, giraffes, rhinos, hippos, primates and big bears from traveling circuses.[67] Recognizing the change in the public's attitudes toward captive animals, Germany's famous Circus Roncalli stopped using

[62] Four Paws Report, "Circuses Without Wild Animals: Bans or restrictions on the keeping of animals in circuses", March 21, 2023, at https://www.four-paws.org/campaigns-topics/topics/wild-animals/worldwide-circus-bans#

[63] Id.

[64] Id.

[65] Id.

[66] "European Parliament shows broad political support to Stop Circus Suffering", *Eurogroup For Animals,* December 16, 2021, at https://www.eurogroupforanimals.org/news/european-parliament-shows-broad-political-support-stop-circus-suffering

[67] Eurogroup for Animals, *Wild Animals*, at 17.

wild animals in 2019 and began using stunning 360-degree, 3D holograms of horses, elephants and other animals in its performances.[68]

In Spain, more than 400 towns and cities have already banned the use of wild animals in circuses. In March 2023, a new national animal welfare law was passed that includes a section dedicated to prohibiting wild animals in circuses.[69] In Brazil, there are bans on the use of animals in circuses in 11 states and in over 20 cities, and in Argentina, more than 20 cities have enacted a ban, including Buenos Aries.[70] In Australia, over 40 local councils have banned wild animal acts, including councils for Hobsons Bay, Surf Coast Shire, Parramata, and Lismore.[71] In Canada, there are local bans in 33 municipal jurisdictions.[72]

In India, the Central Zoo Authority (CZA) revoked its recognition of 21 circuses in 2016 for keeping wild animals and for multiple violations of the Prevention of Cruelty to Animals Act and Performing Animals (Registration) Rules, 2001.[73] The CZA directed all Chief Wildlife Wardens of each state to rehabilitate all elephants rescued from these circuses.[74] In 2020, the last circus in India recognized under the Wildlife Protection Act lost its recognition for using elephants in its performances.[75] Some animals (e.g., dogs and birds) are still being forced to perform in circuses in India and there have been allocations of abuse.[76] One hundred veterinary experts

[68] Katz, Brigit, "A German Circus Uses Stunning Holograms instead of Live Animal Performers", *Smithsonian Magazine*, June 7, 2019.

[69] *See*, Four Paws Report*; see also*, "Stop Circus Suffering", Animal Defenders International, n.d., at https://www.stopcircussuffering.com/circus-bans/; *see also*, "Federal Circus Bill, Worldwide Summary", by n.d., at https://www.federalcircusbill.org/briefings/worldwide-summary/

[70] Id.

[71] Id.

[72] Stop Circus Suffering.

[73] Singh, Vijay, "No more wild animals in circuses, says Central Zoo Authority", *Times of India,* December 7, 2016.

[74] Id.

[75] *See*, Bagchi, Joymala and Kushwaha, Amiya Kumar, "Only Circus Recognized Under Wildlife Act Loses Recognition for Using Elephant Performers", *Business World,* December 22, 2020; *see also*, Subramaniam, G Ganapathy, "Last Indian circus using elephants for shows loses recognition", *The Federal,* December 23, 2020.

[76] *See,* e.g., "Coimbatore police register case against Great Bombay Circus for animal cruelty", *Hindu Bureau,* July 18, 2023.

are urging India's central government to prohibit the use of all animals in circuses.[77]

In 2015, Ringling Brothers agreed to phase out elephant performances by 2018, but that was not enough for its critics. Facing relentless criticism and dwindling audiences, the circus was forced, without legal action, to close down entirely in 2017 after 146 years of operation.[78]

In 2018, New Jersey became the first state in the United States to pass a broad ban on the use of wild and exotic animals in circuses.[79] The law became known as "Nosey's Law," named after a mistreated circus elephant called Nosey.[80] Hawaii,[81] California,[82] and Colorado[83] followed with their own laws to restrict the use of wild animals in circuses. In 2017, Illinois became the first state to ban elephants in any traveling act where the animals are required to perform or entertain.[84] New York followed by enacting the Elephant Protection Act,[85] which prohibits elephants in entertainment acts, including circuses and traveling exhibits.

As of 2022, eight U.S. states, including Rhode Island (2016), Illinois (2017), New York (2017), New Jersey (2018), Hawaii (2018), California (2019), Colorado (2021), and Kentucky (2022), and more than 150 cities and counties in 37 states, have banned or restricted wild animals in circuses.[86] Legislation has also been introduced in Connecticut to ban the

[77] *See*, Pandey, Ashish, "Veterinary experts appeal for prohibition of use of animals in circuses", ***India Today***, January 6, 2020.

[78] Nir, Sarah Maslin and Schweber, Nate, "After 146 Years, Ringling Brothers Circus Takes Its Final Bow", *New York Times*, May 21, 2017.

[79] N.J. Rev. Stat. §§23:2A-16 & 23:2A-10.

[80] After litigation, a court ruled that Nosey can stay permanently at a Tennessee elephant sanctuary. The prior owners of Nosey were also charged with animal cruelty. *See*, Sack, Wendy, "Justice for Nosey: elephant's owners arrested on animal cruelty charges", *The Cullman Tribune*, December 16, 2017.

[81] Hawaii Code R. §§ 4-71-6.5 & 4-71-4.3; Hawaii Rev. Stat. §150A-14.

[82] Cal. Fish & Game Code §§ 2207-2210.

[83] Colo. Rev. Stat. § 33-1-126.

[84] 720 Illinois Compiled Statutes §§ 5/48-11 & 5/5-4.5-55.

[85] N.Y. Agric. & Mkts. Law, Ch. 69, Art. 26, §380.

[86] *See*, "Prohibiting Circuses and Traveling Acts that Use Animals: Using Local Legislation to Protect Animals", *Animal Legal Defense Fund*, n.d., at https://aldf.org/article/protecting-animals-through-local-legislation/prohibiting-circuses-and-traveling-acts-that-use-animals/

use of wild or exotic animals in traveling circus acts.[87] The Traveling Exotic Animal and Public Safety Protection Act was introduced in Congress in 2017 and re-introduced again in 2021, which when enacted, will amend the Animal Welfare Act to prohibit the use of wild and exotic animals in traveling performances nationwide.[88]

States and municipalities are also passing laws to outlaw the use of instruments, such as bull hooks,[89] that are intended to inflict (or threaten) pain on elephants for training purposes or to control the animal. Two states, Rhode Island and California,[90] have banned the use of bull hooks on elephants, and at least 117 cities around the U.S. have enacted similar bans.[91] In 2019, the board of the Association of Zoos and Aquariums voted to phase out the use of bull hooks for the routine care of elephants in zoos.[92] At the federal level, the USDA, known to be lax when it comes to enforcement, made a determination in 2016 that zoos that remove infant exotic cubs (e.g., tigers, lions, jaguars or leopards that are 4 weeks old and under) from their mothers to be handled and fed by the public are in violation of the Animal Welfare Act.[93] However, the USDA continues to permit zoos, like the Natural Bridge Zoo in Virginia, to remain in business, despite having nearly 150 violations, tens of thousands of dollars in

[87] Conn. Gen. Assem., Proposed HB 5800 (2021) and S.B. No. 66 (2021), An Act Prohibiting the Use of Wild Animals in Circuses, Carnivals and Exhibitions.

[88] Traveling Exotic Animal and Public Safety Protection Act of 2021 - H.R.5999 and S.3220, 117th Congress (2021–2022); *see also*, Press Release: Reps. Grijalva, Schweikert & Sen. Menendez Introduce the Traveling Exotic Animal and Public Safety Protection Act to Stop Circus Suffering", *Congressman Grijalva,* November 17, 2021, at https://grijalva.house.gov/reps-grijalva-schweikert-sen-menendez-introduce-the-traveling-exotic-animal-and-public-safety-protection-act-to-stop-circus-suffering/

[89] Bull hooks are rods with sharp, steel tips that are commonly used to train and control elephants.

[90] Reuters Staff, "California Governor Brown signs law banning use of bullhooks on elephants", *Reuters,* August 30, 2016.

[91] Comas, Martin E., "Seminole bans use of bullhooks, torture devices on exotic animals", *Orlando Sentinel,* October 27, 2021.

[92] Brulliard, Karin, "Some of America's top zoos still use bullhooks on elephants. That's about the change", *Washington Post,* August 21, 2019.

[93] Milman, Oliver, "USDA acquiesces to pressure from animal welfare groups to stamp out the use of cubs as entertainment for people who pay sizable sums to meet the animals", *Guardian,* April 5, 2016; *see also,* "USDA Cracks down on Abuse of Tiger Cubs", *Big Cat Rescue,* April 5, 2016, at https://bigcatrescue.org/usda-announces-partial-cub-petting-ban/

fines, and license suspensions.[94] The USDA renewed the license of Cricket Hollow Animal Park (f/k/a Cricket Hollow Zoo) in Manchester, Iowa, despite documented animal deaths, untreated wounded animals, inadequate veterinary care, improper handling of animals, exposure to harsh weather, small, filthy cages, and lack of clean water and food.[95]

While encouraging progress has been made in Europe and elsewhere, many circuses still operate throughout the world. When England banned wild animals in traveling circuses, Environment Secretary, Michael Gove, said that "traveling circuses are no place for wild animals in the 21st century."[96] When Madrid banned the use of wild animals in circuses, Ignacio de Benito, general secretary of the Spanish Socialist Workers' Party, said that, "circus history is part of the cultural heritage but in the twenty-first century, behind the laughter can never hide the suffering of any living being, whether human or animal.[97] In Ireland, the Minister for Agriculture, Michael Creed, said that "[t]he use of wild animals for entertainment purposes in circuses can no longer be permitted," noting that this is "the general view of the public at large."[98] Tien Chiu-Chin, a legislator in Taiwan, argued that, "by exposing our children to wild animals through circus acts, we are setting an incorrect example of how humans should interact with animals."[99]

Tragically, the closure of abusive operations does not always end well for animals. In 2016, the Major of Buenos Aires, Argentina, declared that the capital's 140-year old zoo was "degrading for the animals" and announced that the zoo would be closed and its animals moved to nature

[94] Prater, Danny, "PETA TO USDA: Do Better for Animals Suffering at Roadside Zoos", *PETA*, January 20, 2021.

[95] *See*, "Challenging the USDA for Reissing Roadside Zoo's License", *Animal Legal Defense Fund*, August 6, 2021. Hundreds of animals were previously rescued from "deplorable" conditions. *See also*, Knepper, Hollie, "Several Hundred animals rescued from roadside zoo, 159 in ARL's care", *We are Iowa*, January 9, 2020.

[96] Department of Environment, Food & Rural Affairs, The Rt Hon Michael Gove MP and David Rutley MP, "Gove delivers legislation to ban wild animals in circuses", May 1, 2019. at https://www.gov.uk/government/news/gove-delivers-legislation-to-ban-wild-animals-in-circuses

[97] Starostinetskaya, Anna "Madrid Bans Wild Animal Circuses", *VegNews*, April 16, 2019.

[98] Halpin, Hayley, "The use of wild animals will be banned in Irish circuses from January 2018", *The Journal.ie*, November 9, 2017.

[99] Oung, Angelica, "Lawmakers say no to animals in circus shows", *Taipei Times*, May 8, 2017.

reserves.[100] In the two years following its closure, however, 119 animals died, 12 animals escaped and only 241 were transferred out of the zoo.[101] Still, the captivity of animals for circus entertainment purposes must end and suitable homes must be found for retired animals. In some countries, like Belgium and the Netherlands, circuses have been responsible for finding homes for circus animals.[102] In other countries, nonprofit organizations are assisting in the relocation of circus animals to appropriate sanctuaries and rescue centers.[103] In Portugal, Animal Advocacy Protection (AAP), a member organization of Eurogroup for Animals, entered into a contract with Portuguese authorities to rescue the remaining wild animals in Portuguese circuses.[104]

There have also been positive developments for aquatic animals in captivity. In 2019, Canada's House of Commons passed the Ending the Captivity of Whales and Dolphins Act (also known as the "Free Willy" bill), which outlaws the captivity, breeding, trade, possession and capture of whales, dolphins and porpoises, with fines of up to $150,000 USD.[105] In 2017, France also banned the breeding of dolphins and killer whales in captivity, and while the ban was overturned due to irregularities in the decree,[106] France announced a phase-out in 2020 for the captivity of dolphins and orcas in marine parks.[107] In echoing the sentiments of a growing number of countries, French Ecology Minister, Barbara Pompili, said that France "is now engaged in a major change in the place given to wild animals in our society ... This evolution of perceptions is the mark of a society

[100] Izadi, Elahe, "'Captivity is degrading': Why a major city is shutting down its zoo", *Washington Post,* June 25, 2016.

[101] Kim, Elizabeth Sulis, "Broken promises of Buenos Aires Zoo after mysterious deaths of animals", *Guardian,* July 31, 2018.

[102] Eurogroup for Animals, *Wild Animals,* at 19–20.

[103] Id.

[104] "European Parliament shows broad political support to Stop Circus Suffering", December 16, 2021, at https://www.eurogroupforanimals.org/news/european-parliament-shows-broad-political-support-stop-circus-suffering. David van Gennep, CEO of AAP, said that "[t]he rescue community is always willing to step up and offer solutions to enforcement authorities in implementing these important bans."

[105] Dias, Andrea and Westcott, Ben, "Canada passes 'Free Willy' bill banning whale and dolphin captivity", *CNN,* June 10, 2019.

[106] Reuters Staff, "Top French court reverses ban on breeding whales, dolphins", *Reuters,* January 19, 2018.

[107] Reuters Staff, "France to ban use of wild animals in circuses", *Reuters,* September 29, 2020.

conscious of its responsibility vis-à-vis a fragile nature. It is this movement that we are supporting by announcing the gradual end of the presence of wildlife in circuses, [and] the presence of orcas and dolphins in dolphinariums."[108]

After international outrage over the orca "whale jail" in Russia's Far East,[109] Russia's Prime Minister, Mikhail Mishustin, signed a resolution in 2021 to ban the export of whales, dolphins and porpoises from Russia and President, Vladimir Putin, instructed the government to update its laws.[110] After announcing its intent to ban dolphin captivity in 2017, Mexico City, Mexico also officially banned dolphinariums in 2018[111] and the Guangzhou Zoo in China announced its intent to end animal circus acts in 2017.[112]

Public pressure is also growing in the United States against captive marine mammals. In 2016, California enacted the Orca Protection Safety Act,[113] which bans the breeding of killer whales in captivity for use in entertainment. That same year, SeaWorld announced that it will no longer breed orcas and will focus its efforts on rescue operations of marine mammals in distress that are not able to be released back into the wild.[114] Amid continuing public backlash and criticism following the documentary *Blackfish*, SeaWorld also committed to phase out its orca performances and to fight the commercial fishing of whales and seals and the shark fin trade.[115] The impact of *Blackfish* was also felt by aquariums. In 2016, the Georgia Aquarium also announced that it would no longer seek to acquire

[108] Pallotta, Nicole, "Wild Animals in Traveling Circuses, and Captivity of Orcas and Dolphins in Marine Parks", *Animal Legal Defense Fund*, n.d., at https://aldf.org/article/france-to-end-mink-farming-use-of-wild-animals-in-traveling-circuses-and-captivity-of-orcas-and-dolphins-in-marine-parks/

[109] *See*, Chapter III for more on Russia's "whale jail".

[110] "Government puts temporary ban on export of whales, dolphins and porpoises from Russia", *The White Whale Programme, RU*, August 20, 2021.

[111] Berry, George, "Mexico City bans dolphinariums", *Whale and Dolphin Conservation*, May 8, 2018.

[112] Notwithstanding the fact that the Guangzhou Zoo declined to renew its lease with the Anhui Guangde Animal Circuses' contract, there were initial reports that the circus refused to leave the property and continued operating its shows. It is not clear if or how the dispute was resolved. *See,* e.g., Bossons, Matthew, "Defiant Animal Circus Refuses to Close at Guangzhou Zoo", *Thats Mags*, September 6, 2017.

[113] Cal. Fish and Game Code §4502 (California Orca Protection Act).

[114] Allen, Greg, "SeaWorld Agrees to End Captive Breeding of Killer Whales", *NPR*, March 17, 2016.

[115] Bomey, Nathan, "SeaWorld to phase out killer whale shows, captivity", *USA Today*, March 17, 2016.

dolphins or beluga whales from the wild, but this came only *after* its failed attempts to import 18 wild-caught beluga whales that had been caught pursuant to an arrangement between the Georgia Aquarium and Russia.[116] The aquarium did not anticipate that the National Oceanic and Atmospheric Administration would deny the necessary permit to import the belugas, nor did it expect that a Federal court would uphold that denial.[117] In 2016, the National Aquarium in Baltimore announced that it would relocate its eight bottlenose dolphins to a seaside sanctuary by the end of 2020.[118] In 2019, the National Aquarium acknowledged that the 2020 year-end deadline was no longer realistic due to the challenges of climate change,[119] but efforts to locate and build the sanctuary are continuing.

There have been legal reforms in other entertainment venues as well, including in animal racing venues. In 2018, Florida, once considered the mecca of greyhound racing in the U.S., banned greyhound racing, leaving only a handful of remaining tracks in the United States, several of which closed in 2020.[120] The Greyhound Protection Act was introduced in Congress to ban greyhound racing in the United States and to prohibit foreign racing venues from broadcasting greyhound races in the United States.[121] As of August 2023, the bill remains stalled in Congress.

The Canidrome Greyhound Race Track in Macau, China, once deemed the "world's deadliest track" with an estimated 30 dogs euthanized each month, closed in 2018.[122] According to Grey2K USA Worldwide, the largest nonprofit greyhound protection organization in the world, active commercial dog racing tracks remain in the United States, the U.K.,

[116] Davis, Mark, "Georgia Aquarium: no more whales, dolphins taken from the wild", *Atlanta Journal-Constitution*, June 22, 2016.

[117] Ibid.

[118] Ibid.

[119] Cronin, Dana and Garcia-Navarro, Lulu, "At Baltimore's National Aquarium, Climate Change Presents Challenges Inside and Out", *NPR,* May 5, 2019. The National Aquarium surveyed 50 sites for the sanctuary and found each one unsafe due to conditions such as flooding, fierce storms and algal blooms.

[120] Li, David K., "Dog days of Florida come to an end, with total devise of U.S. greyhound racing within sight", *NBC News,* December 31, 2020.

[121] Greyhound Protection Act of 2021 - H.R.3335, 117th Congress (2021–2022); *see also,* Pacelle, Wayne, "Lawmakers Introduce Federal Legislation to Close the Curtain on a Century of Greyhound Racing in America", *Center for a Humane Economy,* June 21, 2021.

[122] *See generally,* "Asia's last dog-racing track closes", *The Economist,* August 2, 2018.

Vietnam, Australia, New Zealand, Ireland and Mexico,[123] but activists are continuing their work to close down the remaining tracks.[124]

Legal reform is also expanding to protect horses forced to race in the United States. Horse racing has long been plagued with allegations of doping, abuse, and racetrack deaths. In the five-year period ending in 2019, there were more than 5000 reported racehorse deaths in the U.S.[125] At the end of 2020, the Horseracing Integrity and Safety Act was quietly enacted into law, creating uniform standards for thoroughbred racing and bringing with it sweeping changes that are viewed as "the most transformational reform of horse racing in decades."[126] Interestingly, the legal reform was not the result of governmental action; rather, it was reportedly the sport's "moneyed elite" who were concerned with "toothless enforcement" and "widespread doping" in the industry. They turned their findings into federal indictments, and ultimately new legislation.[127] A federal appellate court found a provision in the Horseracing Integrity and Safety Act to be unconstitutional,[128] but Congress passed a technical amendment at the end of 2022 to address the issue.

Worldwide sentiment is also turning against blood sports, evidenced by new laws that are being passed to ban animal fighting. While many countries have already banned dogfighting, in recent years developing countries have also outlawed the cruel spectacle, including Guatemala,[129]

[123] "Greyhound Racing Around the World", *GREYk2 USA Worldwide,* n.d., at https://www.grey2kusa.org/about/worldwide.php

[124] Busby, Mattha, "Activists renew calls to end greyhound racing as 400 die despite lockdowns", *Guardian,* June 26, 2021.

[125] Battuella, Patrick, "Opinion: The Time for horse racing has passed, It's time to outlaw it", *Washington Post,* October 8, 2019.

[126] The Act was part of the omnibus Consolidated Appropriations Act, 2021 (Public Law No. 116-260, December 27, 2020) that Congress passed at the end of 2020; *see also,* Candelaria, Michael, "New law brings sweeping changes to horse racing", *Legal Examiner,* January 15, 2021.

[127] Garcia-Roberts, Gus, "With private eyes and political muscle, horse racing's elite pushed to punish dopers", *Washington Post,* April 29, 2021.

[128] Carroll, Rory, "Horse racing-Appeals court rules horse racing safety law unconstitutional", *Reuters,* November 18, 2022.

[129] "Guatemalan Congress approves animal welfare legislation", *Humane Society International,* March 1, 2017, at https://www.hsi.org/news-media/guatemala-approves-animal-welfare-law-030117/

Mexico,[130] El Salvador[131] and Honduras,[132] as well as jurisdictions within countries, such as Caracas, Venezuela.[133] In 2007, Louisiana became the last state to make cockfighting illegal.[134] In 2014, legislation was passed making it a federal crime to attend an animal fight, with additional penalties if children are brought to the fight.[135] In 2016, the U.S. Sentencing Commission amended sentencing guidelines to increase penalties for animal fighting,[136] and in 2018, the United States enacted into law the Parity in Animal Cruelty Enforcement (PACE) Act, which amended the Animal Welfare Act to prohibit animal fighting (e.g., dogfighting and cockfighting) in U.S. territories. The law was upheld in 2021 by the 9th U.S. Circuit Court of Appeals,[137] and today there are conferences, webinars, and other educational opportunities where prosecutors can learn about animal fighting investigations and how to better prosecute them.

Animal fighting rings that involve other crimes, such as illegal drugs and guns, do tend to get more attention. In 2020, the U.S. Attorney's Office for the Southern District of Georgia announced possible felony or misdemeanor charges for more than 200 individuals participating in, or operating, animal fighting ventures.[138] The raid, dubbed *Operation*

[130] "Yucatan News: Dog Fighting Faces Stiff New Penalties, Mexico Makes Dog Fighting a Felony", *Yucatan Living*, May 1, 2017.

[131] Pacelle, Wayne, "In 2016, HIS struck blows to dog meat trade, factory farming, and more", *The Humane Society of the United States*, December 16, 2016.

[132] "Honduras Bans Use of Animals in Circuses and Dog Fighting", *Animal Equality*, November 12, 2015.

[133] "Caracas, Venezuela bans animal circuses, bullfights, cockfights & dogfights", *Animal Defenders International, Stop Circus Suffering*, n.d., at https://www.stopcircussuffering.com/news/latin-america/caracas-venezuela-bans-animal-circuses-bullfights-cockfights-dogfights/

[134] McCulley, Russell, "Louisiana to be last state to ban cockfighting", *Reuters*, June 27, 2007.

[135] 7 U.S. Code § 2156(a) (Animal fighting venture prohibition).

[136] United States Sentencing Commission, "U.S. Sentencing Commission Approves Significant Changes to the Federal Sentencing Guidelines", April 15, 2016, at https://www.ussc.gov/about/news/press-releases/april-15-2016

[137] Kelleher, Jennifer S., "Court Upholds US Cockfighting Ban, Rejects Challenge in Guam", *Associated Press*, December 22, 2021. The Supreme Court also declined to hear a challenge to the law by individuals and organizations from Puerto Rico who argued that "cockfighting is deeply ingrained in the island's history, tradition and culture."

[138] "More than 200 individuals could face federal felony or misdemeanor charges for operating or participating in animal fighting ventures", *U.S. Attorney's Office for the Southern District of Georgia*, June 22, 2020.

Sunrise, involved the seizure of illegal firearms and drugs and nearly 800 roosters.

There is also growing public condemnation of the centuries old tradition of bullfighting. The blood sport is banned in certain parts of Spain and Ecuador as well as in several smaller Mexican states, and in late 2021, legislation was introduced to ban the sport in Mexico City, Mexico,[139] home to the Plaza de toros Mexico, the world's largest bullfighting ring. It was a court, however, that declared a complete ban on bullfighting in Mexico's capital when the sport was challenged under Mexico City's constitutionally guaranteed right to a healthy environment.[140] In supporting the ban, one judge stressed that "[s]ociety demands that the physical and emotional integrity of all animals, including bulls, be respected"[141] and that "[s]ociety benefits when the physical and emotional integrity of all animals is respected because they are living creatures that form ecosystems and therefore contribute to environmental services that are essential to humans."[142]

Spain's Balearic Islands effectively banned bullfighting in 2017 by prohibiting the killing of bulls and any physical or psychological injury to them.[143] In 2017, Caracas, Venezuela's ban on bullfights became law and in the following year, Maracaibo, the second largest city in Venezuela, announced a ban on bullfighting within its city limits.[144] While bullfighting remains legal in many parts of Spain, government data shows a dwindling public interest in the tradition.[145]

Legal reform to protect animals comes with the promise of legal challenges. In 2014, India's Supreme Court banned *Jallikattu*, a centuries old tradition practiced in the Indian State of Tamil Nadu where participants

[139] Sieff, Kevin, "The last bullfight? Mexico City weighs a ban", *Washington Post*, December 14, 2021.

[140] The association Justicia Justa requested the ban on bullfighting based on Mexico City's local constitution, which guarantees the right to a healthy environment. *See*, "Court in Mexico City permanent bans bullfighting in the capital", *Le Monde*, June 18, 2022.

[141] Id.

[142] "Bullfighting season 2022–2023 canceled in Mexico City", *CAS International*, December 15, 2022.

[143] Reuters Staff, "Spain's Balearic Islands vote to outlaw killing bulls at fights", *Reuters*, July 24, 2017.

[144] Day, Carly, "Bullfighting Has Just Been Banned in This Venezuelan City", *Lady Freethinker*, January 5, 2018.

[145] Valdivia, Ana Garcia, "Will Bullfighting Survive The Next Decade in Spain?" *Forbes*, December 30, 2019.

attempt to "tame" bulls by grabbing and holding onto them until they stop. The court ruled that the tradition violates the Prevention of Cruelty to Animals Act and is in contravention of the constitutional duty which requires that animals be treated with compassion. The ban was reaffirmed by the Supreme Court in 2016.[146] Still, following protracted and widespread protests against the ban in 2017, the State changed the law to allow *Jallikattu*.[147] From 2017 to the end of 2022, a reported 86 people, including participants and spectators, were killed and thousands more injured during the deadly event.[148] In January 2023, at least 5 people were killed during *Jallikattu*, including a 14-year old boy who was a spectator at the event.[149] In 2022, the legality of *Jallikattu* was back before the Supreme Court, where the State argued that the event is a cultural festival with religious significance.[150] In 2023, the Supreme Court upheld the legality of *Jallikattu*, ruling that the law does not violate India's Constitution.[151]

The United States in the only nation on earth where tens of thousands of wildlife are killed for entertainment and prizes.[152] Despite the well-documented link between animal cruelty and violence against humans,[153] it is estimated that 60,000 animals are killed every year in "contests" and "competitions."[154] Project Coyote founder, Camilla Fox, argues (rightfully so) that wildlife killing contests are "blood sports" that are no different from dogfighting and cockfighting,[155] desensitizing participants to

[146] For additional background, *see generally* ClearIAS Team, "Jallikattu: History, Court Rulings, and Controversy", *ClearIAS*, February 11, 2017.

[147] *See*, Safi, Michael, "Tamil Nadu passes order to lift bull-taming ban after angry protests", *Guardian*, January 23, 2017.

[148] *See*, "86 people, 23 bulls killed in bull-taming Jallikattu festival since 2017: PETA India", *India News, CNBCTV18*, December 9, 2022.

[149] Raval, Abhishek, "14-year Old Spectator Gored to Death at Jallikattu Event in Tamil Nadu's Dharmapuri", *Republic World*, January 22, 2023.

[150] "Jallikattu bears religious significance to state's people; no cruelty to animals; Tamil Nadu to SC", *The Print*, November 24, 2022.

[151] Sebastian, Meryl, "Jallikattu: Supreme Court upholds validity of Tamil Nadu law allowing bull-taming sport", *BBC*, May 17, 2023.

[152] Ebersole, Rene, "How killing wildlife in the United States became a game", *National Geographic*, April 27, 2022.

[153] Robinson, Charlie and Clausen, Victoria, "The Link Between Animal Cruelty and Human Violence", *FBI Featured Articles*, April 10, 2021, at https://leb.fbi.gov/articles/featured-articles/the-link-between-animal-cruelty-and-human-violence

[154] Ibid.

[155] Animal Welfare Institute, "Colorado Becomes Sixth U.S. State to Outlaw Cruel and Unsporting Wildlife Killing Contests", May 1, 2020.

violence and perpetuating a culture that devalues life. Public opinion is turning against blood sports. In the last decade, eight states have banned wildlife killing events, including California (2014), Vermont (2018), New Mexico (2019), Arizona (2019), Massachusetts (2019), Colorado (2020), Washington (2020) and Maryland (2021).[156] New York is expected to become the 9th state to end wildlife killing contests.[157] A coalition of 70 conservation scientists have called for an end to wildlife killing contests, refuting arguments often advanced for such contests (e.g., wildlife management; protecting livestock) and citing the important roles that animals have for healthy ecosystems.[158] Some lawmakers are listening. In 2022, legislation was introduced in Congress to prohibit wildlife killing contests on public lands.[159]

The end of the exploitation of captive animals for profit will not happen all at once. It will be achieved incrementally as laws, policies and practices are updated and replaced. In recent years, we have witnessed the cancelation of events which suggests that the public is less tolerant of animal cruelty for entertainment sake: the inhumane King Kong Zoological Park in North Carolina was permanently closed down;[160] a proposed "Great Bull Run" event in Temecula, California was denied a permit;[161] elephant rides were canceled at Angkor Wat in Cambodia;[162] the Stoughton Fair in Wisconsin canceled its pig wrestling event;[163] a festival in Shikoku, Japan ended pig rodeos;[164] and chimpanzee acts at Schwaben Park in Germany

[156] *See generally*, Fishman, Marjorie, "New York to Become Ninth State to End Wildlife Killing Contests", *Animal Welfare Institute*, June 29, 2023.

[157] S.4099/A.2917, An Act to amend the environmental conservation law, in relation to making contests, competitions, tournaments and derbys to take wildlife unlawful.

[158] "Statement in Opposition to Wildlife Killing Contests", *Project Coyote*, n.d., at https://mgaleg.maryland.gov/cmte_testimony/2021/ehe/1JlcVL8zgnTUpVaJODOu_GUTH8v4_nn-N.pdf

[159] Prohibit Wildlife Killing Contests Act of 2022 - H.R. 7398, 117th Congress (2021–2022).

[160] "King Kong Zoo Permanently Shut Down After Being Sued by The Animal Legal Defense Fund", *Animal Legal Defense Fund*, February 23, 2017.

[161] McMillan, Rob, "Great Bull Run event in Temecula cancelled", *ABC7 Los Angeles*, May 8, 2014.

[162] Rizzo, Cailey, "Cambodia's most famous tourist attraction just banned elephant rides", *Business Insider*, November 22, 2019.

[163] Alesia, Tom, "Fair 'forced' to cancel pig wrestling", *Unified Newspaper Group*, June 21, 2016.

[164] Kyodo, "Popular pig rodeo in Shikoku comes to an end", *Japan Times*, August 14, 2016.

came to an end.[165] These incremental changes, when viewed together, reveal a public that is evolving in its attitudes toward animals, and some governments are listening.

After hundreds of animal welfare organizations campaigned against a proposed dolphin park in Da Nang, Vietnam, Vietnam rejected the proposal in 2017.[166] In Cumbria, England, local authorities denied a zoo owner a new license for the South Lakes Safari Zoo after nearly 500 animals died in less than four years.[167] In Moultrie County, Illinois, the public pushed back on a proposed roadside zoo and won.[168] In Israel, an animal welfare group pushed back on proposed construction next to the Jerusalem Zoo, citing loud noise and large amounts of dust, arguing that "[t]he animals do not need to be exposed to the tortures of living next to a huge construction site without any possibility of escape. The right to a life of minimal suffering, even for animals, is more important than real estate gains."[169] The judge agreed.[170]

In 2017, Guadalajara, Mexico became the first city in the world to replace horse-drawn carriages with electric carriages, and other major world cities have since followed, including Cologne, Dubai, Istanbul, Mumbai, and Santo Domingo.[171] The number of cities that have banned horse-drawn carriages is increasing around the world and includes Barcelona, Spain; Delhi, India; Oxford, England; Old San Juan, Puerto Rico; Prague, Czech Republic; Melbourne, Australia; and Montreal, Canada.[172] A growing number of cities in the United States are also ban-

[165] Whitworth, David, "Schwaben Park, Germany", *Interpark,* August 25, 2019, at https://interpark.co.uk/schwaben-park-germany/

[166] "Vietnam's rejection of dolphin park shows no place for cruelty in entertainment", *AnimalsAsia,* November 17, 2017, at https://www.animalsasia.org/us/media/news/news-archive/vietnams-rejection-of-dolphin-park-shows-no-place-for-cruelty-in-entertainment.html

[167] Perraudin, Frances, "Cumbrian zoo boss refused new license after hundreds of animal deaths", *Guardian,* March 6, 2017.

[168] "Central Illinois Wildlife Park Cancelled After Opposition by Neighbors and Animal Legal Defense Fund", *Animal Legal Defense Fund,* June 30, 2015.

[169] Eisenbud, Daniel, "Judge blocks new neighborhood next to Biblical Zoo over animal welfare", *Jerusalem Post,* April 25, 2017.

[170] TOI Staff, "Court scraps plan for new neighborhood next to Jerusalem zoo", *Times of Israel,* April 22, 2017.

[171] Forel, Elizabeth and Wagner, Susan, "Electric 'Horseless' Carriages – the Wave of the Future", *Compassionate & Responsible Tourism,* n.d., at https://compassionatetourism.org/compassionate-responsible-tourism-2/

[172] Ibid.

ning horse-drawn carriages, including Chicago, Illinois; Key West, Florida; and Asheville, North Carolina.[173] In Petra, Jordan, horse carriages are being replaced with electric golf carts,[174] and in Honduras, a judge imposed the highest fine ever for the mistreatment of work horses.[175]

The persistent negative press has led many businesses to cut ties to SeaWorld. In 2019, British Airways announced that it would no longer offer its customers the option of booking tickets for attractions that involve captive animals, joining other travel companies that have severed ties with SeaWorld, including, inter alia, Air Canada and WestJet Airlines,[176] Southwest Airlines,[177] United Airlines, Virgin Holidays and AAA Northeast.[178] Trip Advisor,[179] Booking.com,[180] Airbnb,[181] Thomas Cook[182] and Expedia[183] also ended their business ties with SeaWorld, so that their brands would not be associated with animal cruelty. The Miami Dolphins also ended their contract with SeaWorld.[184] SeaWorld hasn't been the only target. Hundreds of companies, tour businesses and parks have stopped

[173] Ibid.

[174] "Four Paws Helps Ending Animal Cruelty at UNESCO World Heritage Site", *Four Paws*, November 11, 2021, at https://www.fourpawsusa.org/our-stories/press-releases/four-paws-helps-ending-animal-cruelty-at-unesco-world-heritage-site

[175] "Judge rules against offender of Animal Protection and Welfare Law of Honduras for mistreating their work animals: The ruling follows complaint by HSI", *Humane Society International*, n.d., at https://www.hsi.org/news-media/honduras-horse-abuse-fine-051018

[176] The Canadian Press, "Air Canada, WestJet latest companies to cut ties to SeaWorld ahead of whale bill", *Canada's National Observer*, October 30, 2018.

[177] Associated Press, "SeaWorld, Southwest Airlines Ending Partnership", *NBC News*, July 31, 2014.

[178] Weisberg, Lori, "British Airways, other travel sites stop selling SeaWorld tickets", *San Diego Union-Tribune*, August 13, 2019.

[179] Bilbao, Richard, "TripAdvisor cuts ties with SeaWorld, other attractions with whales and dolphins", *Orlando Business Journal*, October 2, 2019.

[180] Ticketing Business News, News Editor, "Booking.com Cuts Ticketing Ties with Captive Animal Attractions", *Ticketing Business*, October 19, 2019.

[181] Smith, Kat, "Airbnb Will No Longer Offer Experiences That Harm Animals", *Live Kindly*, n.d., at https://www.livekindly.co/why-airbnb-banned-animal-experiences/

[182] Vaughan, Henry, "Thomas Cook to Stop Selling Tickets to SeaWorld Over Animal Welfare Concerns", *Independent*, July 29, 2018.

[183] Carr, Jemma, "Changing Fins Expedia Bans 'cruel' travel holidays to see captive dolphins and whales perform after backlash", *Sun*, November 7, 2021.

[184] Sentenac, Hannah, "Miami Dolphins End Contract with SeaWorld", *Miami New Times*, January 26, 2015.

selling tickets for elephant rides, including Trip Advisor,[185] Booking.com,[186] Fodor's,[187] Airbnb[188] and Pacific Delight Tours.[189] In late 2021, Canada's accreditation authority for zoos banned elephant rides.[190]

Companies go to great lengths to avoid controversy. The Iditarod Trail Sled Dog Race, the world's best known sled dog race, has faced reports of cruelty and doping since the release of the documentary *Sled Dogs*[191] that put the spotlight on the death and injury of many dogs.[192] As a result, ExxonMobil, Alaska Airlines, Chrysler, Wells Fargo and Jack Daniel's have ended their sponsorships of the event.[193] Few companies or individuals want to be associated with animal cruelty. HBO canceled the horse racing series, *Luck*, after reports proved that older and arthritic horses had been used in deadly racing sequences.[194]

As the landscape for entertainment venues continues to change, incredible animal rescues are happening. After *The Great Bear Show* ended, the bears were sent to a newly restored habitat sanctuary.[195] Ben and Booger, two bears at a roadside zoo in North Carolina, were rescued and taken to a habitat sanctuary in Colorado.[196] Ricki the Bear, who lived 16 years in a small concrete and chain link cage outside of an ice cream shop in

[185] Sablich, Justin, "TripAdvisor to Stop Selling Tickets to Many Animal Attractions", *New York Times*, October 11, 2016.

[186] Gybels, Marianne, "Our commitment to the protection of animals", *Booking.com*, August 20, 2019.

[187] Taylor, Mia, "Fodor's Joins Growing List of Travel Brands that Oppose Elephant Rides", *Travel Pulse*, September 25, 2019. Airbnb states that "[y]ou will never find an Airbnb Experience where you can kiss a dolphin or ride an elephant."

[188] "Introducing Airbnb Animal Experiences", *Airbnb*, October 3, 2019.

[189] Cogswell, David, "Why Are Tour Operators Cancelling Elephant Rides", *Travel Pulse*, November 30, 2016.

[190] Taekema, Dan, "Canadian zoo accreditation body bans elephant rides. Advocates say change is overdue", *CBC News*, December 16, 2021.

[191] Sled Dogs: The Cold Truth About Man's Best Friend (2016), directed by Fern Levitt. *See also*, Jenkins, Gavin, "The Iditarod is hounded by cruelty allegations, infighting and a doping scandal", *Washington Post*, February 28, 2018.

[192] Payne, Marissa, "Iditarod dog race blames PETA for loss of major sponsor", *Washington Post*, May 26, 2017.

[193] Thiessen, Mark, "ExxonMobil becomes latest sponsor to sever Iditarod ties", *Associated Press*, January 21, 2021.

[194] Tracy, Ben, "Behind HBO's scrapping of 'Luck'", *CBS News*, March 15, 2012.

[195] Rapanut, Kimberly, "Bears find refuge in Arizona after life in Texas traveling act", *Republic*, May 17, 2018.

[196] Associated Press, "Wild Animal Sanctuary takes custody of bears allegedly mistreated by N. Carolina zoo", *Denver Post*, December 21, 2017.

Pennsylvania, was moved to the same Colorado sanctuary.[197] Rangeela and Sridevi, Nepal's last known 'dancing bears', were rescued.[198] Videos and images of animals released into freedom in natural habitats are magical moments, and we need many more of these.

Animals in Research

Kristin Kreisler has told the story of a terrified little beagle, named Beatrice, with an ID tattoo number inside her ear, who broke free from a research facility.[199] Whenever any male in a white lab coat came near, she would roll onto her back, raise her legs in the air, and urinate in submission. Beatrice did learn to trust again, making her one of the few lucky ones.

When it comes to research involving animals, the mistreatment by humans is shocking. On November 3, 1957, Laika, a stray dog from the streets of Moscow, was launched into orbit by the Soviets on the spacecraft Sputnik 2.[200] Laika was never expected to survive, nor was any provision made for her recovery. The experiment aimed to determine whether a human could survive being launched into orbit. There are varying accounts as to how Laika died, including overheating. The official government claim was that she was euthanized before oxygen ran out. Certainly, strays die every day, and many other species have been launched into space,[201] but many found sending the homeless dog to its lonely death to be especially heartbreaking. Sadly, little has changed. In 2016, Russian scientists were forcing dogs to "breath" underwater to test new liquid breathing technology.[202] The United States engages in research torture too, though it generally takes place behind closed doors.

[197] Animal Legal Defense Fund, "Former Roadside Zoo Bear, Ricki, Reunites with Rescuer Whose Lawsuit Freed Her from Concrete Cage", April 25, 2019.

[198] Bale, Rachael, "Nepal's Last Known Dancing Bears Rescued", *National Geographic*, December 17, 2017. Sadly, there were reports that Sridevi died before getting to the sanctuary in India. It's not clear why the bears were sent to the zoo instead of the intended sanctuary in India.

[199] Kristin von Kreisler, *Beauty in the Beasts, true stories of animals who choose to do good*. J. P. Tarcher (2001), at pp. 4–7. ISBN 1-58542-158-8.

[200] *See*, "NASA Space Science Data Coordinated Archive: Sputnik 2" (NSSDCA/COSPAR ID: 1957-002A), National Aeronautics and Space Administration, n.d., at https://nssdc.gsfc.nasa.gov/nmc/spacecraft/display.action?id=1957-002A

[201] For a historical discussion of animals launched into space, *see*, Dohrer, Elizabeth, "Animals in Space", *Space.com*, January 27, 2022, at https://www.space.com/animals-in-space

[202] "Dogs learn breathing underwater as Russian scientists test liquid respirational technology", *TASS Russian News Agency*, July 19, 2016.

In laboratories all over the world, animals are poisoned, burned, cut, shocked, starved, blinded, isolated, maimed, infected with diseases, and subjected to a host of other cruel experiments.[203] It is estimated that more than 115 million animals are used worldwide in research every year,[204] and in the United States, nearly 800,000 dogs, cats, primates, pigs and other animals covered by the Animal Welfare Act are used in research every year, with roughly 71,370 subjected to "unalleviated pain."[205] Incredibly, this estimate does not include roughly 95% of the animals used in research. The Act defines "animal" as any live or dead dog, cat, monkey (nonhuman primate mammal), guinea pig, hamster, rabbit, or such other warm-blooded animal,[206] so rats and mice are excluded from the protection of the Animal Welfare Act. The United States is behind many other countries in terms of its protection of animals used in research. Except for the West African nation of Gabon, it is the only country in the world where research on chimpanzees is explicitly permitted.[207]

Perhaps worse than the physical pain is the psychological torment and isolation of life in a research laboratory. The public was horrified at the sight of emotionally traumatized baby monkeys screaming and shaking with terror while being subjected to cruel "material deprivation experiments,"[208] but laws permitted this abuse long after any purported

[203] "Animals Used for Experimentation Factsheets", *PETA*, n.d., at https://www.peta.org/issues/animals-used-for-experimentation/animals-used-experimentation-factsheets/

[204] Taylor, K., et al., "Estimates for Worldwide Laboratory Animal Use in 2005", Alternatives to Laboratory Animals: ATLA vol. 36(3) (2008):327–42. https://doi.org/10.1177/026119290803600310

[205] Chen, Ingfei, "How Much Pain Should Animals Endure for Science", *Atlantic*, June 8, 2018. The USDA Annual Report Animal Usage by Fiscal Year (Total number of animals research facilities used in regulated activities) reflects 797,546 animals used in research laboratories in 2019.

[206] 7 U.S.C. § 2132(g) (2012).

[207] Coghlan, Andy, "Most chimp experiments unnecessary, says US Panel", *New Scientist*, December 16, 2011; *see also*, de Waal, Frans B. M., "Research Chimpanzees May Get a Break", *PLOS Biology* 10(3), March 27, 2012. https://doi.org/10.1371/journal.pbio.1001291

[208] Krisch, Joshua and Fox, EJ, "Is This Top Scientist Torturing Baby Monkeys", *Vocativ*, February 3, 2015. In "maternal deprivation" studies, monkeys who are predisposed to depression and other mental illnesses are further traumatized by taking them away from their mother at birth and then subjecting them to "years of terrifying and painful experiments." NIH announced an end to the maternal deprivation studies in 2015.

benefit was obtained.[209] On the rare occasions when the public becomes aware of the cruelty involved with animal research, the pharmaceutical industry has been known to use "scare tactics" to prevent laws from being modernized.[210] A 2018 poll concluded that Americans are divided over using animals in research,[211] but it was an abstract exercise with little value. When people are confronted with photographs of research facilities and harsh facts about the treatment of animals in them, opinions quickly change.

Academic pressure to use animals in veterinary and other biomedical programs, however, is coming to an end. Institutions that fail to provide humane alternatives can find themselves subject to liability, as the University of Colorado discovered when a medical student successfully sued the university for $95,000 after she failed physiology for refusing an assignment that involved giving a lethal injection to an anaesthetized dog. The court also required the university to offer alternatives to future students with similar objections.[212]

The United States is not alone in failing in this area. Many were horrified when news broke of New Zealand researchers tying pigs to a surgical table and killing them at close range in the head to study blood-spatter patterns.[213] Following negative press, the Institute of Environmental Science and Research announced that experiments of this nature will no longer be conducted.[214] Most animal research activity would not withstand public scrutiny, which incentivizes researchers to keep the cruelty hidden behind closed doors.

[209] *See*, King, Barbara J., "Still Now, Should Lab Monkeys Be Deprived Of Their Mothers", *NPR*, September 11, 2014.

[210] Rollin, Bernard E. and Benson, G. John, *The Well-Being of Farm Animals, Challenges and Solutions. Issues in Animal Bioethics Series* (Blackwell Publishing, 2004), at 6.

[211] *See*, e.g., Strauss, Mark, "Americans are divided over the use of animals in scientific research", *Pew Research Center*, August 16, 2018.

[212] *See*, Knight, Andrew, "Conscientious Objection to Harmful Animal Use within Veterinary and Other Biomedical Education", *Animals* 4, No. 1: 16–34 (2014). https://doi.org/10.3390/ani4010016

[213] The study was conducted at the University of Otago and the University of Auckland contributed research to the study. *See*, Associated Press, "Researchers Shoot Pigs in the Head in Blood-Spatter Study", *NBC News*, September 16, 2015.

[214] Otago Daily Times, "Live pigs shot in head at University of Otago", *New Zealand Herald*, September 17, 2015.

Perhaps the greatest tragedy is that animal-based research is highly unreliable.[215] According to the National Center for Advancing Translational Sciences, 95% of drugs that pass animal trials fail during human clinical trials.[216] Billions have been spent on cancer research,[217] yet cancer research has a 96.6% failure rate.[218] The system is broken but research grants and other funding sources incentivize researchers to continue with inefficient and unreliable research. Encouragingly, the legal landscape is changing.

Recent Developments for Animals in Research

There is a strong global consensus that testing on animals for cosmetics should be banned.[219] Laws have taken several forms—some ban the sale of cosmetics (or their ingredients) that have been tested on animals, while others ban animal testing itself. Some bans apply only to animal testing within the country, while other bans extend to cosmetics tested on animals in other countries. To date, more than 40 countries have adopted some form of the ban on cosmetic testing on animals, including all 27 countries in the European Union and Australia, Colombia, Ecuador, Guatemala, Iceland, India, Israel, Mexico,[220] New Zealand, Norway, South Korea, Switzerland, Taiwan, Turkey, and the U.K.[221] In 2023, Canada joined the

[215] Akhtar, Aysha, "The Flaws and Human Harms of Animal Experimentation", *Cambridge Quarterly of Healthcare Ethics*, October 24, 2015, 407–419.

[216] *See*, "About New Therapeutic Uses", *National Center for Advancing Translational Sciences*, n.d., at https://ncats.nih.gov/ntu/about#

[217] *See*, e.g., "Funding for Research Areas", *National Cancer Institute*, January 26, 2022 (reflecting research dollars spent from 2014–2019).

[218] Chi Heem Wong, Kien Wei Siah, Andrew W. Lo, "Corrigendum: Estimation of clinical trial success rates and related parameters", *Biostatistics*, 20(2), April 2019, at 366. https://doi.org/10.1093/biostatistics/kxy072

[219] The U.S. Federal Food, Drug, and Cosmetic Act defines "cosmetics" as products that are "for cleansing, beautifying, promoting attractiveness, or altering the appearance". 21 U.S.C. §321(i).

[220] Mexico was the first country in North America to ban cosmetic animal testing. *See*, Romaine, Jenna, "Mexico becomes first North American country to ban animal testing for cosmetics", *The Hill*, September 8, 2021.

[221] *See*, "Cosmetics animal testing FAQ" *The Humane Society of the United States*, n.d., at https://www.humanesociety.org/resources/cosmetics-testing-faq. Some states in Brazil have also banned cosmetic testing on animals.

growing number of countries that have banned cosmetic animal testing.[222] In 2019, China approved two new non-animal tests for testing cosmetic ingredients,[223] and in 2021, it changed its laws to exclude "general cosmetics" (as defined by Chinese law) that are imported into China from its animal testing requirements if certain conditions are met.[224] Similar legislation has been proposed in South Africa.[225] Still, policy changes can have a profound impact on laws. Despite a 25-year ban on cosmetic testing in the U.K., the government changed its policy to allow animal testing for makeup ingredients, a move that has outraged even cosmetic companies.[226]

In 2018, the European Parliament adopted a resolution calling for a global ban on animal testing for cosmetics.[227] The EU has also been updating their laws and policies[228] with the ultimate goal of developing alternatives to animal testing, including approaches using "stem cells, engineered tissues, organ-on-chip, genomic techniques, computer modelling and artificial intelligence" because "[d]ecades of biomedical research using animal

[222] Bill C-47, Budget Implementation Act, 2023, No. 1, and the Food and Drugs Act were amended to ban cosmetic animal testing. *See*, News Release, "Health Canada Announces the End of Cosmetic Animal Testing in Canada", *Government of Canada*, June 27, 2023, at https://www.canada.ca/en/health-canada/news/2023/06/health-canada-announces-the-end-of-cosmetic-animal-testing-in-canada.html

[223] Daliday, Ellen, "China approves non-animal cosmetic testing methods", *Chemical Watch*, April 17, 2019, at https://chemicalwatch.com/76640/china-approves-non-animal-cosmetic-testing-methods

[224] For more on China's animal testing requirements, *see* Pinto, Marta, "China's New Animal Testing Policy", *Critical Catalyst*, April 23, 2021; *see generally*, "China Eases on Animal Testing Requirements By Way of New Cosmetics Regulations", *Fashion Law*, March 5, 2021.

[225] Republic of South Africa, Animal Protection Amendment Bill, amending section 1 of Act 71 of 1962, as amended by section 12 of Act 7 of 1991; *see generally*, Prance-Miles, Louise, "New Legislation Proposal Could Spell The End of Animal Testing in South Africa", *Global Cosmetics News*, September 24, 2020.

[226] Stallard, Esme, "Animal tests for make up ingredients allowed", *BBC*, May 10, 2023.

[227] European Parliament Resolution of 3 May 2018 on a global ban to end animal testing for cosmetics (2017/2922(RSP)), at https://www.europarl.europa.eu/doceo/document/TA-8-2018-0202_EN.html

[228] *See*, Directive 2010/63/EU of the European Parliament and of the Council of September 22, 2010 on the protection of animals used for scientific purposes. The Recitals note that "animal welfare is a value of the Union that is enshrined in Art. 13 of the Treaty on the Functioning of the European Union. *See also*, "Alternatives to animal testing and safety assessment of chemicals", *European Union Science HUB*, n.d., at https://joint-research-centre.ec.europa.eu/scientific-activities-z/alternatives-animal-testing-and-safety-assessment-chemicals_en

models have produced no effective cures for many prevalent and debilitating diseases."[229] In September 2021, members of the European Parliament strongly urged the EU to implement an action plan to accelerate the phase-out of animals used in research and testing, with calls for funding and training for researchers, scientists and technicians,[230] reflecting the deep commitment of Europeans to improve the welfare of animals. Based on a 2016 survey, 90% of Europeans agreed that, "it is important to establish animal welfare standards that are recognized across the world" and 89% agreed that the "EU should do more to promote a greater awareness of animal welfare internationally."[231] In the same year, a record 8,342,438 signatures were delivered to the United Nations, calling for a worldwide ban on animal testing for cosmetics.[232] The movement to ban cosmetic testing on animals worldwide has never been stronger.

The Humane Cosmetics Act was first introduced into the U.S. Congress in 2015 and was re-introduced in 2021.[233] Unfortunately, it has not been enacted into law despite the fact that nearly 80% of Americans support the bill,[234] despite over 500 cosmetic brands already use non-animal based testing,[235] and even though, as of July 2020, 900 companies supported a federal ban on cosmetic animal testing.[236] The Act would end the testing of cosmetics on animals and ban the sale of cosmetics tested on animals. Ten states have passed legislation to ban cosmetics tested on animals, including California, Hawaii, Illinois, Louisiana, Maine, Maryland,

[229] *See*, "On a 30-year mission to replace animal tests with alternative methods", *EU Science HUB*, June 3, 2021, at https://joint-research-centre.ec.europa.eu/jrc-news/30-year-mission-replace-animal-tests-alternative-methods-2021-06-03_en, quoting Maurice Whelan, head of the EU Reference Laboratory for alternatives to animal testing (EURL ECVAM). Since 1991, EURL ECVAM has been working to develop and promote alternative scientific methods to replace animal-based research.

[230] "MEPs demand EU action plan to end the use of animals in research and testing", *News, European Parliament*, September 19, 2021.

[231] "Special Eurobarometer 442, Attitudes of Europeans toward Animal Welfare", *European Commission*, March 2016.

[232] Whitehouse, Lucy, "Animal testing global ban: UN receives major petition", *Cosmetics Design Europe*, October 5, 2018.

[233] Humane Cosmetics Act - H.R.6207 and S. 3357, 117th Congress (2021–2022).

[234] *See*, Engebretson, Monica and Macneil-Brown, Jessie, "Americans are united against animal testing for cosmetics", *The Washington Examiner*, December 16, 2019.

[235] *See*, "Humane Cosmetics Act", *Animal Welfare Institute*, n.d., at https://awionline.org/content/humane-cosmetics-act

[236] Starostinetskaya, Anna, "900 Companies Now Support a Federal Ban on Cosmetic Animal Testing", *VegNews*, July 30, 2020.

Nevada, New Jersey, Oregon,[237] New York and Virginia.[238] Significantly, it is the private sector that is fueling the demand for cruelty-free cosmetics. The market share of cruelty-free cosmetics is expected to increase by an impressive $5.87 billion (USD) from 2022 to 2027.[239]

Countries are also taking concrete steps to end animal suffering in non-cosmetic research settings. The legal protection afforded to animals in research settings varies widely from no legal protection, in countries like Iran [240] and Azerbaijan,[241] to extensive legal protection, in a country such as Switzerland.[242] Still, despite having some of the strictest laws in place, a reported 550,000 animals perished in Swiss laboratories as a result of animal testing in 2020.[243] A nationwide referendum was held in 2022, which would have made Switzerland the first country to completely ban all scientific and medical research on animals.[244] While the initiative failed to pass, it placed animal welfare on the national agenda, igniting dialogue on the ethics of animal testing, not only in Switzerland but in other countries as well.

In South Korea, toxicity tests on animals will no longer be required.[245] In Canada, Health Canada terminated its mandatory year-long pesticide safety testing on dogs.[246] Japan announced the end of its year-long pesticide poisoning tests on beagle dogs.[247] Brazil updated its agricultural

[237] House Bill 3212, Relating to testing cosmetics on animals (82nd Oregon Legislative Assembly – 2023 Regular Session), signed by the Governor on July 31, 2023.

[238] *See generally*, "Cosmetics testing FAQ, What is the HSUS doing to end cosmetics animal testing", *The Humane Society of the United States*, n.d., at https://www.humanesociety.org/resources/cosmetics-testing-faq; *see also*, Tarrant, Tavleen, "10 states have now banned the sale of cosmetics tested on animals", *CNN*, December 18, 2022.

[239] "Vegan Cosmetics Market by Distribution Channel, Type, and Geography – Forecast and Analysis 2023–2027", *technavio,* December 2022, at https://www.technavio.com/report/vegan-cosmetics-market-industry-analysis

[240] World Animal Protection, Iran.

[241] World Animal Protection, Azerbaijan.

[242] World Animal Protection, Switzerland.

[243] Revill, John, "Swiss to vote on becoming first country to ban animal testing", *Reuters*, February 20, 2022.

[244] Ibid.

[245] Buxton, Amy, "South Korea Will No Longer Require Toxicity Tests on Mice and Guinea Pigs", *Plant Based News*, September 22, 2022.

[246] Harris, Sophia, "Health Canada to drop required pesticide safety test using beagles", *CBC News*, March 6, 2016.

[247] Smith, Kat, "Japanese government stops testing pesticides on dogs", *Green Times*, July 18, 2018.

pesticides regulation to end the year-long poisoning test in dogs.[248] The Royal Australasian College of Surgeons agreed to phase out live animals for its Early Management of Severe Trauma program.[249] India has banned the repeat of animal testing for new drugs that were tested abroad,[250] has banned animal testing on soap and detergent products,[251] and has revised its pesticide testing regulation to permit modern cell-based alternatives to animal testing.[252] In 2017, the Dutch government announced that animal testing for research would be phased out by 2025,[253] and the government of the Brussels-Capital region in Belgium announced a ban on experiments involving dogs, cats and primates effective as of January 1, 2020 and by January 1, 2025, a general ban on all animal testing for educational and safety purposes.[254] By 2021, animal testing in Brussels had already dropped by one-third compared to the prior 5 years.[255] Still, a reported 437,275 animals perished in Belgium laboratories in 2020.[256] In 2021 the European Parliament adopted a Resolution calling on the European Commission to establish an action plan to phase out the use of animals in

[248] "HSI celebrates Brazil's elimination of cruel dog-poisoning test and other major reforms to pesticide regulation", *Humane Society International / Brazil*, August 2, 2019, at https://www.hsi.org/news-media/brazil-ends-dog-test-major-pesticide-regulation-reforms/

[249] "Live animals for trauma training no longer an option", *Hospital and Healthcare*, April 28, 2017, at https://www.hospitalhealth.com.au/content/clinical-services/article/live-animals-for-trauma-training-no-longer-an-option-271620839

[250] Johana, Shirley, "Indian Health Ministry Bans Repeat Animal Testing for Drugs", *Med India*, March 18, 2016.

[251] Dutta, Arnab, "Govt bans animal testing for soaps and detergents", *Business Standard*, April 20, 2016.

[252] Mukherje, Sanjeeb, "Rabbits no longer required to test pesticide poisoning on humans", *Business Standard*, January 12, 2018.

[253] Oziel, Clelia, "Dutch government plans to stop animal testing by 2015", *Chemical Watch*, January 5, 2017, at https://chemicalwatch.com/51958/dutch-government-plans-to-stop-animal-testing-by-2025

[254] Hoahing, Cheryl A., "Brussels Banning Animal Testing on Cats, Dogs, and Primates", *Inquisitr*, July 18, 2018. The 2025 ban would exempt the rare instances where the experiments are important and no other alternatives are available.

[255] Walker, Lauren, "Animal testing in Brussels dropped by one-third in five years", *Brussels Times*, September 27, 2021.

[256] *See*, Carter, Dylan, "Nearly half a million animals killed in Belgian laboratories in 2020", *The Brussels Times*, July 15, 2022.

experiments.[257] These developments reflect a growing sensitivity to animal testing.

The past decade has also witnessed positive changes in the United States for animals used in research. In 2012, the National Institute of Health (NIH) agreed to release more than 100 chimpanzees at the New Iberia Research Center to a Louisiana sanctuary after an independent report found virtually no scientific need for biomedical research on chimpanzees.[258] The following year, NIH announced a significant reduction in the use of chimpanzees in agency-supported biomedical research. In 2015, NIH announced a complete termination of its funding for biomedical research on chimpanzees, with all federally owned chimpanzees being eligible for retirement at sanctuaries[259] and the Harvard Medical School officially closed its National Primate Research Center.[260] The U.S. Fish and Wildlife Service also issued a final rule to give all chimpanzees endangered status under the Endangered Species Act,[261] bringing to an end the shameful era of taxpayer funded invasive testing on chimpanzees. In early 2022, Huey and Pancake, the last two chimpanzees deemed "eligible" for release by NIH, arrived at the Chimp Haven chimpanzee sanctuary.[262]

In the United States, laws tend to follow only when there is clear public support for change, and even then, they may not pass. In 2018, Senator Cory Booker introduced The Primate Protection and Research Modernization Act of 2018 to "prevent unnecessary and unethical animal

[257] See, "Plans and Actions to Accelerate a Transition to Innovation without the Use of Animals in Research, Regulatory Testing and Education", *European Parliament*; Strasbourg, France: 2021; *see also*, "A win for animals! The European Parliament votes in favour of a comprehensive plan to phase-out experiments on animals", *Eurogroup for Animals*, September 16, 2021.

[258] Stoller-Conrad, Jessica, "Research Chimps Permanent Retirement Home", *NPR*, December 18, 2012.

[259] "NIH Will No Longer Support Biomedical Research on Chimpanzees", *National Institutes of Health*, November 17, 2015.

[260] "Closure of the New England National Primate Research Center", *National Institutes of Health*, June 11, 2015.

[261] "Final Rule to List All Chimpanzees as Captive and Wild as Endangered, Questions and Answers", June 16, 2015. Prior to the Final Rule, captive chimps were listed as "threatened", but wild chimps were treated as "endangered".

[262] Greenfieldboye, Nell, "The NIH is 'largely finished' moving its former research chimps to a sanctuary", *NPR*, January 27, 2022. NIH claimed that the remaining chimps are too ill or fragile to be moved to a sanctuary and that some chimps could be moved but they are socially bonded to an ill or fragile chimp.

testing practices on primates."[263] The bill was supported by numerous legal scholars, scientists and other professionals,[264] yet despite the well-documented similarities between chimpanzees and humans,[265] and the fact that every nation that has passed protective laws has mentioned the special moral standing of apes,[266] the bill has not been passed into law. Aside from Gabon, the United States is the only nation with chimpanzees in biomedical research facilities.[267] A shameful 68,257 nonhuman primates were used in research in 2019, and an additional 40,269 primates were held as a part of the laboratories' breeding colonies.[268] The abuse of companion animals in research tends to generate more public outrage.

In 2017, the public and lawmakers were outraged when news broke that the Veterans Administration was conducting painful and unnecessary experiments on dogs.[269] The report led to investigations and the end of several Veterans Administration projects,[270] as well as the introduction of the Preventing Unkind and Painful Procedures and Experiments on Respected Species (PUPPERS) Act of 2019.[271] In 2021, the Preventing Animal Abuse and Waste (PAAW) Act of 2021[272] was introduced, which would prohibit any research that could kill or cause significant pain or distress to dogs, but as of early 2023, neither bill has been enacted into law. In 2021, the Veterans Administration was again accused of animal

[263] Primate Protection and Research Modernization Act of 2018 - S.3773, 115th Congress (2017–2018).

[264] Cory Booker, "Booker Legislation Seeks to End Unethical and Unnecessary Testing on Primates", December 18, 2018, at https://www.booker.senate.gov/news/press/booker-legislation-seeks-to-end-unethical-and-unnecessary-testing-on-primates

[265] de Waal, Frans B. M., Research Chimpanzees.

[266] de Waal, Frans B. M., Research Chimpanzees.

[267] de Waal, Frans B. M., Research Chimpanzees.

[268] The USDA Annual Report Animal Usage by Fiscal Year (Total number of animals research facilities used in regulated activities) reflects 68,257 nonhuman privates used in research laboratories in 2019; *see also*, "Nonhuman Primates", *Animal Welfare Institute*, n.d., at https://awionline.org/content/non-human-primates

[269] Brulliard, Karin, "Dog experiments at VA necessary for 'only a few areas of research.' Panel says in sweeping report", *Washington Post*, July 1, 2020.

[270] Ibid.

[271] Preventing Unkind and Painful Procedures and Experiments on Respected Species Act of 2019 or the PUPPERS Act of 2019 - H.R. 1155, 116th Congress (2019–2020).

[272] Preventing Animal Abuse and Waste Act of 2021 or the PAAW Act of 2021 - H.R.6186, 117th Congress (2021–2022); *see also*, Nancy Mace, "Rep. Mace Introduces Bipartisan Bill to End Testing on Dogs", December 8, 2021 at https://mace.house.gov/media/press-releases/rep-mace-introduces-bipartisan-bill-end-testing-dogs

abuse due to its spending millions of dollars to injure and kill healthy cats who exhibited "distress, seizures, bloody urine, and even depression" from the research.[273] The lack of action at the federal level has led some states to take action. In 2022, Virginia lawmakers passed new regulations which would prohibit the sale of dogs to a breeding facility if the facility has a single critical violation or three or more non-critical violations.[274] The regulations are aimed at a beagle breeding facility in Cumberland, Virginia, with years of federal animal welfare violations, inhumane conditions and hundreds of animal deaths.[275] Animal research takes place behind closed doors for a reason.

Industries know that the public does not like animal cruelty, even when it is in the form of animal testing. In one instance, after news broke that small animals were being forced to participate in so-called swim tests to avoid drowning, many companies ended the research, including Pfizer, AstraZeneca, Johnson & Johnson, Sage Therapeutics, AbbVie, Roche and Novo Nordisk A/S.[276] Pressure from groups and individuals has led thousands of companies and organizations to halt (or commit to halt) research projects involving animals, including Kellogg's,[277] CoverGirl,[278] Volkswagen,[279] Dove,[280] Bioqual,[281] Strauss Group,[282] the University of

[273] Xiao, Bing, "VA Continues to 'Torture' Cats in Medical Research, Rights Group Claims", *Military.com*, August 5, 2020.

[274] *See*, Masters, Kate, "Virginia lawmakers pass new regulations for controversial beagle breeding facility", *Virginia Mercury*, March 8, 2022.

[275] *See*, Fobar, Rachel, "Hundreds of beagles died at facility before government took action", *National Geographic*, May 20, 2022; *see also*, Masters, Kate, "New Violations found at Va. beagle breeding center, which recorded 300 'unknown' puppy deaths", *Virginia Mercury*, November 15, 2021.

[276] "Pfizer bans forced swim tests in animal rights win", *Pharma Manufacturing News*, November 1, 2019.

[277] *See*, e.g., Webber, Jemima, "Kellogg's Ends Animal Testing After 65 Years", *Live Kindly*, September 2019.

[278] *See*, e.g., Parsons, Sarah, "CoverGirl to become 'world's largest' cruelty-free make-up brand", *Cosmetics Business*, November 5, 2018.

[279] *See*, e.g., Prashant S. Rao and Melissa Eddy, "Volkswagen Vows to End Experiments on Animals", *New York Times*, June 4, 2018.

[280] *See*, e.g., "Dove and PETA: Together Against Animal Testing", *Dove*, n.d., at https://www.dove.com/uk/stories/about-dove/sign-to-support.html

[281] *See*, e.g., Vastag, Brian, "Era of chimp research ends at controversial Maryland lab", *Washington Post*, June 29, 2012.

[282] *See*, e.g., Jerusalem Post Staff, "Second largest Israeli food and beverage company bans animal testing", *Jerusalem Post*, January 17, 2020.

Wisconsin-Madison,[283] the University of Missouri,[284] the Medical College of Georgia,[285] Vanderbilt University,[286] Texas A&M University,[287] the University of Washington,[288] and the Tuskegee University College of Veterinary Medicine.[289] More than 100 airlines, including US Airways, Virgin Atlantic, Air France and EgyptAir, have also stopped transporting monkeys for animal research.[290] Testing on animals is becoming more widely condemned with each passing year. Private sector changes are driving legal reform, making the legal landscape ripe for change.

The U.S. Food and Drug Administration (FDA) has acknowledged that animal testing in connection with new drugs is inadequate[291] and in 2020, it launched a new program to approve human-based biology methods for use in drug development,[292] but it still needs to more fully embrace

[283] *See,* e.g., Guarino, Mark, "University of Wisconsin closes laboratory, ending cat experiments", *Reuters,* January 26, 2015.

[284] *See,* e.g., Stagno, Barbara, "University of Missouri ends shocking eye experiments on beagles, Alternatives to Animal Testing, Experimentation and Dissection – An Animal Rights Article from All-Creatures.org", *All-Ctreatures.Org,* November 2017. The University of Missouri confirmed via email to CAARE that the experiments have permanent ended, but independent confirmation of this representation is not available.

[285] *See,* e.g., News Release, "Following Physicians' Campaign, Medical College of Georgia Halts Animal Use for Surgery Training", *Physicians Committee for Responsible Medicine,* October 23, 2020.

[286] *See,* e.g., News Release, "Physicians' Multi-Year Campaign Succeeds in Stopping Animal Use for Doctor Training at Vanderbilt University", *Physicians Committee for Responsible Medicine,* February 9, 2021.

[287] *See,* e.g., Gubbins, Teresa, "Texas university stops breeding golden retrievers for experiments", *Culture Map Dallas,* September 16, 2019.

[288] *See,* e.g., News Release, "UW Replaces Animals in Deadly Training Lab Following Years of Pressure from Physicians, Local and State Legislators", *Physicians Committee for Responsible Medicine,* November 5, 2021.

[289] *See,* e.g., News Release, "Doctors Congratulate Tuskegee University on Ending Lethal Dog Use, Urge Auburn to Follow Suit", *Physicians Committee for Responsible Medicine,* January 15, 2021.

[290] Buxton, Amy, "EgyptAir Will No Longer Transport Monkeys For Animal Testing", *Plant Based News,* August 11, 2022.

[291] "Animal Testing: Why the FDA is Exploring More Alternatives", *Healthline,* August 19, 2022.

[292] News Release, "FDA Launches Program to Approve Human Biology-Based Methods for Use in Drug Development", *Physicians Committee for Responsible Medicine,* December 2, 2020.

the safer and more efficient non-animal research models.[293] At the end of 2022, the United States enacted into law the FDA Modernization Act 2.0, Reducing Animal Testing Act, which ends FDA's requirement that drugs be tested on animals before they are used in human clinical trials. This law is permissive, however, not restrictive. It does not ban animal testing, but it allows manufacturers to use more advanced, non-animal testing methods to evaluate the safety and effectiveness of a drug, such as "organ-on-chip" advances that are revolutionizing research.[294] The new law was long overdue and critically needed to update the 1938 Federal Food, Drug, and Cosmetic Act that has resulted in billions of wasted research dollars and billions of dogs, primates, rabbits and mice being subjected to experimentation, pain and death.[295] Aysha Akhtar, M.D., co-founder and CEO. of the Center for Contemporary Sciences,[296] considers the FDA Modernization Act 2.0 as a "great first step" to replace animal testing with more "human-relevant methods", noting that drug manufacturers will still need to submit testing methods to the FDA for approval. Aysha says that while historically, the FDA has been "extremely slow to accept non-animal testing methods," she believes that drug companies will use the more effective "non-animal testing methods", and eventually, as the FDA and companies become more comfortable with "advanced methods", they will replace animal testing.

The enactment of the FDA Modernization Act 2.0 is another example of how, in the United States, it is public pressure that drives private sector changes, and it is private sector pressure that drives legal reform. Researchers are developing much more effective and safe non-animal testing models, including cell-based (in-vitro) tests and computer models,

[293] For a discussion on how bioprinting could help in the development of new therapies and drugs with higher efficacy, *see* Fonseca, Ana Clotilde, et al., "Emulating Human Tissues and Organs: A Bioprinting Perspective Toward Personalized Medicine", *Chem. Rev.* 2020, 120 (19), 11093–11139, September 16, 2020. https://doi.org/10.1021/acs.chemrev.0c00342

[294] Hudson, Aaron, "Organ-Chips and Omics Advance Cancer Research", *Genetic Engineering & Biotechnology News*, February 2, 2022.

[295] Gatenholm, Erik, "The FDA Modernization Act Can Leverage Technology to Accelerate Drug Discovery and Save Millions of Animals", *Forbes*, December 20, 2021.

[296] The Center for Contemporary Sciences, a 501(c)(3) organization, works with the scientific community, lawmakers and the private sector to replace outdated animal testing methods with effective technologies.

and have created life-like human tissues as alternatives to animal testing.[297] Organ-on-chip technology has been proved to outperform animal models in safety and could generate billions in new R&D productivity.[298]

These important changes come on the heels of other significant reforms. In 2018, the FDA permanently ended its nicotine addiction studies on monkeys after four monkeys died,[299] and in 2019, the USDA ended its controversial and deadly toxoplasmosis research program that has killed thousands of cats over the decades.[300] In 2016, the Toxic Substances Control Act was updated to, inter alia, reduce and ultimately replace chemical testing on animals, which will spare millions of animals from cruelty,[301] and in 2019, the Environmental Protection Agency (EPA) issued a directive to reduce funding and animal toxicity testing (e.g., chemicals, pesticides) by 30% by 2025 and to eliminate it altogether by 2035.[302]

When the research on animals is complete, the industry practice is to euthanize the animals. In recent years there has been a movement at the state level to pass "Beagle Freedom" legislation, which requires that animals used in research held for adoption following completion of the research.[303] In 2014, Minnesota made history when it became the first state to allow dogs and cats used in research to be adopted after the conclusion of research. Since that time, other states have passed similar laws, including California, Connecticut, Delaware, Illinois, Maryland,

[297] "Groundbreaking technique helping to pave the way for advances in personalized medicine", *McMaster University*, November 30, 2016.

[298] *See*, e.g., MedTech Intelligence Staff, "Liver-Chip Successfully Identifies Drug Toxicity, Outperforms Animal and 3D Models", *MedTech Intelligence*, January 2, 2023.

[299] Kaplan, Sheila, "Citing Deaths of Lab Monkeys, F.D.A. Ends an Addiction Study", *New York Times*, January 26, 2018. Three monkeys died from anesthesia and one from a type of gastric bloat.

[300] Romo, Vanessa, "USDA Terminates Deadly Cat Experiments, Plans to Adopt Out Remaining Animals", *NPR*, April 2, 2019.

[301] Frank R. Lautenberg Chemical Safety for the 21th Century Act, 114th Congress, Public Law (June 22, 2016).

[302] EPA Press Office, "EPA Finalizes Guidance to Waive Toxicity Tests on Animal Skin: Guidance is expected to save up to 750 animals from unnecessary testing annually", *Environmental Protection Agency*, January 19, 2021, at https://www.epa.gov/newsreleases/epa-finalizes-guidance-waive-toxicity-tests-animal-skin#. In the press release, the EPA also announced $4.25 million in funding for five universities to develop non-animal testing models for evaluating chemical safety.

[303] "Help Pass The Beagle Freedom Bills", *Beagle Freedom Project*, n.d., at https://bfp.org/state/

Massachusetts, Nevada, New York, Rhode Island, Washington, Oregon and Virginia. In addition, bills are pending in other states, including Colorado, Indiana, New Jersey, Texas and Wisconsin.[304] When an educated public gets involved, positive changes can happen for animals. As of January 2022, 21 states have enacted laws or have adopted policies to permit K-12 students to elect humane alternatives instead of animal dissection.[305]

The case for a ban on animal testing for cosmetics is relatively easy, but what about animal research in connection with pharmaceuticals and medical research that purportedly benefits humans? Americans are divided on the issue of animal research[306] despite intensive lobbying efforts and advertising by the pharmaceutical industry. If you or a family member are facing a serious illness or disease, you are right to expect reliable, effective and safe medical treatments. Animal-based research models, however, have been proven to be of little relevance for humans.[307]

Dr. John J. Pippin, director of academic affairs for the Physicians Committee for Responsible Medicine,[308] warns that many reports have shown that animal research as a means of developing safe and effective treatments for humans is unreliable, and that "entire fields of medical discovery have derived little or nothing of value for humans from decades of animal experimentation."[309] As Dr. Pippin explains, "[m]any of the major causes of morbidity and mortality among humans are eye-opening examples of this failure of animal experimentation, including but not limited to HIV/AIDS, stroke, cancers … and numerous other neurological, immunological, cardiovascular, and endocrine (most prominently diabetes

[304] Ibid.

[305] "Student Choice Laws", *American Anti-Vivisection Society*, n.d., at https://aavs.org/animals-science/laws/student-choice-laws/

[306] Strauss, Mark, "Americans are divided over the use of animals in scientific research", *Pew Research Center*, August 16, 2018. A 2018 poll showed that 52% Americans were opposed using animals in scientific research while 47% of Americans favored it; *but see*, "Animal research support rises in US", *European Animal Research Association*, July 6, 2020.

[307] Bailey, Jarrod, "Biomedical Research Must Change – But a Shift Toward Human-specific Research Methods is Only Part of What Is Needed", *Alternatives to Laboratory Animals*, 2021, Vol. 49(3), 69–72. https://doi.org/10.1177/02611929211030417

[308] Dr. John J. Pippin has authored or co-authored more than 70 articles and abstracts that have been published in leading medical journals, and is a frequent speaker at law schools, bar associations and numerous medical organizations.

[309] Pippin, John J., "Animal Research in Medical Sciences: Seeking a Convergence of Science, Medicine, and Animal Law", 54 S. Tex. L. Rev. 469 (2013), at 474–475.

mellitus) diseases."[310] Citing a FDA report that indicated a 92% failure rate for drugs that tested safe and effective in preclinical trials, including animal testing, Dr. Pippin notes that the efficacy of animal testing for pharmaceutical drug testing is even more dismal.[311]

Dr. Pippin warns that while some drugs test safe with animals, many do not test safe for humans, and of the drugs that receive FDA approval, about half are later withdrawn or relabeled "for serious or lethal adverse effects not detected during animal testing."[312] As Dr. Pippin explains "it takes on average more than 100 drugs that are safe and effective in preclinical testing (including animal testing) to produce just one unique, effective, and safe drug for humans, which then works only in a minority of patients and is not curative for most disease categories."[313] As further evidence that animal testing for new drugs is "extremely unreliable", Dr. Pippin cites numerous instances where drugs tested safe during animal trials but were later found to be harmful to humans, including the arthritis drug Vioxx (rofecoxib), which resulted in an estimated 140,000 heart attacks and 60,000 deaths in the U.S., and the diabetes drug Avandia (rosiglitazone), which was reported to increase the risk of heart attacks, strokes, heart failure and cardiovascular deaths, causing as many as 100,000 deaths.[314]

A "paradigm shift" is underway to replace unreliable and cruel animal models with more modern technology that better represents human anatomy.[315] Animal research has consistently proved to be ineffective at predicting drug safety in humans, and research institutes and drug companies are moving away from testing on animals in pre-clinical research[316] and toward new developments in computer modeling, tissue engineering and other "bio-convergence" technologies that have made animal testing

[310] Id.

[311] Id., at 497. Dr. Pippin also cites Professor Robin Lovell-Badge of the MRC National Institute for Medical Research, London, who calculated clinical trial failure rate to be 94%. Id., at 498.

[312] Id., at 498.

[313] Id., at 499.

[314] Id., at 499–500.

[315] Pawlowski, J., et al., (2019). Modernizing biomedical training: replacing live animal laboratories with human simulation. In *Animal Experimentation: Working Towards a Paradigm Change*, (pp. 549–566). Brill.

[316] Nawrat, Allie, "Are we nearing the end of animal testing in pharma?" *Pharmaceutical Technology*, October 3, 2019.

obsolete.[317] Replicas of human bodies, such as the TraumaMan, are helping to modernize trauma training.[318] The message from the 2020 Advances in Cell and Tissue Culture international conference is clear. Non-animal research models that "faithfully replicate human physiology at cellular, tissue and organ level" are critical to developing highly effective, safe and low cost therapies, and "human-relevant *in vitro* models have the potential to replace animal models."[319] We need antiquated laws to catch up with new technologies, and for the health and safety of people, we need laws that ban animal testing altogether.

Animals Raised for Food

In 1906, Upton Sinclair published the novel *The Jungle*, which took readers into Chicago's meatpacking industry.[320] Sinclair wanted to educate the public on the appalling conditions and cruelty in the meat industry, but it would take another 100 years for the information age to help the public truly understand how much farm animals suffer. Farm animals are deliberately kept out of the public's sight by industries and governments. Some suggest that there is a "media blackout" on issues that involve farm animal welfare.[321] The public is better informed today, but many people are still not fully aware of how badly farm animals are treated. This is due in large part to deceptive marketing practices.

Federal and state laws in the United States prohibit false and misleading advertising.[322] However, consumers are inundated with false and misleading images of happy (indeed, blissful!) farm animals on food packing labels

[317] Gatenholm, Erik, "The FDA Modernization Act Can Leverage Technology to Accelerate Drug Discovery and Save Millions of Animals", *Forbes*, December 20, 2021.

[318] Belisomo, Randi, "TraumaMan helps doctors save humans, spares animals", *Reuters*, September 25, 2015.

[319] Singh, Bhumika, et al., "Towards More Predictive, Physiological and Animal-free In Vitro Models: Advances in Cell and Tissue Culture 2020 Conference Proceedings", *Alternatives to Laboratory Animals,* 2021, Vol. 49(3), 93–110. https://doi.org/10.1177/02611929211025006

[320] Upton Sinclair, *The Jungle*. New York, Amereon House (1995).

[321] *See,* e.g., Rollin, Bernard E. and Benson, G. John, *The Well-Being of Farm Animals, Challenges and Solutions: Issues in Animal Bioethics Series,* Blackwell Publishing (2004), at 6.

[322] The Federal Trade Commission Act prohibits false and misleading advertising. 15 U.S.C. §§41–58. For an example of a state law that prohibits false advertising, *see,* e.g., CA Bus & Prof Code §17500 (2021).

that humane-wash their true existence.[323] Walk down any aisle in the grocery store and you will find examples of "humane-washing"[324] that seek to mislead consumers about the realities of industrial animal agriculture. Meat, dairy and egg producers know that consumers are willing to pay a premium for "humanely raised" food.[325] And, given the relatively small fines imposed for deceptive advertising, those producers may decide that the additional profits are worth the legal risk, especially when so many others are doing it and the Federal Trade Commission is not challenging deceptive labels. The onus falls on cash-strapped nonprofits to challenge billion dollar companies.[326] Moreover, industry-funded organizations conduct misinformation campaigns to malign animal-free products[327] and work to pass unconstitutional restrictions on plant-based food labels.[328] Humane-washing and misinformation campaigns distort the market by enticing consumers to purchase products that they would not have purchased if they were better informed. This occurs despite clear congressional interest in informed decision-making by consumers. In upholding the constitutionality of country-of-origin disclosure requirements on meat producers, the Court of Appeals for the D.C. Circuit acknowledged

[323] The Animal Legal Defense Fund defines humane-washing as the practice of making a misleading claim about the treatment of animals or the conditions in which they are born, raised or killed. *See*, "How False Advertising Lawsuits Help Animals", *Animal Legal Defense Fund, Legal Resource*, n.d., at https://aldf.org/article/how-false-advertising-lawsuits-help-animals/

[324] Examples of humane-washing include representations that a product is "responsibly raised", "all natural", "humanely raised", "free-range", "pasture raised", "ethically raised", "thoughtfully raised", "responsibly raised", "humanely treated", "family farmed", "sustainably raised" and "natural".

[325] *See,* e.g., Thibault, M., Pailler, S. & Freund, D., "Why Are They Buying It?: United States Consumers Intentions When Purchasing Meat, Eggs, and Dairy With Welfare-related Labels", *Food ethics* 7, 12 (2022). https://doi.org/10.1007/s41055-022-00105-3; *see also*, Kelso, Alicia, "Consumers are willing to pay a premium for animal welfare certifications", *Grocery Dive*, July 17, 2018.

[326] *See,* e.g., "FTC Challenge: Boar's Head "Humanely Raised" Labels Deceive Consumers", *Animal Welfare Institute*, February 23, 2021.

[327] *See,* e.g., O'Connor, Anahad, "Fake Meat v. Real Meat", *New York Times*, December 2, 2020.

[328] Turtle Island Foods SPC v. Michael G. Strain, U.S. District Court, Middle District of Louisiana (No. 20-00674-BAJ-EWD), striking down Louisiana's Act No. 273, *Truth in Labeling of Food Products Act*, as an unconstitutional restriction on free speech under the First Amendment. The law prohibited plant-based meat products from being marketed as "burgers" and "sausages".

Congress's interest in "enabling customers to make informed choices based on characteristics of the products they wished to purchase, including the United States supervision of the entire production process for health and hygiene."[329] Denying the public full and accurate information about animal agriculture denies consumers the right to make informed decisions and it distorts private markets. The reality is that factory farms are dark, cramped, dirty and diseased[330] cesspools of misery, deprivation and despair.

It is estimated that every year more than 70 billion land animals are killed for food globally,[331] of which 10 billion land animals are farmed in the United States.[332] In 2017, it was estimated that between 51 and 167 billion *farmed* fish were killed globally for food,[333] and between 2007 and 2016, the number of wild fish caught was estimated to be 1–3 trillion.[334] Profits drive the treatment of animals in the United States. Profitability is allowed to take precedence over animal welfare because the legal system provides little to no protection.

Farm animals endure horrific physical pain and mental anguish during their short lives, including extreme confinement and deprivation,[335] castration, hot-iron branding and painful mutilations, such as the docking of tails of pigs, sheep and dairy cattle, cutting of horns off cattle, and cutting of beaks off chickens, all without anesthesia or anything for pain relief. Pigs are amongst the most intelligent animals on earth yet they are routinely subjected to tail docking, teeth clipping and surgical castration, all without anesthesia, and these procedures compromise the health and

[329] Am. Meat Inst. v. U.S. Dep't of Agric., 760 F.3d 18 (D.C. Cir. 2014).

[330] *See*, Chittilapally, Joslyn, "How factory farming breeds deadly viruses and epidemics", *LifeGate*, April 16, 2022, describing how animals can be carriers of harmful viruses, bacteria, parasites and fungi that can spread to people.

[331] Sanders, Bas, *Global Animal Slaughter Statistics and Charts*, Faunalytics, October 10, 2018.

[332] "Livestock and Meat Domestic Data," *USDA Economic Research Service*, April 27, 2023.

[333] "Numbers of farmed fish slaughtered each year", *Fish Count (UK)*, n.d. at http://fishcount.org.uk/fish-count-estimates-2/numbers-of-farmed-fish-slaughtered-each-year

[334] *See*, "Reducing suffering in fisheries", *Fish Count*, n.d., at http://fishcount.org.uk/

[335] For further information on state legislative initiatives to ban the extreme confinement of farm animals, *see* "Farm Animal Anti-Confinement Legislation", *Animal Welfare Institute*, n.d., at https://awionline.org/content/farm-animal-anti-confinement-legislation

welfare of the animals.[336] In the EU, where the practice of tail docking of pigs is illegal,[337] there are still significant compliance concerns among member states.[338]

In the United States, the meat and dairy industries successfully lobbied lawmakers to exclude all animals raised for food from the protection of anti-cruelty laws without any legal or ethical justification. Anti-cruelty laws exempt otherwise cruel practices if they are "common" or "customary" in the industry, such as tail docking, castration and branding.[339] As industries continue to move away from such animal cruelty, the "common practices" exclusion should one day not apply.

The extreme confinement of farm animals began in the twentieth century as a means to boost productivity and convenience, but it came at an enormous cost to the lives of animals.[340] Pigs are forced to live immobilized in tiny gestation crates. Egg laying hens are forced to live on the equivalent of a piece of paper their entire lives. Dairy cows are tethered to stalls that prevent any movement, socialization or natural behaviors. Calves are isolated away from mothers in tiny veal crates. The modern agricultural model houses billions of animals so tightly that they experience stress, frustration, discomfort, injury, disease and death.

As troubling as factory farms are, the export of live animals for slaughter is worse. It is estimated that nearly 2 billion farm animals are packed into ships and onto trucks every year for delivery to other countries.[341] The journeys can take days or weeks, during which time animal waste builds up to levels that can make lying down treacherous. The filth, poor ventilation, excessive heat and cramped conditions are more than many

[336] Morgan, Liat, et al., "Physiological and economic benefits of abandoning invasive surgical procedures and enhancing animal welfare in swine production", *Scientific Reports*, November 6, 2019.

[337] Council Directive 2008/120/EC of 18 December 18, 2008 laying down minimum standards for the protection of pigs (Codified Version), Ch. 1, Sec. 8.

[338] Foote, Natasha, "Routine illegal pig-tail docking continues unabated in the EU", *EURACTIV*, September 30, 2020.

[339] *See*, e.g., "Legal Protections for Animals on Farms", *Animal Welfare Institute*, n.d., at https://awionline.org/sites/default/files/uploads/documents/FA-AWI-Legal Protections-AnimalsonFarms-110714.pdf

[340] For a discussion of convenience versus animal welfare, see Tennenhouse, Erica, "What a Delay on Canada's Gestation Crate Ban Will Mean for Pig Welfare", *Forbes*, January 9, 2021.

[341] Levitt, Tom, "Two billion and rising: the global trade in live animals in eight charts", *Guardian*, January 20, 2020.

animals can bear, and many die during the journey.[342] Others succumb to infections, stress, or injury. The journeys themselves are also not without risk. Mechanical failures, capsizing, fires and rough weather have all claimed the lives of livestock at sea. In Australia, the failure of regulators to take action against live exporters has resulted in mass animal casualties over the years.[343] Despite tragedy after tragedy, the industry continues today, though public awareness is creating change. In 2023, a Brazilian court banned the export of live cattle, ruling that, "[a]nimals are not things. They are sentient beings, that is individuals who feel hunger, thirst, pain, cold, anguish, fear."[344]

Notwithstanding all of the issues associated with animal agriculture, including human and animal rights violations and environmental devastation, the federal government and states in the United States spend billions of dollars subsidizing the meat and dairy industries,[345] in the form of disaster payments, crop insurance, counter-cyclical payments, water subsidies, below market loans and insurance and research assistance.[346] Animal agriculture has far too much political influence (even bringing milkshakes to lawmakers in an effort to win political favor!![347]) and has profited far too long from government subsidies. There is growing discomfort with the business-as-usual approach to farm bills. Strong congressional interest in an alternative protein legislative agendas[348] and legislation proposals like the *Peas, Legumes, and Nuts Today Act (PLANT Act)*, introduced to

[342] *See,* e.g., K. Oanh Ha, Kevin Varley and Bloomberg, "'We don't look at the cargo or animal welfare': Grisly deaths of 1800 shipped cows fuel calls for live animal export ban", *Fortune*, July 8, 2021.

[343] "Live exports: mass animal deaths going unpunished as holes in system revealed", *Guardian*, April 9, 2018.

[344] Mano, Ana, "Brazil court bans live cattle exports over animal welfare concerns", *Reuters*, April 27, 2023, citing judge Djalma Gomes.

[345] *See,* e.g., Press Release, "USDA Provides Payments of nearly $800 Million in Assistance to Help Keep Farmers Farming", *U.S. Department of Agriculture*, October 18, 2022.

[346] Simon, David Robinson, *Meatonomics: How the Rigger Economies of Meat and Dairy Make You Consume Too Much – and How to Eat Better, Live Longer, and Spend Smarter.* California, Conari Press, 2013, at 79. ISBN 978-1-57324-620-0.

[347] Bustillo, Ximena, "Congress gears up for another farm bill. Here's what's on the menu", *NPR*, February 2, 2023.

[348] Ataman, Deniz, "Plant-based and cellular agriculture leaders raise awareness on Capital Hill for sustainable food production ahead of 2023 Farm Bill", *Food Navigator*, April 28, 2023.

support plant-based food production,[349] show that at least some lawmakers understand the need for revolutionary change in the nation's food system.

Government investment in the explosion of more environmentally friendly and convenient plant-based meat and dairy options is good policy. They do not pose the same zoonotic disease risks and environmental degradation as animal agriculture. At minimum, farm subsidies must be redirected to plant-based proteins and non-slaughtered meat. A 2021 report concludes that alternative proteins could support 9.8 million jobs and $1.1 trillion in economic value worldwide by 2050 and that a shift away from animal products toward a more diversified protein sector could yield $5.5 trillion in climate mitigation benefits by 2050.[350] Innovative legal solutions are also needed and statutory frameworks are already in place in the Internal Revenue Code to incentivize certain investments by the private sector. The federal low-income housing tax credit (LIHTC) program under I.R.C. §42, for instance, provides a federal income tax credit to encourage the development of low-income housing rental properties in the United States. The LIHTC program is one of the most successful and widely supported programs in the country and it has created millions of affordable housing units. Similar public-private ventures could be used to modernize the nation's food supply to support more planet friendly options for the twenty-first century.

Recent Developments for Animals Raised for Food

In the last decade, farm animals have been on the agenda as never before. Worldwide, laws are being adopted to protect farm animals, with most changes focusing on the extreme confinement of animals. To date, a handful of countries have banned or have committed to ban battery cages for egg laying hens (e.g., Austria, the Czech Republic, Germany, Luxembourg,

[349] Cervera, Marc, "US Plant Act poised to accelerate alternative protein and propel the burgeoning industry", *Nutrition Insight*, July 31, 2023.

[350] "Global Innovation Needs Assessment: Protein diversity, *Vivid Economics*, November 1, 2021, at 4, at https://www.climateworks.org/wp-content/uploads/2021/11/GINAs-Protein-Diversity.pdf

Australia[351] and Bhutan[352]). Some countries have banned or have placed restrictions on the confinement of sows (e.g., Austria, Sweden, the U.K., Norway, Switzerland, Canada,[353] New Zealand[354] and Germany).[355] While these new laws reflect important trends toward improving animal welfare, the reality is that most of the world's egg laying hens (about 6.5 billion) and tens of millions of sows still remain in cages, as do millions of other farm animals.[356] The global community, however, is becoming increasingly uncomfortable with this confinement.

In response to the European Citizens' Initiative "End the Cage Age", supported by 1,397,113 citizens across the European Union,[357] the European Commission in 2021 announced plans for a legislative proposal by 2023 to ban cages by 2027 for a number of farm animals, including sows, calves, rabbits, ducks, geese, and egg-laying hens.[358] This initiative shows that the European public cares deeply about the welfare of farm animals. Inhumane confinement not only thwart animals' natural instincts, but also seriously harm animals' welfare and cause immense suffering.[359] The movement to install CCTV in slaughterhouses has gained traction in

[351] The ban in Australia does not come into effect until 2036. *See*, Bourke, Latika, "Australian hens to remain in battery cages for another 14 years", *The Sydney Morning Herald*, August 19, 2022; *see also*, Dahlstrom, Michael, "Australia announces ban on battery cage eggs", *Yahoo News*, August 18, 2022.

[352] "Brutan bans confinement cages for egg-laying hens", *Far East Agriculture*, August 27, 2012, at https://fareasternagriculture.com/live-stock/poultry/bhutan-bans-confinement-cages-for-egg-laying-hens

[353] *See*, National Farm Animal Care Council, Code of Practice for the Care and Handling of Pigs (2014), at 11. ISBN 978-1-988793-26-9 (electronic book text).

[354] *See generally*, RNZ, "Pig farrowing crates: Govt. seeks feedback on banning or limiting use", *New Zealand Herald*, April 28, 2022.

[355] *See generally*, "End The Cage Age, Why the EU Must Stop Caging Farm Animals", *Compassion in World Farming*, n.d., at 5 and 18, at https://www.ciwf.org.uk/research/animal-welfare/end-the-cage-age-why-the-eu-must-stop-caging-farm-animals/

[356] Moens, Jonathan, "The worst horrors of factory farming could soon be phased out of Europe", *Vox*, September 29, 2021.

[357] For more on the initiative, *see* "End the Cage Age", *Compassion in World Farming*, n.d., at https://www.endthecageage.eu/

[358] Press release, "European Citizens' Initiative: Commission to propose phasing out of cages for farm animals", *European Commission*, June 30, 2021. In order to become law, the proposal would also need to be approved by the European Parliament and the European Council.

[359] End The Cage Age, at 3–4.

recent years in some countries, including Israel,[360] England,[361] Spain[362] and the Netherlands,[363] with artificial intelligence being developed for better monitoring capabilities.[364]

New laws are also prohibiting cruel practices. Foie gras (i.e., fatty liver), which involves force feeding ducks and geese several times a day through metal tubes shoved down the birds' throats,[365] is so cruel that its production and/or importation is illegal in many countries, including India,[366] Australia,[367] Germany,[368] Italy,[369] the U.K.,[370] Denmark,[371] Finland,[372] Norway,[373] Luxembourg,[374] Austria,[375] Croatia,[376] Turkey,[377] Poland,[378]

[360] Government of Israel, "The Ministry of Agriculture is ordering the installation of cameras in abattoirs and slaughterhouses that will broadcast live to a Ministry control room", December 12, 2015.

[361] Policy Paper, "Action Plan for Animal Welfare", *U.K.* Government, May 12, 2021; *see also*, "CCTV becomes mandatory in all abattoirs in England", *England, Department for Environment, Food & Rural Affairs*, May 4, 2018.

[362] *See*, "Spain introduced video surveillance in slaughterhouses to ensure humane treatment, an EU first", *Euro News*, August 23, 2022.

[363] "Animals in slaughterhouses better monitored by innovative camera surveillance", *Vion Food Group*, January 25, 2021.

[364] Ibid.

[365] The production of foie gras can cause animals to suffer pneumonia, injuries to beaks and throats and organ failure. *See*, Johnson, Kim, "What is Foie Gras", *Animal Equality*, July 26, 2019.

[366] Patel, Atish, "India bans Import of Controversial Foie Gras", *The Wall Street Journal*, July 7, 2014.

[367] "Dishing up foie gras ruffles feathers", *ABC News*, September 10, 2018.

[368] "Foie Gras: Where is it Actually Banned?", *Fine Dining Lovers*, May 16, 2016.

[369] Southey, Flora, "'Foie gras production is not cruel': Resistance against proposed UK ban on foie gras imports", *Food Navigator*, May 21, 2021; *see also*, "Foie Gras: Where is it Actually Banned?", *Fine Dining Lovers*, May 16, 2016.

[370] Caro, Mark, *The Foie Gras Wars: How a 5000-Year-Old Delicacy Inspired the World's Fiercest Food Fight*, Simon and Schuster (2009), at 33.

[371] Ibid. *See also*, "Foie Gras: Where is it Actually Banned?", *Fine Dining Lovers*, May 16, 2016.

[372] Ibid. *See also*, Southey, Flora, Foie gras production is not cruel; *see also*, Foie Gras: Where is it Actually Banned?

[373] Ibid.

[374] Caro, Mark, *The Foie Gras Wars*, at 33; *see also*, "Foie Gras: Where is it Actually Banned?

[375] Caro, Mark, *The Foie Gras Wars*, at 33.

[376] Caro, Mark, *The Foie Gras Wars*, at 33.

[377] Caro, Mark, *The Foie Gras Wars*, at 33.

[378] Southey, Flora, Foie gras production is not cruel. *See also*, Foie Gras: Where is it Actually Banned?

the Czech Republic,[379] Sweden,[380] Switzerland,[381] Argentina[382] and Israel.[383] The mass culling of male chicks by maceration or asphyxiation is common practice because the industry considers the chicks to be an unwanted byproduct of the egg industry, [384] but as of January 1, 2022, this practice is illegal in Germany, France and Switzerland.[385] Israeli researchers have also developed "gene-edited hens" that could revolutionize the egg industry (and prevent the slaughter of billions of male chicks) by laying eggs from which only female chicks can hatch.[386]

Switzerland has joined New Zealand in banning the boiling of live lobsters,[387] and in Italy, lobsters may not be kept on ice in restaurant kitchens because it causes unjustifiable suffering.[388] Bear bile farming, which involves invasive and traumatic methods to extract bile from a bear's gallbladder, cause unimaginable physical and psychological suffering.[389] Sedated or restrained bears are repeatedly injured with long needles until the gallbladder is located and bile is extracted. In 2017 Vietnam agreed to close all remaining bear bile farms,[390] and at the end of 2021, Vietnam's Son La Province was reported to be free of captive bile farming bears after

[379] Ibid.

[380] Ibid.

[381] Caro, Mark, *The Foie Gras Wars*, at 33; *see also*, Foie Gras: Where is it Actually Banned?

[382] Animal Health, Resolution No. 413/2003, August 25, 2003 (prohibition on force-feeding birds); *see also*, Foie Gras: Where is it Actually Banned?, *Fine Din.*

[383] Foie Gras: Where is it Actually Banned?

[384] Male chicks are considered by industry to be an unwanted byproduct of egg production because they cannot lay eggs and are not suitable for meat.

[385] Southey, Flora, "France and Germany first countries to ban chick culling", *Food Navigator*, July 22, 2021; Vuilleumier, Marie, "Switzerland bans shredding of male chicks", *SWI Swissinfo.ch*, September 20, 2019.

[386] Ghosh, Pallab, "Gene-edited hens may end cull of billions of chicks", *BBC*, December 13, 2022.

[387] Bachmann, Helena, "Switzerland makes it illegal to boil a lobster", *USA Today*, February 18, 2018.

[388] Reuters Staff, "Italian court says lobsters must not catch cold before cooking", *Reuters*, June 16, 2017.

[389] *See*, "Five things you need to know about bear bile farming", *Animals Asia*, November 1, 2021.

[390] "Breaking News: Vietnam agrees plan to close all bear bile farms", *Animals Asia*, July 19, 2017, at https://www.animalsasia.org/us/media/news/news-archive/breaking-news-vietnam-agrees-plan-to-close-all-bear-bile-farms.html. While bear bile farming was made illegal in 1992, households were permitted to keep the bears on the government's behalf provided that they agree not to extract bile. This effectively allowed the industry to continue.

the last bear was moved to a sanctuary.[391] It is reported, however, that many bile farms continue to operate illegally in Vietnam.[392]

Cambodia passed the country's first Law on Animal Health and Production, which prescribes rules for the humane treatment of livestock.[393] In India, the Animal Welfare Board and several High Courts have declared battery cages illegal[394] and the Union Ministry of Shipping banned the export of livestock from all sea ports.[395] India also adopted new rules to improve conditions for animals sold at livestock markets.[396] In the UAE, the use of electroshock devices like cattle prods is now prohibited.[397] In 2021, the U.K. announced its *Action Plan for Animal Welfare*, calling for an end to live animal export, enhanced health and welfare support for farm animals and further review of space requirements.[398] In South Africa, the Government of the Western Cape's Health Department is promoting more plant-based eating,[399] while in Germany, meat was banned at official functions.[400] Even a "Milk is Inhumane" advertisement

[391] Bender, Kelli, "Bear Kept in Narrow Cage for 20 Years Moves to Spacious Sanctuary to 'Find Her Bear Friends'", *People*, December 14, 2021.

[392] "Bringing an End to Bear-Bile Farming in Vietnam", *Animal Welfare Institute*, AWI Quarterly, Fall 2022.

[393] Sothear, Kang, "First Animal Health, Production Law Passed", *Cambodia Daily*, December 17, 2015.

[394] Law Commission of India, Report No. 269, Transportation and House-keeping of Egg-laying hens (layers) and Broiler Chickens, July 2017, at http://www.latestlaws.com/wp-content/uploads/2017/10/Law-Commission-Report-No.-269-Transportation-and-House-keeping-of-Egg-laying-hens-layers-and-Broiler-Chickens.pdf

[395] Kateshiya, Gopal, "Despite boom, govt bans all livestock exports from ports indefinitely", *Indian Express*, August 10, 2018.

[396] Pacelle, Wayne, "India adopts remarkable set of new animal protection policies", *The Humane Society of the United States*, May 26, 2017.

[397] Webster, Nick, "Pet abandonment now punishable by law in the UAE", *National News*, December 13, 2018.

[398] Policy Paper, "Action Plan for Animal Welfare", *U.K.* Government, May 12, 2021, Sec. 6 (Farm Animals).

[399] Wellness Team, "Wow! Learn Live Eat Play: Annual Community Report 2019, Western Cape on Wellness (Wow!), January 2019 – December 2019, Creating a Culture of Wellness Together", dated September 2020, at 7.1.1. https://www.westerncape.gov.za/western-cape-on-wellness/files/atoms/files/WoW%21%20Annual%20Community%20Report%202019.pdf

[400] EcoWatch, "Functions to 'Set a Good Example for Climate Protection'", *Eco Watch*, February 23, 2017, at https://www.ecowatch.com/germany-ban-meat-2280180857.html

was upheld by U.K.'s Advertising Standards Agency.[401] China also announced policies to reduce meat consumption in China by 50%.[402] In Switzerland, a basic legal principal is that no person, including farmers and researchers, may "improperly subject an animal to pain, suffering, harm or fear", and "when dealing with an animal, its dignity, i.e., its inherent worth, must be respected".[403] In practice, this has meant that castration and removal of horns must be done under anesthesia.[404]

We share a special bond with dog and cat companions, yet they face the same dangers and cruelty that farm animals face. Until recently, the public in the United States has not been aware that in some cultures, dogs and cats are considered food. It was not until 2018 that the United States enacted the Dog and Cat Meat Prohibition Act to prohibit the slaughter, transport, purchase and sale of dogs and cats for human consumption.[405] In a rare display of solidarity, the House of Representations adopted a resolution urging all nations to outlaw the dog and cat meat trade,[406] even as it sanctions the meat trade of equally sentient animals.

It is estimated that 30 million dogs are victims of the dog meat trade every year across Asia.[407] In some countries, like Canada[408] and the U.K.,[409] the slaughter and sale of dog meat is illegal but consumption is not. In South Korea, an estimated 2 million dogs are killed annually for food, and while a court ruled in 2018 that the killing of dogs for meat is illegal, the consumption of dog meat is still legal.[410] In Vietnam, it is estimated that 1

[401] Clarke, Josie, "Controversial 'milk is inhumane' advert approved by watchdog", *Independent,* July 28, 2017.

[402] O. Milman and S. Leavenworth, "China's plan to cut meat consumption by 50% cheered by climate campaigners", *Guardian,* June 20, 2016.

[403] Misicka, Susan, "How well are Swiss animals protected?", *SWI Swissinfo.ch,* January 18, 2020.

[404] Id.

[405] Dog and Cat Meat Trade Prohibition Act of 2018, 115th Congress, December 20, 2018.

[406] U.S. Housing of Representatives, Res. 401 – Urging all nations to outlaw the dog and cat meat trade and to enforce existing laws against such trade, 115th Congress (2017–2018).

[407] "Shutting Down the Dog Meat Trade", *Humane Society International,* n.d., at https://www.hsi.org/news-media/stop-dog-meat-trade/

[408] Hopper, Tristin, "It's totally legal to eat cats and dogs in Canada", *National Post,* October 1, 2021.

[409] The Dog Meat (Consumption) (Offences) Bill of U.K. Parliament, first reading February 19, 2019, failed to complete its passage through the Parliament.

[410] Brady, Heather, "South Korea Rules Killing Dogs for Meat Illegal, But Fight Continues", *National Geographic,* July 3, 2018.

million cats, including strays and pets, are slaughtered every year for their meat.[411] Still, dog meat consumption is rapidly declining in South Korea, with 84% of citizens rejecting dog meat.[412] The Gyeonggi province shut down the largest dog slaughterhouse in South Korea in 2018,[413] and South Korea's President, Moon Jae-in, is contemplating a ban on dog meat consumption.[414] The change in attitudes toward a tradition that has lasted for more than a thousand years is credited to the sharp increase in pet keepers in South Korea.[415]

In 2017, Taiwan became the first nation to ban the consumption of dog and cat meat in East Asia[416] and the country has been enforcing the new law with fines and jail sentences.[417] The dog meat trade is also illegal in Indonesia, and while the geography of the country makes enforcement difficult,[418] a court did sentence a dog meat trader to jail in 2021.[419] There are also indications that China is considering a ban on dog meat due to the risk of disease transmission and animal welfare.[420] While dog and cat meat consumption continues in many places across the globe, there is a growing backlash against the practice. In 2018, Egypt faced global outrage after reports revealed that the government was planning to export stray animals

[411] Four Paws International, "First Report of its Kind Released Exposing the Cat Meat Trade in Vietnam", *Global Newswire*, August 12, 2020.

[412] "New poll shows 84% of South Koreans reject eating dog meat as HIS rescues nearly 200 dogs from meat farm that 'smells of death'", *Humane Society International*, October 22, 2020,athttps://www.hsi.org/news-media/new-poll-shows-majority-of-south-koreans-reject-eating-dog-meat-as-hsi-rescues-nearly-200-dogs-from-meat-farm/

[413] Wilkinson, Bard and Seo, Yoonjung, "South Korea closes largest dog meat slaughterhouse", *CNN,* November 22, 2018. The largest dog meat slaughterhouse in South Korea in 2018 was Taepyeong, which killed hundreds of thousands of dogs every year.

[414] Shin, Hyonhee, "S. Korea's Moon hints at dog meat ban amid debate over animal rights", *Reuters*, September 27, 2021.

[415] Maresca, Thomas, "South Korean dog meat farms closing as attitudes change", *UPI World News*, October 28, 2020.

[416] Wang, Serenitie, "Taiwan bans eating dog and cat meat", *CNN,* April 12, 2017.

[417] *See,* e.g., Yang, Sophia, "Vietnamese migrant workers in Taiwan fined NT$1 million for preparing dog meat", *Taiwan News*, January 1, 2017.

[418] *See*, Pierson, David, "Why the dog meat trade persists in Indonesia, despite consumption being illegal", *Los Angeles Times*, May 24, 2020.

[419] "Indonesia jails dog meat trade in landmark case", *Times of Malta*, October 21, 2021.

[420] Standaert, Michael, "China signals end to dog meat consumption by humans", *Guardian*, April 9, 2020. Citing concerns over animal welfare and disease transmission, China's Ministry of Agriculture and Rural Affairs has prepared a draft policy that would forbid canine meat, calling dogs "special companion animal[s]".

to Asian countries where they would be consumed as food,[421] and in 2016, a petition with 11 million signatures was presented by Chinese and international campaigners calling for an end to the annual dog meat festival in Yulin, China, where dogs are beaten to death in slaughterhouses.[422] Many Americans are disturbed by the practice of eating dogs and cats, but the United States is #1 in meat consumption in the world.[423]

Investigations into farm animal cruelty in the United States, Canada, Brazil and Mexico are educating the public about what farm animals endure,[424] and members of the public are demanding accountability. In Canada, three men who worked at Chilliwack Battle Sales, the largest dairy factory farm in Canada, were imprisoned (and the owner fined) for beating and whipping cows with chains.[425] In Spain, the highest penalty for farm animal abuse in the nation's history was handed out to men who beat pigs with iron bars, stabbed them with swords, and cut open a fully conscious pig to remove her piglets.[426] In the U.K., a farmer was jailed for 18 months for gross abuse and neglect of hundreds of animals,[427] and the owners of a California slaughterhouse agreed to pay a $497.3 million judgment in connection with an animal cruelty case that led to the largest beef recall in history.[428] Exposure of such cruelty is leading countries to enact better laws to protect farm animals, like Zapopan, Mexico, the first

[421] Sherbini, Ramadan Al, "Uproar in Egypt over 'plan' to export stray animals", *Gulf News*, December 27, 2018.

[422] Denyer, Simon, "Activists gather 11 million signatures against China's infamous dog-meat festival", *Washington Post*, June 10, 2016.

[423] Smith, Rob, "These are the countries that eat the most meat", *World Economic Forum*, August 29, 2018.

[424] *See*, e.g., "Investigation: Animal Equality Exposes Suffering on Brazilian Pig Farm", *Animal Equality*, July 21, 2020, at https://animalequality.org/news/investigation-animal-equality-exposes-suffering-on-brazilian-pig-farm/; "Undercover Investigations", *Mercy for Animals*, at https://mercyforanimals.org/investigations/

[425] Ip, Stephanie, "More jail time sought for three convicted in Chilliwack cow abuse case", *Vancouver Sun*, June 16, 2017.

[426] Animal Equality, "Unprecedented Sentence in One of the Worst Cases of Animal Cruelty Ever Documented", *PR Newswire*, September 27, 2016.

[427] "Bristol animal cruelty farmer jailed for 18 months", *BBC*, November 4, 2019. The RSPCA inspector, who found hundreds of dead and dying animals, called the case the worst case of animal cruelty she had ever seen.

[428] Chiem, Linda, "Slaughterhouse Owners Hit With $500 M Judgment in FCA Case", *Law360*, November 16, 2012.

city in Mexico to criminalize cruelty to farm animals.[429] Exposure to such cruelty is also leading the public to embrace plant-based options. After an investigation into cruelty in Italy's lamb industry, lamb consumption dropped by 70% during Easter.[430]

The barbaric practices inflicted on animals raised for food are often justified as a necessary evil because the factory farm model is needed to feed a growing population. The reality is that the model is actually anchored in convenience and profit. Many members of the public understand this and are demanding better treatment of farm animals, and companies are responding. Companies are adopting policies to require cage-free sourced eggs. To date, thousands of brands,[431] retailers,[432] food manufacturers,[433] restaurants and food chains, [434] food service companies,[435] pharmacies,[436] restaurant operators,[437] entertainment venues,[438] airlines,[439]

[429] Sharma, Aman, "Fifteen of Animal Equality's Most Important Victories, *Animal Equality*, December 27, 2021.

[430] "Because of You 2016 was a Kinder Year for Farmed Animals", *Animal Equality,* December 20, 2016.

[431] Unilever, Sodexo, Inc., Compass Group, Yum! Brands, Conagra, and Dunkin are among the many brands that have committed to use only cage-free eggs. *See*, "Egg track 2021 Report" prepared by Compassion in World Farming.

[432] Walmart, 7 Eleven and Whole Foods are among the retailers that have committed to use cage-free eggs. *See*, "Egg track 2021 Report" prepared by Compassion in World Farming, at 10.

[433] Nestle, Kraft Heinz Company, General Mills, Kellogg's, Hormel Foods, Mars, Pepsico and Hershey are among the many food manufacturing companies that have committed to use cage-free eggs. *See*, Compassion in World Farming, "Egg Track 2021 Report", at 50–52, at https://www.ciwf.org.uk/media/7447947/2021_eggtrack_report_final.pdf

[434] Many restaurants have committed to use cage-free eggs, including McDonalds, Burger King, Taco Bell, Darden, Subway, TGI Fridays, The Cheesecake Factory, Panera Bread, Krispy Kreme, Caribou Coffee, Starbucks Coffee, Peet's Coffee, Einstein Bros. Bagels and Jack in the Box. *See*, Egg track 2021 Report.

[435] Aramark, Corp., Sodexo, Inc. and Compass Group are among the food service companies who have committed to use cage-free eggs. *See*, Egg track 2021 Report for additional companies.

[436] *See,* e.g., "Cage-Free Egg Statement", CVS Pharmacy, n.d., at https://www.cvshealth.com/policies/cage-free-egg-statement; *see also*, "Walgreens Cage Free Egg Statement", Walgreens, n.d., at https://www.walgreens.com/topic/information/cage-free-eggs.jsp

[437] Alsea, a restaurant company with multiple brands, committed to use cage-free eggs worldwide. *See*, Egg track 2021 Report, at 18.

[438] The Walt Disney Company, Six Flags, Inc. and SeaWorld Parks & Entertainment have committed to use cage-free eggs. *See*, Egg track 2021 Report.

[439] *See,* e.g., Lazare, Lewis, "United Airlines messages American and Delta: We have cage-free eggs and you DON'T!", *Business Journals*, November 21, 2017.

hotels,[440] cruise ships,[441] grocery stores,[442] and other businesses have committed to use cage-free eggs. In the last decade, many companies have announced plans to eliminate the use of gestation crates from their supply chains, but sadly, some companies have weakened or removed their commitments.[443] Other companies have pledged to remove tail docking practices from their supply chain, though many commitments remain aspirational only.[444]

A number of companies have also adopted "animal welfare" policies, many of which refer to the "Five Freedoms" for animals, which include freedom from hunger and thirst; freedom to express natural behavior; freedom from discomfort; freedom from pain, injury and disease; and freedom from fear and distress.[445] Nestle,[446] Walmart,[447] Aramark,[448]

[440] Marriott, Hyatt, Hilton, Wyndham, Radisson, Mandarin Oriental, Langham Hospitality Group, The Peninsula Hotels, Best Western and Choice Hotels are among the many hotels that have pledged to serve only cage-free eggs. *See*, "Three More Hotel Brands Make Cage-Free Egg Commitments", *Lodging Magazine*, August 4, 2020.

[441] Norwegian Cruise Line Holdings, which operates Norwegian Cruise Line, Oceania Cruises and Regent Seven Sea Cruises, announced that it will only use cage-free eggs by the end of 2025. *See*, "Norwegian Cruise Line Holdings to Switch to 100% Cage-Free Eggs", *Cruise Industry News*, November 6, 2022.

Carnival Corp., Royal Caribbean and Norwegian Cruise Line have also made commitments to go cage-free across its global operations. *See*, Ross, Aaron, "Carnival Introduces Global Cage-Free Policy", *The Humane League*, January 13, 2022.

[442] A number of grocery stores have pledged to use only cage-free eggs, including Whole Foods, Kroger and Publix. *See*, Egg track 2021 Report.

[443] Burger King, Panera Bread, Chipotle, Bon Appetit and The Cheesecake Factory have adopted policies for gestation crate-free pigs, *but see*, "Quit Stalling 2021: Are Companies Making Good on Promises to End Sow Confinement?", *World Animal Protection*, 2021, at https://www.worldanimalprotection.us/news/quit-stalling-new-report-shows-companies-may-be-misleading-customers-false-promises-pig

[444] *See*, e.g., Unilever's Farm animal welfare statement, which states that for 20% of its global dairy population, they "cannot yet guarantee that the practice [of tail docking] does not take place."

[445] *See*, "Five Freedoms: the gold standard of animal welfare", *American Humane*, October 17, 2016.

[446] "Appendix to The Nestle Supplier Code: Nestle Commitment on Farm Animal Welfare", *Nestle*, n.d., at https://www.nestle.com/sites/default/files/2022-03/nestle-commitment-farm-animal-welfare-appendix.pdf

[447] "Walmart Policies and Guidelines: Animal Welfare – Swine Assurance Position", *Walmart*, n.d., at https://corporate.walmart.com/policies

[448] "Aramark Establishes Animal Welfare Policy: In collaboration with Humane Society of the United States, new principles and policies address multiple issues impacting treatment of animals", *Aramark*, April 29, 2015, at https://www.aramark.com/newsroom/news/aramark-establishes-animal-welfare-policy#

Panera Bread[449] and Hilton[450] are among the companies that have adopted the Five Freedoms in their policy statements, yet in many cases, the policies use soft language, like "working with", "we aim" and "our goal".[451] Other companies have committed to comply with the Global Animal Partnership's *5-Step Animal Welfare Program*, which focuses on health and productivity, natural living and emotional well-being,[452] but some companies have failed to provide commitment deadlines or updates.[453] Companies are more likely to make meaningful changes that can be seen by consumers, such as when Nabisco changed its 116-year old package for Barnum's Animals to remove cages,[454] or when Whole Foods stopped selling rabbit meat,[455] but it is clear that the public is driving positive changes for animals. In the United States, two areas of legal reform have emerged: one aims to protect farm animals from cruelty and the second aims to promote non-animal protein sources.

Federal laws in the United States do not protect farm animals from abuse and cruelty. Moreover, the Humane Methods of Slaughter Act does not protect 98% of animals raised for food.[456] The USDA only has about 105 inspectors for the entire country,[457] rendering proper enforcement of the laws impossible. Absent media coverage, the USDA rarely takes action. In 2008, video footage showed forklifts and electric shocks being used on

[449] "Animal Welfare", *Panera Bread*, n.d., at https://www.panerabread.com/en-us/food-values/food-beliefs/animal-welfare.html

[450] "Animal Welfare Policy Statement", *Hilton*, April 2021, at https://cr.hilton.com/wp-content/uploads/2021/04/Hilton-Animal-Welfare-Statement.pdf

[451] *See,* e.g., Subway's commitment to "aspire to have a pork supply chain that is considerate of animal welfare concerns" in Quit Stalling 2021, at 16.

[452] "The 5-Step Animal Welfare Program", *Global Animal Partnership*, n.d., at https://www.globalanimalpartnership.org/5-step-animal-welfare-rating-program

[453] Quit Stalling 2021, at 3.

[454] Meyer, Zlati, "Nabisco uncages its animal crackers after 116 years", *USA Today*, August 21, 2018.

[455] Ryan, Chloe, "Whole Foods Market halts sale of rabbit", *Food Navigator USA,* September 20, 2015.

[456] Even though poultry accounts for roughly 98% of animals raised for food, they are afforded no protection under the Humane Methods of Slaughter Act. *See,* 7 U.S.C. §1902 (Humane Methods), which limits humane slaughter laws to "cattle, calves, horses, mules, sheep, swine, and other livestock", the latter of which has been interpreted to not include poultry.

[457] David S. Favre, Forward in *What Animal Law can Learn from Environmental Law.* Washington, D.C.: Environmental Law Institute, 2015, at page xxv.

cows who were too sick or weak to walk to their own slaughter.[458] The incident led to the largest recall of beef in U.S. history.[459] The following year, the USDA issued a new rule barring downed cows from entering the food supply[460] but it did so only because of massive public backlash and negative media attention. In 2021, U.S. Senator Cory Booker re-introduced The Farm System Reform Act,[461] which, if passed, would place a moratorium on large factory farms. While a reduction in the number of concentrated animal feeding operations (CAFOs) could help reduce the number of suffering animals, the bill does not include specific protections for farm animals, such as a ban on extreme confinement or physical trauma, such as tail docking. In 2023, the PIGS Act of 2023[462] was introduced, which, if enacted, would amend the Animal Welfare Act to ban the confinement of pregnant pigs, but measures are also being introduced in Congress in an effort to stop States from enacting animal welfare laws.[463]

In 2022, the USDA proposed new animal welfare standards for organic animal agriculture, which if implemented would prohibit physical alternation procedures (e.g., debeaking; tail docking) and set standards for living conditions "to better reflect the needs and behaviors of the different species, as well as related consumer expectations."[464] While the improved conditions would not apply to non-organic animal agriculture, it would improve conditions for the more than 186 million farm animals raised annually under the USDA's National Organic Program.[465] Still, a level legal field where all animals raised for food would benefit from the improved conditions would better serve both people and animals.

[458] Weiss, Rick, "Video Reveals Violations of Laws, Abuse of Cows at Slaughterhouse", *Washington Post*, January 30, 2008.

[459] The Westland/Hallmark Meat Packing Company in California agreed to recall 143 million pounds of beef. *See,* Pifer, Jen, "USDA orders recall of 143 million pounds of beef", *CNN*, February 17, 2008.

[460] Doering, Christopher, "U.S. finalizes ban on cattle too sick to walk", *Reuters,* March 14, 2009.

[461] Farm System Reform Act of 2021 - S.2332, 117th Congress (2021–2022).

[462] PIGS Act of 2023 - H.R. 2939, 118th Congress (2023–2024).

[463] *See,* e.g., Exposing Agricultural Trade Suppression Act - H.R. 4999, 117th Congress (2021–2022).

[464] USDA Agricultural Marketing Service proposed rule, National Organic Program (NOP); Organic Livestock and Poultry Standards, 7 C.F.R. §205.

[465] ASPCA, "USDA Urged to Strengthen Farm Animal Welfare by Finalizing Long-Awaited Organic Standards", *PR Newswire*, October 27, 2022.

At the state level, many anti-cruelty laws exempt practices, such as castration and tail docking without anesthesia, that are commonly performed on farm animals. Only a fifth of the states have passed laws to protect farm animals. Legislation by ballot initiatives have proven to be successful means of adopting laws to protect animals because citizens, not politicians beholden to special interests, control the outcome. In 2018, California's Proposition 12 (Farm Animal Confinement Initiative), which was supported by a coalition of more than 500 public health, food safety, consumer protection, and animal welfare organizations, was approved by California voters by a strong margin.[466] The new anti-cruelty law was enacted in part due to food safety concerns. Factory farms are, after all, cesspools for disease.[467] The law requires larger cages for pigs, calves and chickens. The new law sparked a flurry of legal challenges, but to date, the challenges have been decided in favor of California, including a case before the Ninth Circuit Court of Appeals that upheld the constitutionality of California Proposition 12 in 2021 following a challenge by the National Pork Producers Council and American Farm Bureau Federation.[468] The challengers petitioned the Supreme Court to review the case. On March 28, 2022, the Supreme Court agreed to hear the case,[469] and in May 2023, the U.S. Supreme Court upheld the decision of the 9th Circuit Court to dismiss the pork industry's lawsuit against California's Proposition 12.[470] The pork industry has spent millions to stop California's animal welfare measures, and it is not about to let a Supreme Court decision stop it. It found a few lawmakers who were willing to introduce legislation in

[466] Cal. Health & Safety Code §§25990–25994 (December 19, 2018). The law also requires animal products that are imported into California to meet the same standard.

[467] For more on how factory farms threaten human health, *see*, Robbin Marks, *Cesspools of Shame, How Factory Farm Lagoons and Sprayfields Threaten Environmental and Public Health.* Natural Resources Defense Council and the Clean Water Network, July 2001.

[468] National Pork Producers Council; American Farm Bureau Federation v. California Department of Food & Agriculture; California Department of Public Health and Attorney General of California, as Defendants, and The Humane Society of the United States; Animal Legal Defense Fund; The Humane League; Farm Sanctuary; Compassion in World Farming; and Compassion Over Killing, as Intervenor-Defendants, *Ninth Cir. Ct. of Appeals,* July 28, 2021 (holding that Proposition 12 does not violate the dormant Commerce Clause of the U.S. Constitution).

[469] North America Meat Institution v. Rob Bonta, Attorney General of the State of California, et al., Supreme Court, No. 20–1215.

[470] National Pork Producers Council et al. v. Ross, Secretary of the California Department of Food and Agriculture, et al., U.S. Supreme Court No. 21-468, May 11, 2023.

Congress that would prohibit states and local governments from adopting animal welfare measures.[471] It is not surprising that the industry would take such dramatic measures to defeat the will of the people. Industries that exploit and profit from animals will spend millions of dollars and decades challenging any legal improvement for animals. What is disturbing is that the Biden Administration's Department of Justice filed an amicus curiae brief supporting the pork industry's effort to invalidate California's law![472]

Other states have also faced relentless litigation over animal welfare measures. In 2016, 77.64% of Massachusetts voters voted "yes" on *Question 3* to support the ban on the sale of eggs, veal or pork from farm animals who lack sufficient space to lay down and turn around.[473] Thirteen states sued the state of Massachusetts, arguing that Question 3 violates the Commerce Clause of the U.S. Constitution, but the Supreme Court denied certiorari,[474] so the ban stands.

In 2021, Nevada became the ninth U.S. state to ban cages for egg-laying hens, following California, Colorado, Massachusetts, Michigan, Oregon, Rhode Island, Utah and Washington.[475] As of January 2022, ten U.S. states restrict or ban the use of gestation crates (Arizona, California, Colorado, Florida, Maine, Massachusetts, Michigan, Ohio, Oregon and Rhode Island) and nine states have banned veal crates (Arizona, California, Colorado, Kentucky, Maine, Massachusetts, Michigan, Ohio and Rhode Island).[476] With only 14 states having laws that ban battery cages,

[471] EATS Act of 2023 - S.1488, 118th Congress (2023–2024); EATS Act of 2023 - H.R. 3183, 118th Congress (2023–2024).

[472] For more on the administration's disturbing position, *see*, Robinson, Nathan J., "Why is the Biden Administration Helping the Pork Industry Maintain its Cruel and Abusive Practices?", *Current Affairs*, October 16, 2022.

[473] Mass. Gen. Laws Ann., Ch. 129; App. §§1-3, 1-5 (Cum. Supp. 2023); *see generally*, Schoenberg, Shira, "Massachusetts voters ban farm animal confinement, vote Yes on 3", *Mass Live*, November 9, 2016. For ballot results, *see*, https://ballotpedia.org/Massachusetts_Minimum_Size_Requirements_for_Farm_Animal_Containment,_Question_3_(2016).

[474] Schoenberg, Shira, "US Supreme Court: States cannot sue Massachusetts in high court over cage-free egg law", *Mass Live*, January 8, 2019.

[475] Fatka, Jacqui, "Nevada joins list of states mandating cage-free eggs", *Farm Progress*, June 10, 2021.

[476] *See*, "View State Farm Animal Protection Laws", *The United States Humane Society*, n.d., at https://www.humanesociety.org/resources/farm-animal-protection-faq#problems

gestation crates and veal crates, 72% of states still permit the physical and psychological abuse of farm animals. [477]

California is the only state that has banned foie gras,[478] and it withstood 15 years of litigation before the Supreme Court declined to review a challenge to the ban in 2019.[479] California's foie gras ban was back in court in 2021, however, with legal arguments focusing on out-of-state sales and whether the ban covers foie gras from non-force fed animals.[480] In 2019, New York City banned foie gras,[481] and litigation was threatened the same year.[482] Industries can be relentless in their efforts to bury new laws with protracted litigation.[483] Legal reform for animals in the United States is invariably opposed by taxpayer subsidized industries with deep pockets.

The World Bank has warned that with respect to animal welfare, "failure to keep pace with changing consumer expectations … could put companies and their investors at a competitive disadvantage."[484] Recognizing the clear reputational risks associated with animal cruelty, Citigroup also warned that animal cruelty is a "headline risk" to restaurant companies.[485] Dutch Bank, Rabobank, the world's largest private agricultural financer, recommends against the extreme confinement of farm animals.[486]

[477] *See*, "Farm Animal Confinement by State", *ASPCA*, n.d., at https://www.aspca.org/improving-laws-animals/public-policy/farm-animal-confinement-bans. The states include Arizona, California, Colorado, Florida, Kentucky, Maine, Massachusetts, Michigan, Nevada, Ohio, Oregon, Rhode Island, Utah and Washington.

[478] Cal. Health & Safety Code §§ 25980–25984 (2011).

[479] Hurley, Lawrence, "U.S. Supreme Court rejects challenge to California foie gras ban", *Reuters*, January 7, 2019.

[480] Mackay, Nate, "Ninth Circuit files into debate over California foie gras ban", *Courthouse News Service*, October 18, 2021.

[481] J. Mays and A. Nierenberg, "Foie Gras Served in 1000 Restaurants in New York City, is Banned", *New York Times*, July 17, 2021.

[482] Crowley, Chris, "New York Foie Gras Producers React to Ban: 'The Law is So Completely Screwed Up'", *New York Grub Street*, October 31, 2019.

[483] The enforcement of California's Proposition 12 was held up until the Supreme Court could rule on its constitutionality. *See*, Flynn, Dan, "Prop 12 put off until after SCOTUS ruling", *Food Safety News*, December 2, 2022.

[484] Rowland, Michael Pellman, "Farming's Cage-Free Future", *New York Times*, October 10, 2016.

[485] "Risk Mitigation for Investors and Insurers", *Farms Initiative*, n.d., at https://www.farms-initiative.com/best-practice/risk-mitigation-for-investors-and-insurers/

[486] "Rabobank focuses explicitly on sustainability in livestock farming", *Rabobank*, n.d., at https://www.rabobank.com/en/about-rabobank/background-stories/food-agribusiness/rabobank-focuses-explicitly-on-sustainability-in-livestock-farming.html

The public's demand for animal-free foods is driving companies to invest billions in plant-based food products,[487] and investors are pushing food companies to meet that challenge. Citing weak welfare standards and environmental and sustainability concerns, 40 investors, managing $1.25 trillion dollars in assets, urged 16 global food companies to source protein products from plants instead of animals[488] to meet the exploding demand. A report by Bloomberg Intelligence, *Plant-Based Foods Poised for Explosive Growth,* projects a $162 billion dollar plant-based foods market by 2030,[489] with the plant-based meat market alone projected to reach $8.3 billion dollars by 2025.[490] The global plant-based meat market was valued at $5.06 billion dollars in 2022 and it is expected to exceed $20.76 billion dollars by 2030.[491] Today, most restaurants in the United States have vegan options, including most fast food restaurants,[492] and Disney added more than 400 new vegan meals at its theme parks.[493] The exploding plant-based meat market comes at a time when the World Health Organization has warned that eating red and processed meat is "carcinogenic to humans".[494]

The private sector is also developing technology for meat eaters. Cultivated meat (also referred to as lab-grown or cell-based meat) is a game changer. Using processes like cellular agriculture and tissue

[487] "Investing in the Movement: Plant-Based Food is the New Blank", *Network News Wire,* August 24, 2021.

[488] Jessop, Simon, "Investors urge food companies to shift from meats to plants", *Reuters,* September 26, 2016.

[489] "Plant-based Foods Market to Hit $162 Billion in Next Decade, Projects Bloomberg", *Bloomberg,* August 11, 2021.

[490] "Plant-based Meat Market by Source (Soy, Wheat, Pea, & Other Sources), Product (Burger Patties, Strips & Nuggets, Sausages, Meatballs, & Other Products), Type (Beef, Chicken, Pork, Fish, & Other Types), Process, and Region - Global Forecast to 2025", *Markets and Markets,* n.d., at https://www.marketsandmarkets.com/Market-Reports/plant-based-meat-market-44922705.html

[491] Coherent Market Insights, "Global Plant Based Meat Market to reach US $20.76 bn by 2030, says Coherent Market Insights (CMI)", *Globe Newswire,* January 17, 2023.

[492] Dean, Grace, "Fast-food chains are finally taking vegan food seriously", *Business Insider,* January 16, 2022.

[493] Oliver, David, "Disney World, Disneyland to debut hundreds of vegan options. When are they coming?", *USA Today,* September 24, 2019.

[494] "Cancer: Carcinogenicity of the consumption of red meat and processed meat", *World Health Organization,* October 26, 2015, at https://www.who.int/news-room/questions-and-answers/item/cancer-carcinogenicity-of-the-consumption-of-red-meat-and-processed-meat

engineering, muscle cells extracted from animals are placed in conditions where cells multiply and eventually develop into meat that is molecularly identical to meat from slaughtered animals. Scientists envision a future where a single turkey cell could be turned into enough muscle to create over 20 trillion turkey nuggets.[495] Some believe that the disruption to animal agriculture will be profound, with animal products being replaced by superior and cheaper alternatives that will trigger a death spiral for and ultimate collapse of the cattle farming industry.[496] The vision of slaughter-free meat is coming into focus.

Countries are investing heavily in both cultured meat and plant-based proteins. China has invested $300 million dollars in Israeli technology companies that are developing laboratory-grown meat from animal cells,[497] and Denmark plans to invest $195 million dollars to increase plant-based foods.[498] The European Commission is investing $11 billion dollars for research into more sustainable food products, like meat substitutes and plant-based proteins,[499] and researchers at universities are also working to develop plant-based meat alternatives.[500] In 2020, Singapore issued the world's first regulatory approval for lab-grown meat,[501] and in 2021, the

[495] Wang, Brian, "Lab grown meat prices have dropped 30,000 times in less than four years and are about 3–4 times more expensive than regular ground beef", *Next Big Future*, February 19, 2017.

[496] Tubb, Catherine and Seba, Tony, "Rethinking Food and Agriculture 2020–2030: The Second Domestication of Plants and Animals, the Disruption of the Cow, and the Collapse of Industrial Livestock Farming", *Industrial Biotechnology*, April 2021. https://doi.org/10.1089/ind.2021.29240.ctu

[497] Surkes, Sue, "China makes massive investment in Israeli lab meat technology", *Times of Israel*, September 17, 2017.

[498] De Lorenzo, Daniela, "Denmark Plans to Spend $195 Million to Boost Plant-Based Foods. Can It Do So While Remaining a Top Pork Producer?", *Forbes*, November 22, 2021.

[499] "Communication From The Commission To The European Parliament, The Council, The European Economic and Social Committee and the Committee of the Regions, A Farm to Fork Strategy for a fair, healthy and environmentally-friendly food system", *European Commission*, May 20, 2020, at https://eur-lex.europa.eu/legal-content/EN/TXT/?uri=CELEX%3A52020DC0381; *see also*, Starostinetskaya, Anna, "EU to Promote Plant-Based Shift With $11 Billion "Farm to Fork Strategy", *Veg News*, May 20, 2020.

[500] *See*, e.g., McAleer, Keith, "UC Berkeley Sutardja Center Launches new lab to take on $1 trillion meat industry", *Berkeley*, August 17, 2017.

[501] Lucas, Amelia, "Singapore issues first regulatory approval for lab-grown meat to Eat Just", *CNBC*, December 1, 2020.

USDA announced that it is investing $10 million dollars to create an Institute for Cellular Agriculture at Tufts University for the research and development of cellular agriculture.[502] In 2022, China launched its *Five-Year Plan for Bioeconomy Development*, which calls on the country to develop new "synthetic proteins" to reduce the impact that animal agriculture has on the environment,[503] and the world's largest cultivated meat factory is under construction in the United States.[504] Meat companies are even investing in plant-based meats![505]

In 2022, the FDA approved the sale of cultivated meat ("slaughter-free" or "lab-grown" meat), marking the first lab-grown meat to come to market in the United States.[506] Still, the United States is at a global competitive disadvantage because of archaic laws that subsidize the failing meat and dairy industries with billions in taxpayer dollars,[507] while providing little to no subsidy to plant-based options and cultivated meat. Notwithstanding the massive subsidies, the disruption to the dairy market is already clear. Since 2003, more than half of the licensed dairy operations in the United States have closed.[508]

[502] Starostinetskaya, Anna, "The USDA Just made its First Investment in Lab-Grown Meat", *Impact Lab*, November 4, 2021.

[503] Rees, Tom, "Cultivated Meat is Coming to Countries Around the Globe", *Euromonitor International,* November 21, 2022.

[504] Ramirez, Venessa Bates, "The World's Biggest Cultured Meat Factory is Under Construction in the U.S.", *Singularity Hub,* December 14, 2022.

[505] Cargill invested in Memphis Meats and Aleph Farms. *See*, "Protein Innovation: Cargill invests in cultured protein". January 24, 2020, at https://www.cargill.com/story/protein-innovation-cargill-invests-in-cultured-meats

[506] Wiener-Bronner, Danielle, "Lab-grown meat is cleared for sale in the United States", *CNN,* June 21, 2023; *see also*, Toeniskoetter, Clare, "Lab-Grown Meat Receives Clearance from F.D.A.", *New York Times*, November 17, 2022.

[507] Meatonomics, at 89 (discussing the annual $38.4 billion U.S. subsidy to the meat and dairy industries).

[508] *See,* "USDA Report: U.S. Dairy Farm Numbers Continue to Decline", *Farm Bureau,* February 26, 2021; *see also*, "Milk Production", *National Agricultural Statistics Service, Agricultural Statistics Board, USDA*. ISSN: 1949–1557.

Animals in Fashion

The global skin trade is responsible for the deaths of billions of animals every year and no animal is safe.[509] In Africa, elephants, tigers and donkeys are slaughtered for their hides.[510] The global trade of wild animal skins involves tens of thousands of species and is driving many species toward extinction.[511] Like their counterparts on factory farms, furbearing animals are confined to tiny, barren, filthy cages with no opportunity to engage in natural behaviors. Just as animals raised for food, animals farmed for their fur lack legal protection too.

Millions of animals are also trapped and killed every year in the United States by indiscriminate, bone-crushing traps (e.g., steel-jaw leg-hold traps; Conibear traps) that not only cause excruciating injuries and death to targeted species but also injury and death to companion animals, endangered species and children.[512] The United States is an outlier when it comes to dangerous leg-hold traps. According to a study by the Law Library of Congress, more than 100 countries have banned controversial steel-jaw traps.[513]

Aside from the industry's brutal treatment of animals, the most unfortunate legal aspect of fur farming is that the fur industry is allowed to use "greenwashing" as a means of sanitizing their environmentally destructive trade. Real fur is also being marketed as faux fur.[514] The Federal Trade

[509] While estimates of fur trade victims are often quoted as being in the range of 100–150 million annually, this estimate includes the billions of rabbits that are killed in China solely for their fur based on my discussions with individuals with statistical information on the fur trade in China.

[510] *See,* e.g., Scigliano, Eric, "Asian Elephants Are Now Being Killed For Their Skin", *National Geographic*, November 29, 2017; *see also*, Phelan, Jessica, "6 endangered animals poachers are hunting into extinction", *USA Today,* July 31, 2015; *see also*, Yee, Amy, "Donkeys Are Dying Because China Wants Their Hides For a Traditional Remedy", *NPR*, April 30, 2019.

[511] Guglielmi, Giorgia, "Sweeping extent of global trade in wild animals revealed", *Nature*, October 7, 2019.

[512] "Legislation to Ban Brutal and Indiscriminate Body-Gripping Traps Reintroduced", *Animal Welfare Institute*, October 18, 2021, at https://awionline.org/press-releases/legislation-ban-brutal-and-indiscriminate-body-gripping-traps-reintroduced

[513] "Laws on leg-hold animal traps around the world", *Law Library of Congress (U.S.). Global Legal Research Directorate.* Washington, D.C., August 2016, at https://www.loc.gov/item/2016479005/

[514] *See*, e.g., Danovich, Tove, "Faux fur is a staple of the fashion industry. But what's marketed as fake might actually be all too real", *Grid*, January 10, 2023.

Commission in the United States prohibits unfair or deceptive environmental marketing claims.[515] However, fur trade associations falsely promote fur as "green", "natural" and the "responsible" choice",[516] despite using highly toxic chemicals (needed to prevent the decay of animal skins) that can cause cancer and other health detriments.[517]

Human Rights Watch warned in their *Toxic Tanneries* report that tannery pollution creates dangerous working conditions and serious health issues, with anecdotal evidence of elevated cancer rates among workers working with chemicals.[518] The World Health Organization has warned that the health of many Bangladesh residents is threatened by tannery pollution, with a significant number of tannery workers suffering from pollution-related gastrointestinal and dermatological diseases and 90% of workers dying before they reach age 50.[519] People who live and work near tanneries in Hazaribagh and Kamrangirchar in India also die before they reach age 50.[520] Toxic chemicals have been found in fur on garments intended for children under the age of 36 months.[521] Animal fur is neither green, natural, nor a responsible choice.

[515] *See*, 16 C.F.R. § 260 (2012) – Guides for the Use of Environmental Marketing Claims.

[516] The Fur Council of Canada claims that "fur is green" on its website, https://www.furisgreen.com/. The International Fur Trade Federation promotes fur as sustainable on its website, https://www.wearefur.com/sustainability-campaign-2021/. The Hong Kong Fur Federation describes fur as the "natural" and "responsible" choice on its website, http://www.hkff.org/furFacts1.php

[517] Chemicals such as formaldehyde, chromium, naphthalene, sulfuric acid, toluene, ammonia, chlorine, lead, copper, zinc, and chlorobenzene are used to "dress" and "dye" animal skins. *See*, Humane Society of the United States, "Toxic Fur: The Impacts of Fur Production on the Environment and Risks to Human Health," January 29, 2009, at https://www.furfreealliance.com/wp-content/uploads/2019/09/HSUS_EN_Toxic-fur-Report-2009.pdf

[518] Richard Pearshouse, *Toxic Tanneries: The Health Repercussions of Bangladesh's Hazaribagh Leather*. Human Rights Watch, October 2012, https://www.hrw.org/report/2012/10/09/toxic-tanneries/health-repercussions-bangladeshs-hazaribagh-leather#

[519] John Maurice, "Tannery Pollution Threatens Health of Half-Million Bangladesh Residents," *Bulletin of the World Health Organization*, Vol. 79, Issue 1, January 2001.

[520] Sarah Boseley, "Child Labourers Exposed to Toxic Chemicals Dying before 50, WHO Says," *Guardian*, March 17, 2017.

[521] The chemicals included chrome VI (Hexavalent), chrome III (Trivalent), formaldehyde, and nonylphenol ethoxylate. *See*, LAV, "Toxic Fur 2," December 15, 2014, at https://www.bontvoordieren.nl/wp-content/uploads/2016/09/2014-LAV-Toxic-Fur-2-EN-1.pdf

Like factory farming, fur farming causes severe environment degradation. Governmental reports by Nova Scotia Environment have found that nutrient runoff (a primary cause of which is animal manure[522]) from mink farms has "seriously degraded" lakes in the Carleton River watershed areas of Digby and Yarmouth Counties,[523] with some causing blue-green algae known to be toxic to humans and wildlife.[524] The mink industry in Nova Scotia has also caused eutrophication[525] of several of the freshwater lakes.[526] In Leningrad, Russia, the carcasses of thousands of skinned animals are known to have been dumped alongside waterways.[527] In Daying, China, rivers are so severely contaminated by fur and leather processing chemicals that they are brown and black.[528] The magnificent Ganges River in India has been polluted by tanneries.[529] Nutrient pollution is a "leading cause of degradation of United States water quality," causing depletion of dissolved oxygen that fish and other aquatic life need to survive and increasing "harmful algal blooms, which may endanger human health."[530] In the

[522] U.S. Environmental Protection Agency, "Nutrient Pollution: Sources and Solutions," n.d., at http://www.epa.gov/nutrientpollution/sources-and-solutions

[523] Brylinsky, M. and Sollows, J, *Results of the 2013 Water Quality Survey of Eleven Lakes Located in the Carleton River Watershed Area of Digby and Yarmouth Counties, Nova Scotia*, prepared for Nova Scotia Environment, June 2014, Summary, at https://novascotia.ca/nse/surface.water/docs/carleton-river-watershed-survey-2013.pdf

[524] Brylinsky and Sollows, at 1.

[525] Eutrophication occurs when excess nitrogen and phosphorus occurs in water. *See*, Water Resources Mission Area, "Nutrients and Eutrophication", *USGC*, March 3, 2019, at https://www.usgs.gov/mission-areas/water-resources/science/nutrients-and-eutrophication

[526] *See*, David Suzuki Foundation, *The Impacts of the Mink Industry on Freshwater Lakes in Nova Scotia: An Overview of Concerns* (technical brief), April 25, 2011, at 1. The report found that several lakes "artificially eutrophied as a result of nutrient inputs from human activities, with some developing blue-green algae (cyanobacteria) blooms."

[527] Stewart, Will, "'I Have No Sympathy for the Animals … I Feel a Deep Satisfaction': Barbarity of Russian Fur Farms Where Thousands Are Slaughtered to make $1 m coats and blankets then left to rot in stinking corpse mountain", *Daily Mail*, May 10, 2016.

[528] Wei, Xu "Fur and Leather Industry Leads to Hair-Raising Pollution Problems," *Shanghai Daily*, May 16, 2015.

[529] The Ganges river is polluted with heavy metals, such as chromium, a chemical agent used in leather production. *See,* McBride, Pete "Industry on the Banks: Deep Inside Kanpur's Tanneries," *National Geographic*, August 6, 2014.

[530] *See*, "Preventing Eutrophication: Scientific Support for Dual Nutrient Criteria", U.S. Environmental Protection Agency, February 2015, at https://19january2017snapshot.epa.gov/sites/production/files/documents/nandpfactsheet.pdf

United States, the EPA considers nutrient polluted lakes, rivers and other waterways with highly toxic algal blooms to be "one of America's most widespread, costly and challenging environmental problems."[531] Nutrient pollution contaminates groundwater used by millions of people.[532] All of this occurs while the fur industry makes profits by deceptively claiming that fur is "green."

The reality is that animal skins come with a much higher environmental cost than other textiles. A groundbreaking, independent research report compared mink fur to other common textiles, including cotton, polyester fabric, and polyacrylic fabric, with respect to 18 areas of environmental concern.[533] The report found that mink fur scored worst (by 2–28 times!) in terms of its environmental impact in 17 of the 18 areas of environmental concern.[534] The environmental cost of using animal skins and fur is so great that even the fashion industry agrees that non-animal textiles are better for the environment. A 2017 report, *Pulse of the Fashion Industry*, found that of 14 common fashion materials, animal products are among the most environmentally detrimental in terms of global warming, water scarcity, eutrophication, and abiotic resource depletion, and that synthetic leather has only a third of the environmental impact of cow leather.[535] The fur industry's defense of fur is that faux furs contribute to marine plastic

[531] "Indicator Reference Sheet – March 6, 2022: Nutrient and Sediment Yield", *U.S. Environmental Protection Agency*, March 6, 2022, at https://www.epa.gov/system/files/documents/2022-03/nutrient-sediment-yield-indicator-reference-sheet-20220306_508.pdf

[532] Ibid.

[533] Marijn Bijleveld, Marisa Korteland, and Maartje Sevenster, *The Environmental Impact of Mink Fur Production* (CE Delft, January 2011), at https://www.furfreealliance.com/wp-content/uploads/2021/06/CE-Delft-The-environmental-impact-of-mink-fur-production.pdf. The environmental areas of concern included climate change, water depletion, minerals depletion, fossil depletion, ozone layer depletion, ionizing radiation, agricultural land occupation, urban land occupation, freshwater ecotoxicity, marine ecotoxicity, particulate matter formation, terrestrial ecotoxicity, freshwater eutrophication, marine eutrophication, terrestrial acidification, human toxicity, photochemical oxidant formation, and natural land transformation. CE Delft is an independent research and consultancy organization that specializes in developing structural and innovative solutions to environmental problems.

[534] Bijleveld, Korteland, and Sevenster, *Environmental Impact*, at 47.

[535] Sebastian Boger et al., *Pulse of the Fashion Industry*. Global Fashion Agenda and the Boston Consulting Group, 2017, at 77 & 80. The report was commissioned by Global Fashion Agenda and the Boston Consulting Group and focused on environmental and sustainability issues as they relate to the fashion industry.

pollution. Plastic pollution is a serious crisis, but it is not caused by faux fur. Marine plastic pollution in oceans comes principally from land-based sources (e.g., inadequate waste disposal and management; industrial activities; sewer overflows; and littering) and the fishing industry (e.g., lost or discarded fishing nets).[536]

Fur farming can also spread zoonotic diseases, like COVID-19. Since April 2020, more than 450 mink farms in North America and Europe have been impacted by COVID-19 outbreaks, and sadly, more than 20 million animals have been culled to prevent the spread of COVID-19.[537] The European Centre for Disease Prevention and Control has warned that COVID-19 outbreaks on fur farms could result in new variants of concern and could compromise the effectiveness of vaccines.[538] The high environment and public health cost of using animals in fashion is driving historic changes for animals exploited by the clothing industry.

Recent Developments for Animals in Fashion

The past few decades have seen transformative changes for furbearing animals. Since 2000, a growing number of countries have banned fur farming, including England and Wales (2000),[539] Northern Ireland (2002),[540] Scotland (2002),[541] Austria (2004),[542] Croatia (2007),[543] Bosnia and

[536] See, "Marine plastic pollution", *International Union for Conservation of Nature*, November 2021, at https://www.iucn.org/resources/issues-brief/marine-plastic-pollution

[537] *See*, "COVID-19 on Mink Farms", *Fur Free Alliance*, n.d., at https://www.furfreealliance.com/covid-19-on-mink-farms/; *see also*, "HSI/Canada applauds BC government's decision to ban mink farming", *Humane Society International*, November 9, 2021, at https://www.hsi.org/news-media/hsi-canada-applauds-bc-governments-decision-to-ban-mink-farming/

[538] "ECDC to assess risk associated with spread of SARS-CoV-2 in mink farms," *European Centre for Disease Prevention and Control*, November 6, 2020.

[539] *See*, Fur Farming (Prohibition) Act 2000, UK Public General Acts, 2000, c 33, §§1–7; *see generally*, "Fur Market in Great Britain", U.K. Department for Environment Food & Rural Affairs, last updated September 20, 2021.

[540] Northern Ireland, Fur Farming (Prohibition) (Northern Ireland) Order 2002.

[541] Scotland, Fur Farming (Prohibition) Act (2002).

[542] Austria, Federal Act on the Protection of Animals of 2004 (Animal Protection Act – TSchG), §25(5).

[543] Croatia, The Animal Protection Act, Art. 4, §23 (December 1, 2006), superseded by Animal Protection Act of 2017, Art. 5, §21.

Herzegovina (2009),[544] the Netherlands (2013),[545] Slovenia (2013),[546] Macedonia (2014),[547] the Czech Republic (2017),[548] Norway (2018),[549] Belgium (2018),[550] Luxembourg (2018),[551] Serbia (2019),[552] Slovakia (2019),[553] Estonia (2021),[554] France (2021),[555] Italy (2021),[556] Latvia (2022)[557] and Ireland (2022).[558] Sweden (2005),[559] Switzerland (2008)[560]

[544] Bosnia and Herzegovina, Law on the Protection and Welfare of Animals, Ch. 1, Art. 4, §(bb) (2009).

[545] Netherlands, Prohibition of Fur Farming Act of 4 January 2013, Art. 2.

[546] Slovenia, Animal Protection Law (official consolidated text), Art. 15, 22 (eff. December 18, 1999).

[547] Republic of Macedonia, Law (General provisions for treatment of animals), Art. 4.

[548] Czech Republic, Act on the Protection of Animals Against Cruelty, Collection of Laws 246/1992 (May 29, 1992), as amended in 2017.

[549] Norway, Fur Farming Prohibition Act (2018).

[550] Wallonia Animal Welfare Code, Art. D.21, 2° (October 4, 2018); Brussels Animal Welfare Code, Art. 9bis; Flanders Animal Welfare Code. Art. 9bis §1.

[551] Luxembourg, Law on the Protection of Animal Life, Security and Welfare (June 6, 2018).

[552] Serbia, Animal Welfare Act, Section II (General Protection of Animal Welfare), Art. 7, §37.

[553] Slovakia, Decree on Identification, Registration and Conditions of Farm Breeding of Animals (Collection of Laws No. 178 of 2012), Ministry of Agriculture and Rural Development of the Slovak Republic), §22 ods., 4pism (g).

[554] Estonia, Animal Protection Act, s. 4 (Keeping animals for the purpose of production of fur), RT 1, 16.06.2021.

[555] On September 29, 2020, France announced an immediate ban on any new American mink farms and the end of American mink farming with a 2025 deadline. *See,* "Barbara Pompili announces new measures in favor of captive wildlife", French Government, at https://www.ecologie.gouv.fr/barbara-pompili-annonce-nouvelles-mesures-en-faveur-faune-sauvage-captive

[556] Italy, Budget Law 2022, Amendment No. 157.04.

[557] Latvia, Amendments to the Animal Protection Act, OP No. 2022/191A.2 (September 22, 2022), adding Art. 13.1 to Ch. II.

[558] Ireland, Animal Health and Welfare and Forestry (Miscellaneous Provisions) Act of 2022 (Act 4 of 2022); *see generally*, "A Guide to Fur Bans Around the World", *Respect for Animals*, n.d., at https://respectforanimals.org/a-guide-to-fur-bans-around-the-world/; *see also,* "Fur Bans", *Fur Free Alliance*, n.d., at https://www.furfreealliance.com/fur-bans/. The dates reflect the date of the bans. The effective dates may differ.

[559] Sweden, Animal Welfare Act (Code of Statutes No. 2018:1192), §2 (Good animal environment and natural behavior), June 20, 2018. Fox and chinchilla fur farming have been phased out due to the stricter regulations.

[560] Switzerland, Animal Welfare Ordinance (TSchV) of 23 April 2008.

and Germany (2017)[561] effectively regulated fur farming out of existence by mandating greater animal welfare standards that made fur farming an unprofitable industry.[562] In 2022, Malta announced a ban on the production of fur with immediate effect.[563] Fur farming bans are under consideration in other countries, including Lithuania, Poland and Romania.[564] Legislation has also been introduced into the House of Commons of Canada, which if enacted, would outlaw all fur farms in Canada.[565] In Europe, a citizens initiative, Fur Free Europe Initiative, received a staggering 1,502,319 signatures to ban fur farming in the European Community. The Initiative was submitted to the European Commission in 2023.[566] Despite the enactment of successful legal reforms to protect fur-bearing animals, animals are still languishing in captivity on fur farms. Despite the 2016 ban on new mink farm operations in Spain, for instance, extensions have been granted to farmers which has allowed the doubling of the number of female minks at one farm.[567]

Other countries have instituted partial bans on fur farming, including Hungary (mink, foxes, polecats and coypu are banned),[568] Spain (new mink fur farms are banned), New Zealand (minks are effectively banned),[569] Denmark (foxes and raccoon dogs are banned)[570] and Japan (new mink

[561] Germany, Law for the implementation of EU regulations on bans and restrictions on trade in certain animal products as well as on keeping and selling bans in certain cases (Animal Products Trade Prohibition Act – TierErzHaVerbG), §3 (Fur Animals).

[562] Ibid.

[563] Subsidiary Legislation 439.09, Farm Animals (Protection) Regulations, 30th September 2003, Legal Notice 266 of 2003, as amended by Legal Notices 187 of 2022 (Prohibition of fur farming).

[564] *See*, Fur Bans.

[565] An Act to prohibit fur farming, Bill C-247 (First Session, Forty-fourth Parliament) first reading February 8, 2022.

[566] Apelblat, A., "European Citizens Initiative on Fur Free Europe presented to the European Commission", *Brussels Times*, July 2, 2023.

[567] Casamitjana, Jordi, "Animal Rights Group Exposes the Cruelty of Mink Farming in Spain", *Vegan FRA*, January 25, 2023.

[568] Hungary, Annex to Decree 32 of 1999 (lll. 31.) of the Ministry of Agricultural and Regional Development on animal protection rules to be respected during animal husbandry.

[569] The importation of minks into New Zealand is prohibited under the Biosecurity Act 1993 No 95 (as of 30 August 2021) Public Act, effectively banning mink fur farming.

[570] Denmark, Act banning the keeping of foxes (no. 469 of 2014), superseded by Animal Welfare Act (No. 133 of 2020).

farms are banned).[571] In 2016, the last fur farm in Japan, Otsuka, closed down, citing a decline in the demand for fur.[572] The United States has not banned fur farming but it did enact the Dog and Cat Protection Act of 2000 to protect dogs and cats from the fur trade.[573] The law bans the manufacture, distribution, importation and sale of products made with dog or cat fur.

The COVID-19 pandemic has led to further closures of mink farms, as mutated forms of the virus from farmed minks have reportedly infected workers.[574] In 2021, British Columbia announced a phase out of its mink fur industry "due to ongoing public-health risks associated with COVID-19."[575] In the United States, Covid-19 outbreaks have been found on mink farms in a number of states, including Michigan, Wisconsin, Utah and Oregon, and COVID-19 infected minks escaped from an Oregon farm risking the infection of wild animals.[576] Researchers warn that COVID-19 virus transmission is rapid among minks and that virus mutations have resulted in a novel "mink-associated variant" that was identified in both minks and humans.[577] Mink farms are the perfect breeding ground for COVID-19,[578] and the public health risks associated with mink fur farming has gotten the attention of lawmakers. In 2021, the Minks are Superspreaders Act was introduced in the U.S. House of Representatives to ban the sale, possession or transportation of captive

[571] Invasive Alien Species Act, Law No. 78 (June 2, 2004), as amended, bans the importation and breeding of minks as an invasive alien species that threatens biodiversity and human safety; *see generally*, A Guide to Fur Bans Around the World; *see also*, Fur Bans.

[572] Starostinetskaya, Anna, "Last Fur Farm Closes in Japan", *Veg News*, December 8, 2016.

[573] Dog and Cat Protection Act of 2000, Public Law 106–476, codified at 19 U.S.C. §1308 (November 9, 2000).

[574] Liss, Cathy, "Mink farms can be COVID-19 super spreaders", *Statesman Journal*, March 29, 2021.

[575] News Release, "Mink farming phase out planned in B.C.", *British Columbia, Agricultural, Food and Fisheries*, November 5, 2021.

[576] Liss, Cathy, "Mink farms can be COVID-19 super spreaders", *Statesman Journal*, March 29, 2021.

[577] Sharun, Khan, et al., "SARS-CoV-2 infection in farmed minks, associated zoonotic concerns, and importance of the One Health approach during the ongoing COVID-19 pandemic", *The Veterinary Quarterly*, Vol. 41,1 (2021), at 50–60. https://doi.org/10.1080/01652176.2020.1867776

[578] For background, *see* Keen, Jim, "Jim Keen: Mink farms are a perfect breeding ground for COVID-19", *The Salt Lake Tribune*, August 1, 2022.

mink and their pelts.[579] In 2023, the Mink: Vectors for Infection Risk in the United States (VIRUS) Act was introduced with the stated goal of protecting public health and safety by outlawing mink fur farming.[580]

In a stunning rebuke of the fur trade, Israel became the first country in 2021 to ban the sale of fur for fashion.[581] When Luxembourg banned fur farming, the government declared that animals will no longer be treated as a "thing."[582] The Dutch Advertising Standards Authority forced fur brand *Airforce* to remove its "ethical" and "responsible" labels on jackets with fur trim.[583]

The European Union has also taken a firm stand against the abuse of seals. In 2009, the European Union banned all seal products produced in the EU or imported into the EU, with the regulation stating that, "[s]eals are sentient beings that can experience pain, distress, fear and other forms of suffering."[584] Canada and Norway sought to overturn the ban by filing a complaint with the World Trade Organization, but the ban was ultimately upheld.[585] In 2018, India's Directorate General of Foreign Trade

[579] MINKS are Superspreaders Act - H.R. 4310, 117th Congress (2021–2022); *see generally*, Animal Wellness Action, "U.S. House Passes Sweeping Ban on Mink Farming Citing Cruelty and Contagion Risks", *Globe Newswire*, February 4, 2022.

[580] If enacted, the law would compensate mink farmers as they transition out of the industry. MINK Virus Act - H.R. 3783, 118th Congress (2023–2024).

[581] The new law has exceptions for animal fur used for educational or religious purposes. *See*, "Ban on animal fur sales! Minister of Environmental Protection Gila Gamliel signs regulations forbidding trade in usage of furs for fashion industry in Israel", Israel Ministry of Environmental Protection, October 6, 2021; *see also*, Hernandez, Joe, "Israel Has Become The 1st Country To Ban The Sale of Most Fur Clothing", *NPR*, June 14, 2021. While other countries had banned fur farming, Israel took the unprecedented step of banning the sale of fur.

[582] *See*, "Luxembourg 10th European Country to Ban Fur Farming", *Fur Free Alliance*, June 15, 2018, at https://www.furfreealliance.com/luxembourg-10th-european-country-ban-fur-farming/

[583] "Advertising Standards Authority Reprimands 'Animal-Friendly Fur' Labels", *Fur Free Alliance*, July 30, 2017, at https://www.furfreealliance.com/advertising-standards-authority-reprimands-animal-friendly-fur-labels/

[584] "Regulation (EC) No. 1007/2009 of the European Parliament and of the Council, of 16 September 2009, on trade in seal products", at https://eur-lex.europa.eu/legal-content/EN/TXT/?uri=CELEX:32009R1007

[585] Dispute Settlement, "DS401: European Communities – Measures Prohibiting the Importation and Marketing of Seal Products", *World Trade Organization*, June 18, 2014, at https://www.wto.org/english/tratop_e/dispu_e/cases_e/ds401_e.htm

joined 36 other countries that have banned the commercial trade in seal products, including the United States, Taiwan, Russia and all 28 European Union member states.[586] In 2017, India banned the importation of exotic animal skins, including minks, foxes, chinchillas, and reptiles such as crocodiles and alligators.[587] New Zealand recently banned "mulesing," a barbaric procedure in the wool industry where large chunks of skin and fresh are carved out from sheeps' backsides, without painkillers, to reduce flystrikes.[588] The public, aware of the cruelty involved with fur farming, is demanding change, and companies are stepping up.

The list of major clothing brands that have committed to stop using animal fur continues to grow and includes, inter alia, Armani, Valentino, Gucci, Versace, Ralph Lauren, Calvin Klein, Prada Group, Phillip Lim, Coach, Tommy Hilfiger, Burberry, Michael Kors, Diane Von Furstenberg, Jimmy Choo, Donna Karan & DKNY, Yoox Net-a-Porter, Hugo Boss, Stella McCartney, Kate Spade, Furla, The Kooples, Tom Ford, Vivienne Westwood, Maison Margiela, Kering (including Alexander McQueen, Balenciaga, and Bottega Veneta), Jean Paul Gaultier, Oscar de la Renta, and more recently Dolce & Gabbana.[589] Canada Goose, the epitome of the fur industry, announced in 2020 that it would no longer use "new" fur in its products,[590] but consumers were not satisfied. On June 24, 2021,

[586] "Victory! India bans the import of seal fur and skins: Humane Society International/India and People for Animals applaud the decision", *Humane Society International*, April 3, 2018, at https://www.hsi.org/news-media/india-bans-seal-skins-import-040318/

[587] Guinebault, Matthieu, "India bans imports of reptile skins, mink and fox furs", *Fashion Network*, January 6, 2017.

[588] *See*, Frost, Kristen, "New Zealand prohibits the practice of mulesing in sleep", *Farm Online*, September 10, 2018.

[589] *See generally*, "Retailers who do not use fur", *Animal Defenders International*, February 2, 2022, at https://www.ad-international.org/fur/go.php?id=4486&ssi=19; *see also*, Vidalon, Dominique and Spencer, Mimosa, "Luxury group Kering to ditch fur completely", *Reuters*, September 24, 2021; *see also*, Kratofil, Colleen, "Luxury Fashion Brands That are anti-Fur", *People*, June 30, 2021; *see also*, Gabardi, Chiara Spagnoli, "20 of the Biggest Fur Free Fashion Brands", *Eluxe Magazine*, October 22, 2022; *see also*, Penrose, Nerisha, "Your Complete Guide to Fur-Free Fashion Designers and Retails", *Elle*, October 22, 2019.

[590] Testa, Jessica, "Canada Goose Will Stop Buying Fur – Sort Of", *New York Times*, July 1, 2021.

Canada Goose announced that it will be fur free,[591] and at the end of 2022, Lion Farms, the largest mink farm in North America, announced it was closing.[592]

François-Henri Pinault, Chairman and CEO of Kering, voiced the sentiment of the fashion industry when he said that "[t]he time has now come to take a further step forward by ending the use of fur in all our collections. The world has changed, along with our clients, and luxury naturally needs to adapt to that."[593] Burberry's CEO, Marco Gobetti, agrees, acknowledging, "I don't think it is compatible with modern luxury and with the environment in which we live."[594] Jean Paul Gaultier was more blunt when he dropped fur from his collections, calling fur farming, "absolutely deplorable."[595] One report estimates that nearly 69% of the most profitable luxury brands have banned animal fur.[596]

Department stores are also committing to stop selling fur, including Saks Fifth Avenue, Nieman Marcus, Bergdorf Goodman, Bloomingdale's, Macy's, Gap, Forever 21 and Nordstrom. Nordstrom has also agreed to stop selling products with exotic animal skins (e.g., snakes, alligators, lizards, crocodiles, ostriches, sharks, kangaroos and stingrays).[597] Association

[591] Nguyen, Amy, "Canada Goose Plans To Go Fur-Free by 2022 – Will The Alternative Material be Sustainable", *Forbes*, June 27, 2021.

[592] Hirsh, Sophie, "Ohio Mink Farm Shutting Down, Just Weeks After Activists Freed 10,000 of Their Minks" *Green Matters*, December 22, 2022.

[593] Vidalon, Dominique and Spencer, Mimosa, "Luxury group Kering to ditch fur completely", *Reuters*, September 24, 2021.

[594] Amed, Imran, "Burberry Stops Destroying Product and Bans Real Fur", *The Business of Fashion*, September 6, 2018.

[595] *See*, "Jean Paul Gaultier Drops Fur, Calls Industry 'Absolutely Deplorable'", *EcoWatch*, November 12, 2018.

[596] Hakansson, Emma, "Cruelty is Out of Fashion, An Overview of the fashion industry's policies on wild animal products", Collective Fashion Justice with input from World Animal Protection, at 16.

[597] *See*, Retailers who do not use fur; *see also*, Balu, Nivedita, "Luxury retailer Nieman Marcus to stop selling products by early 2023", *Reuters*, June 30, 2021; *see also*, Benveniste, Alexis, "Nordstrom will no longer sell fur and exotic animal skins", *CNN*, September 29, 2020.

with animal fur is becoming so unsavory that fashion weeks,[598] magazines[599] and modeling agencies[600] are adopting fur-free policies.

Companies are also dropping alpaca wool,[601] badger hair,[602] mohair,[603] angora[604] and down.[605] Innovative technologies are replacing leather using non-animal materials such as mushroom fibers,[606] pineapple leaves, tree leaves, waxed cotton and cork.[607] A few companies have pledged to cease using exotic animal skins (e.g., pythons, crocodiles, lizards, alligators), including Prada, Chanel, Victoria Beckham, Vivienne Westwood and Diane von Furstenberg,[608] but the market for exotic animal skins remains strong. The exotic animal skin market is fraught with compliance issues,

598 *See,* e.g., Conlon, Scarlett, "Helsinki fashion week to ban leather as vegan fabrics catch on", *Guardian*, August 17, 2018; *see also*, "London Fashion week to go fur-free for the first time", *BBC*, September 7, 2018.

599 *See,* e.g., Franklin, Jonathan, "Elle magazine says it will ban fur from its publications worldwide", *NPR*, December 2, 2021; *see also*, Harris, Taylor, "InStyle Bans Fur", *Fashion Week Daily*, April 3, 2018.

600 *See,* e.g., Gush, Charlotte, "Linden Staub becomes the first agency to go FUR FREE", *Linden Staub*, March 22, 2018.

601 Williams-Sonoma, Pottery Barn, West Elm, Lands' End, White House Black Market, Valentino, Ascena Retail Group (with brands Ann Taylor, Loft, Land Bryant), ESPRIT, and others have banned alpaca fur. *See,* e.g., Turk, Robyn, "Ascena Retail Group to stop using alpaca fur across brands", *Fashion United*, November 25, 2020; *see*, Chua, Jasmin Malik, "Williams-Sonoma Drops Alpaca Fleece after PETA Expose", *Sourcing Journal*, May 17, 2021.

602 As of January 2021, nearly 100 brands have banned badger hair, including L'Oréal Group, Procter & Gamble and Morphe. *See*, Caldwell, Georgina, "L'Oréal Group Bans Animal Hair Brushes", *Global Cosmetic News*, January 20, 2021.

603 Hundreds of brands, including Lacoste, Ralph Lauren and Diane Von Furstenberg, have banned mohair. *See,* e.g., Pointing, Charlotte, "Lacoste Joins 340 Brands and Ditches Mohair", *Live Kindly*, n.d., at https://www.livekindly.co/lacoste-fast-retailing-co-ditch-mohair/

604 More than 425 brands have banned angora wool. *See*, "Some of the 425+ brands that have banned Angora Wool", *PETA*, December 21, 2021, at https://www.peta.org/living/personal-care-fashion/more-brands-ban-angora/

605 For a list of some of the companies that have stopped using down, *see* "The Major Brands That are Ditching Down", *PETA UK*, November 24, 2020, at https://www.peta.org.uk/blog/major-brands-ditching-down/

606 Roberts-Islam, Brooke, "Mushroom-Based 'Leather' Is Now A Scalable Alternative To Animal Leathers, Poised For Market Disruption", *Forbes*, April 1, 2021.

607 Wolfe, Isobella, "Leaves, Mushrooms, Bark and More: 8 Innovative Eco-Friendly Leather Alternatives", *Good on You*, March 9, 2020.

608 "The Exotic Skins Trade", *Four Paws*, n.d., at https://www.fourpawsusa.org/campaigns-topics/topics/wild-animals/exotic-skins

with illegal wildlife tainting markets. Based on information obtained under the Freedom of Information Act, between 2003 and 2013, more than 5600 illegal wildlife items destined for Gucci, Ralph Lauren, Michael Kors and other brands were seized by the U.S. Fish and Wildlife Service at ports of entry.[609] Law enforcement studies have concluded that less than 1 in 10 illegal wildlife products are actually seized,[610] so the number of illegal wildlife products imported into the United States is likely much higher. Still, some progress is being made for exotic animals. In 2023, Macy's confirmed that it will no longer sell leather items from ostriches, alligators, lizards and snakes.[611]

Compliance has also been a major issue with California's ban on kangaroo-derived products. A 2020 investigation by the Center for a Humane Economy found that a staggering 93% of "dominant" online retailers were sending kangaroo leather into the state in violation of California law.[612] In response, California's Department of Fish and Wildlife claimed to be overwhelmed with policing more "egregious" animal products such as rhino horn and ivory.[613] Each year, roughly 2 million kangaroos are killed for their skins (e.g., to make soccer shoes) and for their meat (e.g., for pet food), despite the catastrophic impact of Australia's 2019/2020 wildfires on wildlife populations.[614] A few brands have banned kangaroo leather, including Prada, Versace, and Chanel.[615] In 2021, the Kangaroo Protection Act of 2021 was introduced in the United States Congress to ban the importation, sale or trade of kangaroo skins and products.[616] The bill remains stalled in Congress.

[609] Nuwer, Rachel, "Luxury fashion brands had thousands of exotic leather goods seized by U.S. law enforcement", *National Geographic,* May 22, 2020.

[610] Ibid.

[611] Douglass, Rachel, "Macy's to cut reptile and ostrich leather from stores", *Fashion United*, February 13, 2023.

[612] Visontay, Elias, "Nike and Puma flouting California ban on selling kangaroo leather goods, animal rights group claims", *Guardian*, July 31, 2020.

[613] Ibid.

[614] "Australian Wildlife & Nature Recovery Fund, Respond, Restore and Build a Resilient Future", *WWF*, April 2022 Final Report, at 2; *see generally*, "Kangaroos Are Not Shoes, The Issue", *Center for a Humane Economy*, at https://centerforahumaneeconomy.org/kangaroos-are-not-shoes-campaign/

[615] Sharma, Saumya, "Luxury fashion giant Prada has banned Kangaroo skins; Valentino to stop using Alpaca wool", *Hindustan Times*, August 24, 2020.

[616] Kangaroo Protection Act of 2021 - H.R. 917, 117th Congress (2021–2022).

West Hollywood, California[617] and Berkeley, California[618] were the first cities to ban the sale of animal fur apparel within their city limits. After San Francisco became the first major city to ban the sale of fur,[619] California became the first state, in 2019, to ban the sale of fur.[620] In Massachusetts, the sale of animal fur is prohibited in the Town of Wellesley,[621] the Town of Weston,[622] Brookline,[623] Plymouth,[624] Cambridge[625] and Lexington.[626] Legislation has also been introduced at the state level in Massachusetts to prohibit the sale or trade of animal fur products.[627] Other states are

[617] City of West Hollywood Ordinance, §9.51.020 Sale of fur products (Ordinance No. 11–877, 11.21.2011).

[618] Berkeley Municipal Code, Ordinance No. 7539-N.S., adding Ch. 9.22 to the Berkeley Municipal Code to Prohibit the Sale of Fur Products Within the City of Berkeley, adopted on 3.28.2017.

[619] San Francisco Health Code, Sec. 1D.1 "Animal Fur Products Ordinance", added by Ord. 55-18, File No. 171317, App. 4/13/2018.

[620] AB-44 Fur products: prohibition (2019–2020), An act to amend, repeal and add Section 3039 of, and to add Section 2023 to, the Fish and Game Code, relating to fur products, signed into law on October 12, 2019; *see generally*, Friedman, Venessa, "The California Fur ban and What it Means for You", *New York Times*, October 14, 2019.

[621] Town of Wellesley, Town Bylaw Amendment, Article 53A, Fur Products, effective October 28, 2021. The law exempts used fur by a private party, non-profit organization or a second-hand store, fur used in a religious practice and fur used for traditional tribal, cultural, or spiritual purposes by a member of a federal or state recognized Native American tribe; *see generally*, O'Laughlin, Frank, "Wellesley becomes first community outside of California to ban fur sales", *WHDH*, October 29, 2020.

[622] Town of Weston, Annual Town Election, May 8, 2021, Article 34 (Fur Ban Bylaw), adding new Section XXXVIII.

[623] Town of Brookline, Annual Town Meeting, April 2, 2022, General Bylaws, Art. 8.40 (Trade in Fur Products).

[624] Town of Plymouth, Amendment to The Bylaws, to add new Article VI (Fur Products) to Ch. 23 (Animals).

[625] Cambridge Municipal Code, Ch. 6.24 (Sale of Fur Apparel Products) (Ordinance #2022–17). The law exempts used fur by a private party, non-profit organization or a second-hand store, fur used in a religious practice and fur used for traditional tribal, cultural, or spiritual purposes by a member of a federal or state recognized Native American tribe.

[626] Town of Lexington, Annual Town Meeting 2023, Article 31: Fair Trade Restrictions – Fur Products (Citizen Petition), amending Chapter 9 of the Code of the Town of Lexington to add new Section 9-8 (Trade in Fur Products).

[627] Commonwealth of Massachusetts Bill H.849, 193rd (Current) (An Act Prohibiting the Sale of Fur Products) and Bill S.590, 193rd (Current) (An Act Prohibiting the Sale of Fur Products).

considering a similar ban on the sale of fur, including New York,[628] Hawaii,[629] Connecticut,[630] Rhode Island[631] and Oregon,[632] and Washington[633] is considering a ban on the production of fur.[634] Ann Arbor, Michigan,[635] Boulder, Colorado[636] and Hallandale Beach, Florida[637] have also passed local laws banning the sale of fur. Legislation has been introduced in Oregon to phase out mink farms after COVID-19 infected minks escaped from fur farms.[638]

The Public Safety and Wildlife Protection Act[639] was introduced (and re introduced) in Congress after a 12-year old North Carolina boy was severely injured by a Conibear trap while playing outside.[640] The Act would ban the interstate shipment of Conibear and steel-jaw leg-hold

[628] State of York, Prohibition of Fur Products, SB 5439 (2021–2022).

[629] Hawaii S.B. No. 682, S.D.1 H.D. 2 (A Bill for an Act Relating to Animal Fur Products).

[630] Schaeffer-Helmecki, Jessica, Legislative Research Report on "Fur Sales Bans", December 11, 2019.

[631] An Act Relating to Criminal Offenses – Trade in Animal Fur Products Act, HB 5258, SB 746 (2023).

[632] 82nd Oregon Legislative Assembly, A Bill for an Act, Relating to the trade of fur products, House Bill 3390 (2023).

[633] Prohibiting activities related to the production and manufacturing of fur products, HB 1718 (2021–22).

[634] *See generally*, "Testimony of the Department of Commerce and Consumer Affairs Before the Housing Committee on Judiciary and Hawaiian Affairs, Tuesday, March 16, 2021 2:00 p.m., Via Videoconference, On the following measure: S.B. 969, S.D. 2, Relating to Animal Fur Products", *State of Hawaii, Office of Director Dept. of Commerce and Consumer Affairs,* at https://www.capitol.hawaii.gov/sessions/Session2021/Testimony/SB969_SD2_TESTIMONY_JHA_03-16-21_.PDF

[635] Ann Arbor, Michigan, Code of Ordinances, Title VII, Ch.91 (Sale of Animal Products), adopted by Ordinance No. ORD-21-26, adopted August 16, 2021; *see generally,* Witsil, Frank, "Ann Arbor retailers banned from selling new fur, a first for Michigan, *Detroit Free Press,* August 17, 2021.

[636] Boulder, Colorado, Municipal Code, Ch. 6, §5–6-17 (Fur Products), adopted by Ordinance No. 8480, adopted August 17, 2021.

[637] Hallandale Beach, Florida, Code of Ordinances, Ch. 6, Art 1, Div. 3 (Trade in Fur Products), adopted by Ordinance No. 2021-024 on November 17, 2021.

[638] Liss, Cathy, "Mink farms can be COVID-19 super spreaders", *Statesman Journal,* March 29, 2021.

[639] H.R. 5578 – Public Safety and Wildlife Protection Act, 117th Congress (2021–2022), re-introduced on October 15, 2021.

[640] *See,* "Legislation to Ban Brutal and Indiscriminate Body-Gripping Traps Reintroduced", *Animal Welfare Institute,* October 18, 2021, at https://awionline.org/press-releases/legislation-ban-brutal-and-indiscriminate-body-gripping-traps-reintroduced

traps, bringing the United States into conformity with over 100 other countries that have banned the traps.

California also enacted into law the Wildlife Protection Act of 2019, which prohibits commercial and recreational fur trapping.[641] Comprehensive legal reform is needed in the area of trapping to protect wildlife and people.

Wildlife

Wildlife trafficking is a sophisticated, billion dollar global business that is driven by greed and poverty.[642] The scale of illegal wildlife trafficking is tremendous, ranking only behind narcotics, weapons and human trafficking in international crimes.[643] According to a 2016 report by the International Criminal Police Organization (INTERPOL) and United Nations Environment Programme, the market value of all environmental crimes (e.g., illegal wildlife trafficking; illegal fisheries; forestry sector crimes) is estimated to be $91–258 billion (USD) annually.[644] The World Bank assessed the annual value of wildlife crimes to be much higher at $1–2 trillion dollars when taking into account the damage to the ecosystems, species' abilities to sequester carbon, and the loss of governmental revenue.[645] Wildlife trafficking syndicates are well-organized and well-

[641] AB-273 Fur-Bearing and nongame mammals: recreational and commercial fur trapping: prohibition, September 4, 2019, at https://leginfo.legislature.ca.gov/faces/billTextClient.xhtml?bill_id=201920200AB273

[642] Ragnhild Aslaug Sollund defines the wildlife "trade" as the "legal and illegal abduction, possession, processing, acquiring or transporting of free-born animals for the purpose of purchasing, importing, exporting, selling, bartering or exchanging them through theming them as captives" and defines animal "trafficking" as "the legal and illegal trade, smuggling, abduction, theriocide and collection of animals pertaining to (often endangered) animal species, either alive or by turning them into products." *See*, Sollund, Ragnhild Aslaug, The Crimes of Wildlife Trafficking, Issues of Justice, Legality and Mortality", Routledge, Taylor & Francis Group (2019), at 3.

[643] "Fact Sheet: Elephant Ivory and Rhino Horn Bans". *National Caucus of Environmental Legislators*, July 27, 2021, at http://www.ncelenviro.org/resources/elephant-ivory-and-rhino-horn-bans-fact-sheet/

[644] *See*, "Anti-wildlife trafficking operation results in global arrests and seizures", *INTERPOL*, March 2, 2017, at https://www.interpol.int/en/News-and-Events/News/2017/Anti-wildlife-trafficking-operation-results-in-global-arrests-and-seizures#

[645] "Illegal Logging, Fishing, and Wildlife Trade: The Costs and How to Combat It", *The World Bank Group*, October 2019, at 18. The report notes that more than 90% of the value estimate is derived from value that is not priced by the market, such as the value of ecosystems.

funded, and poachers are well-trained and willing to risk their lives for lucrative profits. Together they destroy families and villages, wiping out entire herds of animals, and killing anyone who tries to stop them.

Every year, millions of animals are the victims of poachers, trophy hunters, and legal and illegal trafficking. Some species of animals, including elephants and rhinos, are under such tremendous assault by humanity that they are being pushed to extinction.[646] The United Nations estimates that more than 7000 different species of animals are trafficked illegally,[647] with more than 1 million species at risk of extinction,[648] and INTERPOL warns that wildlife crime is rising 5–7% annually.[649] Endless conflicts between wildlife authorities and poachers underscore the fact that conservation is akin to war.[650] The consequences are severe. Global biodiversity is being lost at a much faster rate (100 to 1000 times faster) than natural extinction.[651]

There is a widespread consensus among scientists that humanity is facing a 6th mass species extinction.[652] The mass extinction is only the 6th to occur in roughly 540 million years, and it will annihilate many forms of life on the planet or result in their extinction by the end of this century.[653] Many experts believe that this extinction event is "the first to be caused by

[646] *See*, Sieff, Kevin, "'Tape their beaks': Wildlife trafficking case offers glimpse into clandestine animal trade from Mexico", *Washington Post*, September 11, 2021, citing comments from Juan Carlos Cantu, director of programs at Defenders of Wildlife in Mexico.

[647] United Nations Office on Drugs and Crime (UNODC), *World Wildlife Crime Report, Trafficking in Protected Species,* 2016, at pp. 3 and 13. PDF ISBN: 9789210580557.

[648] "World is 'on notice' as major UN report shows one million species face extinction", *United Nations, UN News, Global perspective Human stories,* May 6, 2019, at https://news.un.org/en/story/2019/05/1037941

[649] "Wildlife crime: closing ranks on serous crime in the illegal animal trade", *INTERPOL,* December 21, 2020, at https://www.interpol.int/News-and-Events/News/2020/Wildlife-crime-closing-ranks-on-serious-crime-in-the-illegal-animal-trade

[650] *See.* e.g., Hammer, Joshua, "The Fight Against Elephant Poachers is Going Commando", *Smithsonian Magazine*, June 2016.

[651] Dasgupta, Partha, "The Economics of Biodiversity: The Dasgupta Review Headline Messages", February 2021, at 1. ISBN 978-1-911680-31-4.

[652] For a critical analysis of whether the current biodiversity crisis amounts to the start of a Sixth Mass Extinction, *see*, Cowie, Robert H., et al., "The Sixth Mass Extinction: fact, fiction or speculation", *Biological Reviews*, 2022. The researchers note that invertebrate animals receive far less attention than vertebrate animals when examining the loss of biodiversity, and even the world's primary record of species extinctions, the IUCN Red List of Threatened Species, is biased toward mammals, birds, and amphibians.

[653] Ripple, William J., et al., World Scientists' Warming to Humanity: A Second Notice.

a single organism—us."[654] The Anthropocene epoch, the era of significant human influence on the planet's ecosystems and climate, will be known for its biological devastation.[655] Research suggests that this Anthropocene extinction crisis is far worse than we have thought, with nearly half of 71,000 studied animal species in decline.[656] Research also shows that the extinction crisis is accelerating as a result of the increase in the human population and consumption rates.[657]

Tanzania was once the largest home to elephants in East Africa, but the country's leaders failed to act to stop poaching (and rejected offers for help), with the result that nearly 70% of its elephant population was lost to poachers between 2008 and 2014.[658] Botswana, now home to the largest elephant population in Africa, adopted an unofficial "shoot-to-kill" strategy in 2013 as a means of stopping the mass slaughter of its wildlife.[659] Botswana had once been considered to be the last great refuge for elephants,[660] but in recent years, rhinos and elephants have been poached in Botswana at such alarming numbers that Botswana has been forced to evacuate rhinos to undisclosed sanctuaries and areas.[661]

[654] United Nations Development Programme, *Human Development Report 2020, The next frontier, Human development and the Anthropocene*. New York, 2020, at 3. ISBN: 978-92-1-126442-5.

[655] For more on the biological annihilation, *see*, Gerardo Ceballos, et al., "Biological annihilation via the ongoing sixth mass extinction signaled by vertebrate population losses and declines", *PNAS*, July 10, 2017. https://doi.org/10.1073/pnas.1704949114

[656] Finn, Catherine, et al., "More losers than winners: investigating Anthropocene defaunation through the diversity of population trends", *Biological Reviews*, May 15, 2023. https://doi.org/10.1111/brv.12974

[657] Ceballos, Gerardo, et al., "Vertebrates on the brink as indicators of biological annihilation and the sixth mass extinction", *PNAS*, Vol. 117, No. 24, June 1, 2020. https://doi.org/10.1073/pnas.1922686117; *see also*, Ceballos, Gerardo, et al., "Accelerated modern human-induced species losses: Entering the sixth mass extinction", *Science Advances*, Vol. 1, Issue 5, June 19, 2015. https://doi.org/10.1126/sciadv.1400253

[658] Rice, Mary, "Botswana's elephant crisis – no time for pride and arrogance with such a pressing need for action", *Environmental Investigation Agency*, July 6, 2020, at https://eia-international.org/blog/botswanas-elephant-crisis-no-time-for-pride-and-arrogance-with-such-a-pressing-need-for-action/. It was "widely acknowledged" that individuals in the Wildlife Decision were involved with the poaching and trafficking of ivory, but no one was ever charged.

[659] Smith, Sonja, "Ex-Botswana president explains 'shoot to kill'", *Namibian*, December 2, 2020.

[660] Nuwer, Rachel, "Poachers are Invading Botswana, Last Refuge of African Elephants", *New York Times*, July 1, 2019.

[661] Rice, Mary, Botswana's elephant crisis.

In South Africa, home to the world's largest rhino population, rhinos are killed at alarming rates every year (448 in 2022,[662] 451 in 2021,[663] 394 in 2020 and 594 in 2019[664]). Between 2013 and 2017, more than 1000 rhinos were killed annually in South Africa.[665] In Kenya, poachers can receive life sentences, but the country's 2013 Wildlife Conservation Act has failed to deter poaching.[666] Despite harsh penalties, poaching has reached critical levels in Kenya, threatening the survival of both elephants and rhinos and threatening the livelihoods of millions of people who depend on tourism to make a living.[667] Millions in Kenya live in poverty,[668] and poverty fuels the recruitment (by bribes or by threat) of underpaid wildlife rangers, police and military personnel to participate in wildlife crimes.[669] Wildlife trafficking even increased in some areas during the COVID-19 pandemic as tourist spots emptied out and workers lost their livelihood.[670]

By losing species and populations within species, researchers fear that humanity is losing "intricate ecological networks involving animals, plants, and microorganisms" and vital "pools of genetic information," with "cascading catastrophic effects on ecosystems, worsening the annihilation of

[662] "Rhino poaching sees slight decline in South Africa", *Reuters*, February 7, 2023.

[663] Raghavan, Sudarsan, "The perilous 1000-mile journey to save Africa's endangered black rhinos", *Washington Post*, October 27, 2022.

[664] "The department report back on rhino poaching in South Africa in 2020", *Forestry, Fisheries and the Environment, Republic of South Africa*, dated February 1, 2021, at https://www.dffe.gov.za/mediarelease/rhinopoaching_sa

[665] *See*, "South African poaching explained", *Save the Rhino* (website), n.d., at https://www.savetherhino.org/rhino-info/poaching-stats/

[666] Lajka, Arijeta, "Wildlife poaching in Kenya is not punishable by death", *Associated Press*, December 27, 2019.

[667] Fiesta Warinwa, Erustus Kanga, and William Kiprono, "Fighting Wildlife Trade in Kenya", *United Nations UN Chronicle*, n.d., at https://www.un.org/en/chronicle/article/fighting-wildlife-trade-kenya

[668] In 2021, over 7.8 million people in Kenya lived in extreme poverty, with up to 6.6 million living on less than $1.90 U.S. dollars a day in rural regions. *See*, "Number of people living in extreme poverty in Kenya from 2016 to 2021" at https://www.statista.com/statistics/1229720/number-of-people-living-in-extreme-poverty-in-kenya-by-area/

[669] Fiesta Warinwa, Erustus Kanga, and William Kiprono, Fighting Wildlife Trade in Kenya.

[670] *See*, e.g., Koju, Narayan Prasad, et al., "COVID-19 lockdown frees wildlife to roam but increases poaching threats in Nepal", *Ecology and Evolution*, Vol. 11, Issue 14, at 9198–9205. https://doi.org/10.1002/ece3.7778; *see also*, "The Pandemic is a gift to poachers in Africa", *Economist*, March 31, 2021.

nature."[671] The call to address this "biological annihilation," which will have "serious ecological, economic and social consequences," is growing louder, even as signs point to "ever more powerful assaults on biodiversity ... painting a dismal picture of the future of life, including human life."[672] Drivers of species loss (beginning with those with the most impact) include (1) habitat loss (i.e., changes in land and sea use); (2) exploitation (e.g. hunting, fishing, harvesting, logging); (3) climate change; and (4) pollution,[673] each requiring swift action to address.

Existing international agreements have failed to prevent the collapse of the planet's biodiversity. The Convention on International Trade in Endangered Species of Wild Fauna and Flora (CITES) is a key international agreement adopted by 180+ nations to help ensure that international trade does not threaten biodiversity and species survival.[674] With insufficient funding, noncompliance, and no mechanism for enforcement, however, some compare the holes in CITES to Swiss cheese.[675] CITES has been further criticized for failing to protect vulnerable species.[676] A 2018 study found that, from 2006 to 2015, 2,009,377 kg of meat, 1,558,794 million animal skins, and 1,393,003 million live animals and plants were legally exported from Africa to Asia,[677] further calling into question the effectiveness of CITES.

[671] *See*, Gerardo Ceballos, Paul R. Ehrlich, and Rodolfo Dirzo, "Biological annihilation via the ongoing sixth mass extinction signaled by vertebrate population losses and declines", Instituto de Ecologia, Universidad Nacional Autonoma de Mexico, Mexico City, Mexico and the Department of Biology, Stanford University, Stanford, CA, March 23, 2017, E6094-E6095, at https://pichimahuida.info/area-protegida-privada_files/Sixth%20extinction%20of%20species.pdf

[672] Ibid.

[673] Brondizio, Eduardo S., et al. (Eds.), "Global assessment report of the Intergovernmental Science-Policy Platform on Biodiversity and Ecosystem Services," *IPBES*, May 4, 2019, at xvi. ISBN: 978-3-947851-20-1; *see also*, Pelley, Scott, "Scientists say planet in midst of sixth mass extinction, Earth's wildlife running out of places to live", *CBS News*, January 1, 2023.

[674] For more information on CITES, *see* https://cites.org/eng/disc/what.php

[675] For a discussion on how CITES has failed to protect biodiversity, *see* Pinnock, Don, "CITES has failed the natural world. Here's how it can be fixed", *Daily Maverick*, July 4, 2021.

[676] *See*, e.g., "CITES COP16: Successes and Failures", *Animal Welfare Institute*, AWI Quarterly Spring 2013, at https://awionline.org/awi-quarterly/2013-spring/cites-cop16-successes-and-failures

[677] Outhwaite, Willow and Lauren Brown, Executive Summary of "Eastward Bound, Analysis of CITES-listed flora and fauna exports from Africa to East and Southeast Asia", *Traffic International*, March 2018. ISBN: 978-1-85850-429-2.

The casualties from wildlife trafficking are not limited to animals. Wildlife protection is a dangerous and demanding profession. It is estimated that more than 150 rangers die in the line of duty every year.[678] Rangers and guards are often in the crosshairs of heavily armed poachers, militias/rebels and organized crime syndicates.[679] Over a 16-year period from 2006 to 2021, there were 2351 ranger fatalities, including 42.2% felony deaths and 57.8% deaths from accidents, wildlife attacks, illness or other work-related casualties.[680] The job is so dangerous that 1 in 7 rangers were injured in 2018.[681] Rangers also find themselves as targets at home. Homes have been burned down and rangers have been driven out of their communities for protecting wildlife.[682]

Every day, rangers fight the biodiversity crisis, a crisis that is an existential threat to humanity,[683] but many operations are understaffed, underfunded, and insufficiently trained. The Game Rangers Association of Africa has called for better employment conditions, including medical benefits, counseling services, life insurance, and other support services to rangers and their families.[684] In 2021, the United Nations called on Member States to recognize and support rangers and guards in their fight against illicit wildlife trafficking and to help support their training, equipment and wages.[685] Rangers need specialized training (e.g., first aid; firefighting; survival tactics; handling human-wildlife conflict) and adequate

[678] "Risking Lives to Protect Wildlife and Wildlands: Stories from Rangers in the Field", *The World Bank*, July 30, 2020, citing estimates from the Thin Green Line Foundation.

[679] U.S. Department of the Treasury, "Treasury Sanctions Wildlife Trafficking Organized Crime Group", October 7, 2022.

[680] Asia reported the highest number of ranger fatalities, 643 deaths, followed by Africa with 591 deaths. *See*, Galliers, Chris, et al., "Conservation Casualties: An Analysis of On-Duty Ranger Fatalities (2006–2021)", *Parks Journal*, Vol. 28(1), May 2022, at 39–50.

[681] *See*, "New Survey Finds One in Seven Wildlife Rangers Have Been Seriously Injured in the Line of Duty Over the Past Year", *WWF*, July 31, 2018.

[682] *See,* e.g., Feature Story "Risking Lives to Protect Wildlife and Wildlands: Stories from Rangers in the Field", *The World Bank*, July 30, 2020.

[683] In a 2022 interview, Jan-Niclas Gesenhues, the environmental spokesperson for the Bundnis 90/Die Grunen parliamentary group in the German Parliament, warned that "[t]he loss of biodiversity poses an existential threat to us humans, our livelihoods and prosperity". *See*, "The loss of biodiversity poses an existential threat;" Jan-Niclas Gesenhues in Interview", December 5, 2022, *Heinrich Boll Stiftung*, Washington, D.C., at https://us.boell.org/en/2022/12/05/loss-biodiversity-poses-existential-threat-jan-niclas-gesenhues-interview

[684] *See*, "The 2022 Kasane Ranger Call to Action", *Game Rangers Association of Africa*, n.d., at https://www.gameranger.org/all-media.html

[685] U.N. General Assembly Resolution 75/311, adopted July 23, 2021, §17.

gear and equipment (e.g., personal protective equipment; mosquito nets), as well as measures to improve both their physical and mental well-being (e.g., clean drinking water; adequate vaccinations; stress management).[686] Wildlife trafficking impacts not just the remote parts of the world, it has become an international crisis with global ramifications. As John F. Kerry explained to the Senate Committee on Foreign Relations in May 2012, "[p]oaching is not just a security threat for Africa. It is also a menace to developing economies, and it thrives where governance is weakest. Poachers with heavy weapons are a danger to lightly armed rangers and civilians, as well as to the animals who they target. They operate in remote territories and cross borders with impunity, wreaking havoc on villages and families. … We also know that poaching is interwoven into some of central and east Africa's most brutal conflicts and that many of those combatants are essentially members of criminal gangs preying upon the communities. One begets the other, and they are interrelated."[687] According to the Environmental Crimes Section of the Department of Justice, the criminal acts of poachers, smugglers and black market sellers harms local communities, hinders economic development, destabilizes the environment, threatens security and funnels billions of dollars "to those who perpetrate evil in the world."[688]

The protection of habitats, on which billions of species depend, is also a dangerous job. It may not be possible to ever know the exact number of deaths, but between 2000 and 2019, more than 1700 people were killed protecting the environment, of which 30–40% were indigenous people.[689] The execution of people on the frontlines of the conservation battle has been happening for decades, and the frequency of attacks is increasing.[690] Dorothy Stang, a 73-year old American nun, spent decades defending the human rights of the rural poor in Brazil's Amazon and their right to sus-

[686] Galliers, Chris, et al., Conservation Casualties.

[687] Kerry, John F., "Kerry Statement Senate Foreign Relations Committee Hearing on Ivory and Insecurity: The Global Implications of Poaching in Africa", *U.S. Senate, Committee on Foreign Relations, Washington, D.C.*, May 24, 2012, at https://www.foreign.senate.gov/press/rep/release/kerry-statement_senate-foreign-relations-committee-hearing-on%2D%2Divory-and-insecurity-the-global-implications-of-poaching-in-africa

[688] *See*, "Wildlife Trafficking", *The United States Department of Justice, About the Division, Environmental Crimes Section*" n.d., at https://www.justice.gov/enrd/wildlife-trafficking

[689] *See*, Schwartzman, Steve, "Murder in the rainforest: 1700+ defenders killed, but their legacy lives on", *Environmental Defense Fund*, November 22, 2019.

[690] Press Release: "Global Witness reports 227 land and environmental activists murdered in a single year, the worst figure on record", *Global Witness*, September 13, 2021.

tenance from the rainforest, despite receiving frequent death threats.[691] Her voice made her the target of powerful beef and agribusiness interests that destroy rainforests for cattle grazing and commercial farming.[692]

In 2005, Stang was executed on a dirt road near a remote settlement in northern Brazil by a gunman paid by local cattle ranchers.[693] Stang's legacy was her deep understanding of the connection between the environment and human rights, warning that, "the death of the forest is the end of our lives."[694] In 2021, a newly discovered species of screech owl in the Amazon rainforest was named after Stang, a fitting tribute for someone who would sit outside at night, "look up at the sky and listen to the music of nature."[695]

Some say that little has changed. In 2019, cattle ranchers, farmers and loggers were accused of deforestation and triggering sharp increases in wildfires to exploit wood from the rainforest and to level habitats for meat production.[696] The fate of the planet's tropical rainforests, which perform the critical job of draining heat-trapping carbon dioxide from the atmosphere, should not be left to indigenous people, underfunded police, non-governmental organizations and conservationists. The primary responsibility should rest with governments and the global community, all of which must enact meaningful laws to protect the environment and, equally important, enforce them. Companies and industries that profit from the destruction of habitats with 'don't ask, don't tell' policies also bear responsibility. First and foremost, however, individuals on the frontlines like Dorothy Stang, who are risking their lives to protect wildlife, the environment and humanity from the devastating effects of biodiversity loss, must be protected.

[691] Associated Press, "American nun shot to death in Brazil's Amazon", *NBC News*, February 12, 2005; *see also*, "Expanded Story of Sister Dorothy Stang", *Sisters of Notre Dame De Namur*, n.d., at https://www.sndohio.org/sister-dorothy/expanded-story/

[692] Judge, Ed, "Sister Dorothy Stang: A Martyr for God's Poor and God's Creation", *Holy Cross*, February 12, 2022.

[693] Doce, Nacho and Garcia, Pablo, "Years after nun's murder, church activists face threats in lawless Amazon", *Reuters*, September 12, 2019.

[694] "Sister Dorothy Stang and the Xingu Screech-Owl", *Sisters of Notre Dame De Namur, About the Sisters*, April 16, 2021.

[695] Alves, Lisa, "The screech owl named for Sr. Dorothy Stang is a tribute 'symbolic of her life'", *Global Sisters Report*, May 17, 2021, quoting Sr. Judith Clemens, a Sister of Notre Dame de Namur and friend of the late nun.

[696] Doce, Nacho and Garcia, Pablo, "Years after nun's murder, church activists face threats in lawless Amazon", *Reuters*, September 12, 2019.

Notwithstanding the crisis, some countries, including the United States, Canada, Zimbabwe, Namibia, Zambia, Mozambique, Tanzania, Botswana, and South Africa,[697] still permit or even encourage trophy hunting of endangered wildlife, including elephants, giraffes, lions, leopards and rhinos.[698] Trophy hunting, in turn, leads to illegal poaching, as poachers target private game reserves.[699] The United States again finds itself as an outlier in the international community. It is responsible for 71% of the import demand for animal "trophies," making it the primary driver of trophy hunting.[700] There is a clear inconsistency (some would say hypocrisy) when countries enforce anti-poaching measures against poor indigenous communities but permit the blood sport killing of endangered species by the wealthy and elites. Legalizing animal hunting for "trophies" not only undermines anti-poaching laws, it fosters an underground market for illegal hunts for lucrative profits, and worse, it perpetuates the belief that animals are mere commodities for human sport.

There are largely unsubstantiated claims that trophy hunting aids conservation. However, this ignores the significant concerns associated with it, including declining "trophy" animal populations, reduced quality of hunted species, suppressed immunity, reduced reproductive success, and low fitness levels and nutritional stress that may make animals more susceptible to infections and diseases over time.[701] There are also claims that trophy hunting benefits local communities, but recent studies show that

[697] *See generally* "Killing For Trophies, An Analysis of Global Trophy Hunting Trade", *International Fund for Animal Welfare*, June 14, 2016, at https://www.ifaw.org/resources/killing-for-trophies; *see also*, Froelich, Paula, "Elephants, lions and leopards; 13 countries where rich people hunt endangered animals", *New York Post*, February 8, 2020.

[698] Since 1991, Zimbabwe has sold annual permits that allow wealthy hunters to shoot and kill elephants. *See*, Shahani, Shradha, "500 elephants waiting to be shot as Zimbabwe's hunting season begins", *Conde Nast Traveler*, 4.30.2021.

[699] *See*, e.g., Acharya, Bhargav, "Rhino poaching sees slight decline in South Africa", *Reuters*, February 7, 2023.

[700] *See*, "killing for trophies: an analysis of global trophy hunting trade", *IFAW.*, n.d., at https://www.ifaw.org/resources/killing-for-trophies

[701] Muposhi, Victor K., et al., "Ecological, Physiological, Genetic Trade-Offs and Socio-Economic Implications of Trophy Hunting As A Conservation Tool: A Narrative Review", *The Journal of Animal & Plant Sciences*, 27(1): 2017, at 1–14. ISSN: 1018-7081.

local communities receive little to no benefit from trophy hunting.[702] Trophy hunting is not a large contributor to economies. A recent report found that in eight African countries, trophy hunting contributed at most 0.03% of GDP, compared to overall tourism, which accounted for 2.8% and 5.1% of GDP.[703] More often, there are reports of corruption.[704]

Trophy hunting also negatively impacts tourism. In 2022, Botswana's former president, Ian Khama, strongly criticized the killing of one of the nation's two largest tusked elephant bulls, explaining that the animal was "an elephant that tour operators constantly tried to show tourists as an iconic attraction. Now it is dead. How does it being dead benefit our declining tourism due to poor policies? Our tourism is wildlife based. No wildlife means no tourism, no tourists no jobs, and no revenue stream."[705] There are clearly far more sustainable, eco-friendly and humane ways to support conservation and local communities than killing endangered animals.

Trophy hunting and government sanctioned hunts get a lot of negative press, as they should, but one of the greatest threats to wildlife is roads and highways. It's impossible to know how many animals are killed on roads worldwide each year, but there are estimates. One report estimates that, depending on the country, the number of animals killed each year on roads ranges from hundreds of thousands to several hundred million animals.[706] Another study found that roughly 194 million birds and 29

[702] *See,* e.g., Economists at Large, "The $200 million question, How much does trophy hunting really contribute to African communities?", a report for the African Lion Coalition, prepared by Economists at Large, Melbourne, Australia. (2013); *see also*, Ingeborg Nordbø, Bakyt Turdumambetov & Bilgehan Gulcan, "Local opinions on trophy hunting in Kyrgyzstan", *Journal of Sustainable Tourism*, 26:1, 68–84 (2081). https://doi.org/10.1080/09669582.2017.1319843

[703] The studied countries included Botswana, Ethiopia, Mozambique, Namibia, South Africa, Tanzania, Zambia and Zimbabwe. *See*, Murray, Cameron K., "The lion's share? On the economic benefits of trophy hunting. A report for the Humane Society International", *Economics at Large*, Melbourne, Australia (2017).

[704] Ghasemi, Benjamin, "Trophy hunting and conservation: Do the major ethical theories converge in opposition to trophy hunting?", *British Ecological Society, People and Nature*, October 19, 2020. https://doi.org/10.1002/pan3.10160

[705] Zenda, Cyril, "Controversy Grows Over Elephant Trophy Hunting", *Fair Planet*, July 22, 2022.

[706] Seiler, A., Helldin, J.O., "Mortality in wildlife due to transportation", in the *Environmental Pollution* book series (EPOL, Vol. 10). https://doi.org/10.1007/1-4020-4504-2_8

million mammals may be killed each year on European roads.[707] The estimates for some European countries range from 350,000 to 27 million birds killed on roads annually.[708] In the United States, it is estimated that 1 million animals are killed on roads every year,[709] including mammals, birds, invertebrates and amphibians.[710] Most estimates, however, do not include animals who are mortally wounded but manage to get away from the road. During lockdowns in 2020 due to the Covid-19 pandemic, the number of animals killed on roads declined by more than half.[711] Vehicle collisions with wildlife are very dangerous for drivers and are responsible for many fatalities. State Farm Insurance reports that between July 1, 2019 and June 30, 2020, there were more than 1.9 million insurance claims involving collisions with animals and that, on average, drivers have a 1 in 116 chance of colliding with an animal.[712]

In recent decades, countries have been investing in wildlife corridors for both conservation and for public safety purposes. Wildlife passageways can be found around the globe, with key wildlife corridors in the United States, Canada, Europe, Kenya, Singapore, Mexico, Oslo, Japan, India, Nepal, Russia and China.[713] Many countries are exploring how to reduce vehicle collisions with wildlife. In Australia, researchers are looking at

[707] Grilo, Clara, et al., *Roadkill Risk and Population vulnerability in European birds and mammals*. University of Reading, Frontiers in Ecology and the Environment, June 8, 2020. https://doi.org/10.1002/fee.2216

[708] Erritzoe, Johannes; Mazgajski, Thomasz D.; Rejt, Lukasz, "Bird Casualties on European Roads – A Review", Acta Ornithologica, 38(2): 77–93 (2003). https://doi.org/10.3161/068.038.0204

[709] Seiler, Andreas and Helldin, J-O, "Mortality in Wildlife Due to Transportation", in *The Ecology of Transportation: Managing Mobility for the Environment* (ISBN: 978-1-4020-4504-2), at 166–189. https://doi.org/10.1007/1-4020-4504-2_8; *see also*, Wollan, Malia, "Using Crowds, and GPS, to Chart Roadkill", *New York Times*, September 12, 2010.

[710] Case, Ronald M., "Interstate Highway Road-Killed Animals: A Data Source for Biologists", Wildlife Society Bulletin. 6 (1):8–13. JSTOR 3781058.

[711] Katz, Cheryl, "Roadkill rates fall dramatically as lockdown keeps drivers at home". *National Geographic*, June 26, 2020.

[712] "Don't Veer for Deer: Reduce speed and stay alert to help avoid animal collisions", *State Farm*, October 21, 2020, at https://newsroom.statefarm.com/animal-collision/

[713] Chauhan, Priya, "26 Most Important Wildlife Corridors Across the Globe", *Planet Custodian*, April 1, 2021.

wildlife-proof fences and koala-friendly tunnels.[714] In India, corridors are being developed for elephants to reduce conflicts with humans.[715]

Wildlife corridors are highly effective. When Utah constructed underpasses for animals on a highway that blocked migratory routes, it resulted in a 98.5% reduction in deer mortalities.[716] When Colorado built wildlife crossings in 2016, collisions between animals and vehicles dropped by 90%, and mule deer used the crossing 96% of the time.[717] In 2021, Florida, Colorado and Virginia enacted laws to protect wildlife corridors, while 14 states have either issued executive orders or have introduced wildlife corridor legislation.[718] California budgeted $61.5 million dollars in 2021 to help reduce the 7000+ vehicle collisions that occur every year involving large wildlife.[719] When the United States enacted the Infrastructure Investment and Jobs Act in 2021, it included $350 million in federal funds for new wildlife crossings pilot programs to help reduce vehicle-wildlife collisions.[720]

A 2017 collaborative study at Concordia University examined existing studies on vehicle-wildlife collisions and considered 40 "prevention methods" that are used to reduce the number of animals killed on roads. The study concluded that animal deaths could be reduced 54% by fences alone, and that when coupled with crossing structures, the number of large mammals killed would be reduced by 83%.[721] Fences should never be used, however, in a manner that restricts animals from finding food and water. When the National Park Service erected fences to prevent tule elk

[714] Gibson, Eloise, "Australia's 'road kill' map: The 76-year old making a road kill map of Australia", *BBC Earth*, November 2019.

[715] For more on corridors being built in India, *see*, "Right of Passage: National Elephant Corridors Project", *Wildlife Trust of Indian*, at https://www.wti.org.in/projects/right-of-passage-national-elephant-corridors-project/

[716] Bissonette, John A. and Rosa, Silvia, "An evaluation of a mitigation strategy for deer-vehicle collisions", *Wildlife Biology*, December 1, 2012. https://doi.org/10.2981/11-122

[717] Ukropina, Mitchell, "Colorado wildlife crossings dramatically reduce collisions: Other states should follow example of habitat connectivity", *Colorado Newsline*, October 21, 2021.

[718] *See*, "Landmark Legislation to Protect Wildlife Corridors Passes U.S. House of Representatives", *Center for Large Landscape Conservation*, July 2, 2021.

[719] Garcia, Marissa, "California budgets $61.5 million for wildlife crossings", *High Country News*, July 7, 2021.

[720] Infrastructure Investment and Jobs Act - H.R. 3684, 117th Congress (2021–2022) became law on November 15, 2021 as Public Law No: 117-58.

[721] Concordia University, "How to save animals by reducing roadkill: Collaborative study shows that more comparable data is needed to protect animals", *Science Daily*, April 4, 2017, at https://www.sciencedaily.com/releases/2017/04/170404160107.htm

at the Point Reyes National Seashore from competing with cattle for food and water, dozens died from dehydration and starvation.[722] Failures by government result in the deaths of countless animals.

Authorities in the United States, intentionally and unintentionally, continue to kill millions of animals. The Fish and Wildlife Service is the federal agency responsible for "conserving, protecting, and enhancing fish and wildlife and their habitats."[723] Since 2000, it has killed more than 2 million mammals and 15 million birds.[724] The USDA's Wildlife Services program has been accused of recklessly violating animal protection laws and destroying ecosystems, with profound consequences to biodiversity and the economy.[725] It has been accused of using inhumane and cruel practices, such as torturing and killing dogs and endangered species, using "poison baits, cyanide traps, leghold traps and neck snares," setting animals on fire and suffocating animals with carbon monoxide.[726] It kills wildlife for private farmers if they allege that the animals are competing with farmed animals for land.[727] In 2020 and 2021, the USDA's Wildlife Services program killed more than 1.5 million animals, including 62,537 coyotes, 685 bobcats, 434 black bears, 276 cougars and 2527 foxes in the first year.[728] Cattle ranchers in Mexico kill jaguars to prevent future attacks on their

[722] Associated Press, "Animal rights group sues National Park Service over dying tule elk", *Los Angeles Times*, June 22, 2021.

[723] "Our Statutory Authority and Functions", *U.S. Fish & Wildlife Service*, at https://www.fws.gov/about/mission-and-vision

[724] Bale, Rachael, "This Government Program's Job is to Kill Wildlife", *National Geographic*, February 12, 2016.

[725] Wildlife Services is a program within the USDA's Animal and Plant Health Inspection Service division. The program costs taxpayers more than $100 million per year. *See*, "Wildlife Services' War on Wildlife: Reckless behavior is destroying ecosystems and violating animal protection laws", *Animal Legal Defense Fund*, n.d., at https://aldf.org/issue/wildlife-services-war-on-wildlife/

[726] Ketcham, Christopher, "The Rogue Agency: A USDA program that tortures dogs and kills endangered species", *Harper's Magazine*, 2016, at https://harpers.org/archive/2016/03/the-rogue-agency/

[727] *See*, Wildlife Services' War on Wildlife. The Wildlife Services' wildlife killing costs taxpayers more than $100 million per year.

[728] "Program Data Reports, Program Data Report G – 2020, Animals Dispersed / Killed or Euthanized / Removed or Destroyed / Freed or Relocated", *USDA Animal and Plant Health Inspection Service, U.S. Department of Agriculture*, at https://www.aphis.usda.gov/aphis/ourfocus/wildlifedamage/pdr/?file=PDR-G_Report&p=2020:INDEX:

livestock.[729] Other animals are forced to do unpleasant work for humans: e.g., canaries to test coal mines, donkeys to carry loads, horses for law enforcement, elephants to help with logging, rats to detect land mines, monkeys to pick coconuts.

Countless numbers of animals are victims of catastrophic wildfires, driven in significant part by the climate crisis and by human involvement. In 2019 and 2020, record-breaking wildfires broke out in Australia. Chris Dickman, a professor of ecology at the University of Sydney, estimates that more than 1 billion animals perished as a result of the wildfires, including those killed by the fire and those killed indirectly by starvation, dehydration or habitat loss.[730] A report commissioned by the World Wide Fund for Nature Australia found that nearly 3 billion animals perished or were affected by Australia's wildfires from July 2019 through March 2020, including 143 million mammals, 2.46 billion reptiles, 180 million birds and 51 million frogs, making it "one of the worst wildlife disasters in modern history".[731] The 2020 fire season on the West Coast of the United States was unprecedented, with more than 5 million acres burned in California, Oregon and Washington.[732] Canada's 2023 wildfire season has been the worst on record, with 32 million acres burning so far.[733] Wildfires in Maui in 2023 was one of the deadliest fires in U.S. history.[734] The increasing frequency and severity of catastrophic wildfires are having a devastating impact on wildlife. While there are no official estimates of the number of wildlife affected by the record-breaking fires, ecologists fear lasting damage to habitats, reduced species populations and species extinc-

[729] Maron, Dina Fine, "Mexican cartels are increasingly moving into wildlife crime", *National Geographic*, February 25, 2022.

[730] Chow, Denice, "Scientist estimates that more than a billion animals killed by Australian wildfires", *NBC News,* January 8, 2020. The estimate is based on a 2007 World Wildlife Fund-Australia report on animal density.

[731] Van Eeden, Lily, et al., "Australia's 2019–2020 Bushfires: The Wildlife Toll, Interim Report", *World Wildlife Fund*, 2020, at 1–2.

[732] Migliozzi, Blacki, et al., "Record Wildfires on the West Coast are Capping a Disastrous Decade", *New York Times*, September 24, 2020. In recent years, California has also suffered from historic atmospheric rivers. *See*, Cappucci, Matthew and Brasch, Ben, "Northern California sees historic deluge as atmosphere river slams state", *Washington Post*, January 2, 2023.

[733] Meredith, Sam, "Unprecedented Canada wildfires obliterate previous annual pollution record in just seven months", *CNBC,* August 3, 2023.

[734] Treisman, Rachel, "Maui's wildfires are among the deadliest on record in the U.S. Here are some others", *NPR*, August 15, 2023.

tions.[735] The health of millions of people is also threatened by severe air pollution caused by the wildfires.[736] Dangerous levels of smoke and ozone pollutants from the wildfires can affect the cardiovascular system and the lungs, irritate chronic diseases and lead to premature death.[737]

Historically, state laws in the United States have failed wildlife by permitting the private ownership of wild animals, including big cats and other wild animals[738] and by failing to make enforcement of the law a priority. Baloo (a bear), Leo (a lion), and Shere Khan (a tiger) were rescued in 2001 from deplorable conditions in a drug dealer's basement, each malnourished and riddled with parasites. Due to their deep bond, they were housed together at a sanctuary, where they clung to one another for comfort.[739] Tragically, such stories are not unique, despite hundreds of dangerous incidents in nearly all 50 states since 1990, some of which resulted in serious injuries and death.[740] Only 20 states have comprehensive bans on the ownership of wild or exotic animals as pets.[741] Fortunately, in 2022, the Big Cat Public Safety Act[742] was finally signed into law. The new law prohibits the private ownership of big cats and makes it illegal for exhibitors to permit direct contact with cubs.

Human celebratory activities also threaten wildlife, such as the release of balloons, which can entangle and strangle wildlife and kill animals who

[735] Pennisi, Elizabeth, "As wildfires continue in western United States, biologists fear for vulnerable species", *Science*, September 30, 2020.

[736] Ibid.

[737] Fountain, Henry, "Health Risks of Smoke and Ozone Rise in the West as Wildfires Worsen", *New York Times*, January 5, 2022.

[738] As of August 8, 2022, Alabama, Nevada, North Carolina, Wisconsin and Oklahoma permit the private ownership of big cats as pets. *See*, "State Laws Exotic Cats: State Laws for Keeping Exotic Cats as Pets", *Big Cat Rescue*, August 8, 2022, at https://bigcatrescue.org/state-laws-exotic-cats/

[739] Poole, Shelia, "Update: Shere Khan, beloved Bengal tiger, dies", *The Atlanta Journal-Constitution*, December 18, 2018.

[740] For more on the risk to public safety that private ownership of big cats entails, *see* "Big Cat Public Safety Act", *Animal Welfare Institute*, n.d., at https://awionline.org/legislation/big-cat-public-safety-act

[741] Thirteen states have partial bans that ban some, but not all, non-domestic animals. *See*, "Map of Private Exotic Pet Ownership Laws", *Michigan State University, Animal Legal & Historical Center*, n.d., at https://www.animallaw.info/content/map-private-exotic-pet-ownership-laws

[742] Big Cat Public Safety Act, Public Law No. 117-243, December 20, 2022.

mistake balloons for food.[743] Fireworks can also damage hearing, cause panic, disorientation and stress, and cause the death of animals.[744] Poisonous and harmful particles, such as fine dust (PM10), are released from firecrackers,[745] which can be toxic to wildlife. On New Year's Eve in Beebe, Arkansas in 2010, thousands of red-winged blackbirds fell from the sky. It was believed that the birds were startled by the New Year's Eve fireworks and died of "acute physical trauma" as they flew into chimneys, houses, trees and other objects.[746] The following New Year's Eve saw the same devastation as birds again fell from the sky in Beebe, Arkansas.[747] Fireworks are not just harmful to wildlife, they can trigger PTSD in veterans, torment companion animals and overwhelm some children. It is estimated that one-fifth of companion animals who disappear do so because of loud noises, primarily fireworks and storms.[748] For these reasons, many advocate for silent fireworks.[749] Human activity is so disruptive to wildlife that it is driving animals to be nocturnal to avoid interaction with humans.[750]

[743] *See*, "Balloons and Wildlife: Please Don't Release Your Balloons: An Open Spaces Blog", *U.S. Fish and Wildlife*, August 5, 2015, at https://www.fws.gov/news/blog/index.cfm/2015/8/5/balloons-and-wildlife-please-dont-release-your-balloons#

[744] "How fireworks harm nonhuman animals", *Animal Ethics*, n.d., at https://www.animal-ethics.org/how-fireworks-harm-nonhuman-animals/

[745] Greven, Frans E.; et al., "Air pollution during New Year's fireworks and daily mortality in the Netherlands", *Scientific Reports*, 9, 5735 (2019). https://doi.org/10.1038/s41598-019-42080-6

[746] Robertson, C. "For Arkansas Blackbirds, the New Year Never Came", *New York Times*, January 3, 2011.

[747] McLaughlin, E. "Dead Blackbirds Fall From the Sky Again in Beebe, Arkansas, on New Year's Eve", *ABC News*, January 1, 2012.

[748] "Independence Day can be perilous for pets", *ASPCA*, June 25, 2015, at https://www.aspca.org/about-us/press-releases/independence-day-can-be-perilous-pets

[749] Desmond, Jane, "It's time for silent fireworks", *The Hill*, June 29, 2020.

[750] Gaynor, Kaitlyn M, et al., "The influence of human disturbance on wildlife nocturnality", *Science*, Vol. 360, Issue 6394, June 15, 2018, at 1232–1235. https://doi.org/10.1126/science.aar7121

Recent Developments for Wildlife

The United Nations has called for increased international cooperation and coordination among nations to address the "adverse economic, social and environmental impacts" of poaching.[751] In recent years, the United Nations has raised concerns about the "increasing scale of poaching and illegal trade in wildlife" and the "unprecedented global decline of biodiversity" in recently adopted resolutions, warning that wildlife trafficking contributes to species extinction, destruction of ecosystems, devastation to rural livelihoods, and national instability.[752] Recognizing the link between wildlife and financial crimes, the United Nations has called on Member States to update their national laws to ensure that crimes associated with illegal wildlife trade are treated as "predicate offences" for money laundering.[753]

The United Nations Environment Programme (UNEP) is focusing on biodiversity with working groups within the Conference of the Parties to the Convention on Biological Diversity (COP-15).[754] In 2021, UNEP released a draft of its *Post-2020 Global Biodiversity Framework*, which includes measures to protect land and marine habitats and specific milestones and targets to be achieved by 2030 to build "a shared future for all life on Earth."[755] More importantly, unlike CITES, it is anticipated that the framework will include enforcement mechanics.[756] A second UNEP event in 2021, the United Nations Climate Change Conference (COP-26), focused, in part, on one of the main drivers of biodiversity loss, habitat loss.[757] The event was criticized for serving animal meat, which is driving

[751] *See,* e.g., U.N. General Assembly Resolution 73/343, adopted September 20, 2019, at https://undocs.org/en/A/RES/73/343

[752] Ibid.

[753] Ibid. Predicate offenses are crimes that are components of more serious offences, such as money laundering or racketeering.

[754] "Report of the Conference of the Parties to the Convention on Biological Diversity on its Fifteenth Meeting (Part I)", *UN Environment Programme*, Convention on Biological Diversity (CBD/COP/15/4, Kunming China, October 11–15, 2021, at https://www.cbd.int/meetings/COP-15

[755] Id., at 17.

[756] Id., at Part III (Establish Accountability Mechanisms).

[757] For details on this event, *see*, UN Climate Change Conference UK 2021, at https://ukcop26.org/

deforestation.[758] As of November 12, 2021, COP26 world leaders from 141 countries have vowed to end deforestation by 2030 and the pledge is backed by $19.2 billion dollars in public and private funds.[759] International collaboration is challenging because nations have conflicting priorities, different interests, and are at different stages of development, but these two initiatives prove that progress at the global level can be made.

At the 2022 United Nations Biodiversity Conference (COP15), 188 nations adopted the Kunming-Montreal Global Biodiversity Framework in a further effort to protect biodiversity on earth.[760] The agreement sets forth four long-term goals, including (A) maintaining, enhancing or restoring "[t]he integrity, connectivity and resilience of all ecosystems"; halting "[h]uman induced extinctions"; reducing the extinction rate by tenfold and increasing wild species to healthy levels by 2025; and maintaining and safeguarding genetic diversity within wild and domesticated species; (B) using and managing biodiversity sustainably; maintaining and enhancing "nature's contributions to people"; and helping achieve "sustainable development for the benefit of present and future generations by 2050"; (C) sharing fairly and equitably the benefits (monetary and non-monetary) of "genetic resources, and digital sequence information on genetic resources" to contribute "to the conservation and sustainable use of biodiversity."; and (D) fully implementing the framework with "financial resources, capacity-building, technical and scientific cooperation" and access to technology, in particular for developing countries, to close "the biodiversity finance gap of 700 billion dollars per year."[761] Nations are also endorsing legally non-binding but highly symbolic declarations to safeguard habitats. In 2021, 127 nations signed the Glasgow Leaders' Declaration on Forests and Land Use, to "halt and reverse forest loss and land degradation by 2030."[762]

[758] Buxton, Amy, "World's Largest Climate Crisis Conference Sparks Controversy After Serving Meat", *Plant Based News*, November 12, 2022.

[759] Rannard, Georgina and Francesca Gillett, "COP26: World leaders promise to end deforestation by 2030)", *BBC*, November 2, 2021.

[760] *See*, Andersen, Inger, "Adoption of the 'Kunming-Montreal Global Biodiversity Framework'", *United Nations Environment Programme,* December 19, 2022.

[761] *See*, Kunming-Montreal Global biodiversity framework.

[762] As of November 12, 2021, 144 nations have signed the declaration. *See*, Butler, Rhett, "What countries are leaders in reducing deforestation? What are not?", *Mongabay,* November 5, 2021.

In 2020, a global initiative, "End Wildlife Crime," was launched to address the significant gaps in international law that have allowed wildlife trafficking to flourish.[763] The Initiative includes a broad coalition of experts in law, policy, public health, business, and the environment to provide technical support to reform international law in 2 major respects: the creation of an international agreement to address wildlife crimes; and recognition of risks associated with any wildlife trade in the 'Pandemic Prevention, Preparedness and Response Accord' currently under negotiation by the World Health Organization.[764]

Some countries and regions are also taking separate action to protect biodiversity. In 2021, China announced that it was creating 230,000 square kilometers of national parks and establishing the Kunming Biodiversity Fund, a $230 million dollar international fund to support biodiversity in developing countries.[765] China also removed scales of pangolins, the world's most trafficked mammal, from its 2020 list of approved traditional medicines.[766] In Ghana, 12,132 acres were legally designated as a municipal-level protected area in 2020 for threatened species.[767] Guanay, Bolivia also enacted a new law to protect one-third of its territory, or 273,884 acres of forests, to help fight deforestation,[768] while Turkey established 350 square kilometers of protected area along its Mediterranean coastline to safeguard one of the world's most overfished areas.[769] In

[763] *See*, End Wildlife Crime, at https://endwildlifecrime.org/

[764] Ibid.

[765] Farand, Chloe, "Xi Jinping announced biodiversity fund to help developing nations protect nature", *Climate Change News*, December 10, 2021.

[766] Maron, Dina Fine, "Pangolins receive surprising lifeline with new protections in China", *National Geographic*, June 9, 2020.

[767] Boateng, Caleb Ofori, "Critical Refuse for *the* Togo Slippery Frog", *WFN Supporting Conservation Leaders*, n.d., at https://whitleyaward.org/winners/critical-refuge-for-the-togo-slippery-frog/; *see also*, "20 Wildlife Conservation Wins in 2020", *WFN Supporting Conservation Leaders*, n.d., at https://whitleyaward.org/2021/01/14/20-conservation-wins-in-2020/

[768] Price, Kelly, "In Bolivian Andes, new protected area offers 'a breath of fresh air'", *Conservation International*, March 25, 2021, at https://www.conservation.org/blog/in-bolivian-andes-new-protected-area-offers-a-breath-of-fresh-air

[769] Pocock, Sarah, "New Marine protected areas connect hundreds of kilometers of Turkey's Mediterranean coast", *Fauna & Flora International*, September 25, 2020.

2016, Norway became the first country in the world to implement a complete ban on deforestation.[770]

Countries are tackling poaching and illegal wildlife trafficking, with some countries banning the sale of ivory, including China,[771] France,[772] Hong Kong[773] and the United States.[774] The U.K. aims to ban the import of hunting trophies from elephants, rhinos, and thousands of other threatened and endangered species.[775] In an effort to deter people from buying ivory, nations are publicly destroying stockpiles of ivory, including Vietnam,[776] Sri Lanka,[777] China,[778] France,[779] Kenya[780] and the United States.[781] Countries are also focusing on anti-corruption efforts. In 2022, a Cambodian wildlife official and seven others were arrested for allegedly

[770] Fawzy, Farida, "Norway becomes first country to ban deforestation", *CNN,* June 9, 2016.

[771] "China's ban on ivory trade comes into force", *BBC,* January 1, 2018.

[772] The French Environment Minister signed a decree in 2016 that bans the trade of ivory and rhino horn in France and all French territories. *See*, "France bans all ivory and rhino horn trade", *The Ecologist*, August 19, 2016, at https://theecologist.org/2016/aug/19/france-bans-all-ivory-and-rhino-horn-trade

[773] AFP, "Hong Kong's ban in ivory products comes into force, marking end of once-rampant industry", *Hong Kong Free Press*, January 1, 2022, at https://hongkongfp.com/2022/01/01/hong-kongs-ban-on-ivory-products-comes-into-force-marking-end-of-once-rampant-industry/

[774] The importation of elephant ivory was already prohibited in the U.S. but in June 2016, the U.S. Fish & Wildlife Service issued a new federal rule to implement a near-total ban on the commercial trade of elephant ivory within the U.S. *See*, Arnold, Chris, "New U.S. Ban on Ivory Sales To Protect Elephants", *NPR*, June 2, 2016.

[775] Press Release, "Importing of hunting trophies banned to protect world's threatened species", *U.K. Department for Environment, Food & Rural Affairs, The Rt Hon Lord Goldsmith, and The Rt Hon George Eustice MP*, December 10, 2021.

[776] Vietnam also destroyed rhino horn. *See*, Reuters Staff, "Vietnam destroys mass rhino horns and elephant ivory", *Reuters*, November 12, 2016.

[777] Haviland, Charles, "Sri Lanka destroys poached 'blood' ivory", *BBC*, January 27, 2016.

[778] "China destroys tonnes of ivory in landmark move", *BBC*, January 6, 2014.

[779] "France publicly destroys seized ivory", *BBC*, February 6, 2014.

[780] Nuwer, Rachel, "Kenya Sets Ablaze 105 Tons of Ivory", *National Geographic*, April 30, 2016.

[781] U.S. Department of the Interior, "United States Destroys Confiscated Elephant Ivory in Times Square", June 19, 2015 (last ed. September 29, 2021).

trafficking and selling thousands of endangered monkeys to research facilities in the United States.[782]

The United States is the largest importer of animal trophies in the world, importing more than 10 times the number of trophies than China, the world's second largest trophy importer.[783] In the 5 year period from 2011 to 2015, trophy imports of CITES-listed species into the United States was greater than the sum of the next nine largest importing countries in the world.[784] The United States did ban the import of lion trophies from captive bred lion hunts in South Africa in 2016, but in 2018, the ban was removed to allow applications for trophies to be considered on a "case-by-case basis."[785] Fortunately, government actions can be challenged in courts in the United States, sometimes successfully. The federal Court of Appeals for the DC Circuit upheld the conservation mandate of the Endangered Species Act[786] and invalidated permits for imports of elephant and lion trophies from Zimbabwe and Zambia.[787] Opinion polls indicate that the majority of Americans oppose the importation of "trophies" from "pay to slay" kills,[788] but the actions of a few affluent trophy hunters are allowed to tarnish the country's image for all citizens.

Legal reform for animals will not be achieved by a single new law, but rather, by a series of legal changes that together work to improve the status of animals. In recent years, numerous countries have done that by enacting a variety of wildlife protection laws. China is cracking down on the

[782] The accused, the deputy director of wildlife and biodiversity in Cambodia's Ministry of Agriculture, was arrested while traveling to a CITES conference. *See*, Maron, Dina Fine, "U.S. arrests Cambodian official headed to wildlife summit – for monkey smuggling", *National Geographic*, November 17, 2022; *see also*, Associated Press, "Cambodian wildlife official among eight charged in US with smuggling endangered monkeys", *Guardian*, November 17, 2022.

[783] Sheikh, Pervaze, "International Trophy Hunting", *Congressional Research Service*, March 20, 2019, at 4, at https://crsreports.congress.gov/product/details?prodcode=R45615

[784] Ibid.

[785] *See*, Nuwer, Rachel, "U.S. Lifts Ban on Some Elephant and Lion Trophies", *New York Times*, March 7, 2018.

[786] Endangered Species Act of 1973, 16 U.S.C. § 1531 et seq. (1973).

[787] News desk, "Federal Court invalidates decision for trophy imports to US", *Africa Geographic*, January 2, 2018.

[788] *See*, e.g., Pacelle, Wayne, "Survey of American electorate reveals overwhelming opposition to trophy hunting", *A Humane World*, December 7, 2017.

illegal wildlife trade by closing down online stores and accounts.[789] Vietnam's Administration of Forestry agreed to rescue more than 1000 bears at illegal bear bile farms.[790] France outlawed the import of trophies from African lions,[791] while Luxembourg banned fox hunting.[792] The UAE outlawed the private ownership of wild animals as pets,[793] and Morocco is working to protect its natural habitats and to strengthen anti-poaching initiatives.[794] Britain has deployed soldiers to wildlife reserves in Africa to help fight illegal wildlife trafficking.[795]

British Columbia, Canada, instituted a complete ban on grizzly bear hunting in 2017, eliminating one of the greatest threats to the species.[796] Alberta, Canada, banned the use of spears in big game hunting to prevent "unnecessary suffering."[797] India opened the country's first hospital for elephants[798] and Cuba approved a new animal welfare law in 2021.[799] In Scotland, when legal protection was afforded to beavers, making it illegal to destroy their dams or to kill them without a license, the Scottish Environment Secretary, Roseanna Cummingham, echoed the sentiments

[789] "Chinese police crackdown on illegal online wild animal trade amid COVID-19", *Global Times*, August 26, 2020, at https://www.globaltimes.cn/page/202008/1198880.shtml

[790] While bear bile farming is illegal in Vietnam, many bile farms were operating illegally under a "pet" exception in the law. *See*, AFP, "Vietnam to rescue 1000 bears in bid to end bile trade", *Phys. Org.*, July 19, 2017, at https://phys.org/news/2017-07-vietnam-bile.html

[791] Vaughan, Adam, "France bans imports of lion hunt trophies", *Guardian*, November 19, 2015.

[792] ADW, "Luxembourg fox hunting ban stays", *Luxembourg Times*, December 2, 2019, at https://www.luxtimes.lu/en/luxembourg/luxembourg-fox-hunting-ban-stays-602d6782de135b9236a6c056

[793] *See*, "UAE outlaws keeping wild animals as pets", *BBC*, January 4, 2017; *see also*, "UAE bans keeping wild animals as pets: The new law forbids dealing in and ownership of all types of wild, domesticated and dangerous animals", *Al Jazeera*, January 4, 2017.

[794] Morocco considers poaching to be one of the most serious threats to biodiversity. *See*, Koigi, Bob, "IFAW unveils key partnership with Morocco to tackle illegal wildlife trade", *Africa Business Communities*, August 28, 2017.

[795] "British troops aid Malawi wildlife anti-poaching fight", *BBC*, February 16, 2018.

[796] "Grizzly Bear Hunting Banned in BC", *Nature United*, n.d., at https://www.natureunited.ca/what-we-do/our-priorities/investing-in-people/conservation-victory%2D%2Dgrizzly-bear-hunting-banned-in-bc/

[797] "Alberta bans spears in big game hunting", *CBC News*, February 7, 2018.

[798] Kataria, Sunil, "India's first elephant hospital cheers animal activists, draws tourists", *Reuters*, November 18, 2018.

[799] Acosta, Nelson, "Cuba approves animal welfare law after civil society pressure", *Reuters*, February 27, 2021.

of many people when she said, "we felt it was high time that beavers enjoyed the same legal protection as other species."[800] The UAE banned the possession of dangerous animals.[801] The collective steps taken by countries in recent years to protect animals represents a paradigm legal shift.

Countries are also getting tougher on enforcement. China amended its Wildlife Protection Law to strength protections for wildlife.[802] The law prohibits the production and consumption of certain protected wildlife and contains reporting provisions.[803] In Indonesia, traffickers of wildlife face tougher penalties, including prison sentences of up to 10 years and fines of up to $682,000 (USD).[804]

The European public can be effective at holding governments accountable for animal protection. After a nationwide backlash against British politician, Theresa May, she abandoned her pledge to allow a vote to overturn the ban on using dogs to hunt foxes in England and Wales.[805] When EU President, Jean-Claude Juncker, proposed to weaken the EU's "nature laws" (the Birds and Habitats Directives), around 500,000 people mobilized to save the laws.[806] As a spokesperson for Birdwatch Ireland said, "Our environment is our life-support system, and we must protect it in order to protect ourselves."[807]

The decision by the United States to rejoin the Paris Climate Agreement[808] was a victory for wildlife and biodiversity because climate

[800] Davis, Josh, "Scottish beavers are now a protected species", *National History Museum,* May 1, 2019.

[801] UAE Federal Law No.(22) of 2016, issued on 12/12/2016, Corresponding to 13 Rabi Al-Awwal 1438 H, Regulating the Possession of Dangerous Animals.

[802] Wildlife Protection Law of the People's Republic of China (2022 Version), adopted on December 30, 2022, translated at https://www.chinalawtranslate.com/en/wildlife protectionlaw2022/#

[803] Id. at Articles 6 and 31.

[804] Pratama, Rezza Aji, "New Indonesian law used to crack down on wildlife smuggling", *Earth Journalism Network,* September 11, 2020.

[805] Merrick, Rob, "Theresa May abandons vote on overturning fox hunting ban in face of overwhelming opposition", *Independent,* January 7, 2018.

[806] Carey, Ian, "Major victory for environmentalists as European Commission drop plan to change Nature Laws", *Green News,* December 8, 2016.

[807] Id., quoting Oonagh Duggan, Acting Head of Policy, Communication and People Engagement for Birdwatch Ireland.

[808] Blinken, Anthony J., "The United States Officially Rejoins the Paris Agreement", *U.S. Department of State,* February 19, 2021, at https://www.state.gov/the-united-states-officially-rejoins-the-paris-agreement/

change can potentially impact millions of species.[809] The federal government also enacted the Great American Outdoors Act in 2020,[810] which provides funding for the Land and Water Conservation Fund to protect watersheds and wildlife and to preserve ecosystems for local communities. In 2021, it also reinstated the 2001 Roadless Rule to prohibit road construction and timber harvesting in more than 9 million acres of roadless areas in the Tongass National Forest, the largest national forest in the United States.[811] Most laws in the United States that protect animals, however, get passed at the state level.

In the last decade, states have taken action to ban ivory and/or ivory horn, including New Jersey,[812] New York,[813] California,[814] Washington,[815] Hawaii,[816] Illinois,[817] Nevada,[818] New Hampshire[819] and the District of Columbia.[820] New Jersey passed a law that bans the importation of "trophy animals" into New Jersey,[821] and in 2019, New York enacted historic legislation to protect giraffes by banning the trade of giraffe body parts. The broad legislation gives the New York Department of Environmental Conservation the authority to ban the trade of any species (or parts) that

[809] The U.S. set an ambitious goal to reduce net greenhouse gas emissions by 50–52% by 2030. *See* "The Long-Term Strategy of the United States, Pathways to Net-Zero Greenhouse Gas Emissions by 2050", *U.S. Department of State and the U.S. Executive Office of the President*, Washington, D.C., November 2021.

[810] Public Law No. 116–152 (Great American Outdoors Act), 116th Congress (2019–2020), adopted on August 4, 2020.

[811] Press Release, "USDA Announces Steps to Restore Roadless Protections on Tongass National Forest", *U.S. Department of Agriculture, USDA*, Washington, November 19, 2021, at https://www.usda.gov/media/press-releases/2021/11/19/usda-announces-steps-restore-roadless-protections-tongass-national

[812] New Jersey Statutes Title 23 (Fish and Game, Wild Birds and Animals), 23 § 2A-13.3.

[813] New York State Environmental Conservation Law § 11-0535-a.

[814] California Fish and Game Code, Division 3, Ch. 1, § 2022.

[815] Initiative Measure No. 1401, an Act Relating to the Trafficking of animal species threatened with extinction, filed April 3, 2015.

[816] A Bill For an Act Relating to Natural Resources, Act 125(16) (SB2647 SD1 HD2), enacted on June 23, 2016.

[817] Illinois Public Act 100-0857 (Ivory Ban Act).

[818] Nevada Revised Statutes, Ch. 597.905 (Purchase, or sale of, or possession with intent to sell items made of part or byproduct of certain animals; Prohibition; exceptions; penalties).

[819] New Hampshire Revised Statutes, Title 18 (Fish and Game), Ch. 212-C (Wildlife Trafficking Prevention).

[820] D.C. Law 23-126, Elephant Ivory and Rhinoceros Horn Trafficking Prohibition Act of 2020.

[821] Johnson, Brent, "Christie signs law banning 'trophy animals' in N.J.", *New Jersey*, June 2, 2016.

it considers to be "vulnerable."[822] Oregon passed The Wildlife Trafficking Prevention Act to protect 12 endangered species from trafficking, including elephants, rhinos, whales, tigers, lions leopards, cheetahs, jaguars, sea turtles, sharks and pangolins.[823]

In recent years, legislation by referendum has given voters the ability to make decisions on wildlife matters. As author, Bernard E. Rollin, explains, the America public is not satisfied with how wildlife authorities are managing wildlife. The use of deadly traps, sanctioned hunts, and the lethal control of wildlife populations, including slaughter lactating mother bears, has led to what one official called "'management by referendum', with the public, by right of referendum, usurping the job of wildlife managers."[824] Recent ballot measures approved by the public to protect animals include California's Proposition 67[825] (bans plastic bags that injure and kill sea birds and marine animals), Oregon's Measure 100[826] (bans the intrastate sale of ivory, rhino horns and other wild animals), Washington's Initiative 1401[827] (bans the trade of parts of elephants, rhinos and other animals), and Florida Amendment 1[828] (dedicates funds to conservation and wildlife habitats). However, there can still be attempts to overturn citizen votes, such as efforts in Michigan to overturn a 2006 landslide vote to protect mourning doves from hunting.[829]

The public does not take kindly to indiscriminate and cruel killing of wildlife. When the Idaho Fish and Game Commissioner posted photos of himself with a "family of baboons" that he killed while on an African

[822] For a discussion of this new law, see Pepper, Elly, "Gov Cuomo Signs Historic Bill to Reverse Biodiversity Loss" *NRDC,* December 17, 2019.

[823] Wildlife Trafficking Prevention Act, ORS §498.022.

[824] Rollin, Bernard E. and John G. Benson (Eds.), "The Ethical Imperative to Control Pain and Suffering in Farm Animals" by Bernard E. Rollin in *The Well-Being of Farm Animals, Challenges and Solutions. Issues in Animal Bioethics Series.* Blackwell Publishing, 2004., at 5. ISBN 978-0-8138-0473-6.

[825] *See,* California Proposition 67, Plastic Bag Ban Veto Referendum (2016), at https://ballotpedia.org/California_Proposition_67,_Plastic_Bag_Ban_Veto_Referendum_(2016).

[826] *See,* Oregon Wildlife Trafficking Prevention, Measure 100 (2016), at https://ballotpedia.org/Oregon_Wildlife_Trafficking_Prevention,_Measure_100_(2016).

[827] *See,* Washington Animal Trafficking, Initiative 1401 (2015), at https://ballotpedia.org/Washington_Animal_Trafficking,_Initiative_1401_(2015).

[828] *See,* Florida Water and Land Conservation Initiative, Amendment 1 (2014, at https://ballotpedia.org/Florida_Water_and_Land_Conservation_Initiative,_Amendment_1_(2014).

[829] Baker, Julie, "Baker: There's no good reason to shoot mourning doves and sandhill cranes", *Lansing State Journal,* July 30, 2017.

hunting trip, there was so much public outrage that he was forced to step down.[830] The public is uncomfortable with wildlife "killing contests," where people kill animals for cash and prizes.[831] Since 2014, eight states have banned certain types of wildlife contests, including California (contests for furbearers, game species and nongame mammals), Vermont (coyote contests), Arizona (contests for furbearing species and predators), Massachusetts (contests for furbearer species and predators), New Mexico (coyote contests), Colorado (contests for furbearing species and certain small game species), Washington (contests without a bag limit) and Maryland (contests for coyotes, foxes and raccoons).[832] Proponents of wildlife killing contests argue that the events help manage wildlife populations, but humane and more effective ways are available to do that, such as the EPA's approval of ZonaStat-D to manage deer populations.[833] Research suggests that non-lethal methods of wildlife control (e.g., sterilization; visual deterrents; repellents; diversionary feeding; livestock-guarding animals) are more effective than lethal methods (e.g.. hunting; kill traps; poisoning; destroying litters).[834]

After public backlash, black bear hunts were canceled in Florida and a petition was filed to list the Florida black bear as endangered under the Endangered Species Act.[835] Legal efforts to permit black bear trophy hunts have also been stopped in Connecticut[836] and in New Jersey.[837] In 2018, a Federal judge blocked planned hunts in Idaho and Wyoming and rein-

[830] Chappell, Bill, "Idaho Game Commission Resigns After Killing 'Family of Baboons' in Africa", *NPR*, October 15, 2018.

[831] *See*, "Wildlife Killing Contests", *Animal Welfare Institute*, n.d., at https://awionline.org/content/wildlife-killing-contests

[832] Ibid.

[833] "EPA Approves Immunocontraceptive for Deer Management", *Animal Welfare Institute*, AWI Quarterly, Winter 2017, at https://awionline.org/awi-quarterly/winter-2017/epa-approves-immunocontraceptive-deer-management

[834] Gaworecki, Mike, "Based on available evidence, non-lethal predator control is more effective than lethal means", *Mongabay*, September 8, 2016.

[835] "Petition to List The Florida Black Bear (Ursus americanus floridanus) Under the Endangered Species Act" submitted by the Center for Biological Diversity, et al., to the U.S. Department of Interior and the U.S. Fish and Wildlife Service on March 17, 2016.

[836] Shay, Jim, "Bear hunting bill shot down", *CT Post*, March 15, 2018.

[837] *See,* e.g., Sportelli, Albina and Bruce A. Scruton, "Gov. Murphy: 'No bear hunt this year. Period'", *New Jersey Herald*, September 15, 2021. But see, Nieto-Munoz, "Activists say Governor Murphy is turning his back on bears", *New Jersey Monitor*, September 11, 2023.

stated legal protections for grizzly bears under the Endangered Species Act[838] to reduce the risk of extinction of the animals.[839] When legal protections are removed, animals do face an onslaught by hunters. Grey wolves were removed from the protection of the Endangered Species Act in 2020,[840] and hunters quickly wiped out nearly 20% of Yellowstone's gray wolves with months to go.[841]

Public pressure has forced the cancelation of bobcat hunts[842] and has prevented the trapping and snaring of mountain lions in Wyoming,[843] but states remain battlegrounds when it comes to wildlife protection. When animal protection is enacted, it can become the subject of protracted litigation.[844] Obstruction and challenge by litigation is a common strategy in the United States.

The private sector is critically important to wildlife. In 2021, more than 30 financial institutions, managing more than $8.7 trillion in assets, agreed to tackle deforestation by financing commodity production in a sustainable manner and investing in nature-based solutions.[845] In 2020, the six largest banks in the United States pledged to stop financing gas and oil exploration in the Arctic National Wildlife Refuge.[846] And, in a record

[838] Endangered Species Act, 16 U.S.C. § 1531 et. seq. (1973).

[839] Hughes, Trevor, "Judge reinstates federal protections for grizzly bears, blocks planned fall hunting season", *USA Today*, September 25, 2018.

[840] Press Release, "Endangered Species Act Protections Stripped from Grey Wolves, New Rule Halts Wolf Recovery in Lower 48 States", *Center for Biological Diversity*, October 29, 2020, at https://biologicaldiversity.org/w/news/press-releases/endangered-species-act-protections-stripped-gray-wolves-2020-10-29/

[841] Dawson, Bethany, "Hunters kill almost 20% of Yellowstone's gray wolves, with months to go in the hunting season", *Insider*, January 8, 2022.

[842] *See*, e.g., Fish and Game News Release, "NH Fish and Game Withdraws Bobcat Season", *New Hampshire Center for Public Interest Journalism*, April 13, 2016; *see also*, Garrett, Olivia, "Due to resident opposition, plans dropped for bobcat hunt in Dubuque County", *Cascade Pioneer*, May 26, 2021.

[843] Knudson, Tom, "Wyoming won't legalize mountain lion trapping", *Reveal News*, February 11, 2016.

[844] After legal challenge, the U.S. Appeals Court for the Ninth Circuit ultimately upheld California's ban on the killing mountain lions for trophies. *See*, e.g., Safari Club International v. Cal. Department of Fish and Wildlife, U.S. Court of Appeals for the 9th Circuit (D.C. No. 2:14-cv-01856-JAM-AC), November 15, 2017.

[845] *See*, "Thirty financial institutions commit to tackle deforestation", *Global Canopy*, November 2, 2021, at https://globalcanopy.org/press/thirty-financial-institutions-commit-to-tackle-deforestation/

[846] Frazin, Rachel, "Bank of America pledges no financing for Arctic Oil", *The Hill*, December 1, 2020. Similar commitments were also made by Morgan Stanley, JPMorgan

commitment to support biodiversity conservation, nine philanthropic organizations pledged $5 billion dollars over the next decade to ensure that, by 2030, nearly a third of the planet will be preserved for biodiversity.[847]

Evolving consumer sentiment is driving corporate policy changes. Major airlines, such as Delta, American Airlines and United Airlines, banned big game trophy hunt shipments following the slaughter of Cecil the lion.[848] TripAdvisor announced that it will no longer sell tickets to events "where captive wild or endangered animals are forced to perform demeaning tricks or other unnatural behaviors,"[849] and Instagram instituted an alert system that informs users that certain hashtags may be associated with behavior that harms animals.[850] Stock photo companies, such as Alamy and Dreamstime, are removing all "inappropriate" images of primates. Getty Imagines is removing "inappropriate" images of any wildlife, and Shutterstock is banning photographs that depict monkeys or apes dancing or performing.[851] The private sector is also creating alternatives to trophy hunts. In 2021, the first non-fungible token (NFT)[852] of a horn of a rhinoceros was sold at auction in South Africa for the equivalent of $6850, with the proceeds going to benefit the Black Rock Rhino conservancy.[853]

Chase, Goldman Sachs, Wells Fargo and Citi.

[847] "Private Funders of the New 'Protecting Our Planet Challenge' Announce $5 billion Commitment to Protect and conserve 30% of Planet by 2030", *WCS Newsroom*, New York, September 22, 2021, at https://newsroom.wcs.org/News-Releases/articleType/ArticleView/articleId/16685/Private-Funders-of-the-New-Protecting-Our-Planet-Challenge-Announce-5-Billion-Commitment-to-Protect-and-Conserve-30-of-Planet-by-2030.aspx

[848] Larimer, Sarah, "While airlines ban hunting trophy shipments, UPS says it won't bow to controversy", *Washington Post*, August 4, 2015. *See* Chapter III for more on Cecil the lion.

[849] "Our Animal Welfare Policy", *TripAdvisor*, at https://www.tripadvisor.com/blog/animal-welfare-policy/

[850] Daly, Natasha, "Exclusive: Instagram Fights Animal Abuse With New Alert System", *National Geographic*, December 4, 2017.

[851] Katz, Brigit, "PETA had lobbied against images that perpetuate harmful misconceptions about the animals", *Smithsonian Magazine*, July 5, 2018.

[852] Non-fungible tokens (NFTs) are unique blockchain-based tokens that can be used to represent virtually anything in digital form, the authenticity of which is certified by blackchain technology.

[853] *See*, AFP, "First rhino horn NFT sold at auction in South Africa", *EWN Eyewitness News*, November 12, 2021, at https://ewn.co.za/2021/11/12/first-rhino-horn-nft-sold-at-auction-in-south-africa#

The challenge to protect wildlife is so great, in part, because the lack of economic opportunities in poor and developing countries makes unsustainable development and the market for poached items attractive. Mankind's peaceful coexistence with the animal kingdom, however, is no longer an abstract goal that we can work toward at our convenience. The loss of biodiversity means the loss of "the essential infrastructure that supports all forms of life on earth, including human life."[854]

In July 2021, the United Nations adopted Resolution 75/311, voicing its continued concerns regarding the unprecedented decline in biodiversity and rate of species extinctions, coupled with an "increasing scale of poaching and illegal trade in wildlife" and an ever increasing number of new illicit markets.[855] The Resolution again urged Member States to prioritize wildlife crimes, to strengthen their laws, to strengthen enforcement, and to tackle wildlife trafficking through racketeering, money laundering, fraud, corruption and other financial crime laws.[856] In late 2021, lawmakers in the United States introduced the Wildlife Conservation and Anti-Trafficking Act with the goal of supporting wildlife conservation and improving anti-trafficking enforcement.[857] The Act includes a provision that makes wildlife trafficking violations a predicate offense, as well as important provisions that protect and reward whistleblowers. As of August 2023, however, the bill remains stalled in a politically polarized Congress. The United States did pass the Eliminate, Neutralize, and Disrupt Wildlife Trafficking Act of 2016,[858] which requires the Secretaries of State, Commerce and the Interior to report to Congress on "Focus Countries" (i.e., major source, transit point or consumer of wildlife trafficking products)[859] and "Countries of Concern" (i.e., governments actively

[854] Brondizio, Eduardo, et al. (Eds), "The global assessment report on biodiversity and ecosystem services of the Intergovernmental Science-Policy Platform on Biodiversity and Ecosystem Services", *IPBES*, May 4, 2019. https://doi.org/10.5281/zenodo.6417333

[855] U.N. General Assembly Resolution 75/311.

[856] Ibid.

[857] Wildlife Conservation and Anti-Trafficking Act of 2021 - H.R. 6059, §302, introduced in the U.S. Housing of Representatives on November 19, 2021.

[858] Eliminate, Neutralize, and Disrupt (END) Wildlife Trafficking Act of 2016, P.L. 114-231, §201.

[859] The list of 2021 Focus Countries includes China, India, Indonesia, Nigeria, Brazil, Bangladesh, Mexico, Philippines and Vietnam. For the complete list of 2021 Focus Countries, *see* Report to Congress on the Eliminate, Neutralize, and Disrupt Wildlife Trafficking Act of 2016, P.L. 114-231, Sec. 201 (Unclassified).

engaged in or profiting from trafficking).[860] The United States has not, however, enacted the ProTECT Act of 2019, which would amend the Endangered Species Act to prohibit trophy hunting of any endangered or threatened species in the country and the importation of any endangered or threatened species trophies into the country.[861] A ban on trophy hunting, which legitimizes poaching in the eyes of so many, would give the United States much more credibility in its fight to protect wildlife.

Preventing wildlife trafficking is a tremendous challenge, because where desperate poverty and greed intersect, we will always find animals suffering and exploited. Wildlife protection must be accompanied by laws that support local communities economically, because limited opportunities make wildlife crimes attractive. Wildlife tourism is critical to developing economies, but wildlife trafficking is a global problem that requires a global solution. Combatting poaching has become so difficult that organizations, like the International Anti-Poaching Foundation, have resorted to a military style approach to fight poaching. The organization uses technology, strategies and equipment that are often reserved for warfare, which it believes is necessary to stop poaching.[862] In the past, law enforcement has not viewed wildlife crimes as a priority, but this is changing.[863] The recent work of international organizations shows what can happen when laws are enforced to protect animals.

The International Consortium on Combating Wildlife Crime (ICCWC) is a coordinated global alliance, formed in 2010, with the mission to provide "coordinated support at national, regional and international levels to combat wildlife and forest crime."[864] Five partner organizations work with ICCWC, including the United Nations Office on Drugs and Crime (UNODC), INTERPOL, the World Customs Organization (WCO), the World Bank Group and the Secretariat of the Convention on International Trade in Endangered Species of Wild Fauna and Flora (CITES).[865] Since

[860] The list of "Countries of Concern" includes Nigeria, Cambodia, Madagascar, and Laos. Id.

[861] ProTECT Act of 2019 - H.R. 4804, 116th Congress (2019–2020).

[862] Dunn, M., "Ex-solder takes on poachers with hi-tech help for wildlife". *Herald Sun*, December 21, 2012.

[863] INTERPOL, Wildlife crime: closing ranks on serous crime in the illegal animal trade.

[864] *See*, "Who we are", *International Consortium on Combating Wildlife Crime*, at https://www.iccwc-wildlifecrime.org/who-we-are

[865] For more information on the partner organizations, *see* https://cites.org/eng/prog/iccwc/partners.php

2017, CITES members have been required to report data on all wildlife seizures into a database compiled by UNODC, which as of the date of the 2020 World Wildlife Crime Report includes 180,000 seizures from 149 countries and territories.[866] Since 2017, INTERPOL and WCO have also carried out a series of internationally coordinated operations to fight illegal wildlife and timber trafficking worldwide.

In 2017, *Operation Thunderbird* involved officials from 49 countries and territories and resulted in the recovery of thousands of live animals and 25 tons of various animal parts, including meat, horns, feathers and 50 kg of raw and processed ivory.[867] In 2018, *Operation Thunderstorm* involved officials from 92 countries and led to the seizure of thousands of live animals, 43 tons of wild meat (including meat from elephants, whales, bears and zebras) and 1.3 tons of raw and processed elephant ivory. The operation identified 1400 suspects and triggered arrests and additional investigations worldwide.[868] In 2019, *Operation Thunderball*[869] involved 109 countries and resulted in the recovery of more than 10,000 live animals and thousands of wildlife parts from elephants, rhinos, big cats, marine animals and other species.[870] The crackdown netted nearly 600 suspects from all parts of the globe, triggering arrests worldwide.[871]

In 2020, *Operation Thunder 2020* involved officials from 103 countries and resulted in the recovery of more than 45,500 live animals and plant specimens, including 1400 turtles and tortoises, 6000 turtle or tortoise eggs, 1800 reptiles, 1160 birds, 32 chimpanzees, a white tiger, a jaguar,

[866] UNODC World Wildlife Crime Report, at 9 and 32. CITES governs the trade for over 36,000 protected species.

[867] "Anti-wildlife trafficking operation results in global arrests and seizures", *INTERPOL*, March 2, 2017, at https://www.interpol.int/en/News-and-Events/News/2017/Anti-wildlife-trafficking-operation-results-in-global-arrests-and-seizures

[868] "Wildlife crime: global seizures and arrests in transcontinental operation", *INTERPOL*, June 20, 2018, at https://www.interpol.int/ar/1/1/2018/Wildlife-crime-global-seizures-and-arrests-in-transcontinental-operation

[869] "Wildlife trafficking: organized crime hit hard by joint INTERPOL-WCO global enforcement", *INTERPOL*, July 10, 2019, at https://www.interpol.int/en/News-and-Events/News/2019/Wildlife-trafficking-organized-crime-hit-hard-by-joint-INTERPOL-WCO-global-enforcement-operation

[870] Yuhas, Alan, "Interpol Operation Seizes More Than 10,000 Animals in Anti-Trafficking Campaign", *New York Times*, July 10, 2019.

[871] "Thousands of wild animals seized in smuggling crackdown", *Guardian*, July 10, 2019.

and a four-month old lion cub.[872] The operation resulted in the apprehension of 699 offenders with additional arrests and investigations expected.[873] In 2021, *Operation Thunder 2021* involved officials from 118 countries and again seized thousands of protected wildlife and triggered hundreds of arrests worldwide.[874] The most recent operation, *Operation Thunder 2022*, involved an unprecedented 125 countries, the seizure of thousands of live animals and animal parts, and the identification of 934 suspects and 141 companies involved in illegal sales.[875] The joint INTERPOL and WCO operations are the blueprint for the effective enforcement of anti-poaching laws and prove that strategic global alliances, and cooperation and coordination among nations, are critical to protecting wildlife. ICCWC is building on its success by the launch of its *Vision 2030*, which aims to encourage further collaboration and the exchange of knowledge globally as a means of deterring and detecting wildlife crimes and disrupting and detaining criminals.[876]

Despite the success of these operations, illegal wildlife trafficking remains an urgent threat to both endangered and threatened species and to humanity, with no signs of slowing down. Wildlife traffickers are part of sophisticated global criminal enterprises with expertise, funding and unparalleled recruiting abilities, which explains why poaching is soaring in places like Namibia, which suffered a record number of slain rhinos in 2022.[877] Traffickers thrive in countries with weak laws and limited law enforcement capabilities, which enable traffickers to exploit weaknesses across the globe.[878] According to UNODC in its 2020 World Wildlife Crime Report, traffickers are actively "exploiting legislative gaps between

[872] "Wildlife and forestry crime: Worldwide seizures in global INTERPOL-WCO operation", *INTERPOL*, November 9, 2020, at https://www.interpol.int/News-and-Events/News/2020/Wildlife-and-forestry-crime-Worldwide-seizures-in-global-INTERPOL-WCO-operation

[873] Ibid.

[874] "Global arrests and seizures: WCO-INTERPOL Operation Thunder 2021 strikes wildlife and timber trafficking networks", *World Customs Organization*, November 30, 2021.

[875] "Thunder Operations enforce the Convention on International Trade in Endangered Species of Wild Fauna and Flora (CITES)", *INTERPOL*, December 6, 2022.

[876] Press Release: "Towards a World Free of Wildlife Crime – International Consortium on Combating Wildlife Crime launches its Vision 2030", *ICCWC*, November 28, 2022.

[877] In 2022, poaching increased by 93% in Namibia. *See*, "Rhino poaching soars by 93 percent in Namibia", *Animal Survival International*, February 1, 2023.

[878] UNODC World Wildlife Crime Report, at 12.

countries,"[879] and crime syndicates are "flexible", readily adapting to "policies, capacities and regulatory frameworks [that] differ between countries."[880] The World Bank Group also blames weak governance across public and private sectors, as well as systematic corruption, which enables illegal wildlife to flourish.[881] No one country or group of countries can win the war that is being waged against wildlife. It will take the commitment of every nation to halt the relentless attacks on wildlife. Continued international cooperation is critical to enacting and enforcing laws against crimes that have such catastrophic consequences for biodiversity, global security and human health.

Animals in Religion and Culture

> The thinking man must oppose all cruel customs no matter how deeply rooted in tradition or surrounded by a halo. We need a boundless ethic which will include the animals also.—Albert Schweitzer

Throughout history, animals have been sacrificed in the name of religion, to atone for one's sins, or as an offering to a deity. Animals are also abused and killed by cultural traditions that are passed on from generation to generation.[882] Religion and tradition are deeply engrained into an individual's identity and culture and they remain some of the toughest areas in which to legally protect animals.

Traditions that involve animal abuse can be found in most cultures, many of which involve extreme and shocking animal torture. In the name of "tradition," religious or otherwise, animals have been stuffed into

[879] UNODC World Wildlife Crime Report, at 3.

[880] UNODC World Wildlife Crime Report, at 12.

[881] "Illegal Logging, Fishing, and Wildlife Trade: The Costs and How to Combat It", *The World Bank Group*, October 2019, at 8.

[882] There is considerable overlap between animals abused for entertainment and animals abused for traditions. For the former, *see* "Animals in Entertainment" in this chapter.

men's trousers,[883] forced to consume alcohol,[884] hung from trees,[885] traumatized, injured and killed by firecrackers,[886] had limbs broken,[887] had eyes gouged out,[888] had genitals cut off,[889] had tails hacked off,[890] been stoned,[891] shot down,[892] chased, beaten and stabbed,[893] dragged and

[883] In England, hungry live ferrets are stuffed into men's trousers and held there for hours as an "endurance" or "manliness" test. *See generally*, Katz, Donald, "Inside the sport of putting vicious ferrets in your pants", *NY Post*, May 31, 2014.

[884] During the Tlacotalpan Bull Festival in Mexico, bulls are forced to consume alcohol. *See generally*, Hernandez, Cesar, "240-year-old tradition proves difficult to stop", *Mexico News Daily*, February 2, 2017; *see also*, Rosenblatt, Kalhan, "The running of the booze: Shocking Mexican festival sees bulls plied with alcohol before being unleased on the town and concludes with them drowning in river", *Daily Mail*, January 26, 2016.

[885] During the Hanging of the Galgos in Spain, hunting greyhounds are hung from village trees at the end of each hunting season and some are left to starve. *See generally*, Daly, Natasha, "Traditional Hunting Dogs are Left to Die En Masse in Spain", *National Geographic*, October 26, 2016.

[886] *See generally*, "How fireworks harm nonhuman animals", *Animal Ethics*, n.d., at http://www.animal-ethics.org/how-fireworks-harm-nonhuman-animals/

[887] During the Festival of the Oxen ("Farra do Boi") in Brazil, the limbs of oxen are often broken. *See generally*, Freedman, Joel, "Guest Appearance: Pope Francis must firmly address systemic cruelty to animals", *Finger Lake Times*, August 13, 2022.

[888] During the Festival of the Oxen ("Farra do Boi") in Brazil, hot pepper is rubbed into the eyes of oxen and/or eyes are gouged out. *See generally*, Jha, Rakesh, "7 festivals around the world where animals are brutally killed in the name of tradition", *Inuth*, August 1, 2017.

[889] During the Toro de la Vega in Spain, the genitals of dying animals are often cut off. *See generally*, "El Toro de la Vega: The Shame of Spain", *Saving Earth Encyclopedia Britannica*.

[890] During the Festival of the Oxen ("Farra do Boi") in Brazil, the tails of ox are hacked off. *See generally*, "7 festivals of torture", *News 24*, December 27, 2012.

[891] During the Festival of the Oxen ("Farra do Boi") in Brazil, oxen are stoned. Id. During the Hanging of the Galgos in Spain, some greyhounds are stoned. *See generally*, "The plight of the Spanish Galgos", *Galgo Amigo's Animal Welfare Pages*, at http://www.galgoamigo.com/the-plight-of-the-spanish-galgos.html

[892] An estimated 25 million migratory birds, including, robins, quail, and chaffinches, are illegally killed every year across the Mediterranean region, including in Egypt, Italy, Syria, Lebanon, Cyprus. *See generally*, "The Killing: Unlawfully shot, trapped or glued. Every year around 25 million birds are slaughtered in the Mediterranean. Read our first review of illegal killing of birds in the region", *BirdLife International*. August 2015, at https://www.birdlife.org/wp-content/uploads/2022/05/The_Killing_01-28_low.pdf

[893] During the Tlacotalpan Bull Festival in Mexico, bulls are beaten to death. *See generally*, Reina, Elena, "The Mexican patron saint feast where tired, old bulls are tortured", *El Pais*, February 2, 2016. During the Toro de la Vega in Spain, bulls are chased through the streets and pierced with spears and lances. *See generally*, "Spain wants to end the controversial Toro de la Vega bull festival", *In Spain News*, September 8, 2022. Colombia has a festival where bulls are killed with machetes, rocks, knives and kicks. *See*, Associated Press, "Horrific scenes as bull stabbed and beaten to death at Colombian festival", *The Guardian*, January 5, 2015.

tortured,[894] wrestled and killed,[895] blowtorched and boiled alive,[896] butchered,[897] crushed,[898] tossed into wells to drown,[899] shot from cannons,[900] dropped from planes,[901] submerged into wine,[902] eviscerated by charging bulls,[903] decapitated,[904] quartered and cut in half,[905] set on

[894] During the Pero Palo Festival, Villanueva de la Vera in Spain, donkeys are abused and injured by crowds. *See generally*, 7 festivals around the world.

[895] During Umkhosi Ukweshwama in South Africa, young men chase, wrestle and kill bulls in an enclosure as a coming of age celebration. *See generally*, 7 festivals around the world.

[896] *See*, e.g., Mills, Kelly-Ann, "Inside horror of Yulin dog festival where animals are tortured and boiled alive", *Mirror*, June 24, 2020.

[897] During the "grindadrap" tradition in Faroe Islands, pilot whales are surrounded by boats and forced toward the shore where they are butchered. See generally, White, Robyn, "Faroe Islands Slaughter Begins With Pilot Whales Butchered Alive", *Newsweek,* June 14, 2022.

[898] During the Pero Palo Festival, Villanueva de la Vera in Spain, donkeys are crushed by crowds. *See generally*, Turner, Rachael, "Donkey ridden by 'drunk' man to be dragged through crowds at festival", *Horse&Hound*, February 5, 2018.

[899] During the Hanging of the Galgos in Spain, at the end of each hunting season, some hunting greyhounds are tossed into wells to drown. *See generally*, The plight of the Spanish Galgos.

[900] During Baby Quail Catapulting in Valencia, weeks old baby quails are fired from a specifically made cannon and then shot from the sky. *See generally*, Anthony, Brad, "Top 10 Animal Cruelty Traditions in Spain", *Global Animal Welfare*, November 8, 2014; *see also,* Brackett, Crystal, "14 Barbaric Festivals That Should Be Banned For What They Do to Animals", *Ranker*, September 23, 2021.

[901] During the Turkey Trot festival, live wild turkeys are dropped out of an airplane, a practice known as the "Turkey Drop". *See generally*, Holley, Peter, "The 'barbaric' tradition of throwing live turkeys from planes", *Washington Post*, October 8, 2016; *see also*, Associated Press, "Festival flap: live turkeys dropped from planes in cruel and bizarre American tradition", *South China Morning Post,* October 14, 2017.

[902] During the Krakelingen festival in Belgium, tiny fish submerged into wine and consumed. *See generally*, Castle, Stephen, "A gulp of live fish with your red wine: A ritual draws condemnation", *New York Times*, March 2, 2008.

[903] During Torneos de Lazo in Mexico, horses are eviscerated by charging bulls in rodeo-like event in Yucatan. The spectacle is illegal but it still occurs. *See generally*, "Torneos de Lazo" public display of animal cruelty in Yucatan", *The Yucatan Times*, September 9, 2019.

[904] During Gadhimai Hindu festivals, hundreds of thousands of animals have been beheaded. *See generally*, Osborne, Samuel, "Gadhimai Hindu festival: World's 'largest animal sacrifice' under way in defiance of ban", *Independent,* December 3, 2019.

[905] During the Nem Thuong Pig-Slaughter Festival in Vietnam, screaming pigs quartered and cut in half with large sword. *See generally*, Cuong, Do Manh, "Vietnam's controversial pig slaughtering festival returns behind closed doors", *VN Express International*, February 21, 2018.

fire,[906] and of course, eaten.[907] Humans can be the most violent species on the planet.

Some traditions are not well known, such as the centuries old tradition in the mountains of Galicia, Spain, known as "*rapa das bestas*", or "*shaving the beasts*", which involves herding horses into densely packed pens where they are sheared in a spectacle promoted as a battle of "man versus beast".[908] Other traditions are better known from the attention that they receive in the press. During the "*Toro de Jubilo*" *festival* in Medinaceli, Spain, flammable tar is attached to horns of bulls and then set on fire. The panicked bulls are then released to run through public squares and streets. "Toro de Fuego" means "bull on fire." The bulls' horns are left to burn for hours, scorching the animal's eyes, faces and bodies.[909] During the *Running of the Bulls*[910] (San Fermin Fiestas) in Spain, people run alongside panicked bulls, who are prodded to run down cobblestone streets. The animals are grabbed, hit with sticks and ultimately killed.[911] The spectacles can result in injuries and fatalities to those who participate.[912]

In New York City and in other Jewish communities, the controversial, ancient tradition of *kapparot* occurs, which involves swinging live chickens above the practitioner's head as a means of symbolically transferring sins to the chicken, after which the animal is slaughtered.[913] The conditions under which the birds are held prior to the tradition are deplorable … cramped cages with no food or water and no protection from the elements … and many animals die before the sacrifice begins. The practice

[906] During the Hanging of the Galgos in Spain, at the end of each hunting season, some hunting greyhounds are set on fire. *See generally*, The plight of the Spanish Galgos.

[907] During the Yulin Dog Meat Festival in China, dogs are consumed. *See generally*, Ahluwalia, Ravneet, "Yulin Dog Meat Festival: What is it, how did it start and will activists ever manage to get it banned", *Independent*, June 19, 2020.

[908] For a critical study of this tradition, *see* John Hartigan Jr. *Shaving the Beasts, Wild Horses and Ritual in Spain*. Minneapolis: University of Minnesota Press, 2020, at 6–7. ISBN: 9781452965185.

[909] *See generally*, "Outcry over 'Toro de Jubilo' Burning Bull Festival", *Madrid Metropolitan*, November 16, 2022.

[910] *See generally*, Keeley, Graham, "San Fermin celebrates running of the bulls but is the controversial fiesta in decline", *EuroNews*, August 7, 2022.

[911] Yague, Irene, "Activists protest over Spain's San Fermin bull-run festival", *Associates Press*, July 5, 2022.

[912] *See*, e.g., "With 10 people killed this summer alone, could Spain say adios to bull-running festivals?", *CBS News*, September 6, 2022.

[913] Lee, Jennifer, "Dead Chickens, Amends, and on an Outcry", *New York Times*, October 9, 2008.

divides Orthodox Jews[914] and some rabbis strongly object to kapparot, considering it a pagan ritual that violates religious tenets for the humane treatment of animals.[915] Israel's Environment Ministry has called for money to be donated instead of practicing *kapparot* with live chickens.[916]

Religion has been used throughout history to justify the continued abuse and exploitation of animals, but most religions are united in their creed (if not their practice) that we show compassion to animals.[917] In Buddhism, The Dhammapada says that "[a]ll tremble at violence; all fear death"; and "life is dear to all. Putting oneself in the place of another, one should not kill nor cause another to kill."[918] In Hinduism, the Bhagavad Gita proclaims that a self-realized soul is able to understand the equality of all beings[919] and that "[e]very living creature is a son of the Supreme Lord, and He does not tolerate even an ant's being killed."[920] Islam teaches that "[a]ll creatures are like a family to God,"[921] while Judaism prohibits the unnecessary suffering of animals (*Tza'ar ba'alei chayim*).[922] Pope Francis, leader of the Roman Catholic Church, has decried human activity that is turning the planet into "a polluted wasteland full of debris, desolation and filth"[923] and causing the extinction of thousands of species of animals that will "no longer give glory to God by their very existence, nor convey their

[914] Hagerty, Barbara Bradley, "Swinging Chicken Ritual Divides Orthodox Jews", *NPR*, September 26, 2009.

[915] Lee, Jennifer, "Dead Chickens, Amends, and on an Outcry", *New York Times*, October 9, 2008.

[916] *See*, Surkes, Sue, "Environment minister urges charity instead of 'kapparot' for Yom Kippur", *The Times of Israel*, October 3, 2022; *see also*, Surkes, Sue, "Environment Ministry: Replace cruel chicken 'kapparot' with donations", *Times of Israel*, September 14, 2021.

[917] For a discussion of the treatment of animals in the context of religions, *see* Caruana SJ, Louis, "Different religions, different animal ethics", *Animal Frontiers*, Vol. 10, Issue 1 (January 2020), at 8–14. https://doi.org/10.1093/af/vfz047

[918] The Dhammapada, Ch. 10 (Violence), §§129–130.

[919] The Bhagavad Gita, Verse 5.18: "The humble sage, by virtue of true knowledge, sees with equal vision a learned and gentle brahmana, a cow, an elephant, a dog, and a dog-eater." Translated at https://asitis.com/5/18.html

[920] The Bhagavad Gita As It Is, Ch. 14.16. Translated at https://www.krishna.com/smart-quote-day-august-18-2017

[921] Mishkat al-Masabih, 3:1392 (Narrated By Anas), quoted from Sahih Bukhari.

[922] *See generally*, "Issues in Jewish Ethics: The *Treatment* of Animals, Prohibition Against Cruelty to Animals", *Jewish Virtual Library*, n.d., at https://www.jewishvirtuallibrary.org/judaism-and-the-treatment-of-animals

[923] *See*, Encyclical Letter *LAUDATO SI'* of the Holy Father Francis On Care For Our Common Home, §161. https://www.vatican.va/content/francesco/en/encyclicals/documents/papa-francesco_20150524_enciclica-laudato-si.html

message to us."[924] Pope Francis is also calling for immediate action to address the urgent issue of climate change, which threatens the existence of many animals.[925] Reforming traditions and religious practices that are rooted in animal cruelty will face strong resistance, but change is possible.

Recent Developments for Animals in Religion and Culture

Legal systems are starting to outlaw the sacrifice of animals during festivals. In Nepal, the centuries old *Gadhimai* festival, known as the bloodiest ritualized slaughter on the planet, involved the sacrifice of as many as 500,000 buffalo, goats, pigs, chickens, and other animals,[926] but the number dropped in 2014 after India's Supreme Court ordered the government to halt the illegal export of animals across India's border to the festival.[927] In 2019, Nepal's central government also refused to finance the festival due to the Supreme Court's prohibition on supporting animal sacrifices.[928] Despite the religious festival's long history in Nepal, however, change was possible. In 2015, Ram Chandra Shah, the Gadhimai Temple Trust Chairman, announced a decision to halt animal sacrifices at Gadhimai festivals and "to replace killing and violence with peaceful worship and celebration."[929] A change of this magnitude requires a large public awareness campaign, and in 2016, Nepal's Supreme Court directed government agencies to launch awareness programs to halt the inhumane animal sacrifices at the festival.[930] The massacre continued at the 2019 festival, but far

[924] Id at §33.

[925] Id at §§24–25.

[926] The Gadhimai festival takes place every 5 years. *See generally*, Power, Gabriel, "What is the Gadhimai festival and why is it so controversial?", *The Week*, December 5, 2019.

[927] Sigdel, Chahana, "India apex court restricts export of animals", *The Kathmandu Post*, October 16, 2014.

[928] Sharma, Bhadra, "Nepal's Animal-Sacrifice Festival Slays On. But Activists Are Having an Effect.", *New York Times*, December 6, 2019.

[929] Shah, Ram Chandra, "Gadhimai Temple Trust Chairman, Mr. Ram Chandra Shah, on the decision to stop holding animal sacrifices during the Gadhimai festival", n.d., at https://www.hsi.org/wp-content/uploads/assets/pdfs/gadhimai-temple-trust-statement-ram-chandra-shah.pdf

[930] Samiti, Rastriya Samachar, "Supreme Court directs govt to 'control' Gadhimai sacrifice", *The Himalayan Times*, August 4, 2016.

fewer animals were slaughtered,[931] and efforts are already underway for a "Bloodless Gadhimai" in 2024,[932] with focus on the fundamental Hindu principle of *ahimsa* (non-violence).[933]

Blood festivals are being banned in other countries. In 2016, the "*buffalo stabbing festival*" in Lam Dong Vietnam became the fourth providence to ban ritual slaughter, following bans in Dak Lak, Hue and Nghe An.[934] Buffalo fighting festivals are ending in Vietnam, including festivals in Phuc Tho (Hanoi), Phu Son (Bac Ninh) and in Bao Thang (Lao Cai providence).[935] In Mexico, the *Kots Kaal Pato* festival, which involved hanging up small animals like a "pinata" (or stuffed into a pinata) to be beaten to death, ended. In 2022, *Kots Kaal Pato* was celebrated without the animal cruelty.[936]

Ritual slaughter, which involves the killing of an animal without first stunning the animal, is a legal battleground where the right of religious expression runs right up against progressive measures aimed to reduce animal suffering in death.[937] Countries are weighing the competing rights and the trend is to ban slaughter, unless the animal is first sedated. The list of countries that has placed some form of restriction (to varying degrees) on non-sedated animal slaughter is growing and includes, Sweden, Finland, Norway, Switzerland, Denmark, Belgium (Wallonia and Flemish regions only), Austria, Slovenia, Iceland and Estonia.[938] The bans on ritual slaughter have not been without controversy.

[931] An estimated 30,000 animals were slaughtered in 2014, down from 500,000 in 2009. *See generally*, "Mass animal sacrifice begins despite outcry from activists", *CNN*, December 3, 2019; *see also*, "Gadhimai: Nepal's animal sacrifice festival goes ahead despite ban", *BBC*, December 3, 2019.

[932] Kathmandu Tribune Staff, "Bloodless Gadhimai campaign eyes 2024 to make the festival free from animal sacrifices", *Kathmandu Tribune*, December 9, 2019.

[933] Power, Gabriel, "What is the Gadhimai festival and why is it so controversial?", *The Week*, December 5, 2019.

[934] "Another animal sacrifice festival BANNED in Vietnam", *Animals Asia*, November 23, 2016.

[935] Id.

[936] The festival is now known as San Bartolo. *See generally*, "Citilcum celebrates the Kots Kaal Pato again but this time without animal cruelty", *Yucatan Times*, May 5, 2022.

[937] Ritual slaughter is required by some religions, including Judaism and Islam.

[938] *See generally*, "Legal Restrictions on Religious Slaughter in Europe", The Law Library of Congress, Global Legal Research Center, March 2018; *see also*, Feder, Shira, "All The European Countries Where Kosher and Halal Meat Production Are Now Forbidden", *Forward*, January 7, 2019.

The controversy has raged in Poland, where ritual slaughter was banned in 2002, permitted again in 2004, banned again in 2012 and allowed again in 2014.[939] At that time, the Constitutional Tribunal ruled that the Animal Protection Act must permit religious forms of slaughter to be consistent with Poland's constitutional freedom of religion requirement and with the European Convention on Human Rights.[940] In 2020, the Polish government passed, retracted and vowed to re-introduce a bill that would ban ritual slaughter for the purpose of export, which accounts for the majority of the industry.[941]

In 2020, the European Union's highest court upheld a Belgian ban on halal and kosher slaughter of animals without first being stunned, over the objections of religious groups, noting that scientific evidence had concluded that stunning was the best way to reduce an animal's suffering and that the law allowed "a fair balance to be struck" between animal welfare and freedom of religion.[942] In 2021, the supreme administrative court in Greece annulled a ministerial decision that allowed ritual slaughter without anesthesia citing animal welfare concerns and effectively banning kosher and halal slaughter.[943] When Denmark banned religious slaughter of animals, the Danish minister for agriculture and food was more blunt, stating, "[a]nimal rights come before religion," prompting fierce backlash from Jewish and Muslim communities.[944]

The bans on halal and kosher slaughter are considered by some to be discrimination against minorities or religious persecution. Critics of the bans are quick to point out the hypocrisy of bans on kosher and halal slaughter in light of the plight of many farmed animals. They point to pigs and calves boiled and skinned alive; animals dying in barn fires; animals

[939] *See*, "Legal Restrictions on Religious Slaughter in Europe", *The Law Library of Congress, Global Research Center*, March 2018, at 15.

[940] Judgment of 10 Dec. 2014, Ref. No. K 52/13, by The Constitutional Tribunal In the Name of the Republic of Poland, *at* https://perma.cc/8YUF-VEU6

[941] Liphshiz, Cnaan, "Poland scraps bill barring ritual slaughter, vows to introduce new one". November 7, 2020; *see also*, Liphshiz, Cnaan, "Poland will send its kosher and halal meat export industry in 2025", *The Times of Israel*, October 15, 2020.

[942] "EU Court backs ban on animal slaughter without stunning", *BBC*, December 17, 2020.

[943] Joffre, Tzvi, "Greek court annuls permit for kosher, halal slaughter", *The Jerusalem Post*, October 27, 2021.

[944] Kedmey, Dan, "Denmark Bans Unstunned Kosher and Halal Animal Slaughter", *Time*, July 29, 2015.

suffocating in their own waste; piglets killed by being slammed onto concrete floors; the mass culling of farmed minks during the Covid-19 pandemic by carbon monoxide gassing; ineffective stunning; pigs immersed in carbon dioxide; and the inverted shackling of chickens.[945] Several countries have addressed the last example involving the shackle-and-hoist method of slaughter. In its New Guidelines for Humane Kosher Slaughter, Israel updated its methods of slaughter in 2017 by requiring a rotating restraint device in lieu of the shackle-and-hoist method.[946] Paraguay decided to phase out the shackle and hoist method of slaughter for more humane methods of kosher slaughter.[947] Nonetheless, the charges of hypocrisy do resonate. In the United States, "ventilation shutdown" is routinely used to "depopulate" sick animal populations, who die slow, agonizing deaths from heat stroke and suffocation.[948] Legal reforms are more widely supported when passed from a moral high ground that does not target specific religions. Anti-cruelty laws should apply equally to everyone, regardless of religious affiliation because while freedom of religion is a human right, the freedom is not absolute.[949]

The conflict between religious expression and animal welfare exists in the United States too. Ritual slaughter of animals by groups, such as Santeria,[950] is not uncommon in Florida, where dead animals have been dumped in public places.[951] Ritual slaughter of animals is permitted under Florida's anti-cruelty statute as an expression of religious freedom.[952] A

[945] For criticism of the bans, *see* Kanji, Azeezah, "Kosher and Halal bans: Fur-washing factory farming's brutality", *Al Jazeera*, November 3, 2021.

[946] JTA, "Israel mandates more humane slaughter methods for beef imports, Agriculture Ministry's new guidelines on kosher meat shipments ban shackle-and-hoist method", *The Times of Israel*, May 19, 2017.

[947] Udasin, Sharon, "Paraguay to replace 'shackle-and-hoist' kosher slaughter method", *The Jerusalem Post*, Marcy 27, 2017.

[948] "HPAI Response, Ventilation Shutdown Plus (+) Policy", *USDA*, January 2022.

[949] For examples of when a nation may, nor may not, limit freedom of religious or belief in furtherance of a state interest, *see* Lavery, Kirsten and Cassidy, Elizabeth, "Legislative Factsheet: Limitations on the Freedom of Religion or Belief", *United States Commission on International Religious Freedom*, June 2020.

[950] Santeria, also known as Regla de Ocha or the Lucumi religion, is an Afro-Cuban religion that originated in what today is Nigeria and Benin in West Africa. *See generally*, "Why Is It Called Santeria?" at www.aboutsanteria.com

[951] *See*, e.g., Price, Mark, "Dead pig, chickens dumped along busy Florida street may be ritual sacrifice, cops say", *Miami Herald*, June 8, 2022.

[952] Fla. Stat. §828.22(3) (Humane Slaughter Act) permits the ritual slaughter of certain "livestock", defined to include, inter alia, cattle, calves, sheep, swine, horses, mules, goats and ostriches.

Florida city did attempt to prohibit the killing of animals in public or private rituals, where the primary purpose was not food consumption. The ordinance was challenged on First Amendment free exercise grounds and the matter was litigated all the way up to the Supreme Court, which held that the law was unconstitutional. The decision was due in large part, however, to the fact that the law targeted a specific religious ritual of a specific religious community (i.e., animal sacrifices by the Santeria religious community),[953] with Supreme Court Justice, Anthony Kennedy, explaining that "religious beliefs need not be acceptable, logical, consistent or comprehensible to others in order to merit First Amendment protection."[954] The Supreme Court decision resulted in the practice of ritualistic animal slaughter continuing in Florida. The city can redraft the law to address the constitutional concerns outlined by the Court, but it has not done so. The constitutional right to religious freedom is robust but not absolute.[955] Freedom of religion, for instance, does not permit human sacrifice or sexual assaults. Neutral laws with general applicability that do not target a specific religious practice or specific religious community are less likely to conflict with the First Amendment principles.[956] An across-the-board state ban on wet markets, for instance, that meets the requirements of neutrality and general applicability may (or may not) pass constitutional scrutiny. This legal question may be ripe for consideration. In early 2023, Hamtramck City council in Michigan amended a city ordinance to allow religious animal sacrifice at home.[957]

[953] Church of the Lukumi Babalu Aye, Inc. v. Hialeah, 508 U.S. 520 (1993). The Court stated that the government's legitimate interest in public health and preventing animal cruelty "could be addressed by restrictions stopping far short of a flat prohibition of all Santeria sacrificial practice, such as general regulations on the disposal of organic garbage, on the care of animals regardless of why they are kept, or on methods of slaughter."

[954] In *Church of the Lukumi Babalu Aye, Inc. v. Hialeah*, Justice Kennedy quoted Justice Warren E. Burger in his opinion in *Thomas v. Review Board of the Indiana Employment Security Division*, 450 U.S. 707 (1981).

[955] The First Amendment to the U.S. Constitution provides that "Congress shall make no law respecting an establishment of religion, or prohibiting the free exercise thereof."

[956] The Supreme Court has held that the Free Exercise Clause of the U.S. Constitution allows states to prohibit sacramental peyote use and may deny unemployment benefits to persons discharged for such use. *See*, Employment Div., Dept. of Human Resources of Oregon v. Smith, 494 U.S. 872 (1990).

[957] Smith, Wesley J., "Michigan City Allows Religious Animal Sacrifice", *National Review*, January 11, 2023.

Aquatic Animals

In many ways aquatic animals are the least like us, and we have the least amount of interaction with sea life, yet humanity has waged a sustained and brutal assault on oceans and sea animals. Humanity's treatment of aquatic animals and the oceans is so appalling that some compare it to an undeclared war.[958]

As a practical matter, it is not possible to know the exact number of animals who live in the ocean, but in 2010, a group of 2700 scientists from more than 80 countries undertook a 10 year collaborative research effort to conduct a census to assess the diversity and abundance of marine life.[959] Despite identifying over 6000 potential new ocean species and 17,000 species that live in the deep sea where no light penetrates,[960] scientists estimate that 91% of all ocean species have yet to be classified[961] and believe that more than 80% of oceans are unmapped and unexplored.[962] The census concluded that we still do not know how many species live closest to us along the shoreline (defined by the census as the shoreline out to a depth of around 65 feet), though estimates widely range from 178,000 to more than 10 million species.[963] Scientists also discovered that while there are 38,000 different kinds of microbes in a single liter of seawater, a staggering 90% of the large predators in the ocean have disappeared as a result of fishing.[964]

The emerging consensus is that fish are sentient and can experience pain. The American Veterinary Medical Association has stated that, given fish sentience and cognition, fish should be afforded pain relief to the same extent that it would be provided to terrestrial vertebrates.[965] Recent

[958] Conathan, Michael, "Trump's War on Oceans", *CAP*, June 8, 2017.

[959] *See generally*, The Census of Marine Life, *Smithsonian*, n.d., at https://ocean.si.edu/ecosystems/census-marine-life/census-marine-life-overview

[960] The Census of Marine Life.

[961] Carilo Mora, et al., "How Many Species are there on Earth and in the Ocean?", *PLOS Biology*, August 23, 2011. https://doi.org/10.1371/journal.pbio.1001127

[962] *See*, "How much of the ocean have we explored? More than eighty percent of our ocean is unmapped, unobserved, and unexplored", *National Ocean Service National Oceanic and Atmospheric Administration*, n.d., at https://oceanservice.noaa.gov/facts/exploration.html#

[963] The Census of Marine Life.

[964] The Census of Marine Life.

[965] Jonathon Balcombe, *What a Fish Knows (The Inner Lives of our Underwater Cousins)*. Scientific American / Farrar, Straus and Giroux, 2016, at p. 83.

research tells us that there is an abundance of intelligence in fish, whose memories and cognitive abilities in some species can match or exceed the memories and cognitive capabilities of "higher" vertebrates, including nonhuman primates.[966] Whales use sonar to find food; sea cucumbers can shapeshift; and an octopus can change its skin color. In the wild, manta rays show their curiosity of divers and are playful.[967] The sea animal kingdom is brimming with abilities that exceed human capabilities.

Sea animals face cruelty as much as terrestrial animals. In 2017, three men shot a shark with a revolver, tied it to the back of their boat, and dragged it to its death.[968] The incident led to public outrage and extensive media coverage, but little media coverage is afforded to the millions of sharks who have their fins sliced off for soup. Many sharks are then tossed back into the ocean to die a cruel death of blood loss or suffocation.[969] Shark fins are considered a delicacy in China and parts of Asia, and tens of millions are killed for their fins or other body parts every year.[970] In 2019, Canada banned the import and export of shark fins,[971] and at the end of 2022, the Shark Fin Sales Elimination Act[972] was signed into law in the United States, making the trade, transport and sale of shark fins illegal. Fourteen states have also banned the sale and possession of shark fins, including California, Delaware, Florida, Hawaii, Illinois, Maryland, Massachusetts, Nevada, New Jersey, New York, Oregon, Rhode Island, Texas and Washington, along with three U.S. territories (Guam, American Samoa and the Commonwealth of the Northern Mariana Islands).[973] In

[966] Brown, Culum, "Animal minds: Not just a pretty face", *New Scientist*, June 11, 2004, at 42–43.

[967] Blog, "Manta ray brain power blows other fish out of the water", *Oceana*, July 25, 2017, at https://oceana.org/blog/manta-ray-brainpower-blows-other-fish-out-water-10/

[968] Selk, Avi, "Three men who laughed as they dragged a shark behind a motorboat could go to prison", *Washington Post*, December 13, 2017.

[969] What a Fish Knows, at 223.

[970] *See generally*, Worm, Boris, et al., "Global catches, exploitation rates, and rebuilding options for sharks", *Marine Policy*, Vol. 40, 2013, at 194–204. https://doi.org/10.1016/j.marpol.2012.12.034

[971] Government of Canada Customs Notice 21-02, Fisheries and Oceans Canada (DRO)'s prohibition on the importation and exportation of shark fins, dated February 9, 2021, at https://www.cbsa-asfc.gc.ca/publications/cn-ad/cn21-02-eng.html

[972] The Shark Fin Sales Elimination Act of 2021 (H.R.7776) was signed into law as a part of the National Defense Authorization Act.

[973] For the governing statutes and statutory penalties, *see* "Shark Finning Legislation", *Animal Welfare Institute*, n.d., at https://awionline.org/content/shark-finning

addition to direct cruelty, habitat destruction is another way that sea animals are abused.

Research reveals that half of the world's coral reefs have been lost or destroyed since the 1950s, driven by overfishing, climate change, ocean acidification and pollution.[974] The finding is deeply disturbing because coral reefs help to protect nearly 200 million people from storm surges and waves.[975] Approximately 25% of the fish in the ocean depend on coral reefs, as do over half a billion people who depend on them for food, income and protection.[976] A 2020 study found that globally, nearly two-thirds of coral reef shark and ray species, who are an important part of coral reef ecosystems, are at risk of extinction.[977] The oceans are in crisis.

Aquatic animals face many threats, including oil spills. When 205 million gallons of oil and 225,000 tons of methane were spilled into the Gulf of Mexico during the BP Deepwater Horizon catastrophe in 2010, the Center for Biological Diversity estimated that the spill likely injured or killed around 82,000 birds (of 102 species), 6165 sea turtles, up to 25,900 marine mammals and a vast unknown number of fish.[978] Ten years after the catastrophe, bottlenose dolphins are experiencing higher rates of lung disease and heart issues, similar to symptoms experienced by clean-up workers and Coast Guard personnel who had exposure to the oil.[979] In 2022, it was reported that the methane leak from the sabotaged Nord Stream Pipeline would likely be the largest known gas leak to occur over such a

[974] *See*, Eddy, Tyler D., et al., "Global decline in capacity of coral reefs to provide ecosystem services", *One Earth*, September 17, 2021. https://doi.org/10.1016/j.oneear.2021.08.016. *See also*, Berwyn, Bob, "Big Reefs in Big Trouble: New Research Tracks a 50 Percent Decline in Living Coral Since the 1950s", *Inside Climate News*, September 17, 2021.

[975] World Wildlife Fund, "Living Planet Report 2020, Bending the Curve of Biodiversity Loss", at p. 70, at https://files.worldwildlife.org/wwfcmsprod/files/Publication/file/279c656a32_ENGLISH_FULL.pdf?_ga=2.200774702.1234671991.1682881068-272343723.1682881068

[976] *See*, "Coral reef Ecosystems", *National Oceanic and Atmospheric Administration*, U.S. Dept. of Commerce, February 1, 2019, at https://www.noaa.gov/education/resource-collections/marine-life/coral-reef-ecosystems

[977] Sherman, C. Samantha, et al., "Half a century of rising extinction risk of coral reef sharks and rays", *Nature Communications*, January 17, 2023.

[978] *See*, "A Deadly Toll: The Devastating Wildlife Effects of Deepwater Horizon – and the Next Catastrophic Oil Spill", *Center for Biological Diversity*, n.d., at https://www.biologicaldiversity.org/programs/public_lands/energy/dirty_energy_development/oil_and_gas/gulf_oil_spill/a_deadly_toll.html

[979] *See*, Meiners, Joan, "Ten years later, BP oil spill continues to harm wildlife – especially dolphins", *National Geographic*, April 17, 2020.

short period of time, with immediate harm to both marine life and to human health.[980] Sea life also suffers from the harmful efforts to locate oil and gas. As Oceana explains, the seismic air gun blasting that is employed to locate oil and gas beneath the ocean floor injures and kills millions of marine animals, from the tiniest zooplankton at the base of the food chain to the largest sea mammals.[981]

Marine mammals and other sea life, including threatened species, are also harmed and killed by exploding bombs, underwater sonar, torpedo testing, projectiles firing at seven times the speed of sound, and other planned military exercises.[982] Organizations have long warned that sonar can be deafening to marine mammals, the equivalent of 2000 jet engines, causing physical trauma and strandings.[983] In so-called explosion drills, the United States military uses live explosives to test the durability of warships. In June 2021, in a 'mine is bigger than yours' display of military power, the Navy released footage of a "full ship shock" trial, which involved the detonation of a 40,000 pound bomb in the Atlantic Ocean. The blast caused the ocean to pour up toward the sky and triggered a 3.9 earthquake.[984] Despite the devastation, destruction and deaths caused by military exercises over oceans, the Navy received a 5 year permit in 2018 to conduct military exercises from Southern California to Hawaii.[985] The Center for Biological Diversity warns that naval military training exercises involving sonar and explosions will disturb marine mammals "millions of times" every year, a disturbing prediction given that strikes by vessels are already a leading cause of whale deaths in California.[986] Animals are the unwitting participants in humanity's conflicts. Both the United States and

[980] Larson, Christina, "'Unprecedented' Nord Stream Pipeline Leaks Will Ravage Marine Life, Harm Climate", *Huffington Post*, September 30, 2022.

[981] *See generally*, "Seismic Airgun Blasting: Seismic airgun blasting threatens marine life, coastal communities and local economies", *Oceana*, n.d., at https://oceana.org/our-campaigns/seismic-airgun-blasting/

[982] Associated Press, "Navy testing criticized for impact on marine life", *Peninsula Daily News*, July 31, 2020.

[983] Liptak, Adam, "Supreme Court Rules for Navy in Sonar Case", *New York Times*, November 13, 2008.

[984] Romaine, Jenna, "Massive explosion set off by US Navy may have injured or killed marine life", *The Hill*, June 23, 2021.

[985] Center for Biological Diversity, "Navy to Reexamine Effects of Pacific Training Exercises on Endangered Whales, Exercises off Southern California, Hawaii Under Review After Deadly Ship Strike", July 15, 2021.

[986] Ibid.

Russia have used whales, dolphins and sea lions, fitted with intelligence gathering equipment, for military purposes.[987]

The Supreme Court has weighed in on the interest of the Navy to conduct training exercises, without taking prescribed precautions to protect marine mammals, and concluded that national security concerns of military preparedness outweigh the injuries to marine mammals.[988] The Navy acknowledged that the exercises could physically harm or kill 466 marine mammals and result in 170,000 disturbances or disruptions to the natural behavioral patterns of marine mammals. Noting that the Navy had used mitigation measures in the past "to reduce the harmful effects of its active sonar", Supreme Court Justices, Ruth Bader Ginsburg and Justice David H. Souter, strongly dissented, noting that "[s]onar is linked to mass strandings of marine mammals, hemorrhaging around the brain and ears, acute spongiotic changes in the central nervous system, and lesions in vital organs."[989] In fact, "noise" pollution in oceans has gotten so loud that dolphins must shout at times just to be heard![990]

The Supreme Court case was not the final word on Naval use of sonar technologies. In 2016, the Ninth federal Circuit Court of Appeals ruled that the Navy's use of low-frequency active sonar in the Pacific Ocean during peacetime training exercises violated the federal Marine Mammal Protection Act[991] by causing mass strandings of marine mammals and the separation of calves, heightened stress responses, hearing damage and disruption of communication, feeding and mating practices.[992] As of 2023,

[987] *See,* e.g., Ismay, John, "Why Whales and Dolphins Join the Navy, in Russia and the U.S.", *New York Times Magazine*, April 30, 2019.

[988] Winter, Secretary of the Navy, et al. v. Natural Resources Defense Council, Inc., et al., 555 U.S. 7 (2008). The District Court had imposed certain "mitigation" conditions on the Navy, such as requiring a shutdown of sonar if a marine mammal is spotted within a certain distance.

[989] Winter, Secretary of the Navy, et al. v. Natural Resources Defense Council, Inc., et al., 555 U.S. 7 (2008). Justice Ginsburg also noted that the Navy had violated the National Environmental Policy Act, which requires environmental impact statements to be prepared by the government before proceeding with significant actions that could impact the environment.

[990] Noise pollution increases the stress of marine mammals and interferes with their ability to find food. *See*, Tucker, Flora, "The Ocean Got so Loud That Dolphins Must Now 'Shout' Over Noise Pollution", *Impakter,* January 19, 2023.

[991] Marine Mammal Protection Act, 16 U.S.C.A. §§ 1361-1423 h.

[992] Natural Resources Defense Council, Inc., et al., v. Penny Pritzker, Secretary, U.S. Department of Commerce, et al., 828 F.3rd. 1125 (2016).

the Navy is still conducting training and equipment testing, and while it remains subject to the requirements of the Marine Mammal Protection Act and the limitations of any issued permits, environmental groups remain concerned that the Navy still does not sufficiently mitigate its impact on marine life.[993] Moreover, the Navy is still using sonar and detonating bombs at sea, injuring and killing marine mammals, which the National Marine Fisheries Service indicates qualifies as permitted 'military readiness activities' pursuant to the Marine Mammal Protection Act.[994] The impact is devastating, yet there are still far greater threats.

An estimated 96 million tons of wild fish are captured globally every year, despite the serious threat of overfishing to oceans.[995] Globally, freshwater species have declined a staggering 83% on average since 1970.[996] Many countries still subsidize the fishing industry despite its devastating impact on biodiversity.[997] The Marine Stewardship Council estimates that over a third of the world's fish stocks are overfished, even as a third of the global catch is wasted.[998]

A little known tragedy of the fishing industry is "bycatch." Fish and sea animals, including protected species who are not the target of commercial fishing, get caught up in the large nets that indiscriminately catch dolphins, whales, sea turtles, seabirds, countless coral and a huge number of other non-target fish and sea animals.[999] Commercial fishing lines can be 75 miles in length, and a single modern fishing vessel can catch 50 tons of sea animals in just a few minutes by using huge indiscriminate fishing nets

[993] Smiley, Sage, "Navy training and testing in Southeast Alaska will stay at similar levels for the next 7 years", *KSTK Wrangell*, October 4, 2021.

[994] Duhamel, Frederik-Xavier, "U.S. renews navy's right to harm marine mammals during testing and training off Pacific Coast", *CBS News*, November 17, 2020.

[995] Independent Group of Scientists appointed by the Secretary-General, *Global Sustainable Development Report 2019: The Future is Now: Science for Achieving Sustainable Development*. United Nations, New York, 2019, at 12.

[996] *See*, "69% average decline in wildlife populations since 1970, says new WWF report", *WWF*, October 13, 2022, citing WWF's "Living Planet Report 2022" at https://livingplanet.panda.org/en-US/

[997] Countries spend billions on subsidies to support fishing industries, even though overfishing is draining the oceans. *See*, Woody, Todd, "The sea is running out of fish, despite nations' pledge to stop it", *National Geographic*, October 8, 2019.

[998] Jardim, Ernesto, "Five things you need to know about the state of the world's fish", *Marine Stewardship Council*, June 10, 2020; *see also*, "Biodiversity and fishing", *Marine Stewardship Council*, n.d., at https://www.msc.org/what-we-are-doing/oceans-at-risk/biodiversity-and-fishing

[999] What a Fish Knows, at 220.

that are each 30 miles in length.[1000] A highly destructive fishing method is "bottom trawling," which drags metal rollers across the ocean floor, randomly catching and destroying everything in its path.[1001] The impact is devastating. A 2014 report by the Natural Resources Defense Council found that the estimated number of marine mammals killed or seriously injured by fisheries exceeds 650,000 every year.[1002] While the United States touts its "dolphin-safe" standards,[1003] and while the World Trade Organization (WTO) ruled in 2017 that U.S. "dolphin-safe" labeling requirements complied with WTO rules,[1004] lawsuits filed against canned tuna producers allege that longlines and "fish aggregating devices" harm and kill dolphins.[1005] The 2014 report also concluded that virtually every fish product imported into the United States violates the Marine Mammal Protection Act, which requires that no whales, dolphins or other marine mammals be killed or seriously injured (in excess of U.S. standards) by the fishing technology.[1006] The law is simply not enforced, with tragic consequences.

For tuna fishing, it is estimated that 145 other species are routinely killed, including various species of shark, whales, dolphins and turtles.[1007] Safran Foer, an American novelist, makes the case for food labeling requirements that would alert customers as to the number of animals killed for the product, such as "26 pounds of other sea animals were killed and tossed back into the ocean for every 1 pound of this shrimp."[1008]

[1000] Jonathan Safran Foer, *Eating Animals*. Little Brown and Company, 2009, at pp. 19 and 35. ISBN-13: 9780316086646.

[1001] What a Fish Knows, at 213.

[1002] Smith, Zak, et al., "Net Loss: The Killing of Marine Mammals in Foreign Fisheries", Executive Summary, *Natural Resources Defense Council,* January 2014, at https://www.nrdc.org/sites/default/files/mammals-foreign-fisheries-report.pdf

[1003] Dolphin Protection Consumer Information Act, 16 U.S.C. §1385. The "dolphin-safe" designation in the U.S. generally requires that dolphins not be encircled when catching tuna and that no dolphins be seriously injured or killed in the sets used to catch tuna.

[1004] Office of the United States Trade Representative, "U.S. Dolphin Safe-Labeling Requirements Found Compliant with WTO Rules", October 26, 2017, at https://ustr.gov/about-us/policy-offices/press-office/press-releases/2017/october/us-dolphin-safe-labeling-0

[1005] *See*, e.g., Mill, Matthew R. and Jasnow, Dan, "False, Reminding Brands Not to Bite Off More Than They Can Chew", *Arent Fox Schiff,* February 7, 2020; *see also*, Gibson, Kate, "Tuna brands accused of making false 'dolphin-safe' claims", *Money Watch,* May 16, 2019.

[1006] Smith, Zak, Net Loss: The Killing of Marine Mammals.

[1007] Foer, Jonathan Safran, *Eating Animals*, at pp. 49 and 50.

[1008] Foer, Jonathan Safran, *Eating Animals*, at p. 49.

Consumers should have the right, and perhaps the duty, to understand the impact of their product choices. While the amount of bycatch has been dropping in recent decades as the result of better fishing equipment, it is estimated that bycatch still accounts for 10–40% of total global fish caught, depending on how "bycatch" is defined.[1009] It is also estimated that 20% of wild-caught fish at stores, restaurants and waterfront docks is illegally caught, while nearly 90% of global fisheries are over or fully exploited.[1010] Illegal fishing is so widespread that it impacts the food security of many nations and has surpassed piracy as a global threat.[1011] The moral cost of seafood is high, as nations are discovering. In 2016, a coalition of countries established 598,000 square miles of protected area in Antarctica's Ross Sea, becoming the world's largest marine reserve.[1012] The reserve is thought to be the planet's last unspoiled area and it will be safeguarded from commercial fishing for 35 years,[1013] but it will not be immune from other threats, such as rising ocean temperatures that adversely impact marine species and ecosystems.[1014]

There is consensus among researchers that oceans have warmed and that acidification (i.e., a reduction in the pH caused principally by uptake of carbon dioxide[1015]) is increasing at the surface. Ocean warming, ocean acidification and deoxygenation, all of which are a threat to marine life and sea habitats, are the result of carbon dioxide and other greenhouse gas

[1009] Dirk Zeller, et al., "Global marine fisheries disregards: A synthesis of reconstructed data", *Wiley Online Library, Fish and Fisheries,* June 26, 2017. https://doi.org/10.1111/faf.12233; *see also*, What a Fish Knows, at 221.

[1010] Issue Brief, "How to End Illegal Fishing: From coastal waters to the high seas, criminals are robbing the oceans and hurting economies", *PEW*, December 12, 2017, at https://www.pewtrusts.org/en/research-and-analysis/issue-briefs/2017/12/how-to-end-illegal-fishing

[1011] Grady, John, "Coast Guard: Illegal Fishing Has Surpassed Piracy as a Global Threat", *USNI News,* January 19, 2023.

[1012] Howard, Brian Clark, "World's Largest Marine Reserve Created Off Antarctica", *National Geographic*, October 27, 2019.

[1013] "Marine Protected Area in Antarctica's Rose Sea: Covering are area of 600,000 square miles in the Ross Sea, the new MPA will be protected from commercial fishing for 35 years", *NOAA Fisheries, International Affairs,* n.d., at https://www.fisheries.noaa.gov/national/international-affairs/marine-protected-area-antarcticas-ross-sea

[1014] For additional information on ocean warning, *see*, "*Climate Change 2021: The Physical Science Basis*", Sixth Assessment Report of the Intergovernmental Panel on Climate Change, August 7, 2021, at https://www.ipcc.ch/report/ar6/wg1/

[1015] Wikipedia defines "ocean acidification" as an ongoing decrease in the pH value of the Earth's oceans, caused by the update of carbon dioxide (CO_2) from the atmosphere."

emissions caused by human activities[1016] and we are already seeing the damage. According to a 2021 Canadian study, an estimated 1 billion marine animals along the coast of Vancouver have died as the result of record-setting temperatures in the Pacific coast region.[1017] The impact of human activity on oceans is catastrophic. If global warning continues, mass extinctions will follow, but scientists believe that it is possible to reduce extinction risks by more than 70% by reversing greenhouse gas emissions.[1018]

Like overfishing and climate change, pollution has profound effects on aquatic life, so much so that "dead zones" (i.e., hypoxic areas with too little or no oxygen) are developing in oceans that are incompatible with marine life. The primary cause of dead zones is nutrient (e.g., nitrogen and phosphorus) pollution caused by human activity.[1019] According to the EPA, in the United States, nutrients from concentrated animal feeding operations, large farms and row crops contribute the most nutrient pollution to the dead zone in the Gulf of Mexico.[1020] A 2008 report found that there are more than 400 dead zones around the planet involving more than 245,000 square kilometers.[1021] The dead zone in the Gulf of Mexico

[1016] For a comprehensive report on the impact of climate change on oceans, *see,IPCC, 2019; IPCC Special Report on the Ocean and Cryosphere in a Changing* Climate [H.-O. Pörtner, et al. (eds.)]. Cambridge University Press, Cambridge, UK and New York, NY, USA, at https://doi.org/10.1017/9781009157964

[1017] *See,* e.g., Shivaram, Deepa, "Heat Wave Killed an Estimated 1 Billion Sea Creatures, and Scientists Fear Even Worse", *NPR*, July 9, 2021; *see also*, Einhorn, Catrin, "Like in 'Postapocalyptic Movies': Heat Wave Killed Marine Wildlife in Masse", *New York Times,* July 23, 2021; *see also*, Cecco, Leyland, "'Heat dome' probably killed 1 bn marine animals on Canada coast, experts say", *Guardian*, July 8, 2021.

[1018] Penn, Justin L. and Deutsch, Curtis, "Avoiding ocean mass extinction from climate warming", *Science,* Vol. 376, Issue 6592, April 28, 2022, at 524–526. https://doi.org/10.1126/science.abe9039

[1019] *See*, "What is a dead zone?", *National Ocean Service, National Oceanic and Atmospheric Administration of the U.S. Department of Commerce,* n.d., at https://oceanservice.noaa.gov/facts/deadzone.html

[1020] U.S. Environmental Protection Agency, *The Facts about Nutrient Pollution*, n.d., at https://www.epa.gov/sites/default/files/2015-03/documents/facts_about_nutrient_pollution_what_is_hypoxia.pdf

[1021] Diaz, Robert J. and Rosenberg, Rutger, "Spreading Dead Zones and Consequences for Marine Ecosystems", *Science*, Vol. 321, Issue 5891, August 15, 2008, at 926–929. https://doi.org/10.1126/science.1156401

is one of the largest in the world, covering more than 8500 square miles.[1022] In 2018, 23 million salmon died off the coast of Chili, only to be followed by thousands of dead sardines, mammals and birds.[1023] Dead zones are putting the aquatic world at risk and the problem extends beyond our oceans.

In 2021, record numbers of manatees died of starvation in Florida because fertilizer and sewage runoff in the Indian River Lagoon caused their main food staple, seagrass, to die.[1024] Despite efforts to help manatees, deaths by starvation continued into 2022.[1025] The Center for Biological Diversity, Defenders of Wildlife and Save the Manatee Club have filed a lawsuit against the U.S. Fish and Wildlife Service for failing to finalize a critical habitat designation for Florida manatees in violation of the Endangered Species Act.[1026] Aquatic animals face many challenges, and pollution is among the greatest.

One of the greatest challenges facing ocean life is marine plastic pollution, which includes abandoned, lost and discarded fishing gear and plastic pollution from land sources, all of which originate from human activities.[1027] It is estimated that a staggering 4.8 to 12.7 million metric tons of plastic waste are dumped into the ocean each year.[1028] Researchers warn

[1022] Malmquist, David, "Dead Zones, Lack of oxygen a key stressor on marine ecosystems", *Virginia Institute of Marine Science*, n.d., at www.vims.edu/research/topics/dead_zones/

[1023] McKenna, John, "Dead zones in our oceans have increased dramatically since 1950", *World Economic Forum*, January 18, 2018.

[1024] A record 1101 of Florida's manatees died in 2021. *See*, Allen, Greg, "Manatees are starving in Florida, Wildlife agencies are scrambling to save them", *NPR*, December 2, 2021; *see also*, Guzman, Joseph, "Record number of manatees died in Florida in 2021", *The Hill*, January 7, 2022.

[1025] *See*, Cardona, Maria Alejandra, "Florida manatees dying off at an alarming rate, experts say", *Reuters*, January 19, 2023; *see also*, Fleshler, David, "Florida manatees still starving to death, despite intervention", *Tampa Bay Times*, February 2, 2022.

[1026] Center or Biological Diversity, Defenders of Wildlife, and Save the Manatee Club v. U.S. Fish and Wildlife Service, U.S. District Ct. of D.C., Case 1:22-cv-00246, filed February 1, 2022; *see generally,* Romaine, Jenna, "Conservation groups suing over rise in manatee deaths in Florida", *The Hill*, March 4, 2022.

[1027] "From Pollution to Solution, A Global Assessment of Marine Litter and Plastic Pollution", *United Nations Environment Programme*. 2021, at https://www.unep.org/resources/pollution-solution-global-assessment-marine-litter-and-plastic-pollution

[1028] Jambeck, Jenna R., et al., "Plastic waste inputs from land into the ocean", *Science*, Vol. 347, Issue 6223, February 13, 2015, at 768–771. https://doi.org/10.1126/science.1260352

that if current pollution rates continue, there could be more plastic in the ocean than there are fish by 2050, unless measures are adopted to ban the use of single-use plastic items.[1029] Many people will recall reports about the "Great Pacific Garbage Patch" (also known as the "Pacific trash vortex"), one of the largest accumulations of ocean plastic in the world that is twice the size of Texas. Recent studies estimate that microplastics account for 94% of an estimated 1.8 trillion pieces of plastic in the Garbage Patch.[1030] Plastic pollution is a major issue because it does not biodegrade and it ends up breaking down into smaller and smaller microplastics, which are then ingested by ocean life.[1031] The consequences of marine pollution are devastating. Marine plastic pollution is choking sea animals, and many perish when they get caught up in debris.[1032]

Every year, marine debris results in the death, by drowning, suffocation or starvation, of approximately 100,000 marine annuals, including seals, whales and dolphins.[1033] The less apparent consequence of marine plastic pollution, however, is its impact to humans. As humans consume ocean animals, they are also consuming microplastics eaten by animals. A 2020 study of microplastics involving 5 different types of seafood found plastic in every sample tested by researchers.[1034]

Researchers do not yet know the full health impact that consuming microplastics may have on human health, and the Food and Drug Administration has yet to prescribe any guidelines or limits on the

[1029] *See*, "*The New Plastics Economy, Rethinking the Future of Plastics*", Ellen Macarthur Foundation and the World Economic Forum and Center for Business and Environment, January 19, 2016, at https://ellenmacarthurfoundation.org/the-new-plastics-economy-rethinking-the-future-of-plastics

[1030] "The Great Pacific Garbage Patch Isn't What You Think It is", *National Geographic Resource Library, Background Info*, at https://education.nationalgeographic.org/resource/great-pacific-garbage-patch-isnt-what-you-think

[1031] For a discussion on the impact of sea live consumption of microplastics, *see* Chatterjee, Subhankar and Sharma, Shivika, "Microplastics in our oceans and marine health", *Field Actions Science Reports* [Online], Special Issue 19, March 1, 2019. ISSN: 1867–8521. https://journals.openedition.org/factsreports/5257

[1032] Lewis, Sophie, "A decade of plastic has entangled, choked and drowned over 1500 endangered marine mammals in U.S. waters, new report finds", *CBS News*, November 19, 2020.

[1033] *See*, e.g., "Plastic in our Oceans is Killing Marine Mammals", *WWF*, June 30, 2021.

[1034] Francisca Ribeiro, et al., "Quantitative Analysis of Selected Plastics in High-Commercial-Value Australian Seafood by Pyrolysis Gas Chromatography Mass Spectrometry", July 9, 2020, *Environ. Sci. Technol.* 2020, 54, 15, 9408–9417. https://doi.org/10.1021/acs.est.0c02337

consumption of microplastics, but some potential effects of eating seafood that is contaminated by microplastics include oxidative stress, damage to neurons, which increases the risk of dementia, endocrine disruption, thyroid damage and cancer.[1035] By consuming sea animals, we are consuming what they have consumed and it impacts our health. In 2023, researchers found that the consumption of just a *single* serving of freshwater fish caught in American rivers, streams and lakes per year could be the equivalent of drinking water contaminated with harmful "forever chemicals" for one month.[1036]

Every year, lost and abandoned fishing nets entangle and kill sea animals, including dolphins, seals, sea birds and sea turtles. The Marine Mammal Protection Act has reduced dolphin mortality from about half a million to 20,000, and while other measures have further reduced the death rate, approximately 300,000 dolphins, small whales and porpoises die each year from net entanglement.[1037] In 2018, a major study found that (i) a substantial amount of marine plastic debris originates from land-based sources, (ii) rivers "act as a major transport pathway for all sizes of plastic debris," and (iii) the top 10 rivers responsible for plastic pollution transport 88–95% of the global debris load into the sea.[1038] The study concluded that by reducing the amount of plastic pollution in the top 10 polluting rivers by 50%, we could reduce the total amount of river-sourced debris to 45%.[1039] The European Parliament is tackling the important issue

[1035] "What to know about plastics in seafood", *MedicalNewsToday*, n.d., at https://www.medicalnewstoday.com/articles/plastics-in-seafood#health-risks

[1036] For more on forever chemicals, *see*, Barbo, Nadia, et al., "Locally caught freshwater fish across the United States are likely a significant source of exposure to PFOS and other perfluorinated compounds", *Environmental Research*, Vol. 220, March 2023. https://doi.org/10.1016/j.envres.2022.115165; *see generally*, *see* LaMotte, Sandee, "Locally caught fish are full of dangerous chemicals called PRAS, study finds", *CNN*, January 17, 2023.

[1037] What a Fish Knows, at 222.

[1038] Schmidt, Christian, et al., "Export of Plastic Debris by Rivers into the Sea," *Environmental science & technology*, Vol. 51,21 (October 2017), at 12246–12253. https://doi.org/10.1021/acs.est.7b02368. The 10 rivers include the Yangtze River, which flows into East China Sea near Shanghai; the Indus River, which flows through India and Pakistan into Arabian Sea; the Yellow River, which flows through China; the Hai River, which flows through China; the Nile River, the world's longest river which flows through 11 countries; the Ganges, which flows through India; the Pearl River, which flows through southern China into South China Sea; the Amur/Heilong River, the border between NE China and Russian Far East; the Niger River, West Africa's main river which flows through 5 countries; and the Mekong River, which flows through China, Vietnam, Laos, Cambodia, Thailand, Myanmar.

[1039] Ibid.

of single-use plastics,[1040] but concentrating on pollution from the top 10 polluting rivers would produce much more measurable results.[1041] In 2022, in what was hailed as the most important climate deal since the Paris climate accord, 200 nations agreed to establish a treaty to address marine plastic pollution.[1042]

The United Nations calls the oceans the "lungs of the Earth" for a reason—they produce most of the oxygen we breathe.[1043] The threats facing aquatic animals are without a doubt our own threats. United Nations Secretary-General, Antonio Guterres, acknowledged in early 2023 that we have been "waging a senseless and self-defeating war on nature" with oceans "on the front lines of the battle"[1044] because we will suffer and perish as a result of our own actions. The International Union for Conservation of Nature warns that around 40% of the world's population in coastal communities face physical, economic and food security threats from the degradation of marine and coast ecosystems,[1045] and this is only the tip of the iceberg of what would surely entail devastation of cascading proportions. This is not a war that humanity must merely end … it is a war where the damage must be fully repaired.

[1040] "Directive (EU) 2019/904 of the European Parliament and of the Council of 5 June 2019 on the reduction of the impact of certain plastic products on the environment", *Official Journal of the European Union*, at https://eur-lex.europa.eu/eli/dir/2019/904/oj

[1041] *See generally*, "Around 90% of all river-borne plastic that ends up in the ocean comes from just 10 rivers", *World Economic Forum*, June 8, 2018.; *see also*, Patel, Prachi, "Stemming the Plastic Tide: 10 Rivers Contribute Most of the Plastic in the Oceans", *Scientific American*, February 1, 2018.

[1042] U.N. Resolution 5/14 (End plastic pollution: towards a legally binding instrument), adopted March 2, 2022; *see generally*, "UNAE Resolution – 'End Plastic Pollution' – and IUCN role in implementation of the Treaty", *IUCN*, March 9, 2022; *see also*, Meredith, Sam, "'Most important climate deal since Paris': UN agrees treaty to end scourge of plastic pollution", *Sustainable Future*, March 3, 2022.

[1043] *See generally*, Inciong, Rolando A., "Oceans are the 'lungs of the Earth'", *Business Mirror*, July 1, 2019.

[1044] "UN Secretary-General: 'Ending the ocean emergency is a race we must win'", *The Ocean Race*, January 24, 2023.

[1045] International Union for Conservation of Nature (IUCN), "Issues Brief: The Ocean and Climate Change", November 2017.

Animals in Human Conflicts

One of the greatest stains on humanity is the untold number of animals who have been forced to serve and die in wars and other violent conflicts. It is not possible to know how many animals have been injured and how many have died, but one thing is clear: where there is human conflict, animals are brought in to join the fight. Animals are recruited for their natural abilities, and many have suffered "agonizing deaths from wounds, starvation, thirst, exhaustion, disease and exposure."[1046] The world is now suffering from the greatest number of conflicts since the United Nations was created, with ~ 2 billion people living in countries impacted by conflict,[1047] with devastating consequences for animals.

In World War I, more than 16 million animals served in the areas of transport, communication, reconnaissance, and companionship.[1048] Animals have been used both offensively in conflicts, such as dogs strapped with bombs,[1049] and defensively, such as dogs used to sniff out landmines.[1050] It is believed that more than 8 million horses, donkeys and mules and 1 million dogs died during the World War I.[1051] An elephant named Lizzie from a traveling menagerie was recruited in Britain to serve in World War I. She was forced to carry heavy machinery, munitions and

[1046] *See generally,* Parsons, Laureen, "Animals at War", *Kenora Great War Project*, n.d., at https://www.kenoragreatwarproject.ca/other-resources/animals-at-war/

[1047] Guterres, Antonia, Secretary-General of the United Nations, Forward to "The Sustainable Development Goals Report, 2022", United Nations, 2022. ISBN 978-92-1-101448-8.

[1048] Hoare, Philip, "The animal victims of the first world war are a stain on our conscience", *Guardian*, November 7, 2018; *see also*, Blog, "Animals and World War 1", *Queensferry History Group*, January 11, 2015, at https://queensferry-at-war.weebly.com/interesting-war-facts/animals-and-world-war-1

[1049] During World War II, Russian military trained "anti-tank dogs" to deliver bombs to German tanks. The dogs were trained to recognize the underside of a military tank as a place to find food. A wooden lever mechanism, attached to the back of the dog, would detonate as the dog scurried under the tank, destroying the tank and killing the dog. *See,* e.g., Harvey, Ailsa, "Military animals", *How it Works,* May 29, 2020, at https://www.howitworksdaily.com/military-animals/

[1050] The Marshall Legacy Institute trains "Mine Detection Dogs" to "sniff out" the explosive odors of landmines. https://www.marshall-legacy.org/

[1051] Thompson, Melissa, "Exclusive: The 9 million unsung heroes of WWI: Dogs, horses and carrier pigeons made victory possible", *Mirror*, July 31, 2014.

scrap metal around the city when the war broke out. She wore a special pair of leather boots to help protect her feet at the scrap metal yards.[1052]

By the time that World War II broke out, machines had begun to replace military tasks previously done by animals,[1053] but many animals, including horses, camels, elephants, dogs and pigeons, were still used in conflict.[1054] As panic set in at the start of World War II, the British government urged pet keepers to "take your household animals into the country" and "[i]f you cannot place them in the care of neighbours, it really is kindest to have them destroyed."[1055] The result was devastating: an estimated 750,000 companion animals were put down as a part of Britain's preparation for war.[1056] The grief of losing pets was reflected by In Memoriam notices across the country. One read "Happy memories of Iola, sweet faithful friend, given sleep September 4th 1939, to be saved suffering during the war. A short but happy life—2 years, 12 weeks. Forgive us little pal".[1057] World War II brought unimaginable tragedies to both people and animals.

Zoo animals, already suffering in captivity, suffer more during wars. During World War II, bombings killed 90% of the animals at the Berlin Zoo and hundreds of animals at the Hagenbeck Zoo outside of Hamburg.[1058] Tragically, there were similar stories at other zoos. As author John Kinder wrote, "[f]rom Berlin to London, Tokyo to Paris, Kabul to Baghdad, zoo animals have been bombed, shot, tortured, starved, massacred, and eaten during wartime."[1059]

[1052] *See*, "Lizzie the elephant; how an elephant captured the heart of a city", *The University of Sheffield*, July 7, 2016, at https://www.sheffield.ac.uk/nfca/researchandarticles/lizzieelephant; *see also*, Blog, "Animals and World War 1, Animals Forced Into World War I", *Queensferry at War*, January 11, 2015, at https://queensferry-at-war.weebly.com/interesting-war-facts/animals-and-world-war-1

[1053] Taylor, Alan, "World War I in Photos: Animals at War", *The Atlantic*, April 27, 2014.

[1054] Storey, Neil, "10 Animals That Played an Important Role in the Second World War", *History Hit*, April 13, 2021.

[1055] *See*, Feeney-Hart, Alison, "The little-told story of the massive WWII pet cull", *BBC*, October 12, 2013, quoting from a government pamphlet entitled "Air Raid Precautions Handbook No. 12 (1st Edition), Air Raid Precautions for Animals".

[1056] *See*, Feeney-Hart, Alison, "The little-told story of the massive WWII pet cull", *BBC*, October 12, 2013.

[1057] Id., quoting an In Memoriam notice in the Tail-Wagger Magazine.

[1058] Kinder, John, "Zoo Animals and Modern War: Captive Casualties, Patriotic Citizens, and Good Soldiers" in *Animals and War: Studies of Europe and Northern America*, ed. Ryan Hediger (Boston: Brill, 2013), 45–56.

[1059] Id, at 47.

In the aftermath of the Soviet's withdrawal from Afghanistan in 1989, the Kabul Zoo was heavily damaged and animals were eaten as warring factions battled in Afghanistan.[1060] When Iraq invaded Kuwait on August 1990, Iraqi soldiers indiscriminately killed and injured many mammals, birds, and reptiles at a zoo outside of Kuwait City and ate 75% of the edible animals in the zoo, and when the United States invaded Iraq in March 2003, the Baghdad Zoo was plundered and more than 95% of the captive animals were killed, consumed or left to die of starvation in their cages.[1061] For years, animals at the Taiz Zoo in war torn Yemen have been starving. In 2016, it was reported that 28 critically endangered Arabian leopards had not eaten in 6 days and that 240 other animals were on the verge of starving to death.[1062] By 2021, little had changed, with animals living in squalid conditions and still starving.[1063] Captive animals are dangerous under the best conditions, but unfed animals are more dangerous. In 2021, a Yemeni toddler lost her hand after she reached into a lion's cage in Yemen.[1064] As conflict broke out in Ukraine in 2022, reports again emerged of zoo animals being eaten—this time by Russian soldiers.[1065] Zoos in Ukraine have sustained serious damage during the conflict and most are short of food and supplies,[1066] which will mean death for many animals.[1067]

During the twentieth century, it was not uncommon for zoos to kill animals during wartime.[1068] As John Kinder explained, "zoo professionals have demonstrated an alarming willingness to shoot, gas, pummel, poison,

[1060] Itoh, Mayumi, *Japanese Wartime Zoo Policy: The Silent Victims of World War II*. Palgrave Macmillan, 2010, at 4. ISBN: 978-0-230-11744-0.

[1061] Id., at 3.

[1062] Daly, Natasha, "War-Torn Yemen is Letting Its Zoo Animals Starve to Death", *National Geographic*, December 21, 2016.

[1063] Bunyan, Rachael, "Kings of the jungle reduced to skin and bones: Lions are starving to death at filth-ridden zoo in war-torn Yemen where they are fed once a week and have been 'failed by humans'", *Daily Mail*, July 20, 2021.

[1064] Nasrallah, Tawfiq, "Lion bites off two-year-old girl's hand in Yemen zoo", *Gulf News*, December 12, 2021.

[1065] King, Chris, "Starving Russian soldiers on Ukrainian front line accused of devouring zoo animals', *Euro Weekly News*, November 5, 2022.

[1066] O'Grady, Siobhan and Kostiantyn Khudov, "A blast-stressed elephant and an abandoned lemur: The war within Kyiv's zoo", *Washington Post*, March 6, 2022.

[1067] Winter, Alex, "Ukrainian zoo 'will put down thousands of animals' after Russian shelling", *New York Post*, April 6, 2022.

[1068] Zoo Animals and Modern War, at 56.

starve, even strangle their nonhuman wards in order to preempt their possible escape."[1069] In 1939, the London Zoo destroyed cobras, pythons, anacondas, rattlesnakes and other venomous animals to prevent possible escape during the war.[1070] During World War II, Japanese zoos "disposed of" elephants, lions, tigers, leopards, cheetahs, bears, hippos and other animals.[1071] Zoos have also killed animals in an effort to be humane. During World War I, the Antwerp Zoo killed large cats and bears to prevent their suffering and starvation.[1072] Captive animals at the Gaza Zoo have been victims of the conflict between Israel and Hamas militants over the years,[1073] and in 2020 lions were starving at the Al-Qurashi Park in Khartoum, Sudan.[1074] In war and conflicts, shelter animals also risk death by starvation. In 2022, hundreds of dogs in Ukraine starved to death at a shelter after workers were unable to get to them due to the conflict.[1075]

Military conflicts, training exercises and military-generated contaminants all have profound and devastating consequences on wildlife and ecosystems, including habitat destruction, declines in species populations and loss of biodiversity in aquatic and terrestrial systems.[1076] Landmines are responsible for injuring and killing wildlife, particularly large mammals,[1077] and have pushed some species closer to extinction, including elephants in Africa and leopards in Afghanistan.[1078]

Studies have shown that the bursts of noise from military aircraft, such as sonic booms, can harm wildlife, whose auditory system is more sensitive

[1069] Zoo Animals and Modern War, at 58.

[1070] Itoh, Mayumi, Japanese Wartime Zoo Policy, at 122.

[1071] Itoh, Mayumi, Japanese Wartime Zoo Policy, at 5–6.

[1072] Zoo Animals and Modern War, at 57.

[1073] Pleitgen, Frederik, "Gaza's zoo animals caught in crossfire of Israel-Hamas conflict", *CNN*, August 22, 2014.

[1074] Dahir, Abdi Latif, "Starving Lions in Sudan Spur Campaign to Save Them", *New York Times*, January 22, 2020.

[1075] *See,* e.g., Bazaraa, Danya, "Hundreds of dogs found starved to death at Ukrainian shelter after Russian invasion", *Mirror*, April 2, 2022.

[1076] Lawrence, Michael J., et al., "The effects of modern war and military activities on biodiversity and the environment", *Environmental Reviews*, 23(4): 443–460. https://doi.org/10.1139/er-2015-0039

[1077] *See,* e.g., Westing Arthur H., "Explosive remnants of war in the human environment", *Environmental Conservation*, 23(4): 283–285. https://doi.org/10.1017/S0376892900039102

[1078] *See generally*, Zenda, Cyril, "Demining Efforts Bring Hope for Africa's Wildlife", *Save the Elephants*, January 7, 2022; *see also*, Mydans, Seth, "Mines Main the Ultimate Civilians: Animals", *New York Times*, March 5, 2021.

than that of humans.[1079] The noise from military aircraft can cause ear-drum ruptures and changes in hearing abilities, both temporary or permanent, in wildlife.[1080] Naval blasts and operations involving sonar can adversely impact many aquatic species, causing ear hemorrhaging in, and beach stranding of, dolphins and whales.[1081] Sonars also interfere with the ability of whales to communicate, to reproduce and to detect predators.[1082] At the same time, countries also exploit the extraordinarily abilities of sea animals. Russia has trained belugas to guard naval bases, find lost equipment and assist divers, while the United States has trained dolphins and sea lions to find mines and equipment because sea lions have extraordinary eyesight underwater and the biosonar capabilities of dolphins are far superior than human technology.[1083]

In the name of "peace" and "security," animals and their habitats are being systematically destroyed. The military has a long history of using live animals, including pigs and goats, for "live tissue training" to simulate conditions on a battlefield, during which the animals are shot, cut and have had limbs severed.[1084] One marine, speaking out anonymously, said, "[w]e are compassionate people, trying to save lives but you are part of something that [is] inherently inflicting pain and suffering on an animal".[1085] During Russia's invasion of Ukraine, the world witnessed the devastation that indiscriminate modern weaponry can cause. Ukraine is home to 35% of Europe's biodiversity, despite having just 6% of Europe's

[1079] Manci, Karen M., Douglas N. Gladwin, and Rita Villella, "Effects of Aircraft Noise and Sonic Booms on Domestic Animals and Wildlife: A Literature Synthesis", *U.S. Fish and Wildlife Serv. National Ecology Research Center, Ft. Collins, CO.* 1998. NERC 88/29.

[1080] Lawrence, Michael J., et al., "The effects of modern war and military activities on biodiversity and the environment", *NRC Research Press*, September 14, 2015.

[1081] Id.; *see also*, "Ocean Pollution: The Dirty Facts: Ocean Noise", *NRDC*, June 7, 2022, at https://www.nrdc.org/stories/ocean-pollution-dirty-facts

[1082] Rendell, L.E. and Gordon J.C.D., "Vocal Response of Long-Finned Pilot Whales (Globicephala Melas) to military sonar in the Ligurian Sea", *Marine Mammal Science*, 15, 198–204. https://doi.org/10.1111/j.1748-7692.1999.tb00790.x. *See also*, Miller P.J., et al., "Whale songs lengthen in response to sonar", *Nature*, 405, 903 (2000). https://doi.org/10.1038/35016148

[1083] Guy, Jack and Dixon, Emily, "'Russian spy' whale shines spotlight on military-grade animals", *CNN*, May 4, 2019.

[1084] August, J.W., Payton, Mari. "Marines Speak Out About Using Live Animals in Trauma Training". February 7, 2017.

[1085] Id.

landmass,[1086] and the conflict has created not just a humanitarian disaster but an ecological disaster as well. In fact, the horrors of modern warfare threaten nearly all life on the planet.

The testing of nuclear weapons poses a grave threat to wildlife.[1087] As of the late 1990s, more than 2000 nuclear weapons have been tested around the world, leaving many areas uninhabitable.[1088] The Chernobyl nuclear disaster in 1986 released the largest radioactivity into the environment in world history, and in the immediate aftermath, radiation destroyed wildlife and the environment.[1089] Evacuees were forced to leave companion animals behind, and many were subsequently killed in an effort to prevent the spread of radiation. Some survived the extermination effort, and their descendants live in the Chernobyl Exclusion Zone today.[1090] Despite the fact that the Chernobyl Exclusion Zone is one of the most radioactively contaminated sites in the world, today a diverse array of wildlife thrive in the zone because of the absence of humans.[1091] Wildlife can flourish more in a nuclear disaster zone than when humans are present!

Recent Developments for Animals in Human Conflicts

Legal protection for animals in the context of human conflicts is slow to develop because national security interests are nearly always prioritized over the interests of animals. The United States Department of Defense did approve a long overdue policy in 2023 to reimburse service members

[1086] See, "Fifth National Report of Ukraine to the Convention on Biological Diversity", at https://www.cbd.int/doc/world/ua/ua-nr-05-en.pdf

[1087] *See*, Xiaoping Yang, et al., "Worldwide Nuclear Explosions", *International Geophysics Series*, 81(B), 2003, at https://www.ldeo.columbia.edu/~richards/my_papers/WW_nuclear_tests_IASPEI_HB.pdf

[1088] "International Day against Nuclear Tests, 29 August, Ending Nuclear Testing", *United Nations*, n.d., at https://www.un.org/en/observances/end-nuclear-tests-day/history

[1089] *See*, Beresford, N.A., E.M. Scott and D. Copplestone, "Field effects studies in the Chernobyl Exclusion Zone: Lessons to be learnt", *Journal of Environmental Radioactivity"*, Vol. 211 (2020). https://doi.org/10.1016/j.jenvrad.2019.01.005

[1090] In recent years there have been efforts to help dogs in the Chernobyl exclusion zone. *See*, Berkhead, Samantha, "How the Dogs of Chernobyl Found a Happy Ending", *Moscow Times*, October 31, 2019.

[1091] Canales, Katie, "There's a thriving population of radioactive animals that have taken over the abandoned Chernobyl exclusion zone, even though the area is toxic for humans", *Business Insider*, April 26, 2020.

for pet travel expenses incurred during a permanent change in station,[1092] but the Department of Defense (DOD) has failed to implement its own stated policy of refining, reducing and replacing the use of animals for trauma training.

In 2014, the DOD announced that starting in 2015, it would reduce the number of live animals used in medical training and instead rely more on simulation models for training and education.[1093] As of 2022, however, the DOD has not been able to demonstrate what progress it has made. A study found that the DOD had failed to establish measurable objectives and performance benchmarks to track their progress in reducing the number of animals used in trauma training,[1094] calling into question the DOD's commitment to follow their own guidelines. The DOD still shoots, stabs, burns and conducts amputations on thousands of pigs and goats and 20 vervet monkeys every year to train Army medics, Navy corpsmen and Air Force personnel.[1095] It is estimated that the United States military uses more than 8500 pigs and goats every year in military trauma training.[1096] In 2018, the Coast Guard permanently ended the use of animals in combat trauma training[1097] after a temporary suspension in 2017,[1098] but there is no indication that the other branches of the U.S. military will end the cruel and unnecessary practice.

[1092] "Department of Defense Approves Policy to Reimburse Pet Expenses Due to a Permanent Change of Station", *U.S. Department of Defense*, June 21, 2023.

[1093] Sisk, Richard, "Military Removes Live Animals from Combat Medical Training", *U.S. Military News,* November 12, 2014, at https://www.military.com/daily-news/2014/11/12/military-removes-live-animals-from-combat-medical-training.html#

[1094] The GAO evaluated progress made by the DOD in reducing and replacing the use of live animals for trauma training. *See*, "DOD Animal Use: Objectives and Performance Measures Needed to Monitor Use of Alternatives for Trauma Training", GAO-22-103,992 (report to congressional requesters), May 3, 2022, at https://www.gao.gov/assets/gao-22-103992.pdf

[1095] The Department of Defense claims that the animals are always deeply anaesthetized for the entire process and humanely euthanized after the training. *See*, Martinic, Gary, "Military 'live tissue trauma training' using animals in the US – its purpose, importance and commentary on military medical research and the debate on use of animals in military training", *JMVH*, Vol. 20, No. 4. https://doi-ds.org/doilink/11.2021-29442211/JMVHVol20No4

[1096] *See*, Klimas, Jacqueline, "The military kills 8500 pigs and goats every year for medical training. A new bill would end that", *Washington Examiner*, March 4, 2017.

[1097] Seck, Hope Hodge, "Coast Guard Puts Permanent End to Wounding Animals for Training", *Military*, March 20, 2018.

[1098] Bever, Lindsey, "Coast Guard suspends practice of shooting, stabbing and dismembering animals in trauma training", *Washington Post,* April 28, 2017.

The issue of "live tissue training" has drawn sharp criticism from both sides of the political aisle in the United States. Congressional representatives, Matt Cartwright (D-Pa) and Ted Lieu (D-Cal), expressed serious concerns with the military's live tissue training, which "involves intentionally wounding live animals—usually stabbing, burning and shooting pigs and goats, and sometimes even dogs—and then having trainees crudely attempt to repair the damage".[1099] As the representatives explained, live tissue training "is expensive, obsolete, unnecessary and opposed by most Americans."[1100] In 2017, the Battlefield Excellence through Superior Training Practices Act was introduced in Congress to require human-based methods only for military combat training[1101] but the legislation has not been passed into law.

In this regard, the United States again finds itself as an outlier vis-à-vis some other countries. As of December 2014, nearly 80% of NATO countries did not use animals for purposes of military training.[1102] When the military in Norway applied to use live animals for military training exercises, the application was denied by the Norwegian Animal Research Authority, which found that the need to use animals instead of other alternatives was insufficient.[1103] As is the case with other animal research, by using outdated and inferior training methods for its members, the military is behind the times.

Companion Animals

Humanity's closest bond with the animal kingdom is with companion animals. Dogs and cats are considered to be members of many households, sharing meals and vacations and nearly half sharing sleeping accommodations with their human guardians.[1104] Americans spent billions of dollars

[1099] *See*, Frazin, Rachel, "Lawmakers express concern to DOJ over training involving 'stabbing, burning and shooting' animals", *The Hill*, October 16, 2019, quoting from a letter from Representatives Matt Cartwright (D-Pa) and Ted Lieu (D-Cal) to the Department of Defense.

[1100] Ibid.

[1101] Battlefield Excellence through Superior Training Practices Act or "BEST Practices Act" - H.R. 1243, 115th Congress (2017–2018).

[1102] Economic Voice Staff, "Norway Rejects Military Application to Use Live Pigs in Deadly Training Exercises", *Economic Voice*, December 18, 2014.

[1103] Ibid.

[1104] *See*, "Almost half of Americans sleep with pets", *American Academy of Sleep Medicine*, June 7, 2022, at https://medicalxpress.com/news/2022-06-americans-pets.html

on their companions, lavishing them with toys, treats and daycare.[1105] In 2021, over $123 billion dollars was spent on animal companions, up from $103 billion dollars in 2020.[1106] Our companions provide emotional and social support,[1107] and among millennial women without children, 70% consider their dog or cat to be a child.[1108]

Companions are included in last wills and testaments, fought over in divorces, buried in memorial gardens, and included in cultural traditions and religious practices. The No Kill Advocacy Center reports that 96% of Americans believe that we have a moral duty to protect animals and that we should have strong laws to do that.[1109] While it is true that companion animals are afforded more legal protection than, for instance, farmed animals, in the form of anti-cruelty laws, the notion that our companions are sufficiently protected is false.[1110]

Laws everywhere fail to protect companions from many threats, including homelessness, meat farms, research labs, abuse and death. Rescue animals are especially vulnerable under the law. Neglected and abused dogs are often traumatized, and like humans, they can suffer from post-traumatic stress syndrome, which can make them more defensive and aggressive. Like many rescue dogs, Petey was traumatized by severe neglect and abuse by his former owner. At the veterinarian, when the technician attempted

[1105] The daycare market for animals was valued at $1.12 billion in 2021 and is only expected to grow. *See*, Market Analysis Report, "U.S. Pet Daycare Market Size, Share & Trends Analysis Report by Pet Type (Dogs (Large Breeds, Medium Breeds, Small Breeds), Cats) by Service Type (Day Boarding, Pet Sitting), by Delivery Channel, and Segment Forecasts, 2022–2030", Report ID: GVR-4-68039-943-2, *Grand View Research*, Historical Range: 2017–2020.

[1106] *See*, "Pet Industry Market Size, Trends & Ownership Statistics, Total U.S. Pet Industry Expenditures", *American Pet Products Association*, n.d., at https://www.americanpetproducts.org/press_IndustryTrends.asp

[1107] For more on the role of companion animals in our emotional and spiritual wellbeing, *see* Kateryna, Muliutina, et al., "The Role of Pets in Preserving the Emotional and Spiritual Wellbeing of Ukrainian Residents During Russian Hostilities", *Journal of Religion and Health*, Vol. 62, 500–509 (2023). https://doi.org/10.1007/s10943-022-01669-4

[1108] *See*, Velez, Lily, "As Birth Rates in US Plummet, Are Pets Standing In For Children?", *Veterinarians.org*, January 26, 2023.

[1109] "Statistics", *No Kill Advocacy Center*, n.d., at https://www.nokilladvocacycenter.org/no-kill

[1110] Companion animals have not always been protected under the law. *See*, e.g., Commonwealth v. Massini, 1963 (holding that a cat is not a "domestic animal" for purposes of anti-cruelty statute); *see also*, McKinney v. Robbins, 1995 (holding that "domesticated animals" is limited to livestock, not domestic pets). Statutes have since been updated.

to muzzle Petey, she was bitten. Fortunately for Petey, the new owner advocated for him and had records to show that he was up to date on his rabies shots. Otherwise, Petey could have been euthanized as an aggressive dog so that he could be tested for rabies.[1111] Still, rescues are more fortunate than homeless animals.

While it is impossible to know the exact number of homeless animals in the United States, and estimates do vary,[1112] it is believed that there are around 70 million homeless dogs and cats.[1113] Worldwide, it is estimated that there are 200 million stray dogs[1114] and 480 million homeless cats.[1115] Homeless animals face many threats, including hunger, extreme weather, vehicles, wildlife, disease, abuse and extermination. Stray animals have been subject to mass culling campaigns by many countries, including Pakistan,[1116] Egypt,[1117] Russia,[1118] Indonesia,[1119] Turkey,[1120] Morocco,[1121]

[1111] *See*, "What to do with an animal that has bitten a person", *Centers for Disease Control and Prevention*, n.d., at https://www.cdc.gov/rabies/specific_groups/veterinarians/person_bitten.html#

[1112] *See*, e.g., Meiners, Joan, "Booming feral cat populations are a disaster, science says. Here are 15 reasons why.", *NOLA*, July 3, 2018; *see also*, "How many stray cats are in the United States?", *Animal Control – Stray Cats, Education and Information to help with stray cat issues in the United States*, n.d., at http://www.aaanimalcontrol.com/professional-trapper/howmanystraycats.html

[1113] *See*, e.g., Stancheva, Terry, "Stray Animal Statistics – What Are the Actual Numbers in 2022", *Pawsome Advice*, January 9, 2022.

[1114] *See*, Strand, Patti, "The Global Stray Dog Population Crisis", *National Animal Interest Alliance*, November 17, 2011, citing an estimate from the World Health Organization.

[1115] Cat Insider Editorial Team, "How Many Cats are in the World", *Basepaws*, October 11, 2022.

[1116] "A Mass Culling of Strays in Pakistan: 25,000 Dogs Expected to be Killed in The Next Few Weeks, OIPA International Writes to the Prime Minister", *OIPA*, March 30, 2021.

[1117] "Animal activists outraged over Egyptian government killing of stray dogs", *Al-Monitor*, January 14, 2021.

[1118] Samedova, Evlaliya, "Russia World Cup plan to cull stray dogs outrages activists", *DW*, June 3, 2018.

[1119] Rkaina, Sam, "Horrific video shows officials in Bali SMILING while they cull island dogs on death row", *Irish Mirror*, July 24, 2014.

[1120] Farhoud, Nada, "Campaigners call for Turkey holidays boycott over 'dog genocides'", *Mirror*, January 30, 2022.

[1121] Hooper, Olivia, "Stray Dogs Killed in Morocco Ahead of FIFA Club World Cup", *Morocco World News*, January 26, 2023.

Dubai,[1122] Turkmenistan[1123] and India.[1124] In 2022, Iran reportedly slaughtered 1700 stray dogs at an animal shelter. Proposed legislation in Iran may strip people of the right to have companion animals.[1125] In nearly every country, strays lack the legal right to food, shelter and basic veterinary care.

Of the approximately 6.3 million homeless animals who enter animal shelters in the United States every year, roughly 920,000 are euthanized (down from 2.6 million euthanized in 2011).[1126] A majority of states now ban euthanasia by gas chamber as cruel and inhumane, and states that still use gas chambers receive significant public backlash.[1127] Spay and neuter advocacy and rescue adoption campaigns are making a difference, but the failure of laws to mandate spay and neutering and to ban puppy mills, kitten factories and (until recently) pet store sales has led to the euthanasia of millions of healthy animals. The lack of proper USDA oversight of breeders has allowed shocking instances of cruelty. One Iowa dog breeder was permitted to rack up more than 100 violations of the Animal Welfare Act involving more than 500 dogs before being shut down.[1128] In Iowa, civil fines and license suspensions are rare and a misdemeanor charge of animal neglect in Iowa carries a fine of just $65.[1129] We deny adequate legal protection to our faithful companions, even as we demand so much from them.

[1122] "Dogs and cats killed in Dubai for the Expo: LNDC writes to the Ambassador", *Euro Group For Animals*, September 28, 2020.

[1123] RFE/RL's Turkmen Service, "Turkmen Authorities Hire Children to Help Cull Stray Dogs, Cats", *Radio Free Europe, Radio Liberty*, February 8, 2022.

[1124] *See*, e.g., "India dog cull causes controversy and heartache", *BBC*, September 6, 2015.

[1125] The proposed law views pet ownership as a "destructive social problem" and a sign of decadence. *See*, Averre, David, "Dog shelter worker cries over dead animal after Iranian regime 'raids property and slaughters 1700 canines taken in as strays', *Daily Mail*, August 3, 2022; *see also*, Hamedani, Ali, "The country where having a pet could soon land you in jail", *BBC*, July 19, 2022.

[1126] *See*, "Pet Statistics", *ASPCA*, n.d., at https://www.aspca.org/helping-people-pets/shelter-intake-and-surrender/pet-statistics

[1127] *See*, e.g., Bartov, Shira Li, "Shelter Using Gas Chambers to Euthanize Dogs Sparks Outrage in Viral Video", *Newsweek*, April 29, 2022.

[1128] For the complaint, *see United States of America v. Daniel Gingerich,* Case 4:21-cv-00283-SMR-SHL filed September 27, 2021 in the United States District Court for the Southern District of Iowa, Central Division.

[1129] Kauffman, Clark, "Financial penalties for animal neglect are small, rare and may go unpaid", *Iowa Capital Dispatch*, October 17, 2021.

Guide dogs assist the blind. Therapy dogs provide emotional support in hospital, nursing home and therapy settings.[1130] Service dogs help with daily tasks and assist the disabled, including hearing, sight and mobility impaired individuals.[1131] Police dogs serve our communities. "Crisis response" dogs bring their calming presence to help us during times of disaster, such as in the aftermath of a mass shooting, an act of terrorism or a natural disaster.[1132] Rescue and recovery dogs, like the ones who assisted in the aftermath of 9/11, help us locate survivors and to bring our dead home. Herding dogs shepherd cattle or sheep. Detection or sniffer dogs can find illegal drugs, explosives, missing people, cancer[1133] and Covid-19 infections.[1134] There are compelling reasons why the extraordinary bond between people and their animal companions should be recognized in our laws.

Some guardians will refuse to go to a shelter during hurricanes unless their animal companions are welcomed. During Hurricane Katrina, nearly 50% of people who refused to evacuate did so because they did not want to leave their pets behind, prompting the passage of the Pets Evacuation and Transportation Standards (PETS) Act in 2005.[1135] Many renters will pass on an apartment unless their companions are accepted. With 70% of

[1130] For more on therapy dogs, *see* "What is a 'Therapy Dog'?", *Therapy Dogs of Vermont*, n.d., at https://therapydogs.org/news-articles/benefits-therapy-dogs/what-is-a-therapy-dog/

[1131] A service dog is defined by the American With Disabilities Act as a dog that is "individually trained to do work or perform tasks for people with disabilities." *See*, "ADA Requirements, Service Animals", *U.S. Department of Justice, Civil Rights Division, Disability Rights Section*, February 28, 2020, at https://www.ada.gov/service_animals_2010.htm

[1132] For more on crisis response dogs, *see* "when someone is hurting there are things we can do", *National Crisis Response Canines*, n.d., at https://crisisresponsecanines.org/

[1133] *See*, e.g., Feil, Charlotte, et al., "Sniffer dogs can identify lung cancer patients from breath and urine samples", *BMC Cancer*, 21, 917 (2021). https://doi.org/10.1186/s12885-021-08651-5

[1134] *See*, Bednar, Hailey, "A New Tool in the Toolkit: Dogs Help to Detect COVID-19", *CDC Foundation*, n.d., at https://www.cdcfoundation.org/stories/project-uses-dogs-detect-covid-19

[1135] Pets Evacuation and Transportation Standards Act of 2006, Public Law 109-308, amending the *Robert T. Stafford Disaster Relief and Emergency Assistance Act*, to ensure that the needs of households with animals are addressed by state and local emergency preparedness plans during a major disaster or emergency. *See generally*, "Katrina's Lesson Learned: Animals No Longer Excluded from Storm Evacuations", *Animal Welfare Institute Quarterly* (Winter 2017).

American households having at least one companion,[1136] landlords with pet restrictions miss out on a large number of potential renters. The bond with our companions is so strong that people will risk their own lives to save their animal,[1137] yet our laws still classify them as mere "property."

Dogfighting is a felony in all 50 states,[1138] the District of Columbia, Guam, Puerto Rico and the U.S. Virgin Islands, yet dogfighting continues to be a pervasive problem. In response, the Sentencing Commission increased the recommended minimum prison sentence for animal fighting offenses from 6–12 months to 21–27 months.[1139] Animal fighting crimes seem to be prioritized by law enforcement when they are associated with other crimes, and in fact, animal fighting rings are often linked to a host of other crimes, including, inter alia, illicit weapons, illegal drugs, gambling, extortion, racketeering, arson, assaults, domestic violence, sexual crimes, and child abuse.[1140] There are periodic reports of indictments involving animal fighting rings, but there are far too few in light of the estimated tens of thousands of dog fighters across the United States.[1141] We must do much better.

Recent Developments for Companion Animals

Global animal welfare standards for companion animals are changing. In adopting new animal protection measures in 2018, Luxembourg acknowledged that attitudes toward animals have "substantially changed," requiring a fundamentally new legal approach that recognizes the dignity of animals. Declaring that animals are companions who provide comfort and

[1136] "Pet Industry Market Size, Trends & Ownership Statistics, 2021–2022 AAPA National Pet Owners Survey Statistics: Pet Ownership & Annual Expenses", *American Pet Products Association*.

[1137] *See*, Haglage, Abby, "Why people will give their lives to save their pets", *Yahoo*, February 27, 2018.

[1138] In 2014, South Dakota became the 50th state to enact felony penalties for malicious acts of animal cruelty. *See generally*, "Finally – All 50 States Have Felony Animal Abuse States", *National Coalition on Violence Against Animals"*, March 17, 2014.

[1139] Wheeler, Lydia, "Sentencing commission votes to increase penalties for dog fighters", *The Hill*, April 15, 2016.

[1140] *See*, "The Criminal, Underground World of Dogfighting", n.d., at https://www.aspca.org/investigations-rescue/dogfighting

[1141] The estimates are from the ASPCA. *See*, Press Release: "ASPCA National Poll Reveals Dogfighting Goes Underreported Despite Hundreds of Thousands of Dogs Being Forced to Fight Nationwide", *ASPCA*, April 3, 2018.

moral support, the law recognizes that "[a]nimals are no longer considered as objects but as partners."[1142] This sentiment is being memorialized by a wave of new anti-cruelty laws around the globe.

Some countries, like Lebanon, are enacting first ever animal welfare laws,[1143] while other countries, like Turkey,[1144] the UAE,[1145] Taiwan,[1146] Guatemala[1147] and El Salvador,[1148] are strengthening anti-cruelty laws. In 2018, Russia enacted The Law on Responsible Treatment of Animals to increase the protection of companion animals and strays,[1149] and Greece updated its animal cruelty laws to provide for penalties of up to 10 years in jail.[1150] In China, there are calls for renewed laws to protect companion animals.[1151] In Prague, selfies with animals is considered a form of animal abuse.[1152] Still, not all countries have anti-cruelty laws. In Iran, there have been unsuccessful attempts to pass anti-cruelty legislation.[1153] In Azerbaijan, there have been allegations of violence against those who criticize government sanctioned animal cruelty.[1154]

[1142] The Luxembourg Government, "Animal protection in Luxembourg", Background, at http://gouvernement.lu/en/dossiers/2018/tierschutz.html

[1143] AFP, "Lebanon gets first animal protection law", *Arab News*, August 29, 2017.

[1144] *See generally*, "AK Party introduces Turkey's much-awaited animal rights bill", *Daily Sabah*, July 1, 2021.

[1145] The new UAE law prohibits the abandonment of animals and requires proper food, shelter and veterinary care. *See generally*, Staff Report, "New UAE rule: Failure to care for pets will be punishable by law", *Gulf News*, December 12, 2018.

[1146] The new law strengthens penalties for animal cruelty. *See*, "Animal Protection further enhanced in Taiwan", *Taiwan Today*, April 12, 2017.

[1147] *See generally*, Casagrande, Orsola, "Guatemala Protects Animal Rights: Landmark Legislation in the Fight Against Cruelty", *Global Rights*, March 4, 2017.

[1148] *See*, Ramos, Karla, "Salvadoran Legislature Approves El Salvador Animal Welfare Law", *El Salvador Info*, January 27, 2022.

[1149] Federal Law No. 498-FZ "On responsible treatment of animals", *Russian Federation*, December 27, 2018.

[1150] GCT, "Animal abusers in Greece will face up to 10 years in jail", *Greek City Times*, November 7, 2020.

[1151] Wong, Hayley, "China's 'two sessions' 2023: lawmaker calls for legal protections for pets", *South China Monitoring Post*, March 11, 2023.

[1152] Iolov, Tzvetozar Vincent, "In Prague: taking selfies with animals is a form of abuse', *The Mayor*, August 1, 2023.

[1153] Dehghanpisheh, Babak, "Pressure mounts in Iran for law against animal cruelty after videos cause outrage", *Reuters*, August 18, 2016.

[1154] Geybullayeva, Arzu, "Blood and democracy: the right for animal rights in Azerbaijan", *Global Voices*, October 7, 2022.

Dedicated police divisions, like the one created in Turkey,[1155] are tracking animal cruelty online, while dedicated law enforcement teams, like the Animal Welfare Police Team established in Helsinki, Finland, focus exclusively on animal protection.[1156] Anti-cruelty training is also becoming more prevalent both in the United States and elsewhere,[1157] and animal welfare is being added to public school curricula around the world.[1158]

Countries are also passing laws to crack down on puppy and kitten farming. The U.K. recently passed "Lucy's Law,"[1159] which bans third-party commercial sales of dogs and cats, and some parts of Canada, including Montreal,[1160] Toronto[1161] and Vancouver,[1162] have restricted pet store sales. India has taken steps to regulate animal breeding,[1163] while other countries are adopting measures to protect homeless animals. In 2017, Nepal's Supreme Court banned the killing of street dogs and mandated a nationwide humane management plan for homeless animals.[1164] In India, the Delhi High Court ruled that stray dogs have the right to food (and that citizens have the right to feed them) because animals have the "right to be treated with compassion, respect and dignity." The High Court also reiterated the responsibility that the State and every citizen has to protect

[1155] Kizilkoyun, Fevzi, "Turkey police set up new division to track animal cruelty online", *Hurriyet Daily News*, December 3, 2017.

[1156] Koskela, Tarja, "The Roles of the Finish Authorities Specializing in Animal Welfare Offences", Section 4.1 (Animal Welfare Police in Finland), at https://scandinavianlaw.se/pdf/67-7.pdf

[1157] *See,* e.g., "NSA Releases New Animal Cruelty Resource for Law Enforcement", *National Sheriffs' Association*, November 8, 2018.

[1158] Animal welfare and responsible pet ownership are being introduced in school curriculum in El Salvador. *See,* Ramos, Karla, "Salvadoran Legislature Approves El Salvador Animal Welfare Law", *El Salvador Info*, January 27, 2022. In China, an animal welfare curriculum is being offered. *See,* "Chinese high schools to offer official animal welfare module for the first time ever", *Animals Asia,* January 30, 2018.

[1159] U.K. Department for Environment, Food & Rural Affairs, "Lucy's Law spells the beginning of the end for puppy farming", April 6, 2020.

[1160] Leavitt, Sarah, "New rule forcing Montreal pet stores to get their animals from shelters garners mixed reviews", *CBC News*, June 16, 2018.

[1161] The Staff, "Toronto becomes second Canadian city to ban puppy mill sales in pet stores", *Global News*, September 22, 2011.

[1162] Dunham, Jackie, "Vancouver bans pet shop sales of cats, dogs and rabbits", *CTV News*, June 29, 2017.

[1163] *See generally*, Singh, Rajesh, "Be Aware of Regulations Related to Dog Breeding in India", *Pashudhan Praharee,* October 28, 2022.

[1164] A Humane World, Pacelle, Wayne, "Nepal's Supreme Court ends mass killings of street dogs", *The Humane Society of the United States,* December 8, 2017.

animals from hunger, thirst and malnutrition.[1165] Contrast these rights to Florida, where it is illegal to feed starving manatees.[1166]

Sterilization programs like the ABC (Animal Birth Control) program in India[1167] work but they are often undertaken by underfunded nongovernmental organizations and are voluntary. Legally mandated and fully funded programs would be much more effective in controlling homeless animal populations. The Netherlands proved that managing homeless animals can be done humanely when it became the first nation to solve its stray dog problem, not with mass killings, but with its CNVR (Collect, Neuter, Vaccinate, and Return) program, which the World Animal Protection Agency believes is the most effective model for controlling stray animal populations.[1168]

Anti-mutilation laws are also becoming more common. Many countries have banned cat declawing (or permit it only in extreme cases, such as injury or disease), including Australia, Austria, Belgium, Bosnia and Herzegovina, Brazil, Bulgaria, the Czech Republic, Denmark (excluding Greenland and Faroe Islands), England, Finland, France, Germany, Greece, Ireland, Israel, Italy, Latvia, Lithuania, Luxembourg, Macedonia, Malta, Montenegro, The Netherlands, New Zealand, Northern Ireland, Norway, Portugal, Romania, Scotland, Serbia, Slovenia, Spain, Sweden, Switzerland, Turkey and Wales.[1169] In 2018, Nova Scotia became the first Canadian province to ban cat declawing[1170] and today eight of Canada's 10 provinces have banned declawing.[1171] Some countries have also banned

[1165] The court ruled that the right to feed stray dogs may not impinge upon the rights of others. *See*, Dr. Maya D. Chablani, Plaintiff, v. Radha Mittal & ORS., Defendants, In The High Court of Delhi at New Delhi, June 24, 2021. I.A. No. 4164/2021 In CS (OS) 277/2020, at https://indiankanoon.org/doc/167511972/

[1166] *See*, "Living with Florida Manatees", *Florida Fish and Wildlife Conservation Commission*, n.d., at https://myfwc.com/conservation/you-conserve/wildlife/manatee/

[1167] Nazareth, Keren, and Patel, Piyush, "Animal Birth Control for street dog management: It's time for an upgrade", *Citizen Matters*, August 26, 2022.

[1168] Higher taxes are also imposed on store-bought dogs to encourage homeless dog adoptions. *See*, Sawbridge, Freya, "How did the Netherlands become the first country without stray dogs?", *Dutch Review*, July 27, 2022.

[1169] "Cat-Friendly Cities, States, and Countries Where Declawing is Illegal", *PETA*, September 20, 2022.

[1170] Stackelberg, Marina, "Nova Scotia becomes 1st province to ban cat declawing", *CBC News*, March 15, 2018.

[1171] "Cat-Friendly Cities, States, and Countries Where Declawing is Illegal", *PETA*, September 20, 2022.

ear cropping, including Australia, New Zealand, England and Wales.[1172] In the United States, only two states, New York[1173] and Maryland,[1174] have adopted laws to ban cat declawing, as have nearly one dozen cities.[1175] There has been more progress in the United States with regard to puppy and kitten farming.

To date, 7 U.S. states have adopted laws to ban the retail sale of companion animals, including California,[1176] Maryland,[1177] Illinois, [1178] Maine,[1179] Washington,[1180] New York[1181] and Oregon.[1182] In addition, more than 400 cities and localities have banned the retail sale of companion animals.[1183] Like other animal welfare measures, humane pet sale laws have faced relentless legal challenges by special interests, but to date the laws have all been upheld.[1184] While states have not enacted mandatory spay and neuter laws for pet guardians, nearly two-thirds of states do

[1172] Ear cropping, tail docking and debarking are prohibited in Australia. *See*, "Prohibited procedures to dogs" (Legislative summary), *Victoria State Government, Animal Welfare Victoria*. Ear cropping is also banned in New Zealand. *See*, Animal Welfare (Care and Procedures) Regulations 2018, Section 58D (Prohibition on cropping dogs' ears). Ear cropping is illegal in England and Wales under the Animal Welfare Act 2006, Section 5 (Mutilation).

See generally, "Ear cropping: Dogs need their ears – and here's why". *RSPCA*, at https://www.rspca.org.uk/-/blog-ear-cropping

[1173] NY Agri & Mkts L §318 (2019).

[1174] SB 67/HB 22, Animal Welfare – Declawing Cats – Prohibited Acts (April 21, 2022).

[1175] *See*, e.g., West Hollywood's ban on declawing at Municipal Code §9.49.020. *See generally*, "Cat-Friendly Cities, States, and Countries Where Declawing is Illegal", *PETA*, September 20, 2022.

[1176] Cal. Health & Safety Code, Division 105, Ch. 5, §122354.5.

[1177] Md. Code, Bus. Reg., Title 19, Subtitle 7, §§ 19-701 to 19-707.

[1178] 225 ILCS 605, §3.8.

[1179] MRS Title 7, Ch. 745 (Sale of Dogs and Cats), §4153(3).

[1180] RCW, Title 16, Ch. 16.52, §16.52.360.

[1181] Puppy Mill Pipeline Act - S.1130/A.4283 (Prohibits the sale of dogs, cats and rabbits by retail pet shops), signed by the governor on December 15, 2022.

[1182] House Bill 2915, Relating to sales of certain animals by retail pet stores, signed by the governor on July 27, 2023.

[1183] For a complete list of jurisdictions that have banned retail pet sales, see "States with Humane Pet Sales Laws", *Best Friends*, n.d., at https://bestfriends.org/advocacy/ending-puppy-mills/states-humane-pet-sales-laws

[1184] *See*, e.g., Bailey, Lorraine, "Chicago Ban on Puppy Mill Upheld by 7th Circuit", *Courthouse News Service*, September 22, 2017; *see also*, Lewis, Truman, "Court upholds NYC law targeting puppy mills", *Consumer Affairs*, March 3, 2017.

require sterilization of shelter animals before they are released.[1185] Disturbingly, politicians in some states, such as Indiana, are attempting to block humane pet sale laws.[1186] Such special interest 'ban the ban' attempts are grossly out of step with public sentiment and benefit only a tiny, but wealthy, percentage of constituents who profit from puppy mills. Still, new laws are making a difference. In 2019, Delaware became the first no-kill state for shelter animals.[1187]

In 1829, New York became the first state to adopt anti-cruelty legislation,[1188] but it would be nearly two centuries later before the federal government enacted the Preventing Animal Cruelty and Torture (PACT) Act,[1189] which prohibits intentional cruelty to animals. The United States enacted the Animal Crush Video Prohibition Act[1190] in 2010, but the law is too narrow and does not apply to underlying acts of animal cruelty. The PACT Act enables federal prosecutors to file charges in cases where the cruelty is beyond the reach of a state or in instances where the state lacks resources to prosecute the case. Unfortunately, the law excludes animals raised for food and animals used in medical or scientific research,[1191] despite reports of cruelty in these settings. In 2016, the FBI began tracking animal cruelty cases,[1192] and the Uniform Code of Military Justice was amended to prohibit animal cruelty on United States military bases worldwide.[1193] Americans have a low tolerance for animal cruelty, as one popular

[1185] *See*, "Mandatory Spay/Neuter Laws", *American Veterinary Medical Association*, June 2019.

[1186] Indiana General Assembly (2023 Session), House Bill 1121 and Senate Bill 134, which would prohibit the adoption of an ordinance or regulation that would prohibit the sale of companion animals.

[1187] Jackson, Amanda, "Delaware is being recognized as the first no-kill State for animal shelters", *CNN*, August 11, 2019.

[1188] N.Y. Rev. stat. tit. 6,26 (1829).

[1189] Preventing Animal Cruelty and Torture (PACT) Act, Public Law 116-72 (November 25, 2019).

[1190] Animal Crush Video Prohibition Act, Public Law 111-294, 111th Congress, December 9, 2010. The law replaces the prior Animal Crush Video Prohibition Act of 1999, Public Law 106-152, which was held to be overly broad and unconstitutional by the Supreme Court on First Amendment grounds.

[1191] Public Law 116-72, §48(d)(1)(B) and –(D), November 25, 2019.

[1192] "Tracking Animal Cruelty, FBI Collecting Data on Crimes Against Animals", *FBI News*, February 1, 2016.

[1193] Pacelle, Wayne, "Obama signs executive order closing animal cruelty loophole on U.S. military cases", *Huffington Post*, December 6, 2017.

presidential candidate discovered when he thought that stowing his dog on the roof of his vehicle for a trip was a good idea.[1194]

Recent legal reforms protect both people and their animal companions, including registration and oversight requirements for animal shelters,[1195] state bans on "pet licensing" arrangements (i.e., making animals subject to "repossession" upon nonpayment),[1196] and state laws requiring that cats and dogs used in research be held for adoption once the research is complete. To date, Minnesota, California, Connecticut, Delaware, Illinois, Maryland, Massachusetts, Nevada, New York, Rhode Island, Washington, Oregon and Virginia have enacted so-called Beagle Freedom laws,[1197] which require healthy cats and dogs used in research to be offered up for adoption instead of being euthanized. Beagle Freedom bills are also pending in Colorado, Indiana, New Jersey, Texas and Wisconsin.[1198] There are no federal laws that regulate animal rescues or foster care homes for animals, and very few states have taken up this issue. In 2022, Florida did enact a law to provide subsidized veterinary care for retired law enforcement dogs,[1199] which honors the service of both the animal and his or her handler.

Still, homeless animals have ended up in animal shelters, only to be sold to laboratories for research and euthanized upon completion of the research. Over a half century ago, *Life Magazine* first reported on the unthinking practice of companion animals being stolen and sold to research laboratories.[1200] It would be 56 years later, in 2022, that Congress

[1194] During the 2008 and 2012 U.S. presidential elections, Mitt Romney received negative media attention and was the subject of political attacks for driving a reported 12 hours with his dog secured to the top of his car in a carrier.

[1195] *See,* e.g., State of Connecticut, Regulation of Department of Agriculture Concerning Kennels, Pet Shops, Grooming Facilities, Training Facilities, Animal Importers, and Animal Shelters", §§ 22-344-32 to 22-344-90; *see also*, MD Code, Agriculture, §§ 2-1701 to 2-1707, requiring animal shelters to establish written protocols for dogs and cats that are consistent with the most recent Association of Shelter Veterinarians' Guidelines for Standards of Care in Animal Shelters.

[1196] *See generally*, Lalljee, Jason, "42 states still allow pet leasing – meaning Fido could get repossessed just like your house or car", *Business Insider*, April 16, 2022.

[1197] "Beagle Freedom" laws are named after beagles who are frequently used in research due to their friendly and docile dispositions.

[1198] *See generally*, "Help Pass The Beagle Freedom Bill", Legislation, State Beagle Bill, *Beagle Freedom Project*, n.d., at http://www.bfp.org

[1199] CS/SB 226 (Care for Retired Police Dogs) and CS/HB 25 (Care for Retired Law Enforcement Dogs), eff. July 1, 2022.

[1200] "Concentration Camps for Dogs", *Life Magazine*, February 4, 1966.

would defund licenses for Class B dealers, who obtain animals from shelters, pounds, breeders and other dealers for research. Some states have outlawed "pound seizures" for research purposes, including Connecticut,[1201] Delaware,[1202] Hawaii,[1203] Illinois,[1204] Maine,[1205] Maryland,[1206] Massachusetts,[1207] New Hampshire,[1208] New Jersey,[1209] New York,[1210] Pennsylvania,[1211] Rhode Island,[1212] South Carolina,[1213] Vermont,[1214] Virginia,[1215] and West Virginia,[1216] but the practice is permitted in other states. In 2023, the Pet Safety and Protection Act of 2023 was reintroduced to prohibit the sale of stray and shelter animals for research,[1217] but the legislation would still permit dogs and cats to be bred for research. Dogs and cats from publicly owned shelters and pounds would also not be protected.

Recognizing the indisputable link between child abuse and animal cruelty, a growing number of states, including California,[1218] Colorado,[1219] Connecticut,[1220] Virginia,[1221] Maine,[1222] Massachusetts,[1223] Illinois,[1224]

[1201] C.G.S. § 22-332a (2001).
[1202] 6 Del. C. § 3003F & § 3004F (2014).
[1203] HRS § 143-18 (2001).
[1204] 510 ILCS 5/11 (2005).
[1205] 17 M.R.S. § 1025 (2001).
[1206] MD Code, Criminal Law § 10-617 (2002).
[1207] Mass. Ann. Laws ch. 140, § 151 (2002).
[1208] RSA 437:22 (2002).
[1209] N.J. Stat. § 4:19-15.16 (2002).
[1210] NY CLS Agr & M § 374 (2010).
[1211] 3 P.S. § 459-302 (2002).
[1212] R.I. Gen. Laws § 4-19-12 (2001).
[1213] S.C. Code Ann. § 47-3-60 (2002).
[1214] 13 V.S.A. § 352 (2001).
[1215] Va. Code Ann. § 3.2-6546; § 3.2-6547; § 3.2-6557 (2008).
[1216] W. Va. Code § 19-20-23 (2001).
[1217] Pet Safety and Protection Act of 2023, H.R. 208, 118th Congress (2023–2024).
[1218] Cal. West's Ann. Cal. Penal Code §11199.
[1219] Colo. Rev. Stat. §19-3-304.
[1220] C.G.S.A. §17a-106d; C.G.S.A. §17a-100a.
[1221] VA Code Ann. §63.2-1509.
[1222] 22 Maine Rev. Stat. Ann. §4011-A.
[1223] Mass. Gen. Laws Ann. 119, §85.
[1224] 325 ILCS §5 and §11.8.

Ohio,[1225] West Virginia,[1226] Nebraska[1227] and the District of Columbia,[1228] now have mandatory cross-reporting laws, which require social workers to report animal abuse and animal control to report child abuse. Recognizing that the safety of domestic abuse victims is tied to the safety of their companion animals, the Pet and Women Safety (PAWS) Act was enacted in 2018 to extend federal domestic violence protections to companion animals. As of 2022, 35 states, the District of Columbia and Puerto Rico have passed laws to permit companion animals to be covered by domestic violence protection orders.[1229] Some states, such as Virginia,[1230] Oregon,[1231] and Illinois,[1232] impose criminal liability on parents and guardians who expose children to animal cruelty, and there is a movement in other states to create animal abuser registries, modeled after sex offender registries.[1233]

Failure to provide appropriate supervision and failure to provide appropriate shelter for children both constitute child neglect under state laws. In Pennsylvania, "Libre's Law"[1234] protects dogs who are tethered outside, and in Massachusetts, leaving companions outside during extreme weather is illegal.[1235] Pennsylvania and Massachusetts join a number of other states that have enacted tethering laws, including California,[1236]

[1225] Ohio R.C. §1717.01; R.C.§ 959.07.

[1226] W. Va. Code §7-10-2.

[1227] Neb. Rev. St. §28-1017.

[1228] DC Code §4-1321.02; DC Code §22-1002.01.

[1229] *See*, Wisch, Rebecca, "Domestic Violence and Pets: List of States that Include Pets in Protection Orders", *Michigan State University, Animal Legal & Historical Center*, 2022, listing states that permit companion animals to be included in domestic violence protection orders, with links to state statutes.

[1230] *See*, Va. Code Ann. §3.2-6571(B), imposing criminal liability on parents or guardians who cause a minor to attend animal fighting event.

[1231] Oregon Stat. §167.320.4 (imposing felony criminal liability for knowingly committing animal abuse in the immediate presence of a minor child).

[1232] Illinois Stat. Ch. 720 §5 and §12-33 (imposing felony criminal liability for torturing animals in the presence of a child).

[1233] *See generally*, "Animal Abuser Registries – National Humane Education Society", *The National Humane Education Society*, n.d., at https://www.nhes.org/animal-abuse-registries/

[1234] Libre's Law was part of a comprehensive animal welfare package that was signed into law in 2017. *See*, 18 Pa. C.S.A. §5536 (2017).

[1235] Mass. Gen. Laws ch.140, §174E (eff. November 7, 2018).

[1236] West's Ann. Cal. Health & Safety Code §122,335.

Connecticut,[1237] Illinois,[1238] Maryland,[1239] Michigan[1240] and Nevada,[1241] to protect chained animals. Some municipalities are considering replacing "pet owner" with "pet guardian" in statutes. Rhode Island law, for instance, uses "guardianship" and "ownership" interchangeably.[1242]These reforms tell us what our laws refuse to acknowledge … that our companions are much more like family members than they are "property."

Achieving the proper legal status for animals, a status that respects each animal as an individual with certain fundamental rights, will require a greater understanding and connection with the animal kingdom in a manner that respects their rights and autonomy. It can start by connecting with a single animal, who can be thousands of miles away from us, and that single animal can change how we view the entire animal kingdom.

[1237] C.G.S.A. §§ 22-350a.

[1238] 510 Illinois Compiled Statutes §70.

[1239] MD Code Criminal Law §10-623.

[1240] Michigan Compiled Laws §750-50.

[1241] Nevada Revised Statutes §574.100.

[1242] Rhode Island General Law §4-1-38 (2020). The statute defines "Guardian" as "a person(s) having the same rights and responsibilities of an owner, and both terms shall be used interchangeably."

CHAPTER 3

Media as a Driver of Change

The positive developments discussed in the last chapter are the result of changes in how the public views animals. Social media plays a pivotal role in raising awareness about animal welfare because the platforms are immediate and widespread. It bridges the information gap by bringing attention to issues relevant to animals that are often overlooked by traditional media. At the local level, traditional media coverage of animals (if any) tends to focus on adoption events and other heart-warming stories of survival, which are helpful for companion animals but do little for other animals. At the national level, traditional media does not generally cover issues that impact animals,[1] which has left much of the public unaware of how badly our society treats animals. It typically requires sustained public outrage, an extreme case of animal cruelty, or the involvement of a public figure to garner media attention, and in turn, the attention of lawmakers. Even then, politicians are more likely to get involved when the abuse of animals translates into a risk for humans.

This was the case in 2008 when video footage of extreme cruelty against "downer" cows (those too weak or sick to stand) was reported by the

[1] The New York Times does on occasion cover in-depth stories that impact animals. *See*, e.g., Moss, Michael, "U.S. Research Lab Lets Livestock Suffer in Quest for Profit", *New York Times*, January 19, 2015.

K. C. Moore, *The Case for the Legal Protection of Animals*, The Palgrave Macmillan Animal Ethics Series,
https://doi.org/10.1007/978-3-031-46065-4_3

media,[2] but the coverage focused on the public health risks associated with including downer cows in the food supply rather than the abuse to the animals.[3] There also seems to be more media coverage if the cruelty involves individuals rather than institutionalized cruelty. Actions taken by corporations, even if cruel, have a shroud of legitimacy because of assumptions (*albeit* false) that laws exist to protect animals and that companies will abide by them. Status quo is a powerful impediment to advancing animal protection.

Social media has fueled and accelerated the movement to protect animals in ways only dreamed of by other rights movements. The speed at which information is disseminated, and the number of people that can be reached, is far greater than at any time in history. Activists can quickly mobilize and demand action. In a matter of days or hours, public outrage can be marshaled, awareness can be raised, and in some instances, change can be secured. Italy's plan to cull wild boars in urban areas received quick global backlash in late 2022,[4] and even random acts of animal cruelty can spark fierce outrage on an international scale.[5]

Social media can be a double edged sword. The United Nations warned in 2021 that social media platforms and online marketplaces are being used to facilitate illegal wildlife trafficking, and it urged Member States to strengthen their laws and regulations to prevent illicit trafficking.[6] Still, social media can be an instrument of change, commanding the public's attention and pressuring government officials and business leaders to take action. Pressure from social media has resulted in to the cancelation of

[2] The Washington Post story reported that "downer" cows were subjected to abuse in violation of state and federal laws, including electric shocks and high-powered water sprays up their nose in an effort to get them on their feet. *See*, Weiss, Rick, "Video Reveals Violations of Laws, Abuse of Cows at Slaughterhouse", *Washington Post*, January 30, 2008.

[3] *See*, e.g., Falco, Miriam, "USDA: Reinspection of downed cattle was key issue in beef recall", *CNN*, February 20, 2008.

[4] AFP, "Outrage over Italy's plan to hunt wild boars in cities", *Global Times*, December 22, 2022.

[5] The brutal slaughter of stray dogs in Qatar prompted Sheikha Al Mayassa bint Hamad Al Thani, sister of Qatari's rule, to condemn the brutality as "unacceptable" on social media. *See*, Chapman, Ben, "Outrage in Qatar over shooting of 29 dogs as it prepares for World Cup", *Britain's News Channel*, July 22, 2022.

[6] *See*, U.N. General Assembly Resolution 75/311.

pigeon shoots,[7] "pig wrestling" games,[8] and other abusive events. In the case of some animals, their stories have yielded far greater change than humans alone could have accomplished. The public is often faced with tragic stories about (and statistics on) animals (e.g., the number of elephants and rhinos slaughtered every year). The public seems to connect better with individual animals when their stories are told, and an informed public is essential for legal reform. This chapter tells the stories of some animals who have commanded the attention of the world.

Cecil the Lion

An African proverb holds that "Until the lion has his or her own storyteller, tales of the hunt will always glorify the hunter." This is the story of Cecil the Lion.

Cecil lived primarily at the Hwange National Park in Matabeleland North, Zimbabwe and was being studied along with other lions by scientists from the Wildlife Conservation Research Unit at the University of Oxford. Cecil wore a GPS tracking collar and had been tracked since 2008.[9] On the night of July 1, 2015, an American dentist and trophy hunter named Walter J. Palmer shot and wounded the magnificent lion named Cecil (2002–2015) with a bow and arrow. The mortally wounded animal was left struggling to breathe for hours. The following morning the animal was tracked down and killed with a second bow and arrow. Cecil's body was skinned and his head was removed.[10]

The backlash against the dentist was quick and fierce. Palmer soon found himself at the center of international outrage and protests.[11] By July 2015, Cecil's story was told in approximately 12,000 editorial articles

[7] *See,* e.g., Querry, K., "Sen. Inhofe to end controversial pigeon shoot fundraiser in Oklahoma", August 23, 2017, at https://kfor.com/news/sen-inhofe-to-end-controversial-pigeon-shoot-fundraiser-in-oklahoma/

[8] The Stoughton County Fair in Wisconsin canceled its pig wrestling event after pressure from city officials and animal rights activists. *See*, "Under pressure, Stoughton County Fair cancels pig wrestling", *Associated Press*, June 16, 2016.

[9] For more on Cecil's legacy and the plight of lions, *see*, "Cecil's Legacy – 5 years on", Wildlife Conservation Research Unit, Oxford University, December 21, 2020, at https://www.ox.ac.uk/news/2020-12-21-cecil-lion-s-legacy-five-years

[10] "Cecil the lion: Zimbabwe hunter bailed over killing", *BBC News*, July 29, 2015.

[11] Seven years following the killing of Cecil, the clinic where Walter Palm works was still receiving negative reviews. *See*, Hurley, Bevan, "Cecil the Lion killer dentist Walter Palmer inundated with one star Yelp reviews", *Independent*, October 27, 2022.

published in 125 different languages.[12] In the aftermath of the killing, Karikoga Kaseke, the director of Zimbabwe's Tourism Authority, said that tourism to the country had been booming, but the killing of Cecil had a negative effect on tourism because Zimbabwe was now perceived as a country that did not protect its animals.[13] The tragic killing of Cecil also impacted the livelihood of workers in Zimbabwe, who could have made more money from wildlife tours than a single one-time fee to kill the animal.

Frozen Fish

Social media erupted in 2016 when Space World, a theme park in Kitakyushu, Japan, featured an ice rink with thousands of fish frozen into the ice.[14] The public backlash was swift and harsh, with thousands denouncing the rink as having "an appalling lack of morality," lacking "disrespect for life" and a "graveyard."[15] The theme park quickly apologized on its website, acknowledging that "[w]e have received a lot of opinions, such as 'Using animals as entertainment and in events is bad' and 'Poor fish'. We sincerely apologise [sic]."[16] Space World also indicated that a memorial service would be held for the fish.[17]

Sade

In 2014, Desmond Hague, the former CEO of sports and entertainment catering giant Centerplate, was caught on a hotel elevator security camera kicking and thrashing a small, cowering puppy named Sade.[18] When the video was leaked to news outlets, Centerline initially attempted to defuse

[12] Macdonald, David W., et al., "Cecil: A Moment or a Movement? Analysis of Media Coverage of the Death of a Lion, *Panthera leo*", *Animals* 6, no. 5:26. https://doi.org/10.3390/ani6050026

[13] Chikowore, Frank, "Cecil's death causes tourism drop in Zimbabwe", *USA Today*, July 30, 2015.

[14] Space World in the city of Kitakyushu in South-west Japan featured around 5000 dead mackerel, sprats and other fish that were bought from a local market.

[15] McCurry, Justin, "Anger as Japanese skating rink freezes thousands of fish into ice as gimmick", *Guardian*, November 27, 2016.

[16] Ibid.

[17] Rich, Motoko, "Aquarium on Ice, a Lure for Skaters in Japan, Appalls Them Instead", *New York Times*, November 28, 2016.

[18] McDonald, Jeff, "Desmond Hague was caught on video hoisting Doberman by lease", *San Diego Union-Tribune*, September 2, 2014.

the situation by calling the incident a personal matter. It didn't work. Amid growing public outrage, the company placed Hague on indefinite probation, ordered Hague into therapy and community service, and announced the creation of a foundation to fight animal abuse to be funded with $100,000 of Hague's personal money.[19] It didn't work. Days later Hague was forced to resign.[20] The public had spoken, and the penalty for abusing an animal proved to be far more financially severe than had Hague faced criminal charges.

Caitlyn

In 2015, a 15-month old dog named Caitlyn received worldwide attention when a heartbreaking photo of her muzzle taped shut went viral. Caitlyn's fight to survive, and the precedent setting criminal case that followed, raised worldwide awareness of animal cruelty. The man responsible for Caitlyn's injuries was arrested and sentenced to 5 years in prison, the maximum sentence for animal cruelty in South Carolina. Judge Markley Dennis told the offender "I wish I could give you more [time]".[21]

Caitlyn's story did not end at the trial. She endured multiple reconstructive surgeries and did eventually recover enough to be adopted by a new family. Caitlyn's scars have become a symbol of survival that has resonated with so many, including one domestic violence survivor who viewed her own scars a reminder that she too was a survivor.[22] People Magazine named Caitlyn the "Best Survival Story of 2015,"[23] and the Caitlyn's Anti-Cruelty Fund was established to help end animal cruelty.[24]

[19] Engel, Pamela, "The CEO of a $6 Billion Company was Caught on Camera Kicking a Dog", *Business Insider*, August 27, 2014.

[20] Sullivan, Gail, "Puppy-kicking CEO forced to step down", *Washington Post,* September 3, 2014; *see also*, McDonald, Jeff, "Desmond Hague was caught on video hoisting Doberman by lease", *San Diego Union-Tribune,* September 2, 2014.

[21] Associated Press, "South Carolina man who taped dog's mouth shut sentenced to 5 years", *ABC News*, March 25, 2017.

[22] *See*, Krosse, Dan, "Caitlyn's A-Team", *Carolina Tails, a Charleston Animal Society Publication*, October 2, 2016.

[23] Tyson, Sam, "Caitlyn named People Magazine's 'Best Survival Story' of 2015", *ABC News*, December 14, 2015.

[24] The Caitlyn's Anti-Cruelty Fund was established by the Charleston Animal Society. *See*, "Caitlyn's Anti-Cruelty Fund" at www.charlestonanimalsociety.org/caitlyn/

Hercules (A Dog's Purpose)

In 2017, the movie premiere for *A Dog's Purpose* was canceled by Universal Pictures after a video emerged that appeared to show Hercules, a German shepherd "stunt dog", in distress. Hercules exhibited signs of stress and was struggling to stay afloat as he was forced to perform in turbulent water.[25] The film was expected to gross more than $25 million during its opening weekend but missed its estimate by ~ 20% (~$5 million) as a result of the negative publicity.[26] The director of the film, Iasse Hallstrom, promptly took to twitter to assure the public that he was "very disturbed" by the video,[27] but the damage was done. The video served to reignite public discussion regarding the use of animals in film.

Guggenheim Museum Exhibit

In 2017, an exhibit by Sun Yuan and Peng Yu titled *Dogs That Cannot Touch Each Other* at the Guggenheim Museum in New York faced significant public backlash.[28] The exhibit involved eight American Pit Bull Terriers running toward each other as they were chained onto treadmills. The Guggenheim asked the public, to no avail, to consider the "artistic and political context" of the exhibit, even as it acknowledged that, "the work may be upsetting."[29] The museum faced a barrage of criticism, protests, and an online petition signed by more than 750,000 people.[30] After initially defending the exhibit as "an intentionally challenging and provocative artwork,"[31] the backlash was so intense that the Guggenheim Museum was forced to pull the exhibit. The intense backlash against the exhibit underscored the fact that Americans know when they are witnessing the mistreatment of animals, even when it is presented as "art."

[25] Kaufman, Amy, "'A Dog's Purpose' was supposed to be a hit, until animal-abuse controversy threw the studio's plan out the window", *Los Angeles Times*, January 26, 2017.

[26] Ibid.

[27] Twitter Tweet, Iasse Hallstrom (@HallstromLasse), January 18, 2017, 9:24 pm.

[28] *See*, Haag, Matthew, "Guggenheim Exhibit With Video of Dogs Trying to Fight Stirs Criticism", *New York Times*, September 21, 2017.

[29] Press Release by Guggenheim, "Statement on the video work 'Dogs That Cannot Touch Each Other'", September 21, 2017.

[30] For more on the controversial exhibit, *see* Baecker, Angie, "In Defense of Difficult Art at the Guggenheim's Controversial Exhibition", *Slate*, October 18, 2017.

[31] Press Release by Guggenheim.

Whale Jail

Russia felt the wrath of the international community in 2018 when news of its "whale jail" found its way onto social media. The "whale jail," cramped holding pens in Russia's Far East Nakhodka Bay, held nearly 100 beluga whales and orcas illegally captured for the eventual sale to marine parks in China.[32] National and international outcry erupted, Russian and international animal rights groups lobbied, celebrities started campaigns, and by the end of 2019, all surviving animals were released back into the wild.[33] Russian news agencies reported, in 2019, that criminal charges have been filed against the four companies involved with the capture and captivity of the animals[34] and that one company had been fined nearly $900,000 for its involvement in the "whale jail."[35] The fierce international backlash against the "whale jail," as well as Russia's quick response, underscored the fact that the global community no longer views the extreme confinement of intelligent marine animals as acceptable.

Animal Abuse

Clear instances of animal abuse on social media receive universal public condemnation. In 2022, international outrage erupted when a Greek man was recorded kicking a kitten into the sea after enticing the animal with a piece of fish. The kitten was unharmed by the incident, but the man faces up to ten years in prison and a maximum fine of 50,000 euros if convicted of animal cruelty. The incident prompted Greek Interior Minister, Takis Theodorikakos, to congratulate police for arresting the man and tweeting "[v]iolence against animals is unacceptable."[36] In late 2022, footage of a dog being beaten to death by a shovel by an animal shelter worker in Konya, Turkey sparked outrage and protests. The death of the dog renewed public dialogue in Turkey on the treatment of stray animals and

[32] For additional background, *see* Daly, Natasha, "Release of whales from notorious Russia 'whale jail' complete', *National Geographic*, November 10, 2019.

[33] Id.

[34] "Reports: Criminal Charges Filed in Russian 'Whale Prison' Case", *Radio Free Europe/Radio Liberty*, February 28, 2019.

[35] "Russian 'Whale Jail' Company Slapped with $900 K Fine Over Orca Captures", *The Moscow Times*, June 14, 2019.

[36] "Animal Abuse Incident in Greece Sparks International Outrage", *The Pappas Post*, May 11, 2022.

prompted Turkey's President, Recep Tayyip Erdogan, to condemn the cruelty and to assure the public that "[m]easures have been taken to prevent it from happening again."[37]

Law enforcement officials and social media "influencers" are not immune from public backlash. In 2021, a video of North Carolina police officer, James Hampton, abusing a K-9 police dog named Zuul led to the resignation of the officer after the department recommended that he be terminated. In a statement by the Salisbury Police Department, the department acknowledged that the officer acted in a manner that was inconsistent with his K-9 training and recognized the need to "restore and maintain the public confidence that has been detrimentally affected by this incident."[38] A Instagram "influencer" also felt the public's wrath when she lured a dog to come closer, only to kick it away. An apology was issued but the damage was done. She received universal condemnation and lost most of her followers.[39]

What we learn from these stories is that the public cares deeply about how animals are treated. The public is quick to demand justice for animals and accountability from anyone who has harmed an animal. Social media allows the public observe, learn, and have its voice heard. It permits "fines" to be levied for animal cruelty (e.g., loss of social media revenue; loss of livelihood). Most importantly, an informed and educated public is vital to tackling global challenges, such as climate change, that affect all life on the planet.

[37] Wilks, Andrew, "Killing of dog enflames Turkish animal lovers on issue that divides society", *Al-Monitor*, November 29, 2022.

[38] Statement of the Salisbury Police Department, n.d., at https://salisburync.gov/Government/Police/About-Us/K9-Operations

[39] Kajal Kiran's Instagram account had more than 120,000 followers before the incident. In early 2023, the account had less than 100 followers. *See*, Hobbs, Jack, "Smiling influencer filmed kicking dog apologizes for sharing 'cruel act'", *New York Post*, December 1, 2022.

CHAPTER 4

The Link Between Human Rights and Animal Rights

Cruelty to animals and cruelty to humans are two sides of the same page on which history is written in blood.
—Ulrich Erckenbrecht

It's all connected.

Humanity has a long history of oppression. Human rights violations have persisted well into the twenty-first century, but unprecedented numbers of rights movements have developed momentum in the past five decades for women, minorities, the disabled, LGBTIQ+ communities, indigenous people, children, other marginalized groups, and nature. The United States is still coming to terms with its own human rights concerns, including inhumane immigration policies; racial profiling and injustices; inadequate healthcare for women; ageism; environmental inequalities; and discrimination based on gender identity and sexual orientation.[1] These heinous and dehumanizing prejudices are at times eclipsed by discrimination that underlies war crimes, human trafficking, and death sentences imposed for exercising human rights. Given

[1] *See*, World Report 2021, Events of 2020, *Human Rights Watch*. ISBN 978-1-64421-028-4; *see also*, World Report 2020, Events of 2019, *Human Rights Watch*. ISBN-13: 978-1-64421-005-5.

K. C. Moore, *The Case for the Legal Protection of Animals*, The Palgrave Macmillan Animal Ethics Series,
https://doi.org/10.1007/978-3-031-46065-4_4

the severity of human rights violations around the globe, some dismiss efforts to achieve legal rights and protection for animals. There is an unconscious bias against other species, speciesism, who are considered far inferior to humans, a bias that undermines the universal quest for freedom that is shared by all.

Dismantling systems of oppression that seek to legitimize "us versus them" constructs is critical to every rights movement, but it is especially important for the movement to legally protect animals, because animals are the quintessential "them." The "us versus them" tactic can be found in the playbook of every repressive system in history. We must fight this narrative for people and for animals, because when we defeat it for one group, we empower other groups. It would not be acceptable to criticize someone for advocating for justice in a particular area of human rights, such as gender equality. Still, there is persistent, but unfounded, fear that by advocating for animal rights, attention will be diverted from humans. Legal reform for animals is not a zero sum game (i.e., where rights for animals come at a cost to human rights). Rights movements are synergetic and work in tandem with one another. Rights movements reinforce and provide strength and encouragement to other rights movements, because when one group of oppressed individuals are lifted up, it opens a door through which others may pass. As author and professor, Carrie P. Freeman, explains, "the goal of any social movement is not to pull oneself up to be better than someone else and earn privileges at their expense" but to "dismantle oppressive hierarchies (and worldviews) that have enabled widespread injustice of many types of living beings."[2]

Discrimination of any kind, including species-based discrimination, emboldens and empowers other systems of oppression. Transforming repressive hierarchies that demoralize victims, whether human or nonhuman, is important for each of us. As German social activist, Martin Niemöller, explained, "First they came for the socialists, and I did not speak out—because I was not a socialist. Then they came for the trade unionists, and I did not speak out—because I was not a trade unionist. Then they came for the Jews, and I did not speak out—because I was not a Jew. Then they came for me—and there was no one left to speak for

[2] Freeman, Carrie P., *The Human Animal Earthling Identity*. University of Georgia Press, 2020, at 37. ISBN: 9-780-8203-5819-2. Carrie P. Freeman, PhD is an Associate Professor of Communication at Georgia State University in Atlanta.

me."[3] Humanity will take one giant evolutionary step forward when we accept that victims are victims, regardless of species; that indifference to any form of oppression is a threat to everyone; and that devaluation of any sentient life is a devaluation of us all.

In the aftermath of World War II, the United Nations adopted the Universal Declaration of Human Rights as a "yardstick by which we measure right and wrong" and to "fight against oppression, impunity and affronts to human dignity."[4] The Declaration acknowledges that certain rights are inalienable to every person "at all times, and in all places," including rights to freedom from tyranny, torture, discrimination and fear.[5] Fundamental human rights to "freedom, equality and dignity"[6] are not granted by the United Nations or by any country … they are absolute rights that exist independent of, and apart from, any nation or authority, much like the "unalienable Rights" referenced in the Declaration of Independence.[7] This is true regardless of whether the rights are recognized.

It is no coincidence that International Animal Rights Day is celebrated annually on December 10, which coincides with the anniversary of the Universal Declaration of Human Rights. In 1978, the United Nations and the United Nations Educational, Scientific and Cultural Organization adopted the Universal Declaration of Animal Rights, recognizing that "[a]ll animals are born with an equal claim on life and the same rights to existence", "[a]ll animals are entitled to respect", and that "genocide has been perpetrated by man on animals".[8] The declaration was not legally binding. As Judge Maria Alejandra Maurico from Argentina would later remind us, issues such as equal voting rights, marriage equality and gender violence have not always been recognized by humanity, and "[t]here is an

[3] Friedrich Gustav Emil Martin Niemöller (1892–1984).

[4] *See*, Universal Declaration of Human Rights, Forward by BAN Ki-moon, Secretary-General of the United Nations, United Nations, 2015.

[5] The Introduction to the Universal Declaration of Human Rights proclaims that there are "inalienable entitlements of all people, at all times, and in all places—people of every colour, from every race and ethic group; whether or not they are disabled; citizens or migrants; no matter their sex, their class, their caste, their creed, their age or sexual orientation."

[6] Id.

[7] The Declaration of Independent, signed on July 4, 1776, states that "[w]e hold these truths to be self-evidence, that all men are created equal, that they are endowed by their Creator with certain unalienable Rights, that among these are Life, Liberty and the pursuit of Happiness".

[8] Universal declaration of animal rights (15 October 1978), solemnly proclaimed in Paris on 15 October 1978 at the UNESCO headquarters, Preamble and Articles 1 and 2.

identical situation with the awareness of animal rights."[9] Still, the declaration carried significant moral authority, reflecting universal values and aspirations of the international community. In the decades that followed, nations would begin to lend legal authority to these principles.

Like humans, animals have certain inalienable rights, such as the right to bodily integrity and the right to be free. These rights exist even if they are not recognized or respected by humans. As humans, we share 98.8% of our DNA sequences with chimpanzees, 96.9% with orangutans, 90% with cats, 85% with mice, 84% with dogs and 80% with cows,[10] but legal systems do not recognize the basic rights to freedom, equality, and dignity of animals, nor do they recognize species-specific rights, such as the right of dolphins to have plastic-free oceans. The systematic and widespread violations of the rights of animals is why many consider the fight for animal rights to be one of the most important rights movements of the twenty-first century.

We need not elevate animals to the moral status of humans to understand that our mistreatment of them has grave implications for our own future. By every metric, we find that violating the rights of animals has severe consequences for humanity. As we will see in this chapter, human rights and animal rights are two sides of the same coin.

Climate Change

All life on the planet, both human and non-human, face existential threats from climate change.[11] Today there is scientific consensus, supported by thousands of peer-reviewed research studies, that human activities are contributing to climate change. In a research study of a

[9] Judge Maurico recognized a chimpanzee as a "legal" person in 2016. *See*, Tercer Juzgado de Garantias de Mendoza, "Presented by A.F.A.D.A. About The Chimpanzee 'Cecilia' – Non Human Individual", File No. P-72.254/15, November 3, 2016.

[10] For further information on the similarities between humans and chimps, *see*, Luskin, Casey, "Human-Chimp Similarity: What Is It and What Does It Mean", *Evolution News & Science Today*, October 20, 2021; *see also*, Deziel, Chris, "Animals That Share Human DNA Sequences". *Sciencing*, July 20, 2018, at https://sciencing.com/animals-share-human-dna-sequences-8628167.html; *see also*, Ramsey, Lydia and Lee, Samantha, "Humans share almost all of our DNA with cats, cattle and mice", *Independent*, April 6, 2018.

[11] The United Nations Framework Convention on Climate Change defines "climate change" as "a change of climate which is attributed directly or indirectly to human activity that alters the composition of the global atmosphere and which is in addition to natural climate variability observed over comparable time periods".

random subset of 88,125 climate-related papers published since 2012, the consensus in the peer-reviewed scientific literature affirming human-driven climate change surpassed 99%.[12] An unprecedented 15,300 scientists from 184 countries have signed a letter entitled "World Scientists' Warning to Humanity: A Second Notice" that warns of the dire consequences of catastrophic climate change due to rising greenhouse gases from burning fossil fuels, deforestation and agricultural production (primarily meat production).[13] In 2023, researchers warned that we are rapidly approaching a collapse of the Atlantic meridional overturning circulation, which helps regulate the planet's climate,[14] and sea surface temperatures hit 100 degrees off the coast of Florida.[15] The United Nations views climate change as the biggest health threat facing humanity,[16] but climate change remains a controversial issue fraught with politics and misinformation in the United States.[17]

Fossil fuels (e.g., coal, oil, natural gas) and deforestation (driven by animal agriculture) are the top contributors to climate change,[18] and the meat and dairy industries contribute to almost 80% of agricultural greenhouse gas emissions.[19] The impact on global warming arises not just from the emission of greenhouse gases, such as methane and nitrous oxide, but also from the loss of terrestrial biomass that occurs when existing

[12] *See*, Lynas, Mark, et al., "Greater than 99% consensus on human caused climate change in the peer-reviewed scientific literature", *Environ. Res. Lett.*, Vol. 16, No. 11, 10.19.2021. https://doi.org/10.1088/1748-9326/ac2966

[13] Ripple, William J., et al., 15,364 scientist signatories from 184 countries, "World Scientists' Warning to Humanity: A Second Notice", *BioScience*, Vol. 67, Issue 12, Dec. 2017, at 1026–2018. https://doi.org/10.1093/biosci/bix125

[14] Ditlevsen, Peter and Ditlevsen, Susanne, "Warning of a forthcoming collapse of the Atlantic meridional overturning circulation", *Nature Communications*, 14, No. 4254 (2023).

[15] Tabuchi, Hiroko, "101 °F in the Ocean Off Florida: Was It a World Record?", *New York Times*, August 18, 2023.

[16] *See*, "Causes and Effects of Climate Change", *United Nations, Climate Action, The Science*, n.d., at https://www.un.org/en/climatechange/science/causes-effects-climate-change

[17] *See*, e.g., Tigue, Kristoffer, "Experts Debunk Viral Post Claiming 1100 Scientists Say 'There's No Climate Emergency'", *Inside Climate News*, August 23, 2022.

[18] Causes and Effects of Climate Change.

[19] Lehner, Peter and Rosenberg, Nathan, "Legal Pathways to Carbon-Neutral Agriculture", *Environmental Law Reporter*, Vol. 47, at 10845, 2017, at http://ssrn.com/abstract=3040919

ecosystems are converted to pastures for grazing animals.[20] Research shows that a phaseout of animal agriculture through the end of the century would yield half of the required net emission reductions needed to limit warming to 2 °C.[21] In short, the science tells us that plant-based diets are essential to avoiding catastrophic climate change, and legal reforms are needed to get us where we need to be. First and foremost, federal and state subsidies to the meat and dairy industries must be re-directed to more climate-friendly plant-based proteins and slaughter-free meat.

According to the World Meteorological Organization, "record atmospheric greenhouse gas concentrations and associated accumulated heat have propelled the planet into unchartered territory, with far-reaching repercussions for current and future generations."[22] 2020 was tied for hottest year on record,[23] and in 2022, carbon dioxide reached a level not seen for millions of years,[24] yet the worst was yet to come. In 2023, record breaking heat waves were felt all over the world,[25] with July 2023 setting a record for the world's hottest month on record.[26] The resulting impact to climate has devastating implications for life on the planet, including warming oceans, rising sea levels, loss of biodiversity and food and water shortages.[27]

[20] Eisen, Michael B. and Brown, Patrick O., "Rapid global phase out of animal agriculture has the potential to stabilize greenhouse gas levels for 30 years and offset 68 percent of CO2 emissions this century", *PLOS Climate,* 1(2): e0000010. https://doi.org/10.1371/journal.pclm.0000010

[21] Ibid.

[22] *See,* e.g., Hubbart, Sarah, "Understanding the New Normal: Extreme Weather and Climate Change", *The National Environmental Education Foundation*, July 30, 2021; *see also*, World Meteorological Organization, "State of Climate in 2021: Extreme events and major impacts", October 31, 2021 (released at UN Climate Change negotiations, COP26, in Glasgow) at https://public.wmo.int/en/media/press-release/state-of-climate-2021-extreme-events-and-major-impacts

[23] Office of the Director of National Intelligence, "Annual Threat Assessment of the US Intelligence Community", April 9, 2021, at 18, at https://www.dni.gov/index.php/newsroom/reports-publications/reports-publications-2021/item/2204-2021-annual-threat-assessment-of-the-u-s-intelligence-community.pdf

[24] Bressan, David, "2022 At Levels Not Seen For Millions of Years", *Forbes*, June 5, 2022.

[25] Borenstein, Seth, "Scientists Link Climate Change to July Heat Waves in Europe, China, and the U.S.", *Time*, July 25, 2023.

[26] Dickie, Gloria, "July 2023 set to be world's hottest month on record", *Reuters*, July 27, 2023.

[27] Causes and Effects of Climate Change.

Climate change affects at least 10,967 species listed on the IUCN Red List of Threatened Species, impacting behavior, genetic composition and the survival of some species.[28] Climate change results in the loss of habitats, food sources, and access to water, all of which drive animals to extinction.[29] The increasing number of floods and wildfires that are destroying ecosystems and habitats are also leaving wildlife with too little food for survival. Scientists warn that climate change may fuel human and wildlife conflicts as competition for resources increases.[30] During the extreme drought in Botswana in 2018, there were a record number of human and wildlife conflicts as lions and other large carnivores preyed on livestock when their natural prey became scarce.[31] In India, blue sheep (or bharal) have moved into lower elevations and are feeding on human crops because climate change has reduced their vegetation.[32] Despite the alarming data, the United States is one of the biggest producers of greenhouse gas emissions.[33]

Scientists agree that climate change is contributing to the increasing frequency and severity of dangerous weather events, including deadly heat waves, droughts and severe flooding,[34] increasingly powerful and deadly

[28] Issues Brief: "Species and climate change", *International Union for Conservation of Nature (IUCN)*, Oct. 2021, at https://www.iucn.org/resources/issues-brief/species-and-climate-change

[29] *See generally*, "the impact of climate change on our planet's animals", *IFAW*, February 28, 2022, at https://www.ifaw.org/journal/impact-climate-change-animals

[30] Urton, James. "Climate change to fuel increase in human-wildlife conflict, UW biologist says", *University of Washington, News Release*, July 7.29.2021, at https://www.washington.edu/news/2021/07/29/human-wildlife-conflict-climate/

[31] Id.

[32] Id.

[33] *See*, e.g., Evans, Simon, "Analysis: Which countries are historically responsible for climate change", *Carbon Brief*, October 5, 2021 (concluding that the US is responsible for the largest share of emissions, more than 509GtCO2 since 1850, or 20% of the global total); *see also*, "2022 Environmental Performance Index Finds World is Not on Track to Meet Climate Commitments", *Yale School of the Environment*, May 31, 2022 (concluding that the US, China, India and Russia are responsible for more than 50% of global greenhouse gas emissions). Note that per capital estimates differ.

[34] Ghebrezgabher, Mihretab G., et al., "Long-Term Trend of Climate Change and Drought Assessment in the Horn of Africa", *Advances in Meteorology*, Vol. 2016. https://doi.org/10.1155/2016/8057641

storms,[35] wildfires,[36] and outbreaks of disease.[37] Warnings of climate catastrophes are coming with increased urgency from all over the globe. Researchers warn that we are now at "code red" on planet Earth, despite repeated warnings from nearly 15,000 scientists from 158 countries that we are facing a climate emergency.[38] In 2022 alone, headlines brought to the forefront the devastation of climate-fueled events: hurricanes (United States, Cuba, Caribbean, Canada); storms (Philippines, Europe, U.K., SE Africa); droughts (Horn of Africa, Europe, China, Brazil); flooding (West Africa, Pakistan, China; E. Australia, Brazil, South Africa, Malaysia); heat waves (India, Pakistan, Arctic, Antarctica); and cyclones (Bangladesh).[39]

Researchers have previously observed the "close ties" between climate change and human health,[40] but recent data indicates that unabated climate change will result in 3.4 million deaths annually by the end of the century.[41] In 2021, an editorial published in more than 200 medical and health journals worldwide warned that a 1.5-degree-Celsius rise in global temperatures is the "greatest threat to global public health", with both direct health consequences (e.g., heat-related deaths; loss of kidney function; skin cancer; cardiovascular and lung disease; pregnancy complications) and indirect consequences (e.g., future pandemics from habitat

[35] Hansen, James, et al., "Ice melt, sea level rise and superstorms: evidence from paleoclimate data, climate modeling, and modern observations that 2 °C global warming could be dangerous", *Atmospheric Chemistry and Physics*, 16, 3761–3812, 3.22.2016. https://doi.org/10.5194/acp-16-3761-2016

[36] Moore, Andrew, "Climate Change is Making Wildfires Worse – Here's How", *NC State University, College of Natural Resources News*, August 29, 2022.

[37] "Our Risk of Infectious Diseases Is Increasing Because of Climate Change", *CDC, National Center for Emerging and Zoonotic Infectious Diseases*, August 2, 2022.

[38] *See*, Ripple, William J., et al., "World Scientists' Warming of a Climate Emergency 2022", *BioScience*, Vol. 72, Issue 12, December 2022, at 1149–1155. https://doi.org/10.1093/biosci/biac083

[39] Rosane, Olivia, "10 costliest climate disasters of 2022", *World Economic Forum, Climate and Nature*, January 5, 2023, discussing the report "Counting the Cost 2022: A Year of Climate Breakdown" prepared by U.K. charity Christian Aid.

[40] Global Sustainable Development Report 2019, at p. xx.

[41] El-Sheikh, Sharm, "New Health Data Shows Unabated Climate Change Will Cause 3.4 Million Deaths Per Year by Century End", *V20 Press Release*, November 12, 2022.

destruction and malnutrition from soil depletion).[42] The United Nations Office for Disaster Risk Reduction and Centre for Research on the Epidemiology of Disasters examined the "staggering rise in climate-related disasters" between 2000 and 2019 and reported that 7348 disaster events worldwide claimed an estimated 1.2 million lives and impacted over 4 billion people,[43] which falls most heavily on the most vulnerable.[44] Citing "clear evidence," the report concludes that climate change is resulting in extreme weather events, including wildfires, droughts (with resulting famines and outbreaks of disease), flooding, hurricanes, and heatwaves.[45] The report voices the frustration felt by so many with the lack of global action, including the failure of industrialized nations to reduce greenhouse gas emissions, lamenting "[i]t is baffling that we willingly and knowingly continue to sow the seeds of our own destruction, despite the science and evidence that we are turning our only home into an uninhabitable hell for millions of people."[46]

In 2023, the United Nations released its updated climate change report, warning that we are quickly approaching a dangerous climate threshold as a result of continued greenhouse gas emissions.[47] Recognizing the interdependence of human societies, climate, ecosystems and biodiversity, the report warns that 3.3–3.6 billion people are highly vulnerable to climate change that will result in more food and water shortages and extreme weather events.[48] The report confirms that greenhouse gas emissions are increasing as a result of human activity, making deforestation one of the planet's most pressing issues. The actions of humans, who consider

[42] *See generally*, Choi-Schagrin, Winston, "Medical Journals Call Climate Change the 'Greatest Threat to Global Public Health'", *New York Times*, September 7, 2021; *see also*, Sommer, Lauren, "Climate Change is The Greatest Threat To Public Health Top Medical Journals Warn", *NPR*, September 7, 2021; *see also*, Dewan, Angela, "More than 230 journals warn 1.5 °C of global warming could be 'catastrophic' for health", *CNN*, September 5, 2021.

[43] "Human cost of disasters, An Overview of the last 20 years (2000–2019)", U.N. Office for Disaster Risk Reduction and Centre for Research on the Epidemiology of Disasters (CRED), October 13, 2020, at 3, 6 and 13.

[44] EPA Press Office, "Climate Change on Socially Vulnerable Populations in the United States", *EPA, News Releases*, September 2, 2021.

[45] Human Cost of Disasters, An Overview, at 7 and 18.

[46] Human Cost of Disasters, An Overview, at 3.

[47] IPCC, "Synthesis Report of the IPCC Sixth Assessment Report (AR6)", draft dated March 19, 2023.

[48] Id. at A.2.2.

themselves to be the most advanced and sophisticated species on the planet, are not only destroying their only home but also the home of millions of other species, and the impact is catastrophic. The climate emergency is spawning legal developments in the United States, albeit slowly. In 2023, the first court decision on climate rights was issued by Hawaii's Supreme Court, which recognized that the right to a stable climate was a human right.[49]

Climate change will have a devastating impact on all life on the planet and to shared ecosystems, but the impact can be limited by simply phasing out animal agriculture and reversing the deforestation that it has caused. Modern science shows that human influence, especially greenhouse gas emissions "has warmed the atmosphere, ocean and land."[50] According to world authorities, we could reduce greenhouse gas emissions by 41–74% by 2030 if we switch to plant-based diets,[51] a strategy far more achievable than ever before given the abundance of climate friendly options. Research shows that cultured meat generates up to 96% lower greenhouse gas emissions than animal meat.[52] The climate emergency requires nothing less than an all-hands-on-board 'Marshall Plan' to restore and expand the planet's forests,[53] and for that, we must change our diets.

Deforestation

Deforestation, the intentional clearing of forested land,[54] is a global threat that destroys biodiversity and exacerbates climate change by increasing the amount of greenhouse gases in the atmosphere. Deforestation is the second biggest human-driven source of greenhouse gas emissions and it is driven primarily by expanding forestry and agriculture, the main

[49] Hijazi, Jennifer, "Hawaii Supreme Court Ruling Bolsters Rights-Based Climate Cases", *Bloomberg Law*, March 17, 2023.

[50] Intergovernmental Panel on Climate Change, Sixth Assessment Report, at 11.

[51] FAO, IFAD, UNICEF, WFP & WHO, "The State of Food Security and Nutrition in the World 2020. Transforming food systems for affordable healthy diets", Rome, FAO, at v. https://doi.org/10.4060/ca9692en

[52] Tuomisto, Hanna L. and Teixeira de Mattos, M. Joost, "Environmental Impacts of Cultured Meat Production", *Envir. Sci. Technol.* 2011, 45, 14, 6117–6123. https://doi.org/10.1021/es200130u

[53] Forests perform the critical role of removing carbon dioxide from the air.

[54] "Deforestation", Encyclopedia Entry, *National Geographic*, at https://education.nationalgeographic.org/resource/deforestation/

commodity groups of which are cattle meat and oilseed products.[55] During the 30 year period between 1990 and 2020, the world lost an estimated 420 million hectares of forest,[56] and between 2015 and 2020, 10 million hectares of forests were lost every year.[57] According to a 2020 report produced by UNEP and the Food and Agriculture Organization of the United Nations, total global forests decreased from 32.5% to 30.8% in the 3 decades between 1990 and 2020,[58] a staggering reduction for such a relatively short period of time.

A key conclusion from the 2020 report is that agricultural expansion continues to be the main driver of deforestation and forest fragmentation.[59] Researchers believe that agriculture is responsible for 60–80% of tropical deforestation.[60] Beef production is the primary cause of deforestation of tropical forests, followed by soybean production, and 70–75% of soy is used to feed livestock.[61] The 2020 report warns that if deforestation and forest degradation continue, there will be a "significant loss of biodiversity."[62] In fact, tropical deforestation is a primary cause of the

[55] Pendrill, Florence, et al., "Agricultural and forestry trade drives large share of tropical deforestation emissions", *Global Environmental Change*, Vol. 56, May 2019, at 1–10. https://doi.org/10.1016/j.gloenvcha.2019.03.002. ISSN 0959-3780.

[56] The net loss of forest area during the 30 year period, taking into account new forest areas, is 178 million hectares, roughly the size of Libya. *See*, FAO, "Global Forest Resources Assessment 2020: Main Report", Rome, at 18. https://doi.org/10.4060/ca9825en

[57] Ibid.

[58] The State of the World's Forests (2020 Edition), produced by the United Nations Environment Programme and the Food and Agriculture Organization of the United Nations, p. 10.

[59] The State of the World's Forests, at 81.

[60] Ritchie, Hannah and Roser, Max, "Deforestation and Forest Loss", 2021. Published online at OurWorldInData.org. at https://ourworldindata.org/forests-and-deforestation; *see also*, Report: *Consumer Goods and deforestation, An Analysis of the Extent and Nature of Illegality in Forest Conversion for Agriculture and Timber Plantations* (Forest Trends Report Series, Forest Trade and Finance, September 2014), at iii.

[61] "What Are The Biggest Drivers of Tropical Deforestation? They May Not be What You Think", *World Wildlife*, Issue Summer 2018, at https://www.worldwildlife.org/magazine/issues/summer-2018/articles/what-are-the-biggest-drivers-of-tropical-deforestation#; *see also*, Schiffman, Richard, "Demand for meat is destroying the Amazon. Smarter choices at the dinner table can go a long way to help", *Washington Post*, March 9, 2022.

[62] The State of the World's Forests, at 9.

world's biodiversity disaster,[63] and habitat destruction is the leading cause of species extinctions.[64] Researchers warn that the Amazon rainforest may have already reached the critical threshold of dieback.[65]

In the United States, habitat loss (whether by degradation, fragmentation, or destruction) is the primary threat to wildlife.[66] Forest fragmentation occurs when a large forest is broken down into smaller and more isolated areas, and it is responsible for "severe biodiversity losses."[67] The significant loss of wildlife along America's highways is testament to the impact that arbitrarily carving up habitats can have on wildlife. While deforestation has been decreasing over the last few decades, it is still contributing to the ongoing loss of biodiversity.[68]

Forests are critically important because trees and plants absorb vast amounts of carbon dioxide from the atmosphere that would otherwise contribute to global warming.[69] According to research, the world's forests are estimated to absorb ~7.6 billion metric tons of carbon dioxide each year, serving as a "net carbon sink" of ~1.5 times the annual amount of emissions in the United States.[70] Global forests are also home to more than 75% of the world's terrestrial biodiversity,[71] 80% of amphibian species, 75% of bird species, and 68% of mammal species.[72] For these animals,

[63] Semper-Pascual, Asuncion, "Biodiversity loss in deforestation frontiers: Linking occupancy modelling and physiological stress indicators to understand local extinctions", *Biological Conservation*, Vol. 236, 2019, at 281–288. https://doi.org/10.1016/j.biocon.2019.05.050. ISSN 0006-3207; *see also*, Ritchie, Hannah and Roser, Max, Deforestation and Forest Loss.

[64] *See*, "Why do animals and plants become endangered?", *USGA*, n.d., at https://www.usgs.gov/faqs/why-do-animals-and-plants-become-endangered#

[65] Boulton, Chris A., et al., "Pronounced loss of Amazon rainforest resilience since the early 2000s", *Nat. Clim. Chang.* 12, 271–278 (2022). https://doi.org/10.1038/s41558-022-01287-8

[66] "Habitat Loss", *National Wildlife Federation*, n.d., at https://www.nwf.org/Educational-Resources/Wildlife-Guide/Threats-to-Wildlife/Habitat-Loss

[67] Haddad, N.M., et al., "Habitat fragmentation and its lasting impact on Earth's ecosystems", *Science advances,* 1, e1500052 (2015). https://doi.org/10.1126/sciadv.1500052

[68] FAO and UNEP, "The State of the World's Forests 2020: Forests, biodiversity and people", Rome, at xvi-xvii. https://doi.org/10.4060/ca8642en

[69] "NASA Satellites Help Quantify Forests' Impacts on Global Carbon Budget", *NASA*, February 3, 2021.

[70] Ibid.

[71] FAO, Forward to "Global Forest Resources Assessment 2020: Main Report", Rome, at https://doi.org/10.4060/ca9825en

[72] FAO and UNEP, The State of the World's Forests 2020, at xvi.

the impact of deforestation is staggering. Every day, 137 species of animals, plants, and insects are lost to extinction.[73] Habitat loss proves deadly for countless animals, who are forced to find new shelter, food and water sources and who must avoid deadly predators and conditions, including traffic, exposure to chemicals, light and noise, and new infections.[74]

Whether deforestation is due to agriculture or urbanization, and whether it is legal or illegal, the result is the same: both human and animal lives are lost. Global forests are the source of food, biofuel, and medicines for more than 1 billion people,[75] and humanity has used more than 28,000 plant species for medicinal use, many of which are only found in forest ecosystems.[76] Forested areas are also home to many people. Indigenous people in the Amazonia depend on the land for their survival and when they are driven from their homes, the rates of malnutrition, alcoholism, disease, and suicide skyrocket.[77]

Deforestation is a global issue that requires a global solution. 'Zero deforestation' commitments are no longer sufficient. Forest preservation and restoration must be coupled with the establishment of new forests and all ecosystems must be protected.[78] In 2021, leaders from more than 100 countries, including the United States, Russia, China, and Brazil, pledged to end deforestation by 2030 for 85% of the world's forests during climate talks in Glasgow.[79] This pledge is backed by $12 billion dollars from a

[73] Nicol, Susan, "The Deadly Effects of Animal Deforestation and Why it's a Major Cause of Concern", *World Animal Foundation*, January 6, 2022.

[74] For more on the impact of habitat loss on wildlife, *see*, Sepp, Tuul, et al., "Urban environment and cancer in wildlife: available evidence and future research avenues", *Royal Society*, January 9, 2019. ISSN 1471-2954. https://doi.org/10.1098/rspb.2018.2434

[75] FAO, Forward to "Global Forest Resources Assessment 2020: Main Report", Rome, at https://doi.org/10.4060/ca9825en

[76] FAO and UNEP, The State of the World's Forests 2020. at xix.

[77] "Background Briefing: Deforestation", *Survival International*, n.d., at https://www.survivalinternational.org/about/deforestation

[78] For more on halting agriculture-driven deforestation, *see*, "Deforestation Position Paper: Preventing Agriculture Driven Deforestation and Conversion of Natural Ecosystems", *Rainforest Alliance*, December 10, 2020.

[79] *See*, "Glasgow Leaders' Declaration on Forests and Land Use", February 11, 2021, *UN Climate Change Conference UK 2021*, committing "to halt and reverse forest loss and land degradation by 2023"; *see generally*, Einhorn, Catrin and Buckley, Chris, "Global Leaders Pledge to End Deforestation by 2023", *New York Times*, November 10, 2021.

dozen countries and $7.2 billion from the private sector.[80] The United States has also released its own plan to conserve global forests, but it does little to address the driver of deforestation, animal agriculture, except for a fleeting mention of payments for "sustainable agriculture."[81] Legislation was introduced in the United States that would ban the importation of products into the country that originate from illegally deforested land,[82] but the bill remains stalled in Congress.

Destroying habitats to produce meat and dairy products comes at a high cost: the catastrophic consequences of deforestation and species extinction. Global scientists agree that humanity must move beyond its animal-based diet to a plant-based diet,[83] which uses 99% less land than animal meat.[84]

Environmental Destruction

Modern industrialized animal agriculture is a catastrophe for the environment and for human health. According to a 2021 report, ~12,700 deaths occur every year in the United States as a result of air pollution from animal agriculture.[85] Similar to communities located near toxic tanneries in India,[86] communities located in proximity to factory farms suffer from serious and chronic health problems and death as a result of contact with contaminated groundwater, polluted air, or pathogens such as parasites,

[80] Moore, Andrew, "COP26 Deforestation Pledge: A Promising Solution with an Uncertain Future", *NC State University, College of Natural Resources News*, November 10, 2021.

[81] "Plan to Conserve Global Forests: Critical Carbon Sinks", *The White House*, n.d., at https://www.whitehouse.gov/wp-content/uploads/2021/11/Plan_to_Conserve_Global_Forests_final.pdf

[82] Forest Act of 2021 - S.2950/H.R.5508, 117th Congress (2021–2022), prohibiting the importation into the U.S. of commodities produced by illegally deforested land.

[83] Ripple, William J., et al., 15,364 scientist signatories from 184 countries, "World Scientists' Warning to Humanity: A Second Notice", *BioScience*, Vol. 67, Issue 12, December 2017, at 1026–2018. https://doi.org/10.1093/biosci/bix125

[84] Tuomisto, Hanna L. and Teixeira de Mattos, M. Joost, "Environmental Impacts of Cultured Meat Production", *Environmental Science & Technology*, 2011, 45, 14, 6117–6123. https://doi.org/10.1021/es200130u

[85] The estimate includes the impact of animal feed production. *See*, Domingo, Nina G. G., et al., "Air quality – related health damages of food", *PNAS*, May 10, 2021. https://doi.org/10.1073/pnas.2013637118

[86] Price, Larry C. and Price, Debbie, M., "India: Toxic Tanneries", *Pulitzer Center*, March 9, 2017.

bacterium, or viruses.[87] In 2019, approximately 7 million deaths occurred worldwide due to air pollution, making it the fourth leading risk factor for premature death."[88] Minority and poor communities in the United States bear the brunt of the health impacts of factory farming,[89] making regulation of the industry an issue of environmental justice.

Notwithstanding the well documented adverse health impact of air pollution from animal waste, in 2008, the EPA issued a final rule that exempted animal agriculture from federal Comprehensive Environmental Response, Compensation, and Liability Act of 1980 (CERCLA)[90] and Emergency Planning and Community Right-to-Know Act of 1986 (EPCRA)[91] requirements that mandate reporting when large quantities of hazardous materials (e.g., ammonia; hydrogen sulfide; methane; nitrous oxide) are released into the environment.[92] In issuing the rule, the EPA joined other federal agencies, like the USDA, that have given favored industries a free pass when it comes to regulatory requirements. In 2017, the D.C. Circuit Court of Appeals vacated the 2008 rule,[93] but the EPA issued a new rule in 2019 to again exempt factory farms from reporting air pollution from animal waste.[94] Like the USDA, which suffered large staff

[87] Hribar, Carrie, "Understanding Concentrated Animal Feeding Operations and Their Impact on Communities" (Ed. Mark Schultz), *Environmental Health*, 2010, at 2–10; *see also*, Wang, Jackie, Nicole Tyau and Chelsea Rae Ybanez, "Farming activity contaminates water despite best practices", *Californian*, August 15, 2017.

[88] Annual Threat Assessment of the US Intelligence Community, at 18.

[89] *See*, Wing, S., Cole, D. and Grant G., "Environmental Injustice in North Carolina's Hog Industry", 108 *Environmental Health Perspective* 225 (2000), at 31. https://doi.org/10.1289/ehp.00108225

[90] CERCLA, 42 U.S.C. §9603 (Notification requirements respecting released substances).

[91] EPCRA, 42 U.S.C. §11004 (Emergency notification).

[92] CERCLA/EPCRA Administrative Reporting Exemption for Air Releases of Hazardous Substances from Animal Waste at Farms, 73 Fed. Reg. 76,948, 76,956/1 (December 18, 2008).

[93] The court rejected arguments that "the source and nature [of air releases from animal waste] are such that ongoing releases make an emergency response unnecessary, impractical and unlikely." *See*, Waterkeeper Alliance, Et Al. v. Environmental Protection Agency, U.S. Court of Appeals for the District of Columbia Circuit, No. 09-1017 (April 11, 2017).

[94] Beitsch, Rebecca, "EPA exempts farms from reporting pollution tied to animal waste", *The Hill*, June 5, 2019.

departures,[95] the EPA has lost people who were disillusioned by the agency's failure to enforce laws against factory farms.[96]

The EPA acknowledges that many rivers, lakes, and streams in the United States are contaminated by nitrogen and phosphorus, primary sources of which are animal manure and fertilizers used in animal agriculture.[97] Excess nutrients are responsible for the increasing number of toxic algae blooms and dead zones, which are incompatible with life.[98] The Centers for Disease Control and Prevention (CDC) warns that during flooding, contaminated floodwaters with animal waste from farms may include pathogens (e.g., E. coli), hormones, antibiotics, chemicals (e.g., ammonia, nitrates, phosphorus), and heavy metals (e.g., zinc, copper) that can cause respiratory and gastrointestinal illnesses.[99] There is no better example of this risk than in North Carolina, where millions of animals have perished in floodwaters over the years. News reports describe the deaths of: 16,000 pigs drowned during Hurricane Fran[100]; 30,000–110,000 pigs and 2 million chickens and turkeys perished during Hurricane Floyd[101]; 2800–5500 pigs and 3.4 million chickens were lost in Hurricane Florence[102]; and 2800 pigs and 1.8 million chickens died during Hurricane

[95] Fobar, Rachel, "USDA accused of ignoring animal welfare violations in favor of business interests", *National Geographic*, October 13, 2021.

[96] Michele Merkel, co-director of Food & Water Justice, left her job as an attorney at the EPA because animal agriculture "has avoided any effective regulation and accountability for a long time." *See*, Flesher, John, "Factory farms provide abundant food, but environment suffers", *Associated Press*, February 6, 2020.

[97] Environmental Topics, Nutrient Pollution, *E.P.A.*, n.d., at https://www.epa.gov/nutrientpollution/issue

[98] "The Effects: Dead Zones and Harmful Algal Blooms", *EPA, Nutrient Pollution* at https://www.epa.gov/nutrientpollution/effects

[99] "Water Contamination from Animal Feeding Operations", *CDC, Water, Sanitation & Hygiene-related Emergencies & Outbreaks, Sanitation and Wastewater*, n.d., at https://www.cdc.gov/healthywater/emergency/sanitation-wastewater/animal-feeding-operations.html

[100] Rivin, Gabe, "Bills Allow Idled Hog Farms to Return Under Old Environmental Standards", *NC Health News*, May 22, 2015.

[101] Reports vary. *See.* e.g., Rivin, Gabe, "Bills Allow Idled Hog Farms to Return Under Old Environmental Standards", *NC Health News*, May 22, 2015, citing 30,000 pig deaths; *but see*, Moon, Emily, "North Carolina's Hog Waste Problem Has a Long History. Why Wasn't It Solved in Time for Hurricane Florence?" *Pacific Standard*, September 16, 2018, citing 110,000 pig deaths.

[102] Reports vary. *See,* e.g., Ferreira, Becky, "At Least 3.4 Million Farm Animals Drowned in the Aftermath of Hurricane Florence", *Vice*, 9.19.2018, citing 5500 pig deaths; *but see*, Polansek, Tom, "Hog deaths, manure flooding from Florence seen surpassing 2016 hurricane", *Reuters*, September 18, 2018, citing 2800 pig deaths.

Matthew.[103] With each new hurricane, there are reports of more death and destruction in North Carolina, with rural counties turned into seas of toxic, bacteria-laden wastelands,[104] but the state has failed to take action to protect its residents and animals due to the influence of powerful farm lobbies.

There is a growing global recognition that much more must be done to protect the planet, as demonstrated by the strong support for the Paris Climate Agreement.[105] International organizations, like INTERPOL and WCO, consider environmental crimes to be serious offenses because of their severe consequences, including forced migration, the emergence of zoonotic diseases, effects on climate change and ramifications for millions of people whose livelihood depends on the environment.[106] A team of worldwide legal experts are advocating for "ecocide" to be recognized as an international crime on par with genocide, war crimes, crimes against humanity, and crimes of aggression.[107]

There is growing evidence that nature has an important impact on human health, including "mental/psychological health, healing, heart rate, concentration, levels of stress, blood pressure, behavior, and other health factors,"[108] and our estrangement from nature has had catastrophic consequences for all life on the planet. The right to a clean, healthy, and sustainable environment is so important that, for the first time in its his-

[103] Polansek, Tom, "Hog deaths, manure flooding from Florence seen surpassing 2016 hurricane", *Reuters,* September 18, 2018.

[104] *See,* e.g., Moon, Emily, "Hurricane Florence has Already Flooded Pits of Toxic Waste in North Carolina", *Pacific Standard,* September 18, 2018.

[105] Paris Agreement to the United Nations Framework Convention on Climate Change, December 12, 2015, T.I.A.S. No. 16-1104.

[106] "Global arrests and seizures: INTERPOL-WCO operation strikes wildlife and timber trafficking networks", *INTERPOL,* November 30, 2021, at https://www.interpol.int/en/News-and-Events/News/2021/Global-arrests-and-seizures-INTERPOL-WCO-operation-strikes-wildlife-and-timber-trafficking-networks

[107] The proposal would define ecocide as "unlawful or wanton acts committed with knowledge that there is a substantial likelihood of severe and either widespread or long-term damage to the environment being caused by those acts". *See,* Fischels, Josie, "How 165 Words Could Make Mass Environmental Destruction an international Crime", *NPR,* June 27, 2021.

[108] *See generally,* "Report of the Special Rapporteur on the issue of human rights obligations relating to the enjoyment of a safe, clean, healthy and sustainable environment", *United Nations General Assembly, Human Rights Council,* A/HRC/34/49, January 19, 2017, § II(B)(1)(17) (Mental Health); *see also,* Jimenez, Marcia P., et al., "Associations between Nature Exposure and Health: A Review of the Evidence", *Int J Environ Res Public Health,* May 2021, 18(9): 4790. https://doi.org/10.3390/ijerph18094790

tory, the United Nations Human Rights Council recognized it as a human right in 2021.[109] Many countries already recognize the right to a healthy environment by law. In fact, more than 150 nations have enshrined the principles of a right to a healthy environment in their national legislation.[110] The United States is unfortunately not among these nations. Some countries view the right to a healthy environment as so important that they have included it in their constitution. Germany's Constitution requires the state, in recognition of its responsibility to future generations, to "protect the natural foundations of life and animals,"[111] while Slovenia's Constitution recognizes a right to a "healthy living environment."[112] Admittedly, constitutional rights to a healthy environment do not always translate into environmental protection. Brazil's Constitution requires the government to "defend and to preserve the environment for present and future generations,"[113] yet deforestation in Brazil hit its highest level in 15 years in 2021[114] as a result of cattle ranching, logging and commodity driven agriculture.[115] That said, the recognition of the importance of the environment in Brazil's highest governing document speaks to the importance of the issue in that country. In the United States, environmental

[109] "Access to a healthy environment, declared a human right by UN rights council", *United Nations, UN News, Global perspective Human stories*, October 8, 2021, at https://news.un.org/en/story/2021/10/1102582. Resolution 48/13 calls on nations to work together to implement this newly recognized right.

[110] Aguila, Yann, "The Right to a Healthy Environment", *IUCN,* 10.29.2021.

[111] Germany's Constitution of 1949 with Amendments through 2012, Art. 20(a) (Protection of the natural foundations of life and animals), *Constitute Project*, at https://www.constituteproject.org/

[112] Slovenia's Constitution 1991 with Amendments through 2013, Art. 72 (Healthy Living Environment), *Constitute Project.*

[113] Brazil's Constitution of 1988 with Amendments through 2017, Chapter VI (The Environment), Art. 225, §1(VII), *Constitute Project.*

[114] Bowman, Emma, "Amazon deforestation in Brazil hits its worst level in 15 years", *NPR,* November 19, 2021; *see also*, Silva Junior, C.H.L., et al., "The Brazilian Amazon deforestation rate in 2020 is the greatest of the decade", *Nature Ecology & Evolution* 5, 144–145 (2021). https://doi.org/10.1038/s41559-020-01368-x

[115] Samuel Blum, et al., "Deforestation in Brazil", *ArcGIS StoryMaps,* July 25, 2019, at https://storymaps.arcgis.com/stories/38535a937f82494a8e37094d9efc6121/print

accountability has become a political battleground.[116] At times, the EPA must be sued to be compelled to enforce the law.[117]

Most people understand that litter kills wildlife[118] and that fossil fuels are dirty, dangerous, and deadly to wildlife.[119] Many are not aware that the "external costs" of inexpensive meat negatively impact society through environmental degradation, depletion of natural resources, decreases in property values, and impact on human health.[120] Major international organizations agree that plant-based diets have less environmental impact than animal-based diets.[121] Despite the negative impact that meat and dairy products have on the environment, the United States has one of the highest per capita meat consumption levels in the world,[122] perpetuated by government subsidies that keep meat and dairy products more affordable and a political culture that shields agricultural industries from environmental accountability. By subsidizing industries that degrade the environment without regulatory accountability, the legal system fails both people and animals.

[116] For more the politics and the environment, *see* Hoffarth, Mark R. and Hodson, Gordon, "Green on the outside, red on the inside: Perceived environmentalist threat as a factor explaining political polarization of climate change", *Journal of Environ. Psychology*, Vol. 45 (March 2016), at 40–49. https://doi.org/10.1016/j.jenvp.2015.11.002

[117] *See*, e.g., Krupnick, Matt, "EPA sued over lack of plan to regulate water pollution from factory farms", *The Guardian*, October 19, 2022; *see also*, "After Long Delay, Groups Sue EPA for Response on Factory Farm Water Pollution Rules", *Center for Food Safety*, October 11, 2022.

[118] *See*, e.g., McSweeney, Eoin, "Covid-19 PPE litter is killing wildlife", *CNN*, 3.30.2021; *see also*, Krosofsky, Andrew, "Plastic Pollution Kills Millions of Animals Every Year", *Green Matters*, January 7, 2021.

[119] Report, "Fueling Extinction: How Dirty Energy Drives Wildlife to the Brink", *Endangered Species Coalition*, n.d., at https://www.endangered.org/campaigns/annual-top-ten-report/fueling-extinction/

[120] More than 10 years ago, David Robinson Simon made the case that animal agriculture imposes at minimum a staggering $414 billion of costs on society that are not paid by producers, including increased health insurance premiums, higher taxes, lower home values and natural resources impacted by factory farms. *See*, Meatonomics at xx.

[121] FAO, IFAD, UNICEF, WFP & WHO, "The State of Food Security and Nutrition in the World 2020.

[122] McCarthy, Niall, "The Countries That Eat the Most Meat", *Statista*, May 5, 2020; *see also*, "Per capital eat consumption by type, 2019", *Our World in Data*, at https://ourworldindata.org/grapher/per-capita-meat-type?country

Loss of Biodiversity

Biodiversity is the beautiful tapestry of nature that supports all life on the planet. It includes the rich variety of all living species, including animals, plants, fungi, bacteria and insects,[123] and is defined by international law as "the variability among living organisms from all sources including … terrestrial, marine and other aquatic ecosystems."[124] Biodiversity is the blueprint for all life on our planet, providing core functions, such as maintaining soil quality, helping with the pollination of crops and plants, and assisting with the decomposition of waste matter.[125] The World Health Organization considers biodiversity and ecosystems to be central pillars of all life on Earth, including human life.[126] Reports on the loss of biodiversity conjure up images of declining animal populations on African savannas, but the threat is much greater. It involves the entire living world. Biodiversity is critically important to humanity. It is "fundamental to human well-being and a healthy planet, and economic prosperity."[127] We depend on it "for food, medicine, energy, clean air and water, [and] security from natural disasters … and it supports all systems of life on earth."[128]

The loss of biodiversity is recognized as one of the planet's greatest threats, a crisis that was unleased by humans that has serious implications for all life on the planet.[129] Research on the crisis is consistent and alarming. In 2019, a team of 145 experts from 50 countries examined roughly 15,000 scientific and government sources to assess the state of the planet's biodiversity. The report found that biodiversity is rapidly declining, ecosystems are deteriorating and 1 million animal and plant species are at threat of extinction, driven by (in descending order of impact): changes in

[123] See, Encyclopedia Entry on "Biodiversity", National Geographic Resource Library.

[124] Convention on Biological Diversity, June 5, 1992. 1760 U.N.T.S. 79; 31 I.L.M. 818 (1992).

[125] Argent, Gemma, "What are the Benefits of Biodiversity?" *Sciencing*, January 9, 2018, at https://sciencing.com/list-6177330-benefits-biodiversity-.html

[126] Biodiversity and Health, *World Health Organization*, June 3, 2015, at https://www.who.int/news-room/fact-sheets/detail/biodiversity-and-health

[127] *See*, Kunming-Montreal Global biodiversity framework, Draft decision submitted by the President, UN Environment Programme, Convention on Biological Diversity, Conference of the Parties to the Convention on Biological Diversity, Fifteenth meeting – Part II, Montreal, Canada, December 7–19, 2022 (CBD/COP/15/L.25, December 18, 2022).

[128] Ibid.

[129] *See*, "Connecting Global Priorities: Biodiversity and Human Health, a State of Knowledge Review", *World Health Organization and the Convention on Biological Diversity*, 2015, at x. ISBN 978-92-4-150853-7.

land and sea use; direct exploitation; climate change; and pollution.[130] Intergovernmental Science-Policy Platform on Biodiversity and Ecosystem Services (IPBES) Chair, Sir Robert Watson, warns that, "[t]he health of ecosystems on which we and all other species depend is deteriorating more rapidly than ever. We are eroding the very foundations of our economies, livelihoods, food security, health and quality of life worldwide."[131]

A 2020 United Nations report further confirmed that biodiversity on earth "is plunging, with a quarter of species facing extinction, many within decades."[132] A World Wildlife Fund 2022 report again confirmed that human activity is destroying biodiversity, warning that more that 1 million species of animals and plants are facing extinction.[133] A 2022 report estimates that at least 1.2 million animal and plant species face extinction,[134] and a 2023 report warns that 40% of animals in the United States are at risk of extinction and that 41% of ecosystems are facing collapse.[135] Scientists warn that efforts in the areas of climate change and biodiversity loss "are not even moving in the right direction."[136]

Monitored wildlife populations have plunged, on average, a shocking 69% from 1970 to 2018, with freshwater species having the largest overall global decline (83%) and Latin America suffering the greatest regional decline (94%).[137] Insect populations are not immune. The "insect apocalypse" threatens critically important services upon which humans depend, including pollination of fruits and vegetables, water purification,

[130] Report: "Nature's Dangerous Decline 'Unprecedented'; Species Extinction Rates 'Accelerating'", *Intergovernmental Science-Policy Platform on Biodiversity and Ecosystem Services (IPBES)*, May 6, 2019.

[131] Chappell, Bill and Rott, Nathan, "1 Million Animal and Plant Species Are At Risk of Extinction, U.N. Report Says", *NRP*, May 6, 2019.

[132] *See*, Human Development Report 2020.

[133] Almond, R.E.A., et al. (Eds), "Living Planet Report 2022 – Building a Nature-Positive Society", *WWF*, at 4 and 16. ISBN 978-2-88085-316-7.

[134] *See*, e.g., "What are the extent and causes of biodiversity loss?", *The London School of Economics and Political Science, Grantham Research Institute on Climate Change and the Environment*, December 2, 2022, at https://www.lse.ac.uk/granthaminstitute/explainers/what-are-the-extent-and-causes-of-biodiversity-loss/#

[135] Brooks, Brad, "Exclusive: Huge chunk of plants, animals in U.S. at risk of extinction", *Reuters*, February 6, 2023.

[136] Global Sustainable Development Report 2019, at xx.

[137] "Living Planet Report 2022", *WWF*, October 13, 2022, at 4 and 32.

decomposition of leaves and wood, dung and carrion removal, soil formation and the control of disease vectors.[138]

Nearly all drivers of biodiversity loss are caused by humans. In fact, 99% of all threatened species are at risk as a result of human activity.[139] Researchers agree that the crisis is driven primarily by overexploitation and agriculture.[140] Humanity is converting the planet's biodiversity-rich forests into pastures for beef production. Humanity is overexploiting other species and polluting their habitats. Humanity is driving climate change by burning fossil fuels and by destroying forests. Humanity is responsible, intentionally or unintentionally, for the introduction of non-native species.[141]

Notwithstanding the alarming research, key habitats that are critical to biodiversity are still being destroyed.[142] Biodiversity in Ukraine, home to 35% of Europe's biodiversity, is being systemically destroyed by the ravages of war and weapons of self-destruction, jeopardizing natural carbon sinks that we need to fight climate change.[143] Ukraine is also home to one-third of the world's most fertile land (the Chernozem soil), and international experts are concerned that the environmental catastrophe unfolding in Ukraine threatens to unleash the worst global food crisis since World War II.[144]

The consequences of the biodiversity loss to humanity will be catastrophic. Research warns that the loss of biodiversity can exacerbate inequalities,[145] raising issues of fairness and justice among nations and people.[146] Biodiversity is so important that the United Nations considers the

[138] Wagner, David L., et al., "Insect decline in the Anthropocene: Death by a thousand cuts", *PNAS*, January 11, 2021. https://doi.org/10.1073/pnas.2023989118

[139] "Biodiversity & Extinction, Biodiversity, Loss and the Extinction Crisis", *Tropical Conservation Fund*, n.d., at https://www.tropicalconservationfund.org/biodiversity.html

[140] Maxwell, S.L., et al., "The ravages of guns, nets and bulldozers", August 10, 2016, *Nature*, 536, 143–145. https://doi.org/10.1038/536143a

[141] "People and Invasive Species", *National Geographic*, June 2, 2022.

[142] Rodrigues, Meghie, "To end illegal deforestation, Brazil may legalize it entirely, experts warn", *Mongabay*, December 20, 2021.

[143] "War in Ukraine has devastating consequences for biodiversity", *IFAW*, February 24, 2023.

[144] Harari, S. and Annesi-Maesano, I., "The War in Ukraine is an Environmental Catastrophe", *The Union*, December 7, 2022.

[145] Global Sustainable Development Report 2019, at xx.

[146] *See*, e.g., McCarthy, Joe, "Why Climate Change and Poverty are Inextricable Linked", *Global Citizen*, February 19, 2020.

protection of biodiversity to be critical to a wide range of human rights, including rights to food, medicine, housing, health, and water.[147] The European Parliament commissioned a study, in 2020, on biodiversity as a human right, which is recognized by Member States by virtue of their participation in The Convention on Biological Diversity and in international human rights treaties.[148] The report details the critical functions of ecosystems, including water and air purification, disease and pest control, soil fertility and resilience to climate change, and warns that the loss of biodiversity can impact food and water availability and the development of medicines, as well as increase life-threatening floods and hurricanes for hundreds of millions of people.[149] Despite the critical role that biodiversity plays, research shows that we are losing vast amounts of biodiversity at a much faster rate than the historical rate of species loss, as much as hundreds or thousands of times faster than historical rates over the last tens of millions of years.[150]

In 2022, the United States acknowledged that the loss of biodiversity presents an existential threat to human health and it reiterated its support for "an ambitious and transformative" global framework that allows biodiversity to thrive,[151] but it has not dedicated sufficient funds to address the crisis. The United States committed $2 billion dollars to help restore the health of streams, rivers and aquatic ecosystems,[152] but the funding is insufficient and initiative does not address the primary source of water pollution (i.e., animal agriculture). A separate initiative, the *America the Beautiful* initiative, commits $1 billion dollars to public-private partnerships to restore and conserve 30% of lands and waters in the United States

[147] *See generally*, "Report of the Special Rapporteur on the issue of human rights obligations relating to the enjoyment of a safe, clean, healthy and sustainable environment", *United Nations General Assembly, Human Rights Council*, A/HRC/34/49, January 19, 2017.

[148] Morgera, Elisa, Study: "Biodiversity as a Human Right and its Implications for the EU's External Action", req. by European Parliament's Subcommittee on Human Rights, April 6, 2020, at v. ISBN: 978-92-846-6489-4. https://doi.org/10.2861/104569

[149] Biodiversity as a Human Right, at 3.

[150] Ceballos, Gerardo, et al., "Vertebrates on the brink as indicators of biological annihilation and the sixth mass extinction", *PNAS*, Vol. 117, No. 24, June 1, 2020. https://doi.org/10.1073/pnas.1922686117; *see also*, "Biodiversity & Extinction, Biodiversity, Loss and the Extinction Crisis", *Tropical Conservation Fund*, n.d., at https://www.tropicalconservationfund.org/biodiversity.html

[151] "Highlighting U.S. Efforts to Combat the Biodiversity Crisis, Fact Sheet, Office of the Spokesperson", *U.S. Department of State,* January 15, 2022.

[152] Ibid.

by 2030,[153] but the initiative does not address one of the primary drivers of the crisis, animal agriculture. In 2021, the U.S. Agency for International Development invested $319.5 million to conserve biodiversity and to help reduce wildlife trafficking,[154] but subsidies to meat and dairy industries result in deforestation and tolerance of trophy hunting drives wildlife trafficking. The United States must significantly increase funding to combat the enormous scale of the biodiversity loss crisis and it must address the root anthropogenic causes of the crisis, including subsidies to the meat and dairy industries that drive pollution, deforestation, and climate change.

The global community recognizes the profound risks that we all face. In 2015, United Nations Member States acknowledged that transformative changes are needed and unanimously adopted the promising "2030 Agenda for Sustainable Development" as a blueprint "to protect the planet from degradation", to ensure that "progress occurs in harmony with nature", and to "ensure that all human beings can fulfil their potential in dignity and equality and in a healthy environment."[155] The Sustainable Development Goals include No Hunger (Goal 2); Clean Water and Sanitation (Goal 6); Sustainable Energy (Goal 7); Responsible Consumption and Production (Goal 12); Climate Action (Goal 13); Sustainable Use of Oceans (Goal 14); and Halting Biodiversity and Land Degradation (Goal 15).[156] In 2022, however, it was reported that climate change, human conflicts, and COVID-19 have placed achievement of the goals in "grave jeopardy."[157] The threats that we face are interrelated and are compounding. In 2020, UNODC published its World Wildlife Crime Report, concluding that humanity's exploitation of nature has led not only to an "unprecedented biodiversity loss and a worsening climate crisis" but also to the emergence of new zoonotic diseases.[158] Humanity's

[153] "America the Beautiful: Spotlighting the Work to Restore, Connect and Conserve 30 Percent of Lands and Water by 2023", *U.S. Department of the Interior*, at https://www.doi.gov/priorities/america-the-beautiful

[154] Id.

[155] United Nations General Assembly, Resolution 70/1 (Transforming our world: the 2030 Agenda for Sustainable Development), adopted on September 25, 2015.

[156] *See*, "The 17 Goals, The 2030 Agenda for Sustainable Development", *United Nations, Department of Economic and Social Affairs, Sustainable Development* (adopted by all United Nations Member States in 2015), n.d., at https://sdgs.un.org/goals

[157] "The Sustainable Development Goals Report, 2022", *United Nations*, 2022, at 3. ISBN 978-92-1-101448-8.

[158] UNODC World Wildlife Crime Report, Trafficking in protected species, May 2020, at 3. ISBN: 978-92-1-148349-9.

relentless and unregulated assault on nature is driving the increasing number of new infections and diseases that infect humans,[159] and it is a crisis of our own making.

Zoonotic Diseases

At the time of this writing, the world is recovering from the worst pandemic since the Influenza Pandemic of 1918. As of July 2023, more than 768 million people have been infected with COVID-19 worldwide and more than 6.9 million have died.[160] While the origins of the virus remain in dispute, experts agree that it resulted from human contact with animals. Whether the virus originated in so-called wet markets or at the infamous Wuhan Institute of Virology, the message is clear: our close contact with (and manipulation of) nature can lead to dire consequences and no one is safe.

Humanity is still reeling from the cascading effects of the pandemic, including economic and supply chain disruptions; record world debt[161]; persistent global inflation; the shuttering of entire industries; rampant inflation; and the loss of livelihoods. The full economic impact is not yet known, but the International Monetary Fund[162] expects the global cost of the COVID-19 pandemic to exceed $12.5 trillion dollars through 2024.[163] In addition, there is the true human cost, which will be felt for years to come: the loss of friends and family; the mental health impact of

[159] Vidal, John, "Pandemics: Humans are the culprits", *UNESCO, The UNESCO Courier"*, e-ISSN 2220-2293, at https://en.unesco.org/courier/2021-3/pandemics-humans-are-culprits#

[160] "WHO Coronavirus (COVID-19) Dashboard, *World Health Organization*, at https://covid19.who.int/

[161] Gaspar, Vitor, et al., "Global Debt Reaches a Record $226 Trillion: Policymakers must strike the right balance in the face of high debt and rising inflation", *IMF Blog*, December 15, 2021.

[162] The International Monetary Fund (IMF) aims to secure prosperity and sustainable growth for its 190 member nations by encouraging trade and economic growth and by further global monetary cooperation. *See*, https://www.imf.org/en/About/Factsheets/IMF-at-a-Glance#

[163] Shalal, Andrea, "IMF sees cost of COVID pandemic rising beyond $12.5 trillion estimate", *Reuters*, January 20, 2022.

lockdowns; the risk of extreme poverty for tens of millions of people[164]; and the educational and developmental impact felt by children all over the world, which the United Nations calls a "global generational catastrophe".[165] Instead of addressing the root cause of the pandemic (e.g., wildlife trade; animal research), the focus has been on eradicating the virus, despite its ability to mutate and the certainty that new pathogens will emerge. Without the rapid development of vaccines for COVID-19, the estimated global cost associated with the virus, including its economic impact, could have been $3.4 trillion dollars per year.[166]

As humans come into greater contact with animals, the incidence of "zoonotic" diseases (i.e., diseases caused by harmful germs like viruses and bacteria that can spread from animals to people and cause illness[167]) increases. In fact, the majority of new infectious diseases, such as COVID-19, are zoonotic and are linked to habitat loss and contact with wildlife.[168] Notwithstanding the risks, the U.S. imports more wildlife than any other nation on earth, including 224+ million live animals and 883 million wildlife specimens every year.[169] These staggering numbers are in addition to the millions of live farmed animals imported into the United States every year,[170] placing its citizens and the global community at risk

[164] Joint statement by ILO, FAO, IFAD and WHO, "Impact of COVID-19 on people's livelihoods, their health and our food systems", *World Health Organization,* October 13, 2020.

[165] *See*, "UN Secretary-General warns of educational catastrophe, pointing to UNESCO estimates of 24 million learners at risk of dropping out', *UNESCO,* June 8, 2020, reporting that in June 2020, 94% of the world's student population (~1.6 billion learners in more than 190 countries) were impacted by the closure of educational facilities at the peak of the pandemic crisis; *see also*, Martinez, Elin, "A Generation of Children Impacted by Covid-19 School Closures: Governments Should Act to Avert a Greater Global Education Crisis", *Human Rights Watch*, March 9, 2022.

[166] Hafner, Marco, et al., "The global economic cost of COVID-19 vaccine nationalism", Santa Monica, CA: RAND Corporation, 2020, at www.rand.org/pubs/research_briefs/RBA769-1.html

[167] "Zoonotic Diseases", *U.S. Centers for Disease Control and Prevention*, at https://www.cdc.gov/onehealth/basics/zoonotic-diseases.html

[168] "Zoonoses: Key Facts", *World Health Organization,* July 29, 2020; *see also*, FAO and UNEP, The State of the World's Forests 2020, at xix.

[169] "End Wildlife Trade, An Action Plan to Prevent Future Pandemics", *Center for Biological Diversity and the Natural Resources Defense Council, Inc.*, May 2020, at 1.

[170] "Livestock and Meat International Trade Data", *USDA Economic Research Service*, updated July 7, 2023, at https://www.ers.usda.gov/data-products/livestock-and-meat-international-trade-data/

for future pandemics. The CDC estimates that more than 60% of known infectious diseases in people are zoonotic and that 75% of emerging infectious diseases in people originate from animals.[171] Zoonotic health threats include the broader category of antimicrobial resistance (i.e., resistance of bacteria, viruses, fungi and parasite to drugs), which has serious global health implications.[172] In the most comprehensive study to date involving more than 204 countries, researchers identified at least 1.27 million deaths in 2019 that were the direct result of antimicrobial resistance.[173] The CDC reports that more than 3 million Americans acquire an antimicrobial-resistant infection each year, resulting in ~50,000 deaths.[174] The destruction of rainforests, animal agriculture, animal research, and humanity's exploitation of wildlife (e.g., exotic pets, food, medicine) all have deadly consequences.[175]

The COVID-19 pandemic also impacted animals. Captive animals at zoos and farmed animals have succumbed to infections,[176] and countries have culled millions of fur farmed animals over fears of mutations of the virus, with Denmark alone culling 17 million minks in November 2020.[177] Disease is an endemic part of industries that exploit animals and mass culls are standard practice. In 2014 and 2015, 50 million chickens and turkeys

[171] "Zoonotic Diseases", *U.S. Centers for Disease Control and Prevention.*

[172] Angulo, F.J. et al., "Antimicrobial resistance in zoonotic enteric pathogens", *Rev Sci Tech*, 23(2) (2004), at 485–96. https://doi.org/10.20506/rst.23.2.1499

[173] Murray, Christopher J. L., et al., "Global burden of bacterial antimicrobial resistance in 2019: a systematic analysis", *The Lancet,* Vol. 399, Issue 10325, at 629–655, February 12, 2022 (pub January 20, 2022). https://doi.org/10.1016/S0140-6736(21)02724-0

[174] "COVID-19: U.S. Impact on Antimicrobial Resistance, Special Report 2022", *CDC,* Atlanta, GA: U.S. Department of Health and Human Services, CDC; 2022, at 3. https://doi.org/10.15620/cdc:117915

[175] For more background on zoonotic diseases, *see generally*, Adekunle Sanyaolu et al., "Epidemiology of Zoonotic Diseases in the United States: A Comprehensive Review", *Journal of Infectious Diseases & Epidemiology.* Vol. 2, November 15, 2016. https://doi.org/10.23937/2474-3658/1510021

[176] See, e.g., Daly, Natasha, "Seven more big cats test positive for coronavirus at Bronx Zoo", *National Geographic*, April 22, 2020; Maron, Dina Fine, "Denmark to cull 15 million mink after coronavirus spillover into humans", *National Geographic,* November 4, 2020.

[177] Bubola, Emma, et al., "Denmark's Leader Apologies for Botched Mink Cull During Pandemic", *New York Times,* July 1, 2022.

in the United States died or were destroyed due to Avian Influenza (HPAI),[178] only to see it infect more than 58 million birds in 2022.[179]

While not all pandemics are caused by human interference with wildlife,[180] many are, including the HIV/AIDS pandemic,[181] plague outbreaks and the Middle East Respiratory Syndrome (MERS).[182] There are also risks in forests, including Malaria, Lyme disease, and Ebola,[183] and every year there are salmonella outbreaks in the United States from animals and animal products.[184] In 2023, swine influenza was spread from pigs at an agricultural fair.[185] The incidence of zoonotic diseases, such as Swine Flu, Avian Flu, Ebola, and Severe Acute Respiratory Syndrome (SARS), is also increasing.[186] In 2020, the CDC warned of a new group of H1N1 swine influenza viruses in China that are "pandemic potential"

[178] Ramos, Sean, "Impacts of the 2014–2015 Highly Pathogenic Avian Influenza Outbreak on the U.S. Poultry Sector", *USDA*, December 2017.

[179] "2022 Confirmations of Highly Pathogenic Avian Influenza in Commercial and Backyard Flocks", *USDA*, April 21, 2023 at https://www.aphis.usda.gov/aphis/ourfocus/animalhealth/animal-disease-information/avian/avian-influenza/hpai-2022/2022-hpai-commercial-backyard-flocks

[180] Cholera originated from microbes living in the water, while tuberculosis originated from microbes living in the soil. *See*, Weiss, Robin A. and Sankaran, Neeraja, "Emergence of epidemic diseases: zoonoses and other origins", *Fac Rev.*, January 18, 2022; 11:2. https://doi.org/10.12703/r/11-2

[181] Acquired immunodeficiency syndrome (AIDS) is caused by two viruses, HIV-1 and HIV-2, both of which are the result of multiple cross-species transmissions of immunodeficiency viruses naturally infecting African primates, with the HIV-1 group being the principal cause of the AIDS pandemic.

[182] *See*, Sharp, Paul M. and Hahn, Beatrice H., "Originals of HIV and the AIDS Pandemic", *Cold Spring Harb Perspect Med.* 2011 Sept;1(1):a006841. https://doi.org/10.1101/cshperspect.a006841

[183] FAO and UNEP, The State of the World's Forests 2020, at xix.

[184] "US Outbreaks of Zoonotic Diseases Spread between Animals & People", *Centers for Disease Control and Prevention: Healthy Pets, Healthy People*", at https://www.cdc.gov/healthypets/outbreaks.html

[185] Goodman, Brenda, "Two people caught swine flu after visiting pig exhibits at agricultural fairs, CDC reports", *CNN*, August 4, 2023.

[186] Adekunle Sanyaolu et al., "Epidemiology of Zoonotic Diseases in the United States: A Comprehensive Review", *Journal of Infectious Diseases & Epidemiology*, Vol. 2, November 15, 2016. https://doi.org/10.23937/2474-3658/1510021

with the ability to infect humans.[187] Still, China is building soaring high-rises to farm even more pigs.[188]

The public health risks associated with animal agriculture do not stop at zoonotic diseases. Animal agriculture forces stressed animals to live alongside dead and diseased animals in such crowded, filthy conditions that antibiotics are needed just to keep them alive.[189] Despite the World Health Organization's warning that antibiotics should not be used in animal agriculture to promote growth or to prevent disease,[190] some countries use ~80% of medically important antibiotics to promote growth or to prevent disease in farm animals.[191] The United States is one of the biggest consumers of antimicrobials in livestock production.[192] Animals raised without antibiotics can still carry antimicrobial-resistant bacteria in their gut, which can pass from the animal into food products.[193] By feeding antibiotics to healthy animals, we are contributing to the rise of deadly new forms of antibiotic resistance[194] and CDC experts are alarmed.[195] The World Health Organization considers antibiotic resistance to be one of the greatest threats to global health and warns that unless urgent action is taken, the world could face a "post-antibiotic era" where people can die from

[187] "CDC Takes Action to Prepare Against "G4" Swine Flu Viruses in China with Pandemic Potential", *CDC*, July 2, 2020. https://www.cdc.gov/flu/spotlights/2019-2020/cdc-prepare-swine-flu.html; *see also*, Cohen, Jon, "Swine flue strain with human pandemic potential increasingly found in pigs in China: New study spotlights influenza virus that could wreak havoc if it adapts to humans", *Science*, June 29, 2020.

[188] Wakabayashi, Daisuke and Fu, Claire, "China's Bid to Improve Food Production? Giant Powers of Pigs", *New York Times*, February 8, 2023.

[189] Aysha Akhtar, *Animals and Public Health: Why Treating Animals Better is Critical to Human Welfare*, Palgrave Macmillan, 2012, Ch. 4.

[190] "Antibiotic resistance", *World Health Organization*, July 31, 2020.

[191] "Stop using antibiotics in healthy animals to prevent the spread of antibiotic resistance", *World Health Organization*, November 7, 2017.

[192] Van Boeckel, Thomas P., et al., "Global trends in antimicrobial use in food animals", *PNAS*, Marcy 19, 2015. https://doi.org/10.1073/pnas.1503141112

[193] "Where Resistance Spreads: Food Supply", *CDC*, n.d., at https://www.cdc.gov/drugresistance/food.html

[194] Moyer, Melinda Wenner, "Travel from the Farm to your Table, Antibiotic-resistant bacteria from livestock pose a deadly risk to people. But the farm lobby won't let scientists track the danger", *Scientific American*, Vol. 315, No. 6, December 1, 2016, at 70–79. www.jstor.org/stable/26047254

[195] "Antibiotic Resistance Threats in the United States, 2019", Atlanta, GA: U.S. Department of Health and Human Services, CDC; 2019, at www.cdc.gov/DrugResistance/Biggest-Threats.html

common infections and injuries.[196] The tendency in the United States is to point to practices in other countries as sources of disease outbreaks, but factory farms in the United States are petri dishes for zoonotic diseases, as evidenced by the 2009 Swine Flu outbreak[197] and the 1997 Bird Flu outbreak, both of which originated from animal agricultural settings.[198]

The CDC warns that climate change is increasing certain health risks, including antibiotic-resistant infections.[199] The COVID-19 pandemic resulted in an increase in antimicrobial resistance as healthcare workers were pushed beyond their breaking points in 2020.[200] Research confirms that antimicrobial resistance is on the rise, but the number of companies and new antibiotics that could combat it is on the decline.[201] Wildlife trafficking is a further complication. The United Nations warned again in 2021 that wildlife trafficking increases the risk that zoonotic diseases will emerge.[202] According to a report from the United Nations Environment Programme and International Livestock Research Institute, loss of habitats and biodiversity, hunting wild meat, and the wildlife trade all increase the risk that new emerging zoonotic diseases will emerge.[203]

In 2022, the United Nations adopted a Resolution affirming, "the health and welfare of animals, sustainable development and the

[196] "Antibiotic resistance", *World Health Organization*, July 31, 2020.

[197] For a history of the Swine Flu (H1N1), *see* Walters, Mark Jerome, "Birds, Pigs and People: The Rise of Pandemic Flus", *Nature Public Health Emergency Collection*, at https://www.ncbi.nlm.nih.gov/pmc/articles/PMC7122937/

[198] For background on the Bird Flu (H5N1), *see* "H5N1 Avian Influenza: Timeline of Major Events", *World Health Organization*, January 25, 2012.

[199] "Our Risk of Infectious Diseases Is Increasing Because of Climate Change", *CDC, National Center for Emerging and Zoonotic Infectious Diseases*, August 2, 2022.

[200] "COVID-19: U.S. Impact on Antimicrobial Resistance, Special Report 2022", *CDC*, Atlanta, GA: U.S. Department of Health and Human Services, CDC; 2022, at 3. https://doi.org/10.15620/cdc:117915

[201] Singh, Bhumika, et al., "Towards More Predictive, Physiological and Animal-free In Vitro Models: Advances in Cell and Tissue Culture 2020 Conference Proceedings", *Alternatives to Laboratory Animals*, 2021, Vol. 49(3), 93–110. https://doi.org/10.1177/02611929211025006

[202] U.N. General Assembly Resolution 75/311.

[203] "Preventing the next pandemic – Zoonotic diseases and how to break the chain of transmission", *United Nations Environmental Program. United Nations*, July 6, 2020, at https://www.unep.org/resources/report/preventing-future-zoonotic-disease-outbreaks-protecting-environment-animals-and

environment are connected to human health and well-being."[204] This "One Health" approach is a collaborative, cross-disciplinary approach that recognizes the interconnectedness of people, animals, and the environment. The approach aims to protect the health of all living beings on the planet and it is recognized by the World Health Organization[205] and by the CDC.[206] Preventing future zoonotic diseases and antimicrobial resistance requires a coordinated and comprehensive legal approach that targets all areas of concern, including animal agriculture, fur farming, animal research, wild animal hunting, the exotic pet trade, deforestation and wildlife trafficking, all of which are largely unregulated in the U.S. The lack of U.S. regulation of animal enterprises, coupled with heavy government subsidies of risky industries (e.g., animal agriculture and research), may explain why the greatest number of new infectious diseases originated in the U.S. during the last half of the twentieth century.[207] Recognizing the connection between animal exploitation and disease, and safeguarding public health from future pandemics and from the threat of emerging zoonotic diseases, must be a legislative priority.[208]

[204] UNEP, EA.5/Res. 1, Nairobi (hybrid), 22 and 23 February 2021 and 28 February – 2 March 2022.

[205] "One Health", *World Health Organization,* at https://www.who.int/europe/initiatives/one-health

[206] "One Health Basics", *CDC,* n.d., at https://www.cdc.gov/onehealth/basics/index.html#

[207] For a comprehensive report on zoonotic risks in the U.S., *see,* Linder, Ann, et al., "Animal Markets and Zoonotic Disease in the United States", *Brooks McCormick Jr. Animal Law & Policy Program, Harvard Law School and Center for Environmental & Animal Protection, New York University,* 2023.

[208] During the Trump administration, environmental rules and regulations that prohibit mining and drilling activities in protected natural reserves were rolled back, increasing the risk of new zoonotic diseases. *See,* Popovich, Nadja, et al., "The Trump Administration is Reversing Nearly 100 Environmental Rules. Here's the Full List", *New York Times,* October 15, 2020.

World Hunger and Water Scarcity

Food is a fundamental human right, yet in 2020, nearly 3.1 billion of the world's population (nearly 40%) was not able to afford a healthy diet[209] and an estimated 720–811 million people went hungry.[210] In 2021, 2.3 billion people were thought to be moderately or severely food insecure[211] and 10.2% of the United States population lacked enough food to meet their needs.[212] Despite humanity's vast accomplishments, we have not been able to secure this most fundamental human right for everyone, but world hunger is not an issue of food scarcity. In fact, there is plenty of food to feed everyone.

The fragility of the world's food system lies with its unsustainable and environmentally destructive animal-based diet. If everyone consumed as much meat as North Americans or Europeans do, many of the world's ecosystems would collapse.[213] Unless current consumption patterns change toward healthier and more climate-friendly plant-based diets, the environmental impact of the global food system could worsen by 50–90%.[214] The current food crisis is only expected to grow. By 2050, the world population is projected to grow to 9.7 to 9.8 billion,[215] requiring an

[209] FAO, IFAD, UNICEF, WFP & WHO, "The State of Food Security and Nutrition in the World, Repurposing Food and Agricultural Policies to Make Healthy Diets More Affordable". 2022. Rome, FAO, at xiv, xix. https://doi.org/10.4060/cc0639en

[210] "Global Issues, Food", *United Nations*, at https://www.un.org/en/global-issues/food

[211] FAO, IFAD, UNICEF, WFP & WHO. The State of Food Security, 2022.

[212] "Food Security in the U.S.", *USDA, Economic Research Service,* at http://www.ers.usda.gov/topics/food-nutrition-assistance/food-security-in-the-u-s/interactive-charts-and-highlights/

[213] University of Bonn, "Meat consumption must fall by at least 75 percent", *Science News,* April 25, 2022, quoting study author Prof. Dr. Matin Qaim of the Center for Development Research at the University of Bonn.

[214] Springmann, Marco, et al., "Options for keeping the food system within environmental limits", *Nature,* 562, 519–525(2018). https://doi.org/10.1038/s41586-018-0594-0

[215] Ruiz, Neil, et al., "Coming of Age", *International Monetary Fund, Finance & Development,* March 2020 (projecting a world population of 9.7 billion in 2050); *but see,* "World Population projected to reach 9.8 billion in 2050, and 11.2 billion in 2100", *United Nations, Dept. of Econ. And Social Affairs,* n.d., at https://www.un.org/en/desa/world-population-projected-reach-98-billion-2050-and-112-billion-2100

increase in global food production of 35% to 56% between 2010 and 2050.[216]

Meat consumption has (regrettably) become a symbol of status and wealth in developed countries, and traditionally it has been a "high-status" food.[217] This perception must change. Some researchers believe that meat consumption in rich countries must decline by a minimum of 75% when taking into account its impact on the environment and on climate,[218] while others see far more benefits to a complete phaseout of animal agriculture.[219] Allowing a smaller amount of meat to remain in the food supply, however, would serve to only increase its price, making it more of a luxury item for the wealthy. From a global perspective, meat is already a luxury item that many cannot afford,[220] even though the world's poor suffer the most from its environmental impact.[221]

Many criticize the USDA's recommended diet as unsustainable and flawed because, as a practical matter, there is simply not enough land to support an animal-based diet for everyone.[222] Animal agriculture accounts for 77% of global farming land, but it supplies only 18% of the world's calories[223] because only a portion of calories fed to animals is returned in meat.[224] This highly inefficient diet cannot support a growing population and it is not good for human health.

[216] Van Dijk, Michiel, et al., "A meta-analysis of projected global food demand and population at risk of hunger for the period 2010–2050", *Nature Food*, 2, 494–501 (2021). https://doi.org/10.1038/s43016-021-00322-9

[217] "The link between meat and social status", *University of Technology, Sydney*, September 7, 2018.

[218] University of Bonn, "Meat consumption must fall by at least 75 percent", *Science News*, April 25, 2022.

[219] Eisen, Michael B. and Brown, Patrick O., Rapid global phase out of animal agriculture.

[220] This is true even if the full amount of its "external costs" are not included in the price. *See generally*, Lymbery, Philip, *Farmageddon: The True Cost of Cheap Meat*. Bloomsbury Publishing plc (2014). ISBN: 978-1-4088-4644-5; *see also*, David Robinson Simon. *Meatonomics*. Conari Press (2013). ISBN: 978-1-57324-620-0.

[221] *See generally*, Seymour, Frances, "Forests and Poverty: Barking Up the Wrong Tree?", *Center for Global Development*, May 8, 2017.

[222] Dockrill, Peter, "There Is Not Enough Land on Earth to Support the Diet Recommended by Authorities", *Science Alert*, August 14, 2018.

[223] Ritchie, Hannah, "Half of the world's habitable land is used for agriculture", *Our World in Data*, November 11, 2019, at https://ourworldindata.org/global-land-for-agriculture#

[224] University of Bonn, "Meat consumption must fall by at least 75 percent", *Science News*, April 25, 2022.

The American Cancer Society warns that evidence of a link between red and processed meats and cancer has existed for decades. Many health organizations recommend limiting or avoiding these foods altogether,[225] but meat remains a highly politicized issue. The Food and Agricultural Organization of the United Nations includes "small amounts of red meat" in its description of a healthy diet,[226] despite dozens of peer-reviewed medical studies that link the eating of processed and red meats to cancer.[227] Red meat is classified as a Group 2A carcinogen, a likely cause of cancer,[228] while processed meats are classified as a Group 1 carcinogen, meaning they do cause cancer.[229] These items should be treated like cigarettes … taxed and discouraged … not subsidized by taxpayers.

There is something acutely disturbing about feeding crops to animals for meat production when the crops could themselves be used to feed people. Research shows that if crops were fed to people instead of farm animals, there would be enough food to feed 10.2 billion people without the environmental damage that accompanies meat production.[230] World hunger can be eliminated, but it will require plant-based diets.

Water is one of the world's most important resources, and the right to water is one of the most basic of human rights.[231] The planet contains vast

[225] "American Cancer Society Guideline for Diet and Physical Activity", *American Cancer Society*, at https://www.cancer.org/healthy/eat-healthy-get-active/acs-guidelines-nutrition-physical-activity-cancer-prevention/guidelines.html#

[226] FAO, IFAD, UNICEF, WFP and WHO, The State of Food Security, 2022, at 71.

[227] *See generally*, Reynolds, Sharon, "Pattern of DNA Damage Links Colorectal Cancer and Diet High in Red Meat", *National Cancer Institute*, July 22, 2021; *see also*, Bingham, S.A., et al., "Does Increased Endogenous Formation of N-nitroso Compounds in the Human Colon Explain the Association between Red Meat and Colon Cancer?" *Carcinogenesis* 17(3) (March 1996): at pp. 515–23. https://doi.org/10.1093/carcin/17.3.525

[228] "Red meat, processed meat and cancer", *Cancer Council*, n.d., at https://www.cancercouncil.com.au/1in3cancers/lifestyle-choices-and-cancer/red-meat-processed-meat-and-cancer/

[229] "Cancer: Carcinogenicity of the consumption of red meat and processed meat", *World Health Organization*, October 26 2015.

[230] Gerten, Dieter, et al., "Feeding ten billion people is possible within four terrestrial planetary boundaries", *Nature Sustainability*, 3, 200–208 (2020). https://doi.org/10.1038/s41893-019-0465-1

[231] The United Nations recognized the right to water as a human right in 2010. *See*, U.N. General Assembly Resolution 64/292 (The human right to water and sanitation), adopted July 28, 2010.

amounts of water, but only ~0.003% is from fresh water sources[232] and large amounts of water are being used unsustainably and unfairly. Researchers at Massachusetts Institute of Technology estimated that 5 billion people (or 52% of the world's projected 9.7 billion population) will reside in water-stressed areas by 2050.[233] More recent studies conclude that the impact will be felt much sooner. The United Nations Children's Fund (UNICEF) reports that 4 billion people now suffer from severe water scarcity at least once a month, and that as soon as 2025, half of the world's population may be living in an area suffering from water scarcity.[234] The United Nations also warns that two-thirds of the global population could reside in "water-stressed countries" as soon as 2025 if consumption patterns continue,[235] and the CDC confirms that worldwide, 2 billion people lack safe drinking water at home.[236] The crisis is so great that the United States announced $49 billion dollars in funding in 2023 to ensure equitable access to water in the United States and abroad.[237]

Estimates vary but the impact of unsafe drinking water is profound. The World Health Organization reports that more than 2 billion people are drinking contaminated water and that ~829,000 die annually as a result of unsafe drinking water, sanitation, and hygiene.[238] A separate study found that ~ 2 million people perish every year as a result of unsafe water,

[232] "Water for Sustainable Food and Agriculture, a report produced for the G20 Presidency of Germany", *Food and Agriculture Organization of the United Nations*, Rome, 2017, at 1. ISBN 978-92-5-109977-3.

[233] Roberts, Alli Gold, "Predicting the future of global water stress: MIT Researches find that by 2050 more than half of the world's population will live in water-stressed areas and about a billion or more will not have sufficient water resources", *Massachusetts Institute of Technology*, January 9, 2014.

[234] "Water scarcity: Addressing the growing lack of available water to meet children's needs", *UNICEF*, n.d., at https://www.unicef.org/wash/water-scarcity

[235] "Water Scarcity – One of the greatest challenges of our time", *FAO of the United Nations,* March 20, 2019, at https://www.fao.org/fao-stories/article/en/c/1185405/

[236] "Global WASH Fast Facts: Access to Clean Water, Sanitation, and Hygiene", *CDC*, n.d., at https://www.cdc.gov/healthywater/global/wash_statistics.html

[237] "FACT SHEET: United States Announces $49 Billion in Commitments to Global Water Security and Sanitation", *United States Mission to the United Nations.* March 23, 2023, at https://usun.usmission.gov/fact-sheet-united-states-announces-49-billion-in-commitments-to-global-water-security-and-sanitation/

[238] Contamination of drink water by feces is the greatest threat to safe drinking water. *See*, "Drinking Water, Key Facts", *World Health Organization*, March 21, 2022, at https://www.who.int/news-room/fact-sheets/detail/drinking-water#

sanitation, and hygiene.[239] Water scarcity is also an issue of gender equality. In what UNICEF calls a "colossal waste" of time, each and every day women and girls spend a staggering ~200 million hours hauling water,[240] impacting educational and work opportunities and putting them at risk of violence.[241] Water is essential for all life, yet water scarcity has become a crisis, in part, of our own making.

There are ways that each of us can conserve water (e.g., water recycling; rainwater harvesting) but we must address one of the largest sources of water usage, and that is animal agriculture. Agriculture uses the vast majority of available freshwater. An estimated 70–80% of freshwater is used for livestock and crop production,[242] and a significant amount of this water is used for the billions of farm animals raised every year and the crops needed to feed them. In the United States, some estimate that animal agriculture uses 36 to 74 trillion gallons of water every year.[243] Others estimate that animal protein requires 100 times more water than plant protein.[244] The Beef Cattle Research Council acknowledges that 1910 gallons of water are required for just one pound of beef,[245] though non-industry estimates are higher. The Water Education Foundation estimates that 2464 gallons of

[239] "Connecting Global Priorities: Biodiversity and Human Health, a State of Knowledge Review", *World Health Organization and the Convention on Biological Diversity*, 2015, at 3.

[240] "UNICEF: Collecting water is often a colossal waste of time for women and girls", *UNICEF*, August 29, 2016.

[241] "Water and Gender", *United Nations, Water Facts*", n.d., at https://www.unwater.org/water-facts/water-and-gender; *see also*, "Why Water is a Women's Issue", *Concern Worldwide US*, April 26, 2021.

[242] *See*, "The Water Footprint of Food", *Food Print*, October 8, 2018 (last updated June 2, 2022), at https://foodprint.org/issues/the-water-footprint-of-food/#easy-footnote-bottom-2-1286, noting that agriculture uses 80% of all water consumed in the U.S.; *see also*, "Nature's Dangerous Decline 'Unprecedented'; Species Extinction Rates 'Accelerating'", *IPBES*, May 6, 2019, noting that "nearly 75% of freshwater resources are now devoted to cop and livestock production"; *see also*, "Water for Sustainable Food and Agriculture, a report produced for the G20 Presidency of Germany", *Food and Agriculture Organization of the United Nations*, Rome, 2017, at 1–2. ISBN 978-92-5-109977-3, noting that agriculture accounts for 70% on average of total freshwater withdrawals.

[243] Libauskas, Rebecca, "Commentary: Animal agriculture's 'water footprint' is putting the planet in peril", *Phys. Org.*, March 16, 2022.

[244] David Robinson Simon. *Meatonomics*. Conari Press (2013), at p. xix. ISBN: 978-1-57324-620-0.

[245] "Facts about water use and other environmental impacts of beef production in Canada", *Beef Cattle Research Council*, February 27, 2019.

water are required to produce just one pound of beef.[246] Regardless of the metric used, it is indisputable that meat production requires an enormous amount of water, and it is not just beef. In Livingston, California, a single chicken processing and slaughterhouse plant uses more than 60% of the city's water (~4 million gallons of water a day),[247] even though California is suffering from record-breaking mega droughts and water shortages.[248] In fact, more than 50% of the country has suffered from drought conditions in the two decades ending in 2020.[249] Some droughts in 2022 were so extreme that farmers were selling cows and destroying crops that had not reached maturity.[250] The frequency of droughts is expected to increase as climate change worsens.

Deforestation compounds the water crisis, because healthy forests reduce runoff, improve water flow regulation, and provide greater water storage.[251] Population growth and climate change will also exacerbate the water crisis as droughts and heat waves continue to dry up rivers throughout the world.[252] Across the western United States, a third of all consumed water is used to feed beef and dairy cattle, and in some western river basins, the amount is over 50%.[253] Animal agriculture is also a primary cause of water degradation in this country.[254]

[246] "Food Facts: How Much Water Does it Take to Produce ...?", *Water Education Foundation*, n.d., at https://www.watereducation.org/post/food-facts-how-much-water-does-it-take-produce

[247] "Challenging Foster Farms Slaughterhouse's Illegal Water Use, Animal Legal Defense Fund v. Foster Poultry Farms", *ALDF*, December 18, 2020.

[248] *See generally*, "California Droughts Compared", *U.S. Geological Surv.*, at https://ca.water.usgs.gov/california-drought/california-drought-comparisons.html

[249] "Solutions to Address Water Scarcity in the U.S.", *Nature Conservancy*, March 31, 2022.

[250] Yurkevich, Vanessa, "American farmers are killing their own crops and selling cows because of extreme drought", *CNN*, August 18, 2022.

[251] Morgera, Elisa, "Biodiversity as a Human Right and its Implications for the EU's External Action", European Parliament Study, at 3. ISBN: 978-92-846-6477. https://doi.org/10.2861/60672

[252] Sullivan, Brian K., "The World's Rivers, Canals and Reservoirs are Turning to Dust", *Bloomberg*, August 26, 2022; *see also*, Croker, Natalie, et al., "The world's rivers are drying up from extreme weather. See how 6 look from space", *CNN*, August 20, 2022, showing impact of heat waves on rivers.

[253] *See generally*, Borunda, Alejandra, "How beef eaters in cities are draining rivers in the American West", *National Geographic*, March 2, 2020.

[254] Environmental Topics, Nutrient Pollution, *United States Environmental Protection Agency*, n.d., at https://www.epa.gov/nutrientpollution/issue

This is a tragedy of our own making because plant-based meats use far less water (up to 99% less water with the popular Beyond Burger) than animal meat.[255] Switching to cultured meat alone could reduce water consumption by 82–96%.[256] All of these factors demand that our laws support sustainable water use and end subsidies to industries that use unsustainable amounts of water and that degrade our waterways. The United States recognizes that water insecurity is a threat to political stability and global economic growth,[257] but policies and laws need to address this threat.

National Security

The world is entering into a dangerous age. Humanity's relentless and systematic destruction of nature and other species has profound consequences for national security.[258] Humans have fought and battled each other over resources for centuries, but the climate crisis of today threatens to unleash devastating and destabilizing resource shortages. Some experts consider climate change to be the greatest threat to humanity.[259] As critical resources such as food and water become more scarce, wars and conflicts will invariably break out.[260] As former United Nations Secretary General, Boutros Ghali, famously predicted, "[t]he next war in the Middle East will be fought over water, not politics".[261]

[255] *See generally*, "Plant-based meat for a growing world", *Good Food Institute*, n.d., at https://gfi.org/resource/environmental-impact-of-meat-vs-plant-based-meat/#

[256] Poirot, Bryce, "Lab Grown Meat – An Emerging Industry", *University of Boulder, Environmental Center*, October 20, 2021.

[257] "Water Insecurity Threatening Global Economic Growth, Political Stability", *U.S. National Intelligence Council's Strategic Future Group*, Global Trends, Structural Drivers of the Future, Environmental and Resource Trends, March 2021.

[258] In law, national security is generally defined to refer "to those activities which are directly concerned with the foreign relations of the United States, or protection of the Nation from internal subversion, foreign aggression, or terrorism". *See*, 5 CFR §1400.102(a)(3).

[259] *See*, e.g., "Climate change the greatest threat the world has ever faced, UN expert warns", *United Nations Press Release*, October 21, 2022.

[260] WWF, Living Planet Report 2020 - Bending the Curve of Biodiversity Loss, at 13. WWF describes biodiversity as a "self-preservation issue" due to its critical role in providing, inter alia, food, water, energy and medicines.

[261] "Talking Point: Ask Boutros Boutros Ghali," *BBC News*, June 10, 2003.

Global water scarcity and water conflicts have become major security concerns for world governments,[262] and water scarcity is considered by many to pose "severe global security risks."[263] Water shortages continue to threaten stability in the Middle East, which in recent decades has suffered the worst droughts in 900 years, with 10 of 17 countries in the region facing "extreme high" water stress.[264] Water scarcity has sparked violence around the globe[265] and its scarcity is being weaponized.[266] In the United States, preventing cyber threats against critical water infrastructure has become an issue of national security.[267] Hunger and conflict is also a vicious cycle, where conflicts destroy agricultural resources, and in turn, food shortages lead to further violence,[268] a situation made worse by a changing climate.

The United Nation's top climate official views climate change as a security issue, explaining that "[c]limate change is the threat multiplier that worsens social, economic, and environmental pressures, leading to social upheaval and possibly even violent conflict."[269] The United States agrees. The intelligence community warned in its 2021 Annual Threat Assessment that "[e]cological degradation and a changing climate will continue to fuel disease outbreaks, threaten food and water security, and exacerbate

[262] Tindall, James A. & Campbell, Andrew A., "Water Security: National & Global Issues", *USGS*, November 2010, at http://pubs.usgs.gov/fs/2010/3106/pdf/FS10-3106.pdf

[263] *See,* e.g., Stuckenberg, Majoro David J., "Water Scarcity: The Most Understated Global Security Risk", *Harvard Law School National Security Journal*, May 18, 2018.

[264] *See generally*, Dilleen, Connor, "Turkey's Dam-Building Could Create New Middle East Conflict", *The Maritime Executive*, November 6, 2019.

[265] Gleick, Peter H., "Water as a weapon and casualty of armed conflict: A review of recent water-related violence in Iraq, Syria, and Yemen", *Wiley Interdisciplinary Reviews: Water* 6, June 4, 2019. https://doi.org/10.1002/wat2.1351

[266] Iran launched a number of cyber-attacks against Israeli water facilities in 2020. *See generally*, Kovacs, Eduard, "Iranian Hackers Access Unprotected ICS at Israeli Water Facility", *Security Week*, December 4, 2020; *see also*, Annual Threat Assessment of the US Intelligence Community, at 14.

[267] "Cyber Security: Water Systems", *U.S. Senate, Republican Policy Committee, Policy Paper*, May 19, 2022.

[268] Haga, Marie, "Breaking the vicious circle of hunger and conflict", *United Nations International Fund for Agricultural Development*, n.d., at https://www.un.org/en/food-systems-summit/news/breaking-vicious-circle-hunger-and-conflict

[269] Espinosa, Patricia, "The Climate Change Story Is a Security Story", *United Nations Climate Change*, February 18, 2017, at https://unfccc.int/news/patricia-espinosa-the-climate-change-story-is-a-security-story

political instability and humanitarian crises."[270] The Assessment reports that the depletion of soil, water and biodiversity will almost certainly increase geopolitical rivalry for scarce natural resources.[271] The climate emergency is also adding to the growing number of migrants, which is itself destabilizing, as extreme weather events force people from their homes and communities.[272] The Assessment does not call out deforestation or animal agriculture but it does cite "poor land management practices" and pollution as threats to human health and social stability and warns that the climate threat will intensify because emissions are continuing to increase.[273] The destabilizing effects of climate change, including droughts, heatwaves and loss of Arctic ice, create cascading global emergencies and global insecurity.

As many struggle to comprehend Russia's invasion of Ukraine,[274] it is illustrative to recall that when Russia annexed Crimea in 2014, Ukraine constructed a dam, which cut off 85% of Crimea's water supply, crippling agriculture and resulting in chronic water shortages.[275] Following Russia's 2021 invasion of Ukraine, Russia restored water to Crimea by destroying the dam.[276] Ukraine, known as the "breadbasket of Europe," has vast agricultural resources, which are incredibly valuable in a climate-challenged world. Ukraine is the third largest exporter of barley, the fourth largest exporter of corn and rye, and the fifth largest exporter of wheat in the world, in addition to other "prolific crops," including legumes, soybeans, potatoes, fruits, and vegetables.[277] This is not to suggest that Russia

[270] Annual Threat Assessment of the US Intelligence Community, at 4.

[271] Annual Threat Assessment of the US Intelligence Community, at 4 and 18.

[272] *See,* e.g., Hubbart, Sarah, "Understanding the New Normal: Extreme Weather and Climate Change", *The National Environmental Education Foundation*, July 30, 2021; World Meteorological Organization, "State of Climate in 2021: Extreme events and major impacts", October 31, 2021 (released at UN Climate Change negotiations, COP26, in Glasgow) at https://public.wmo.int/en/media/press-release/state-of-climate-2021-extreme-events-and-major-impacts; *see also*, Tower, Amali, "2021 Deepened Climate Migration as Survival", *Climate Refugees,* January 7, 2022.

[273] Annual Threat Assessment of the US Intelligence Community, at 18.

[274] Russia has cited several reasons to justify its invasion of Ukraine, including NATO's eastward expansion and Ukrainian genocide against ethnic Russians.

[275] *See generally*, Udasin, Sharon, "How a Ukrainian dam played a key role in tensions with Russia", *The Hill*, March 12, 2022.

[276] "Russian troops destroy Ukrainian dam that blocked water to Crimea – RIA", *Reuters,* February 26, 2022.

[277] Czech, Brian, "Putin the Practical Wants Ukraine Grain", *Steady State Herald,* January 27, 2022.

primarily invaded Ukraine to further its own food and water stability, but countries have gone to war for far less. When viewed, in part, as a resource grab, Russia's invasion and subsequent threats to use weapons of mass destruction show how quickly conflicts over resource shortages could escalate. The conflict also highlights the importance of neutral zones between countries,[278] which could be enhanced by designated and restricted habitats and forests along borders that protect people as well as wildlife and biodiversity.

The United States recognizes transnational crimes, such as illegal wildlife trafficking, as a "significant and growing threat to national and international security, with dire implications for public safety, public health, democratic institutions, and economic stability across the globe."[279] Illegal wildlife trafficking fosters other criminal activities, fuels corruption, undermines the rule of law, triggers conflicts and unrest, and destabilizes global, regional, and local security.[280] The United Nations warned in 2021 that wildlife trafficking is destabilizing to some nations,[281] and Interpol has warned that environmental crimes "can affect a nation's economy, security and even its existence."[282] Transnational organized crimes, such as illicit trade of small arms and light weapons, are linked to illegal wildlife trafficking and threaten national and regional instability in some parts of Africa.[283] Illicit wildlife trafficking presents serious security threats because terrorist

[278] President Putin has cited NATO expansion to include Ukraine as grounds for its February 24, 2022 invasion. *See generally*, Moskowitz, Ken, "Did NATO Expansion Really Cause Putin's Invasion? A seasoned diplomat considers this question in light of his own experience", *The Foreign Service Journal*, October 2022, at https://afsa.org/did-nato-expansion-really-cause-putins-invasion

[279] National Security Council, "Transnational Organized Crime: A Growing Threat to National and International Security", n.d., at https://obamawhitehouse.archives.gov/administration/eop/nsc/transnational-crime/threat

[280] *See generally*, "Study on the interaction between security and wildlife conservation in sub-Saharan Africa", *European Commission,* July 2019. https://doi.org/10.2841/178

[281] U.N. General Assembly Resolution 75/311.

[282] "Wildlife trafficking: organized crime hit hard by joint INTERPOL-WCO global enforcement operation", *INTERPOL*, July 10, 2019.

[283] U.N. General Assembly Resolution 75/311; *see also*, U.S. General Assembly Resolution 73/343.

organizations use profits from poaching to fund terror attacks,[284] making conservation critical to national security.[285]

The United States Department of Justice considers wildlife trafficking, which is often associated with money laundering, criminal conspiracy and other serious crimes, to be a threat to security and a hindrance to economic development.[286] Wildlife crimes are also associated with corruption and tax evasion,[287] as well as fraud, narcotics, smuggling, and murder-for-hire.[288] Poachers and traffickers have been connected to bribery, intimidation, murder, terrorism, and other threats that destabilize communities and national security.[289] Wildlife crimes and drug trafficking often go hand in hand, sharing shipments, smuggling routes and methods of transportation, and reinforce one another, such as when wildlife is exchanged for illegal drugs or when illicit items are hidden in legal shipments.[290] Mexican cartels, for instance, are becoming more involved with illegal wildlife trafficking and are using legal seafood operations to cover up illegal activity.[291] The illegal use, abuse, and exploitation of animals are invariably associated with other criminal activity. This is true at local, national, and international levels. Inexplicably, wildlife crimes are "often overlooked and under-prosecuted" by countries, despite the devastating consequences for public health and global economies.[292] Bringing down the sophisticated crime

[284] "Fact Sheet: Elephant Ivory and Rhino Horn Bans", *National Caucus of Environmental Legislators*, July 27, 2021, at http://www.ncelenviro.org/resources/elephant-ivory-and-rhino-horn-bans-fact-sheet/

[285] WWF, Living Planet Report 2020 - Bending the Curve of Biodiversity Loss, at 6.

[286] Attorney General Jeff Sessions, *Statement on Behalf of the United States at the London Illegal Wildlife Trade Conference*, October 11, 2018.

[287] INTERPOL, Wildlife crime: closing ranks on serous crime in the illegal animal trade.

[288] Department of Justice for the U.S. Attorney's Office for the Western District of Oklahoma. January 22, 2020, quoting Edward Grace, Assistant Director of the U.S. Fish and Wildlife Service, Office of Law Enforcement, when "Joe Exotic" was sentenced to 22 years in prison after being convicted of nine counts of violating the Endangered Species Act, eight counts of violating the Lacey Act for falsifying wildlife records, and two counts of murder-for-hire.

[289] Platt, John R., "Wildlife Trafficking: 10 Things Everyone Needs to Know", *The Revelator*, March 9, 2021.

[290] van Uhm, Dean, South, Nigel and Wyatt, Tanya, "Connections between trades and trafficking in wildlife and drugs". *Trends Organ Crim* 24, 425–446 (2021). https://doi.org/10.1007/s12117-021-09416-z

[291] Maron, Dina Fine, "Mexican cartels are increasingly moving into wildlife crime", *National Geographic*, February 25, 2022.

[292] INTERPOL, Wildlife crime: closing ranks on serous crime in the illegal animal trade.

syndicates that operate the global illegal wildlife trade is one of the world's greatest challenges.[293]

Wildlife trafficking networks are sophisticated criminal enterprises run by financially astute and tech savvy individuals. INTERPOL describes wildlife traffickers as "organized, innovative, [and] well connected," with the ability to sanction "the mass slaughter and capture of protected species in all parts of the world."[294] In his comments on past wildlife operations, INTERPOL Secretary, Jürgen Stock, confirmed that global criminal networks are making billions of dollars in illicit profits every year at a significant cost to the environment, and wildlife crimes are often associated with fraud, money laundering, corruption and violence.[295] Aquatic animals are not immune from traffickers. INTERPOL reports that declining marine fish populations is leading to a surge in "fisheries-related crime," which is often linked to other serious crimes, such as smuggling drugs and illicit products and human trafficking.[296] In fact, modern day slavery and human trafficking are serious issues in the fishing industry, and illegal fishing is one of the greatest threats to humanity's "sustainable use" of ocean resources.[297]

There are many instances where the investigation of wildlife trafficking leads to the discovery of other crimes. In Georgia, an investigation into illegal shark fin trading led to the discovery of a major criminal enterprise involving money laundering and illegal drugs.[298] Animal fighting rings are notoriously associated with illegal gambling and other crimes, including illegal drugs, money laundering and weapons offenses. In a case that

[293] Yuhas, Alan, "Interpol Operation Seizes More Than 10,000 Animals in Anti-Trafficking Campaign", *New York Times*, July 10, 2019, quotes Ginette Hemley, senior vice president for wildlife conservation at the World Wildlife Fund.

[294] INTERPOL, Wildlife crime: closing ranks on serous crime in the illegal animal trade.

[295] "Global arrests and seizures: WCO-INTERPOL Operation Thunder 2021 strikes wildlife and timber trafficking networks", *World Customs Organization,* November 30, 2021; *see also*, Wildlife trafficking: organized crime hit hard by joint Interpol-WCO global enforcement, *Interpol,* July 10, 2019. https://www.interpol.int/en/News-and-Events/News/2019/Wildlife-trafficking-organized-crime-hit-hard-by-joint-INTERPOL-WCO-global-enforcement-operation

[296] "Depleting fish stocks fueling transnational crime", *INTERPOL,* December 15, 2021, at https://www.interpol.int/en/News-and-Events/News/2021/Depleting-fish-stocks-fueling-transnational-crime

[297] Ibid.

[298] Bynum, Russ, "Indictment accuses 12 of illegally trading sharp fins, drugs", *Associated Press*, September 4, 2020.

involved the seizure of 63 dogs from a suspected dogfighting ring, a federal prosecutor confirmed that "[w]e know that animal fighting ventures often entail other forms of illegal activity involving drugs, firearms, and gambling."[299] In fact, prosecutors consider dog fighting to be "a breeding ground for other dangerous criminal activity that undermines the safety of our communities."[300] Based on the hundreds of pit bulls seized in 2021, dog fighting still appears to be thriving in the United States.[301]

Federal law in the United States requires the Financial Crimes Enforcement Network, a bureau of the Department of Treasury, to publish reports that identify "threat patterns and trend information" compiled from reports from financial institutions.[302] In identifying "national priorities" for anti-money laundering and fighting terrorism financing, illicit wildlife trafficking was identified as "a transnational criminal organization-related concern" because of its "strong association" with international criminal organizations and corruption and its "contribution to biodiversity loss, damage to fragile ecosystems, and the increased likelihood of spreading of zoonotic diseases."[303] Wildlife trafficking destroys both human and animal life. Wildlife rangers are killed, illicit profits fund deadly drug and other criminal enterprises, zoonotic diseases claim lives, and the catastrophic impacts of loss of biodiversity and species extinctions will impact all life on the planet.

The global community is mobilizing, adopting new standards of care, taking steps to protect the planet, and passing new laws to protect animals and their habitats. President Putin of Russia dismantled the infamous "whale jail" and President Xi Jinping of China shut down China's domestic ivory market, both in record time, but the United States struggles at both state and federal levels to enact common sense legislation that has the

[299] Department of Justice, U.S. Attorney's Office, Southern District of Georgia, "Federal Agents Seize 63 Dogs from Suspected Dogfighting Ring", March 30, 2018, quoting Acting U.S. Attorney Peter D. Leary for the Middle District of Georgia, at https://www.justice.gov/opa/pr/final-defendants-sentenced-federal-dog-fighting-case

[300] U.S. Department of Justice, Office of Public Affairs, "Final Defendants Sentenced in Federal Dog Fighting Case", September 27, 2021.

[301] Daugherty, Phillis M., "Dog Fighting is Thriving in U.S. – Hundreds of Pit Bulls Seized in 2021", *City Watch*, June 13, 2021.

[302] The report is issued pursuant to Section 6206 of the Anti-Money Laundering Act of 2020.

[303] "Financial Threat Analysis, Illicit Finance Threat Involving Wildlife Trafficking and Related Trends in Bank Secrecy Act Data", *Financial Crimes Enforcement Network*, for data filed between January 2018 and October 2021.

broad support of the public. As a result, the country lags far behind some other nations with respect to the legal protection for animals, risking reputational damage, diminished influence, and alienation from strategic partners. The United States cannot be the global leader it wants to be unless and until it better recognizes the interconnectedness of human rights and animal rights.

National security requires that the United States be a robust international presence on matters of climate change, the environment and on issues of fundamental rights. The U.S. considers itself to be a global leader "for identifying or framing international issues, taking actions to address those issues, [and] setting an example for other countries to follow."[304] Key to the foregoing is the "respect for international law, global rules and norms, and universal values."[305] Unfortunately, the United States has allowed itself to become an outlier compared to some other countries when it comes to the legal protection of animals and the planet, notwithstanding repeated proclamations of American exceptionalism and preeminence. If the United States wants to be a force for stability, it should work with global partners to address the urgent concerns that impact all of humanity, including the loss of biodiversity, species extinction, environmental degradation, marine pollution, and climate change. To address these pressing concerns, the umbrella of legal protection must be extended to animals.

Violence Begets Violence

In recent decades, research on violence has been clear and consistent: there is a strong correlation, referred to as "the link" between animal cruelty and violence toward people, including domestic violence, child abuse, elder abuse, and other violent behaviors.[306]

[304] U.S. Role in the World: Background and Issues for Congress, January 19, 2021. Congressional Research Service Report prepared for Members and Committees of Congress, p. 1.

[305] Id., at 2.

[306] *See generally*, Patterson-Kane, Emily G. and Piper, Heather, "Animal Abuse as a Sentinel for Human Violence: A Critique", *Journal of Social Issues*, Vol. 65, November 3, 2009, at 589–614.

Studies show that in homes that experience domestic violence and child abuse, animal abuse is more prevalent.[307] In a study involving domestic violence shelters, 85% of shelter directors reported seeing cases where animal abuse was disclosed.[308] In a separate study, 48% of battered women reported that animal abuse occurred "often" during the last year and 30% reported that abuse "almost always" occurred.[309] The threat of harm or death to animals is often used as a means to control victims of domestic violence and to ensure their silence.[310] For that reason, many domestic violence victims may, despite the danger, remain in an abusive situation out of fear that their pet may be harmed.[311] A review of twelve independent studies revealed that between 18% and 48% of women facing domestic abuse have delayed leaving the abuser out of fear for their pets or livestock.[312] The National Sheriffs' Association confirms the dangerous and deadly "link", citing a 2017 study where 89% of women involved in an abusive relationship reported that their animals were threatened, harmed, or killed.[313] Homicide is also a leading cause of death for women aged 44 years and younger, with nearly half of female victims killed by intimate male partners.[314]

Animal abuse can be an indicator of elder abuse. In California, a humane investigator was alerted that several dogs had been left behind to starve in an empty apartment. After removing the dogs, the investigator heard

[307] Ascione, Frank and Shapiro, Kenneth J., "People and Animals, Kindness and Cruelty: Research Directions and Policy Implications", *Journal of Social Issues*, 65(3) (2009), at 569–587. https://doi.org/10.1111/j.1540-4560.2009.01614.x

[308] Ascione, Frank R., et al., "The Abuse of Animals and Domestic Violence: A National Survey of Shelters for Women Who are Battered", *Society & Animals*, *5*(3), 1997, at 205–218.

[309] Carlisle-Frank, P., et al., "Selective battering of the family pet", *Anthrozoos,* 17, 26–42 (2004). https://doi.org/10.2752/089279304786991864

[310] Arkow, P, "Form of Emotional Blackmail: Animal Abuse as a Risk Factor for Domestic Violence", *Domestic Violence Report*, 19(4), (2014), at 49–60. Corpus ID: 42401869.

[311] Santiago, Roberto, "DAs Link Pet Abuse, Domestic Violence," *New York Daily News*, November 5, 2022, at www.vachss.com/help_text/archive/pets_dv_nydn.html

[312] Ascione, Frank R, "Emerging Research on Animal Abuse as a Risk Factor for Intimate Partner Violence", In: Kendall-Tackett K. and Giacomoni S. (Eds), *Intimate Partner Violence*. Kingston, NJ: Civil Research Institute, 2007.

[313] *See*, "Animal Cruelty and Domestic Violence", *National Sheriffs' Association,* n.d., at https://www.sheriffs.org/animal-cruelty-and-domestic-violence

[314] Petrosky Emily, et al., "Racial and Ethnic Differences in Homicides in Adult Women and the Role of Intimate Partner Violence: United States, 2003–2014", *MMWR Morb Mortal Wkly Rep*, 2017, 66:741–746. https://doi.org/10.15585/mmwr.mm6628a1

whimpering from a closet, only to find an emaciated elderly man, who had also been left behind by his caretakers.[315] Animal abuse also destroys the innocence of childhoods. Peer-reviewed studies document the impact of violence to animals as an 'Adverse Childhood Experience' with long-term effects on the developing brain.[316] When someone commits animal cruelty, it is thought that their empathy is likely distorted or inhibited, making it easier to disregard the feelings and lives of other animals and humans.[317] Research indicates that a person may become desensitized to abuse or violence if they witness it.[318]

Decades ago, anthropologist, Margaret Mead, made the connection between animal cruelty and the propensity to violence.[319] Studies have since shown that animal abuse may be predictive of future violence.[320] When children witness violence at home, they are at increased risk of being violent against animals.[321] Research confirms the link between a child's history of animal cruelty and patterns of chronic interpersonal aggression later in life.[322] Research also connects animal abuse by children to bullying, aggression, sexual abuse, and school shootings[323] and shows that 50% of rapists and >25% of pedophiles have a childhood history of animal

[315] Lockwood, Randall, "Making the Connection between Animal Cruelty and Abuse and Neglect of Vulnerable Adults", Winter 2002, at https://nationallinkcoalition.org/wp-content/uploads/2013/01/ElderAbuse-Lockwood-.pdf

[316] Phillips, Allie, "Understanding The Link between Violence to Animals and People. A Guidebook for Criminal Justice Professionals", June 2014, at v.

[317] Ascione, Frank R, "Children who are cruel to animals: A review of research and implications for developmental psychology", *Anthrozoos,* 6(4), 226–247. (1993).

[318] Hodges, Cynthia, "*The Link: Cruelty to Animals and Violence Towards People*", Michigan State University College of Law, Animal Legal & Historical Center, 2008.

[319] Mead, Margaret, "Cultural factors in the Cause and Prevention of Pathological Homicide", *Bulletin of the Menninger Clinic,* Vol. 28, Issue 1 (1964). PMID: 14076148.

[320] Phillips, Allie, "Understanding The Link between Violence to Animals and People. A Guidebook for Criminal Justice Professionals", June 2014, at 5. https://ndaa.org/wp-content/uploads/The-Link-Monograph-2014-3.pdf

[321] Currie, Cheryl L, "Animal cruelty by children exposed to domestic violence", *Child Abuse & Neglect,* 30(4), 425–435 (2006). https://doi.org/10.1016/j.chiabu.2005.10.014

[322] Becker, Fiona & French, Lesley, "Making the links: Child abuse, animal cruelty and domestic violence", *Child Abuse Review,* Vol. 13, Issue 6, at 399–414 (2004). https://doi.org/10.1002/car.878

[323] Elkins, Faye, "Animal Cruelty: A Serious Crime Leading to Horrific Outcomes", *USDOJ Publications.* Vol. 12, Issue 3 (2019).

cruelty.[324] Witnessing animal cruelty is so damaging to a child that laws are being enacted to criminalize situations where children are allowed to witness cruelty.[325]

Studies reveal that perpetrators who abuse companion animals tend to use more dangerous forms of violence, including sexual violence, marital rape, and stalking.[326] A police study in Australia revealed that 100% of sexual homicide offenders had a history of animal cruelty.[327] People who commit bestiality against animals are also more likely to commit sexual crimes against people.[328] Animal cruelty is a "significant indicator of violence towards humans, up to and including intimate partner abuse, sexual assault, rape, [and] murder."[329] A comprehensive study involving electronic databases and articles published between 1960 and 2016 found that 97.9% of the research identified a correlation between animal abuse and violence against people.[330] Animal cruelty can destroy respect for life.[331]

[324] Henry, Bill C. & Sanders, Cheryl E., "Bullying and Animal Abuse: Is There a Connection?", *Society and Animals.* 15, 107–126 (2007). https://doi.org/10.1163/156853007X187081

[325] *See,* e.g., the Animal Fighting Venture Prohibition Act (2 U.S.C.A. §2156 and 18 U.S.C.A. §49 (adding enhanced criminal penalties for bringing a child under the age of 16 to an animal fighting event); Oregon: Or. Rev. Stat. Ann. §167.320 (2003) (making it a first-degree felony to commit animal abuse in front of a minor child).

[326] Simmons, Catherine A. & Lehmann, Peter, "Exploring the link between pet abuse and controlling behaviors in violent relationships", *Journal of Interpersonal Violence*, 22(9), 1211–1222 (2007). https://doi.org/10.1177/0886260507303734

[327] Hermann, Henry R., "Killing Humans", in *Dominance and Aggression in Humans and Other Animals.* Ch. 15. Academic Press, 2016. ISBN: 978-0-12-805372-0.

[328] Holoyda, Brian, et al., "Bestiality Among Sexually Violent Predators", *Journal of the American Academy of Psychiatry and the Law*, Vol. 48,3 (2020). https://doi.org/10.29158/JAAPL.003941-20

[329] Johnson, Scott A., "Animal cruelty, pet abuse & violence: the missed dangerous connection", *Forensic Research & Criminology International Journal.* Vol. 6, Issue 5 (2018). https://doi.org/10.15406/frcij.2018.06.00236

[330] Stefany Monsalve, Fernando Ferreira, and Rita Garcia, "The connection between animal abuse and interpersonal violence: A review from the veterinary perspective", *Research in Veterinary Science*, 114, 18–26 (2017). https://doi.org/10.1016/j.rvsc.2017.02.025

[331] Feldman, Irwin, "*Where Violence Begins: Animal Industries and the Cult of Aggression*, n.d., at http://whereviolencebegins.org/aggression.html

Animal cruelty destabilizes communities and contributes to an overall lack of safety.[332] The majority of mass shootings have been associated with domestic violence,[333] which itself is linked to animal abuse. There is a direct connection between mass shootings and animal cruelty.[334] Studies show that 43% of school shooters have a history of animal abuse,[335] including shooters responsible for the massacres at Parkland, Florida and at Columbine High School.[336] Although mass shootings account for a relatively small percentage of all gun deaths in the United States, they have left families devastated and communities in shock. Violence has a tendency to escalate over time, often starting with animals and then moving on to humans. Still, animal abuse as a predictor of mass violence is often overlooked.[337] Animals are on the frontlines when it comes to violence, making animal cruelty a direct threat to everyone. Research on mass shootings is clear: prevent violence against animals and we can prevent at least some violence against people.

Witnessing animal suffering is detrimental to one's sense of well-being.[338] Awareness of institutionalized and government sanctioned cruelty inflicted on animals can cause trauma.[339] Anyone with Internet access

[332] Phillips, Allie & Lockwood, Randall, "Investigating & Prosecuting Animal Abuse: A Guidebook on Safer Communities, Safer Families & Being an Effective Voice for Animal Victims", *National District Attorneys Association*, at https://ndaa.org/wp-content/uploads/NDAA-Animal-Abuse-monograph-150dpi-complete-1.pdf

[333] Gold, Liza H., "Domestic Violence, Firearms, and Mass Shootings", *Journal American Academy of Psychiatry and the Law*, 48(1), 35–42 (2020). https://doi.org/10.29158/JAAPL.003929-20

[334] *See generally*, Levin, Marc, "We Need to Talk About Animal Cruelty and Mass Shooters", *Time*, June 29, 2022.

[335] Arluke, Arnold and Madfis, Eric, "Animal Abuse as a Warning Sign of School Massacres: A Critique and Refinement". *Homicide Studies*, Vol 18, Issue 1, 7–22 (2014). https://doi.org/10.1177/1088767913511459

[336] *See*, Sullivan, Kevin, et al., "Fla shooting suspect had a history of explosive anger, depression, killing animals", *Washington Post*, February 15, 2018; *see also*, Arluke, Arnold, "How reliably does animal torture predict a future school shooter?", *Washington Post*, February 21, 2018.

[337] Rhodes, Wendy, "Police often miss link between animal abuse, mass shootings", *Florida Sun Sentinel*, February 26, 2018.

[338] American Psychological Association, "When working with animals can hurt your mental health", *Science Daily*, August 9, 2019, at https://www.sciencedaily.com/releases/2019/08/190809113026.htm#

[339] *See*, e.g., Lang, April, "Understanding Sensitivity to Institutionalized Animal Abuse", *Social Work Today* n.d., at https://www.socialworktoday.com/archive/exc_0318.shtml

can quickly learn the extent to which humanity tortures and abuses animals, including children. The dehumanizing effects of this knowledge can lead to a devaluation of life, including human life, especially as society continues to learn about the similarities that humans share with the animal kingdom. As Pope Francis explained, "[e]very act of cruelty towards any creature is contrary to human dignity."[340]

States have started to pass laws that require professionals to "cross-report" suspected crimes against companion animals or people (e.g., animal control officers must report suspected child abuse; social workers must report suspected animal abuse). The District of Columbia, Puerto Rico and 36 states have enacted legislation that allows judges to include pets in orders of protection for victims of domestic violence.[341] Some argue that animal abuse by a family member should be considered domestic violence given that the overwhelming majority of people consider companion animals to be members of the family.[342]

Research shows that exposure to the mass and often violent killing of animals has significant mental health consequences.[343] The emotional toll of witnessing animals suffer and die leads to drug and alcohol abuse, severe anxiety, social withdrawal and depression.[344] Criminologists have found a strong link between large slaughterhouses and high crime rates in communities in the United States. One study found that having a slaughterhouse in the community increases both the total number of arrests and the

[340] Encyclical Letter *Laudato Si'* of the Holy Father Francis On Care For Our Common Home at §92.

[341] Wisch, Rebecca F., "Domestic Violence and Pets: List of States that Include Pets in Protective Orders. *Michigan State University, Animal Legal & Historical Center*, at https://www.animallaw.info/article/domestic-violence-and-pets-list-states-include-pets-protection-orders

[342] A Pew Research Center survey found that 85% of dog keepers and 78% of cat keepers considered their companions to be family members. *See*, "Gauging Family Intimacy: Dogs Edge Cats (Dads Trail Both)", *Pew Research Center*, March 7, 2006, at https://www.pewresearch.org/social-trends/2006/03/07/gauging-family-intimacy/#

[343] Slade, Jessica and Alleyne, Emma, "The Psychological Impact of Slaughterhouse Employment: A Systematic Literature Review", *Trauma, Violence, & Abuse,* Vol. 24, Issue 2 (2021). https://doi.org/10.1177/15248380211030243

[344] Eisnitz, Gail A. *Slaughterhouse: The Shocking Story of Greed, Neglect, and Inhumane Treatment Inside the U.S. Meat Industry*. New York: Prometheus Books, 2006. ISBN-13: 978-1-59102-450-7.

number of arrests for violent crimes.[345] The study suggested the existence of a "Sinclair effect" that is unique to slaughterhouse jobs,[346] in reference to the horrific working conditions detailed in Upton Sinclair's 1906 novel *The Jungle*. Slaughterhouse workers are prone to a specific form of post-traumatic stress disorder known as 'perpetration-induced traumatic stress' which occurs when someone participates in causing trauma.[347]

Slaughterhouse work is one of the most physically dangerous and psychologically traumatic jobs.[348] Slaughterhouse workers, who are required to handle dangerous cutting tools on fast moving processing lines, suffer severe injuries, including amputations, blindness, and head traumas.[349] Too often, animals are not properly stunned before they are shackled for slaughter, which creates dangerous conditions for workers as animals thrash and kick.[350] Occupational Safety and Health Administration records reveal that an average of 17 "severe" injuries happen every month in meat plants in the United States.[351] Workers are exposed to zoonotic diseases as they handle animals,[352] and methicillin-resistant Staphylococcus aureus (MRSA) associated with livestock is so prevalent that it is considered an

[345] Amy J. Fitzgerald Linda Kalof, and Thomas Dietz, "Slaughterhouses and Increased Crime Rates: An Empirical Analysis of the Spillover From "The Jungle" Into the Surrounding Community", *Organization & Environment*, 22(2), 158–184 (2009). https://doi.org/10.1177/1086026609338164

[346] Id.

[347] Slade, Jessica and Alleyne, Emma, "The Psychological Impact of Slaughterhouse Employment: A Systematic Literature Review", *Trauma, Violence, & Abuse*, Vol. 24, Issue 2 (2021). https://doi.org/10.1177/15248380211030243

[348] *See*, Dillard Jennifer, "A Slaughterhouse Nightmare: Psychological Harm Suffered by Slaughterhouse Employees and the Possibility of Redress through Legal Reform", *LSN: Transnational Labor Issues (Topic)* (2007); *see also*, van Holland B.J., et al., "Workers' health surveillance in the meat processing industry: work and health indicators associated with work ability", *Journal of Occupational Rehabilitation*, 25(3), 618–26 (2015). https://doi.org/10.1007/s10926-015-9569-2

[349] Human Rights Watch, *Blood, Sweat, and Fear: Workers' Rights in U.S. Meat and Poultry Plants*, January 24, 2005. ISBN: 1-56432-330-7, at https://www.hrw.org/report/2005/01/24/blood-sweat-and-fear/workers-rights-us-meat-and-poultry-plants

[350] *See generally*, Gail A. Eisnitz, *Slaughterhouse: The Shocking Story of Greed, Neglect, and Inhumane Treatment Inside the U.S. Meat Industry*. Prometheus, 2006. ISBN-13: 978-1591024507.

[351] Wasley, Andrew, et al., "Two Amputations a Week: The High Cost of Working in a US Meat Plant", *The Guardian*, July 5, 2018.

[352] Roesel, Kristina and Fries, Reinhard, "Occupational Disease Risks for Handlers of Pigs and Pork", *pig333.com,* April 20, 2018, at https://www.pig333.com/articles/occupational-disease-risks-for-handlers-of-pigs-and-pork_13618/

occupational risk for humans.[353] For these reasons, slaughterhouses target immigrants, refugees, prisoners and other vulnerable groups.[354] Exposing workers to "preventable, predictable, and serious hazards" should be viewed as a human rights violation.[355] Human Rights Watch notes that in slaughterhouses, "[m]any workers suffer severe, life-threatening and sometimes life-ending injuries that are predictable and preventable" and that the United States has failed "to meet its obligations under international human rights standards."[356]

Atrocities against animals are so dehumanizing that one Holocaust survivor described "the striking similarities between what the Nazis did to my family and my people, and what we do to animals we raise for food: the branding or tattooing of serial numbers to identify victims, the use of cattle cars to transport victims to their death, the crowded housing of victims in wood crates, the arbitrary designation of who lives and who dies—the Christian lives, the Jew dies; the dog lives the pig dies."[357] Author Matthieu Ricard explains the parallels: "[t]he common points between genocide and the large scale killing of animals are the devaluation of the victims, the desensitizing of the perpetrators and the mental disassociation operative within them, the methods of extermination, the concealment of the facts by the perpetrators, and the unwillingness to know on the part of those who are in the position to know the facts."[358] By ending violence against animals, we can foster a culture of compassion and empathy that significantly reduces violence against people.

[353] Kalupahana, Ruwani S., "MRSA in Pigs and the Environment as a Risk for Employees in Pig-Dense Areas of Sri Lanka", *Front. Sustain. Food Syst*, Vol. 3 (2019). https://doi.org/10.3389/fsufs.2019.00025

[354] "John Oliver on the US meatpacking industry: 'Things are critical right now'", *Guardian*, February 22, 2021.

[355] *See generally*, Emily A. Spieler, "Risks and Rights: The Case for Occupational Safety and Health as a Core Worker Right," in James A. Gross, ed., *Workers' Rights as Human Rights*. Ithaca: Cornell University Press, 2003.

[356] Human Rights Watch, "Blood, Sweat, and Fear, Workers' Rights in U.S. Meat and Poultry Plants", January 24, 2005. ISBN: 1-56432-330-7.

[357] Dolsten, Josefin, "Holocaust survivor likens treatment of livestock to Shoah", *The Times of Israel,* October 7, 2016, quoting Alex Hershaft.

[358] Ricard Matthieu, *A Plea For The Animals: The Moral, Philosophical, and Evolutionary Imperative to Treat All Beings with Compassion*, Shambhala, 2016, at 155. ISBN-13: 978-1611803051.

Recognizing Our Deep Connection with Animals

Animals enrich our lives immeasurably. We look to our companions for friendship, support, and security,[359] and our relationship with animals improves our mental and physical well-being.[360] Research shows that during the upheaval of the COVID-19 pandemic, companion animals contributed significantly to the well-being of their human companions by lessening the effects of anxiety and depression.[361] During lockdowns, companion animals provided social support and helped many through the psychological impacts of the pandemic.[362]

Research shows that interacting with dogs can reduce stress,[363] positively impact the physical health of guardians,[364] assist in physical and psychological therapy,[365] and aid in the treatment of PTSD.[366] Animals bring

[359] McNicholas, June & Collis, Glyn, "Animals as supports: Insights for understanding animal assisted therapy" (2006), In, A.H. Fine (Ed.), *Handbook on Animal-Assisted Therapy: Theoretical Foundations and Guidelines for Practice,* 2nd ed. San Diego: Academic Press, 49–71.

[360] *See generally,* Roberts, Nicole E., "8 Reasons Pets Improve Your Health and Wellbeing", *Forbes,* May 12, 2019. *See also,* Dasha Grajfoner, Guek Nee Ke, and Rachel Mei Ming Wong, "The Effect of Pets on Human Mental Health and Wellbeing during COVID-19 Lockdown in Malaysia", *Animals: an open access journal from MDPI* vol. 11,92689 (2021). https://doi.org/10.3390/ani11092689

[361] *See,* e.g., Kogan, Lori, R., et al., "The Psychological Influence of Companion Animals on Positive and Negative Affect during the COVID-19 Pandemic", *Animals,* 11(7), 2084 (2021). https://doi.org/10.3390/ani11072084; *see also,* Carr, Dawn, et al., "Dog Walking and the Social Impact of the COVID-19 Pandemic on Loneliness in Older Adults", *Animals,* 11(7), 1852 (2021). https://doi.org/10.3390/ani11071852

[362] Martin, Francois, "Depression, anxiety, and happiness in dog owners and potential dog owners during the COVID-19 pandemic in the United States", *PLoS One,* 16(12) (2021). https://doi.org/10.1371/journal.prone.0260676

[363] *See,* e.g., Abrahamson, Kathleen, et al., "Perceptions of a hospital-based animal assisted intervention programs: an exploratory study", *Complementary Therapies in Clinical Practice,* 25, 150–154 (2016). https://doi.org/10.1016/j.ctcp.2016.10.003. *See also,* Derting, Terry, "Effects of pet therapy on the psychological and physiological stress levels of first-year female undergraduates", *North American Journal of Psychology,* 17, 575–590 (2015).

[364] Friedmann, E., Son, H., & Tsai, C.C. (2010). The animal/human bond: Health and wellness. In A. H. Fine, ed., *Handbook on Animal-Assisted Therapy: Theoretical Foundations and Guidelines for Practice (3rd ed.).* San Diego: Academic Press, pp. 85–107.

[365] *See generally,* "What to know about animal therapy", *Medical News Today,* March 24, 2022, at https://www.medicalnewstoday.com/articles/animal-therapy

[366] Fullerton, Nicole, "Pets & PTSD: How the Human-Animal Bond Complements Treatment for Veterans", *Penn Medicine News,* June 24, 2021.

calm and comfort to a variety of settings, including hospitals,[367] prisons,[368] courtrooms,[369] and in times of disaster.[370] Children receive a wealth of positive benefits from companion animals, including behavioral, educational, and social benefits,[371] while the elderly benefit from an improved quality of life and reduced symptoms of depression, cognitive impairment and behavioral and psychiatric symptoms of dementia.[372] Companion animals help us to better cope with grief and loss, and they can provide comfort to people as they approach the end of life.[373]

Animals play a significant role in family structures, with 95% of guardians viewing their companions as family members.[374] In fact, there are now more households in the United States with companion animals than there are with children.[375] The vast majority of animal keepers believe that their companions are capable of experiencing love, and more than 75% of people seek comfort from their companions, while 40% of people are anxious when separated from their companions during the day.[376] Billions of

[367] *See generally*, McCullough, Amy, et al., "The Use of Dogs in Hospital Settings", *Habri Central Briefs*, January 18, 2016.

[368] Hogle, Pamela S., "Going to the Dogs: Prison-Based Training Programs are Win-Win", *Corrections Today*, 71(4), 69–72 (2009). NCJ No. 228214.

[369] Mariani, Jill, "Courtroom Dogs Help Ensure Victims Voices Are Heard", *ABA, The Public Lawyer Winter 2022*, January 12, 2022.

[370] Robino, Ariann, et al., "Sustained Effects of Animal-Assisted Crisis Response on Stress in School Shooting Survivors", *Human-Animal Interaction Bulletin. CABI International*, October 10, 2022. https://doi.org/10.1079/hai.2022.0019

[371] Geerdts, Megan S., "(Un)Real Animals: Anthropomorphism and Early Learning about Animals", *Child Development Perspectives*, 10(1), 10–14 (2015). https://doi.org/10.1111/cdep.12153; *see also*, Melson, Gail F., "Child Development and the Human-Companion Animal Bond", *American Behavioral Scientist*, 47(1), 31–39 (2003). https://doi.org/10.1177/0002764203255210

[372] Hughes, Michael J., et al., "Companion Animals and Health in Older Populations: A Systematic Review", *Clinical Gerontologist*, 43(4), 365–377 (2019). https://doi.org/10.1080/07317115.2019.1650863

[373] For more on animal-assisted therapy, *see*, Cameron, Melainie, et al., "Working Like a Dog: Exploring the Role of a Therapy Dog in Clinical Exercise Physiology Practice", *Animals*, 12(10), 1237 (2022). https://doi.org/10.3390/ani12101237

[374] Oaklander, Mandy, "Science Says Your Pet is Good for Your Mental Health", *Time*, n.d., at https://time.com/collection/guide-to-happiness/4728315/science-says-pet-good-for-mental-health/

[375] Lautz, Jessica, "A Stunning Stat: There are More American Households with Pets than Children", *National Association of Realtors*, March 13, 2023.

[376] Orth, Taylor, "Dogs, cats, and other pets play a meaningful role in the lives of many Americans", *YouGov America*, May 31, 2022.

dollars are spent on the care and well-being of companion animals, and in return, they provide unconditional love, friendship, and devotion.

Nature and wildlife are also extraordinarily important to one's well-being. In 2019, a law was proposed in New York City that would have prohibited the feeding of birds and squirrels in City parks. The animal welfare issue, it was claimed, was to prevent reliance of park animals on humans as a source of food, and while there is some validity to that point, the real motive behind the bill was complaints by a few residents that the feeding of animals contributed to "nuisance animals" and to animal waste in community areas. The New York City Bar's Animal Law Committee submitted written testimony in opposition to the bill, arguing that feeding birds arose out of "the humanitarianism movement in the nineteenth century that promoted kindness to animals, and since then, the activity of feeding wild birds continues to be popular and in cities, it is one of only a few ways that urban dwellers [can] connect with nature."[377] Connecting with nature is vital to one's well-being, so much so that the World Health Organization has recognized the importance of green spaces rich in biodiversity for physical and mental well-being, noting that it can help treat depression and anxiety.[378] Many local New York City residents, who enjoy the mental health benefits of feeding birds and squirrels, came out in force to oppose the bill, which was ultimately defeated.

Mankind is a highly polarized and divided species. One thing that has proven time and time again to unite many people is animals, even when geopolitical, cultural and religious beliefs have divided them.[379] Public opinion polls reveal that Americans care deeply about the treatment of animals and that a strong majority believes that animals should be afforded significantly more legal safeguards than they currently receive. A 2015 Gallup poll determined that a strong majority, 62%, believe that animals

[377] Written testimony of the Animal Law Committee and the Civil Rights Committee, New York City Department of Parks and Recreation Hearing on Proposed Rule: Prohibition on Feeding Wildlife in Parks, Reference Nos.: DPR-14. March 1, 2019. https://www.nycbar.org/member-and-career-services/committees/reports-listing/reports/detail/opposition-to-proposed-prohibition-on-feeding-wildlife-in-parks-testimony

[378] The World Health Organization, *Report by the Director-General – Health, environment and climate change – Human health and biodiversity*, A71/11. 2018.

[379] *See*, e.g., Winer, Stuart, "Israelis, Palestinians pull together to rescue lion", *The Times of Israel*, August 10, 2016; *see also*, Kamisher, Eliyahu, "Israelis and Palestinians partners to save animal shelter", *The Jerusalem Post*, August 29, 2016.

should be afforded some rights and protection, but nearly one third (32%, up from 25% in 2008) believe that animals should be afforded the *same* rights and protections from harm and exploitation as people. Only 3% thought that animals should receive little protection.[380] Acknowledging that we share 98.8% of our gene sequences with chimpanzees is not an argument against human exceptionalism. Recognizing our similarities with animals, and reforming laws to account for these similarities, *is* human exceptionalism.

As this chapter has demonstrated, there are many reasons to extend meaningful legal protection to the animal kingdom, but perhaps the most important reason is our deep connection with animals. As we learn more about the wondrous lives of animals, we come to appreciate that certain rights and protections should be legally recognized. Rights movements are rooted in the universal desire to prevent suffering, to recognize the dignity and worth of every individual and the desire for a more merciful world. The failure of laws to recognize the interconnectedness of all life on the planet, and the integral relationship between human and animal rights, has had profound implications for humanity.

[380] *See*, Yuhas, Alan, "A third of Americans believe animals deserve same rights as people, poll finds", *The Guardian*, May 19, 2015; *see also*, Riffkin, Rebecca, "In U.S., More Say Animals Should Have Same Rights as People", *Gallup, Social & Policy Issues*, May 18, 2015.

CHAPTER 5

Challenges to Legal Reform

The worst sin towards our fellow creatures is not to hate them, but to be indifferent to them. That's the essence of inhumanity. (George Bernard Shaw, The Devil's Disciple. *London, 1897.)*
George Bernard Shaw

Legal reform does not come easily and it does not come quickly. This is true for every 'rights movement' in the history of the United States and this is especially true for animals. Competing legislative agendas, coupled with limited resources, can complicate the passage of the most widely supported legal reforms. There are biases against animals, both conscious and unconscious, in the form of willful ignorance[1] and speciesism.[2]

[1] Willful ignorance is defined by Wiktionary as a decision in bad faith to avoid becoming informed about something so as to avoid having to make undesirable decisions that such information might prompt.

[2] Speciesism is discrimination against an individual based on his or her species that tends to correlate with other prejudicial attitudes, including sexism and racism. For more on speciesism, *see*, Everett, Caviola L., et al., "The moral standing of animals: Towards a psychology of speciesism", *Journal of Personality and Social Psychology,* June 2019, *116*(6), 1011–1029. https://doi.org/10.1037/pspp0000182. PMID: 29517258.

K. C. Moore, *The Case for the Legal Protection of Animals*, The Palgrave Macmillan Animal Ethics Series,
https://doi.org/10.1007/978-3-031-46065-4_5

Over the years, many arguments have been made in opposition to affording animals greater legal rights, which have created roadblocks to legal reform: animals lack consciousness and the ability to feel[3]; animals lack responsibilities, duties and the ability to enforce rights[4]; animals lack souls and morality[5]; affording animals legal rights will open the "floodgates" of litigation[6]; the right to exploit animals is a human right[7]; and the worldview that humans are special and the only species worthy of legal protection.

As a practical matter, the greatest obstacle to affording animals legal protection is that it may not be "convenient" to humans, but convenience has never been accepted as grounds for denying rights to women, minorities and other protected groups. Rights movements have historically focused on the "interests" of those harmed, not the interest of parties who may be "inconvenienced" by the right. There are also billions of dollars at stake, and industries, armed with legal teams and armies of lobbyists, will employ every tactic to protect their bottom line, including securing the passage of weak animal protection laws.

[3] Rene Descartes (1596–1650), a French philosopher, believed that animals lack the ability to feel and are essentially machines or automata, which has been proved to be false by modern science. For criticism of this 'animal machine' doctrine, *see*, Cottingham, John, "'A Brute to the Brutes?': Descartes' Treatment of Animals", *Philosophy, 53*(206), at 551–559. https://doi.org/10.1017/S0031819100026371

[4] *See*, e.g., Matter of Nonhuman Rights Project Inc. v. Stanley, 49 Misc. 3d 746, 16 N.Y.S. 3d 898, 2015 N.Y. Slip Op 25,257, decided July 29, 2015, quoting reasoning in prior cases for denying a writ of habeas corpus: "legal personhood has consistently been defined in terms of both rights and duties" and the "incapability to bear any legal responsibilities and societal duties" disqualifies chimpanzees from receiving legal rights that are afforded to humans.

[5] For a historical analysis of the impact of animals being viewed as having souls, *see* Bates, Alan W.H., "Have Animals Souls? The Late-Nineteenth Century Spiritual Revival and Animal Welfare", Chapter 3 in *Anti-Vivisection and the Profession of Medicine in Britain: A Social History*, London: Palgrave Macmillan 2017. ISBN: 978-1-137-55696-7.

[6] *See*, e.g., Keim, Brandon, "An Elephant's Personhood on Trial", *The Atlantic*, December 28, 2018.

[7] Mink fur farmers and the Dutch Federation of Noble Fur Holders argued before the Dutch Supreme Court that the ban on fur farms is a breach of the European Convention of human rights. The Supreme Court disagreed and upheld the ban on fur farming. *See generally*, "Netherlands ban on mink breeding, slaughtering upheld in top court case", *NL Times*, December 16, 2016.

Weak Laws

The enactment of weak laws creates challenges to meaningful legal reform. The Animal Welfare Act, one of the few animal protection laws at the federal level, requires minimal (if any) standards of care for animals and it exempts most animals from its coverage.[8] The law excludes the vast majority of animals in research facilities from coverage by defining "animals" to exclude birds, rats, and mice bred for research, even though birds, rats, and mice constitute the largest percentage (~95%) of animals used in research.[9] The law also does not protect farm animals from physical torture and mental anguish they experience on factory farming.

The law is woefully out-of-date, failing to recognize the growing body of scientific evidence on animal sentience. Frankly, industry could not have drafted a better law for themselves. The law may cause more harm than good because it misleads the public into thinking that animals are adequately protected under the law when they are not. There is no "fix" for this law. It is so weak that it must be replaced in its entirety with genuine and meaningful legal protection that extends to every species of animal in every setting. In recent decades many countries have reformed their animal protection laws, and the United States must do the same. The failure of federal laws to protect animals is also further exacerbated by the lack of enforcement of these laws.

Lack of Enforcement

Laws can become meaningless if they are not enforced, or if penalties are so minimal or inconsequential that they lack any deterrent effect. Legislative reforms are undermined if resources are not committed to ensure proper implementation. The "enforcement gap" between laws and their actual enforcement is well documented,[10] and this gap is bigger for

[8] Animal Welfare Act, 7 U.S.C. §2131.

[9] Section 2132(g) of the Animal Welfare Act reads: "[T]he term 'animal' ... excludes...farm animals, such as, but not limited to livestock or poultry used or intended for use as food or fiber, or livestock or poultry used or intended for improving animal nutrition, breeding, management, production, efficiency, or for improving the quality of food or fiber." 'Animal' is similarly defined in the 1985 Amendment. 7 U.S.C. §2132(g) (1988).

[10] *See*, Morton, Rochelle, et al., "Explaining the Gap Between the Ambitious Goals and Practical Reality of Animal Welfare Law Enforcement: A Review of the Enforcement Gap in Australia", ***Animals***, 10(3), 2020. https://doi.org/10.3390/ani10030482

animals. Often, there seems to be an unconscious bias when the victim is an animal, and human victims are nearly always prioritized by law enforcement.

Failure to enforce the minimally protective laws that do exist leads to further victimization of animals, and the results of this failure can be seen all across the United States. Puppy mills are operating with impunity despite gross cruelty and neglect of animals.[11] Backyard butchers and religious practitioners are violating state laws without consequence.[12] Animal fur, including illegal dog and cat fur, is marketed as faux fur.[13] Animal cruelty cases are routinely pled out and discontinued,[14] animal fighting cases are often dismissed,[15] and weak penalties are given for horrific animal torture.[16] Failure to enforce animal protection laws sends the message that violence against animals will be tolerated and it undermines the rule of

[11] Despite anti-cruelty laws in all 50 states, animals are often found in poor conditions and in need of veterinary care. Animals are also deprived of exercise and social interaction. Breeders are rarely held accountable for veterinary care and placement of confiscated animals.

[12] The failure of law enforcement to enforce state anti-cruelty and humane slaughter laws means that it is left to nonprofits to initiate litigation to shut down operations. *See,* e.g., Reyes-Velarde, "Jewish center sued over controversial chicken-killing ritual", *LA Times,* July 26, 2019; *see also,* Echgelmeier, Danice and Hernandez, Roman, "Challenging Backyard Butchers in Florida", *Animal Legal Defense Fund,* n.d., at https://aldf.org/case/challenging-backyard-butchers-in-florida/

[13] Violations are found more often in other countries because the U.S. does not test retail fur products. *See,* e.g., Warfield, Kristen, "Your 'Faux' Fur Coat Might Actually be Real", *The Dodo,* November 21, 2018; *see also,* Blott, Unity, "Exposed: Market traders are caught selling 'faux fur' hats, gloves and coats made from REAL animals slaughtered in overseas factories (and one item even contained traces of CAT)," *Daily Mail,* February 12, 2018; *see also,* Farand, Chloe, "'Faux fur' found in high street shops actually from animals", *Independent,* April 10, 2017.

[14] Cases involving the death or injury of an animal are often pled out, resulting in lighter sentences. *See,* e.g., Keller, Mary Grace, "In two animal cruelty cases, Westminster woman gets probation but no jail time", *Carroll County Times,* December 6, 2019.

[15] According to a 2019 Office of Legislative Research report in Connecticut, during the period from 2008 to 2018, there were only 110 cases of animal fighting and 83 of the cases were dropped or dismissed. *See,* Basile, Jo-Anne and Lefland, Ilene, "Opinion: Few punished for cruel dogfight", *Connecticut Post,* October 28, 2021.

[16] An individual who tortured animals in violation of the *Preventing Animal Cruelty and Torture Act* (Title 18 U.S.C. Section 48) for animal crush videos faced up to seven years in prison and a $250,000 fine but received just 30 months in prison. *See,* Press Release: Kokomo Resident Sentenced for Animal Crushing, U.S. Attorney's Office, Southern District of Indiana, November 10, 2021.

law. Even government agencies tasked with the responsibility of protecting animals fail to enforce the law, and the USDA is at the top of the list.

Failures of a Rogue Agency

The combination of protected industries, which are free to neglect and abuse animals behind closed doors, and lax government oversight and enforcement, makes for a deadly combination for animals, and when it comes to lax government oversight, the USDA is at the top of the list of offenders.

The USDA and its Animal and Plant Health Service (APHIS), which is responsible for administering the Animal Welfare Act nationwide, is too understaffed and underfunded to conduct regular and meaningful inspections of covered facilities, and when it does so, it typically turns a blind eye to cruelty. The story of a beagle breeding facility in Cumberland Virginia offers a glimpse of how APHIS is derelict in its duty and how the USDA is failing its mandate to enforce the Animal Welfare Act.

During the five-year period from 2017 to 2022, Envigo RMS, LLC ("Envigo") received numerous citations and warnings for violating the Animal Welfare Act, including more than 70 severe violations between July 2021 and March 2022 alone.[17] APHIS failed to take any action (such as fines; license suspension; confiscation of dogs) to aid the suffering animals. It took an undercover investigation by a PETA employee to expose the cruelty, which unleashed a public and political backlash against the facility. Recall that some states have criminalized this method of exposing animal cruelty.[18] Despite the backlash, APHIS still took no action. It took the extraordinary decision by the Department of Justice in 2022 to file a complaint against Envigo,[19] which eventually led to a "settlement," which resolved all *civil* claims against Envigo.[20] Pursuant to the settlement, Envigo agreed to shut down the Virginia breeding facility and transfer the

[17] Fobar, Rachel, "Hundreds of beagles died at facility before government took action", *National Geographic*, May 20, 2022.

[18] *See generally*, Barclay, Eliza, "States Crack Down On Animal Welfare Activists And Their Undercover Videos", *NPR*, March 1, 2012.

[19] United States of America v. Envigo RMS, LLC.

[20] Consent Decree, United States of America v. Envigo RMS, LLC, U.S. Dist. Ct. for W. Dist. of VA, Lynchburg Division, Case No. 6:22-00028-NKM, July 15, 2022.

4000 remaining beagles to the United States Humane Society, in what became the largest dog rescue in the history of the United States.[21]

The violations at the Cumberland facility were later described by a U.S. District Court as inadequate nutrition and food infested with mold, feces, maggots and live insects; deaths from cold exposure; lack of veterinary care despite life-threatening illnesses and injuries; skin infections; traumatic wounds and lesions; lameness and foot injuries; ear and eye conditions; and severe dental disease.[22] Over 300 beagle puppies died at the facility from "unknown causes" and many animals were euthanized for minor injuries and medical conditions that could have been easily treated.

Still, amid the thousands of rescue stories and photos that followed the rescue of the Cumberland animals was the realization that the animals had been victimized not once, but multiple times. Envigo admitted no wrongdoing, was neither fined nor penalized,[23] faced no consequences for misleading statements made to government officials,[24] and is free to continue its business involving thousands of animals in its more than 20 *other* locations across North America and Europe, despite a clear pattern of violations that date back decades.[25] The Association for Assessment and Accreditation of Laboratory Animal Care International (AAALAC) had granted accreditation to Envigo, despite only conducting site visits once

[21] *See generally*, Grantham-Philips, Wyatte, "4,000 beagles to be rescued from Virginia breeding facility after animal welfare violations alleged", *USA Today*, July 15, 2022.

[22] United States of America v. Envigo RMS, LLC, U.S. Dist. Ct. of W. Dist. of VA, Case No.: 6:22-cv-00028 (May 21, 2022).

[23] As a part of the settlement, a Transfer Plan governing the transfer of ownership of the beagles required Envigo to pay $100 per Beagle (or $150 per nursing beagle and litter) to help defray adoption costs, but such amount did not cover all necessary medical costs. The HSUS had to agree not to photograph or record the facility or the animals while at the facility. *See*, Transfer Plan dated July 1, 2022 by and between Envigo RMS, LLC and HSUS at https://awionline.org/sites/default/files/uploads/documents/Envigo-Jt-Transfer-Plan.pdf

[24] In a presentation to Virginia officials, the company represented that "animal welfare is a top priority" and that they have a "humane and compassionate approach". *See*, Johnson, Lizzie, "Profit, pain and puppies: Inside the rescue of nearly 4000 beagles", *Washington Post*, October 17, 2022.

[25] Huntingdon Life Services, which merged with Harlan Labs to form Envigo, had violations dating back to the late 1990s, including citations for severe animal suffering that included a dog with an untreated broken leg. *See*, Fobar, Rachel, "Hundreds of beagles died at facility before government took action", *National Geographic*, May 20, 2022.

every three years.[26] APHIS's colossal failure at the Cumberland facility and its subsequent failure to take action against Envigo is standard practice for the agency,[27] but in a move that shocked many lawmakers, the agency renewed Envigo's license. Congressional members condemned the action as "an abdication of the agency's duty to protect animals" and demanded a prompt response from APHIS.[28] A public records request yielded more than 800 pages of internal APHIS inspection records that revealed a sharply divided agency, ill-equipped to handle the issues at the facility.[29] In April 2023, the top animal care official at the USDA who testified before a federal grand jury in 2022 as part of a criminal probe into Envigo's animal cruelty announced her retirement, leaving behind an agency that remains unable to fulfill its mandate to enforce the Animal Welfare Act.

The Envigo matter was not an isolated case. In a separate matter, the USDA cited an Iowa dog breeder for more than 100 violations of the Animal Welfare Act within a six-month period for failing to provide 514 dogs with sufficient food, water, shelter, and veterinary care. During each inspection, the USDA failed to take any action to protect the animals.[30] Legislation has been introduced in Congress that would mandate yearly inspections of licensees, impose significant penalties for violations and require confiscation of any animals harmed as a result of violations of the Animal Welfare Act.[31] Until action is taken at the federal level to address the decades of neglect and failures at the USDA, states must act to protect animals. Following public outrage of the Cumberland breeding facility, Virginia updated its laws to require the standards and penalties that apply

[26] Ibid.

[27] *See,* e.g., Fobar, Rachel, "USDA accused of ignoring animal welfare violations in favor of business interests", *National Geographic,* October 13, 2021.

[28] Correspondence dated September 30, 2022 from the Congress of the United States to Kevin Shea, Administrator of APHIS, at https://www.aspca.org/sites/default/files/2022-10-03_quigley-fitzpatrick_et_al._letter_to_aphis_-_envigo_license_renewal_-_28_signers.pdf

[29] *See,* Lynch, Sarah N., "USDA official who oversaw Envigo beagle inspections to step down – email", *Reuters,* March 27, 2023.

[30] Over 500 dogs had protruding ribs, matted fur, and sunken eyes. *See,* Fernando, Christine, "Iowa breeder banned from selling dogs after 500 rescued amid 'horrific' conditions", *USA Today,* November 5, 2021.

[31] To amend the Animal Welfare Act to increase enforcement with respect to violations of the Act – H.R. 6100, 117th Congress (2021–2022).

to dealers and breeders to also apply to breeders of research animals.[32] A better legal outcome would be to ban animal research altogether.

In 2015, *The New York Times* broke a story on the USDA's callous disregard for animal suffering at the notorious Meat Animal Research Center, a taxpayer funded complex consisting of laboratories and pastures for nearly 30,000 animals in Clay Center, Nevada. Research is conducted on farm animals at the center with one principal goal: to help meat producers realize a higher profit.[33] At the time of the report, a tragic 6500 animals at the complex had starved to death and hundreds of lambs had died after being left outside in the cold, while many other animals were subjected to cruel experiments, physical trauma, and death.[34] Shocking reports, including deadly experiments and the dissection of a live pig by a sadistic researcher who seemed to enjoy the animal's suffering, came to light as insiders came forward.[35] A subsequent report ordered by the Secretary of Agriculture confirmed that procedures were not in place at the facility to minimize the pain and suffering of animals.[36]

The USDA does not monitor the Meat Animal Research Center's handling of animals, even though the agency acknowledged in a 2016 report that animal welfare was not properly monitored at the Center and that the Center needs greater oversight.[37] Farm animals and animals used in research are excluded from protection under the Animal Welfare Act, even at facilities like the Center where research shocked even members of the meat industry.[38] The *New York Times* report also found that over the past three decades, "some employees have reportedly been reluctant to report animal welfare complaints for fear of retaliation or indifference by facility management,"[39] making it precisely the kind of situation where both

[32] Virginia Senate Bill 87 and House Bill 1350, amending Va. Code §3.2-6511.2.

[33] Moss, Michael, "U.S. Research Lab Lets Livestock Suffer in Quest for Profit", *New York Times,* January 19, 2015.

[34] Ibid.

[35] Ibid.

[36] Moss, Michael, "Stricter Oversight Ordered for Animal Research at Nebraska Center", *New York Times,* March 9, 2015.

[37] Farrell, Patrick, "U.S. Animal Research Center Needs More Oversight, Audit Says", *New York Times,* December 20, 2016.

[38] For additional information, *see*, "Meat Animal Research Center: The Animal Welfare Act and Farm Animal Research", *Congressional Research Service* (R44091), October 9, 2015; *see also*, Moss, Michael, "U.S. Research Lab Lets Livestock Suffer in Quest for Profit", *New York Times,* January 19, 2015.

[39] Ibid.

public and private oversight is needed. In response to the *New York Times* article, a congressional investigation was opened and the Secretary of Agriculture ordered the USDA to review and update animal welfare standards for the Center.[40] The Animal Welfare in Agricultural Research Endeavors Act[41] was also introduced in Congress but it has not been enacted into law. As recently as 2022, animals were still dying at the Center.[42]

The USDA has been accused for decades of disregarding the safety and welfare concerns of animals. In 2017, a USDA inspection of the Monterey Zoo found the zoo to be in full compliance with the Animal Welfare Act, despite the fact that almost all of the zoo's medications had expired, despite evidence of neglect, and despite animals in need of veterinary care.[43] Despite criticism, USDA enforcement has gone from bad to worse with declining numbers of enforcement actions.[44] During the first 18 months of the Trump administration, the USDA filed just two complaints,[45] continuing its long-standing culture of disregard for animal suffering. This ineptitude is made worse by favoritism for special interests in the political system.

Even when the Animal Welfare Act is enforced, the fines imposed are so insignificant relative to the amount of money at stake that they provide no deterrence. Shin Nippon Biomedical Laboratories (SNBL), a Japanese-based company that conducts primate research, was ordered to pay $185,000 in connection with dozens of violations over a five-year period,

[40] *See*, Meat Animal Research Center; *see generally*, "MARC Continues to Feel the Heat", *Animal Welfare Institute*, AWI Quarterly (Spring 2015).

[41] The bills would amend the Animal Welfare Act to delete the exemption for farm animals used in agricultural research at federal facilities. *See*, Animal Welfare in Agricultural Research Endeavors Act, H.R. 746, S. 388, 114th Congress (2015–2016).

[42] *See*, e.g., "Complaints made against Meat Animal Research Center", *KSNB Local4*, February 4, 2022.

[43] Fobar, Rachel, "USDA accused of ignoring animal welfare violations in favor of business interests", *National Geographic*, October 13, 2021. An elderly kangaroo was "exhibiting tremors and vision loss" and elephants had a painful skin condition. Animals were also found with overgrown hooves.

[44] Ibid.

[45] This compares to 59 complaints filed by the USDA in 2015 and 2016. *See*, "Administration Remaking AWA into Animal Industry Welfare Act", *Animal Welfare Institute*, AWI Quarterly (Fall 2018).

including acts that led to the deaths of 38 nonhuman primates.[46] The market value of SNBL's parent was nearly $200 million in 2016,[47] so such inconsequential fines give SNBL little incentive to comply with the law. The University of Louisiana paid just $100,000, in 2017, in connection with the mishandling, injury and deaths of animals,[48] a trivial amount relative to millions of dollars available research funding. In one rare case, Santa Cruz Biotechnology was fined a record $3.5 million and was ordered to cancel its research registration for its abuse of animals, but penalties of this magnitude are very rare (the prior record was less than $300,000).[49]

In 2017, as the Director of Public Relations for Fur Free Society, Inc.,[50] I filed a complaint with the USDA regarding the treatment of animals at Ruby Fur Farm in Iowa.[51] Ruby Fur Farm breeds foxes, raccoons, ferrets and other animals for sale as research subjects. Based on the USDA's own inspection reports, which were obtained under The Freedom of Information Act,[52] we learned that temperatures in the metal housing exceeded 100 °F, with blistering heat indexes reaching as high as 122 °F on at least four separate inspection dates. Animals were observed to be in severe heat distress, with many animals panting, drooling, lethargic, breathing heavily, non-responsive to activity around them, and unable to cool off. The owners of the farm were instructed by USDA inspectors on multiple dates to take measures to ensure the proper handling of the animals, but the violations were not corrected.

In the complaint, I asked the USDA to impose the maximum fine of $13,750,000 ($10,000 per violation) against Ruby Fur Farm, for repeated

[46] SNBL paid stipulated fines of $31,852 in 2006, $12,937 in 2008, and $1406 in 2009. *See*, "Despite Serious Allegations, SNBL USA Dodges Significant Penalty from USDA", *Animal Welfare Institute*, December 18, 2016.

[47] Ibid.

[48] McConnaughey, Janet, "Louisiana university to pay USDA $100,000 over primate lab", *Associated Press*, July 21, 2017.

[49] "Biotech firm to pay $3.5 M fine to settle animal-abuse case", *Associated Press*, May 21, 2016.

[50] Fur Free Society, Inc. is a nonprofit organization dedicated to the protection of fur-bearing animals worldwide.

[51] *See*, correspondence dated August 25, 2017 from Fur Free Society, Inc. to Director, Western Region, USDA/APHIS/AC, at http://www.furfreesociety.org/Official_Complaint_8.25.2017.pdf

[52] The Freedom of Information Act, 5 U.S.C. § 552.

and severe violations of the Animal Welfare Act.[53] I also asked the USDA to immediately terminate all licenses issued to the farm, which had allowed hundreds of fur-bearing animals to suffer in dangerous and extreme heat conditions. The story was picked up by the Associated Press and ended up on over 7200 news sites, but the USDA never responded to my complaint, nor did they release any information concerning the animals who were at risk. In 2019 we learned what happened from an article in The Washington Post.[54]

It turns out that a team of USDA veterinarians and specialists were very concerned about the repeated violations by Ruby Fur Farm and the conditions under which the animals were being maintained. They were so concerned that they took the unprecedented step of confiscating ten of the animals, with plans to come back for the remaining ones.[55]

In a textbook case of special interests politics, an industry group in Iowa appealed to a Trump White House advisor, after which Agricultural Secretary, Sonny Perdue (2017–2021), and senior USDA officials intervened in the Ruby Fur Farm investigation (according to five former employees). The inspectors and veterinarians were blocked from taking the remaining animals and were ordered to return the confiscated animals to Ruby Fur Farm.[56] As governor of Georgia, Sonny Perdue was the subject of numerous conflict of interest concerns and ethical complaints, and the State Ethics Commission ruled on at least two occasions that Perdue had violated state ethics laws, including the acceptance of improper campaign contributions.[57] By the time the Ruby Fur Farm investigation came to Perdue's attention, he had a long history of ethics complaints and allegations of political corruption.[58]

[53] The Animal Welfare Act, 7 USC § 2149 (Violations by licensees) provides for penalties of up to $10,000 for each violation, and the inspection reports documented 1375 animal violations at the farm.

[54] Brulliard, Karin and Wan, William, "Caged raccoons drooled in 100-degree heat. But federal enforcement has faded", *Washington Post,* August 22, 2019.

[55] Ibid.

[56] Ibid.

[57] Lipton, Eric and Eder, Steve, "Ethical Lapses Trail Nominee for Agriculture – Conflicts of Interest as Governor of Georgia", *New York Times,* March 9, 2017.

[58] *See*, McCrimmon, Ryan, "Sonny Perdue faces ethics questions over his business holdings", *Politico*, October 15, 2020; *see also*, "Why Former Ag Secretary Sonny Perdue's Compliance With Federal Ethics Rules Still Needs to be Investigated", *American Oversight*, July 2, 2021; *see also*, Eric Lipton and Steve Eder, "Ethics Questions Dogged Agriculture Nominee as Georgia Governor", *New York Times*, March 8, 2017.

The Washington Post story reported that the Ruby Fur Farm investigation was discussed at an internal USDA meeting as an example of the Agency's pro-industry policy, called "teachable moments," that emphasized "education" over "enforcement", a policy that undermines the laws passed by Congress to protect animals. Pursuant to this policy, the USDA inspectors were instructed to use the repeated violations at Ruby Fur Farm as an opportunity to "educate" the owners, notwithstanding the USDA's own mission statement of ensuring "the humane treatment of animals covered by the Animal Welfare Act".[59] According to the Washington Post report, leaders of the USDA's Animal Care division told inspectors to treat those who violate the Animal Welfare Act as "partners" rather than "potential offenders". The USDA essentially sanctioned ignorance of the law as a defense to lawbreaking, which a former USDA assistant director criticized as the "systematic dismantling" of protections at the expense of animal welfare.[60]

In addition to failing to conduct timely inspections, the USDA released a much shorter *Animal Welfare Inspection Guide* in May 2018, cutting more than 150 pages, omitting key provisions, and instructing inspectors to "work with" violators rather than cite them.[61] In early 2019, the USDA also changed its procedures to only require partial "focused" inspections for AAALAC accredited labs (the same group that gave accreditation to the infamous Cumberland beagle facility). It took congressional intervention to get the USDA to restore its database of animal welfare records for public viewing and to mandate recording of all citations on inspection reports.[62] A few years later, when the USDA finally announced the end of its "teachable moments" policy following congressional intervention,[63] it described the policy as addressing "minor, isolated noncompliances" that do not

[59] *See*, "About Animal Care", *USDA Animal and Plant Health Inspection Service, U.S. Department of Agriculture*, September 9, 2022, at https://www.aphis.usda.gov/aphis/ourfocus/animalwelfare/usda-animal-care-overview

[60] Fobar, Rachel, "USDA accused of ignoring animal welfare violations in favor of business interests", *National Geographic*, October 13, 2021.

[61] For background, *see* "Administration Remaking AWA into Animal Industry Welfare Act", *Animal Welfare Institute*, Fall 2018. The 31-page section regarding confiscation criteria has been dropped and replaced by a mere seven lines buried in Appendices.

[62] The congressional requirements were included in the 2020 federal spending bill. *See generally*, "Final Appropriations Bills Contain Groundbreaking New Protections for Animals?", *ASPCA*, December 17, 2019.

[63] Ibid.

impact the welfare or care of the animals.[64] The violations at Ruby Fur Farm, however, were neither "minor" nor "isolated" occurrences. The failure to enforce the law had serious, even lethal consequences for the animals.

Inspection reports for Ruby Fur Farm from 2018 to 2023 reflect continued violations of the Animal Welfare Act, including stagnant water with animal waste and pests that threatened the health of the animals (2018); inadequate enclosures (2019); aerosol spray that threatened the health of animals and food and water contamination (2020); damaged enclosures (2021); enclosures that could injure animals; buildup of excreta, dirt, grime and hair in enclosures that increases the risk of disease; damaged wire flooring with nails and sharp points; and an animal entrapped in (and injured by) a wire panel of its enclosure (2022); and broken wires with sharp points; floors so heavily saturated with urine the wood was spongy; ammonia levels so extremely high that it irritated inspectors' eyes; large piles of feces and large puddles of urine under enclosures; and large amounts of rodent feces on nest boxes and on food containers (2023).[65]

For decades, the USDA has allowed breeders, zoos, circuses, and research laboratories to operate without accountability, accumulating hundreds of citations. Little has changed. Enforcement actions against animal facilities dropped a staggering 90% between 2015 and 2020.[66] Federal agencies that fail to enforce laws duly enacted by elected representatives undermine the rule of law, and it impacts the morale of public servants. Veterinarians and former employees have spoken out about the culture at the USDA, where inspectors fear raising legitimate animal welfare concerns and are told to not cite certain violations or are instructed to "downgrade" the severity of the violation.[67] The disregard for animal welfare was so appalling that there was a "mass exodus" of nearly three dozen USDA inspectors in 2017 and 2018.[68] The public also suffers from the failings of the USDA.

[64] *See*, "Letter to Animal Care Stakeholders Regarding Teachable Moments", *USDA Animal and Plant Health Inspection Services, U.S. Dept. of Agriculture,* July 28, 2022.

[65] USDA Inspection Reports (U.S. Department of Agriculture, Animal and Plant Health Inspection Service), dated January 10, 2023, August 2, 2022, July 21, 2022, April 18, 2022, January 27, 2022, February 10, 2021, March 3, 2020, May 9, 2019, and September 19, 2018.

[66] Fobar, Rachel, "USDA accused of ignoring animal welfare violations in favor of business interests", *National Geographic*, October 13, 2021.

[67] Ibid.

[68] Ibid.

In 2017, the USDA abruptly removed from public access all inspection reports that document many violations of the Animal Welfare Act by thousands of zoos, research laboratories, dog breeding operations and other covered facilities, citing "privacy" concerns,[69] even though "privacy" has not been cited by other law enforcement agencies as grounds to withhold the names of offenders.[70] After national outcry and congressional involvement, some inspection reports were restored, albeit heavily redacted to remove information critical to enforcement,[71] thereby rendering analysis by the public all but impossible. In fact, more than 90% of the restored inspection reports, involving over 3000 animal breeders and dealers, were redacted to protect the identity of the offenders, leaving the public with little to no transparency.[72] In 2023, the *Better CARE of Animals Act* (S-2555, 118th Congress) was introduced in Congress, which would provide the Department of Justice with the same enforcement authority as the USDA. Still, many question whether the USDA should be dismantled and replaced in part by an agency that is dedicated solely to the enforcement of the Animal Welfare Act. That would be a good start.

Citizen Suits

In the aftermath of the COVID-19 pandemic, we are more aware that the health of animals has critical implications for public health, yet the public has no rights when animal agriculture threatens human health. There is precedent in environmental law in the United States for allowing private citizens to commence "citizen suit" actions against those who violate the law.[73] Under the Clean Water Act,[74] for instance, actions may be com-

[69] Brulliard, Karin, "USDA abruptly purges animal welfare information from its website", *Washington Post*, February 3, 2017.

[70] In certain circumstances, the names of juveniles can be withheld in police reports but the names of adult offenders are generally released to the public.

[71] *See generally*, Daly, Natasha and Bale, Rachael, "We Asked the Government Why Animal Welfare Records Disappeared. They Sent 1,700 Blacked-Out Pages", *National Geographic*, May 1, 2017.

[72] "Administration Remaking AWA into Animal Industry Welfare Act", *Animal Welfare Institute*, Fall 2018.

[73] For a comprehensive analysis of citizen suits, see Gordon, Stacy L., "The Legal Rights of All Living Things: How Animal Law can Extend the Environmental Movement's Quest for Legal Standing for Non-Human Animals", in "What Can Animal Law Learn From Environmental Law?" *Environmental Law Institute* (2015), at 211–241.

[74] Citizen Suits, 33 U.S.C. § 1365(a).

menced by a private citizen against a business entity or governmental agency for violations of the statute. There is no comparable provision in animal law. While environmental laws can be enforced directly against the person or entity causing the harm, the Animal Welfare Act exempts the commercial animal industry, the area that presents significant animal welfare concerns, from its coverage.[75] Protecting the environment and animals are equally important as a public health matter. By amending animal protection laws to permit citizen suits, we could help prevent another public health catastrophe like COVID-19. Affording the public standing in courts to act on behalf of animals provides another layer of protection against public health risks, which could be especially effective when coupled with monitoring rights (e.g., CCTV in slaughterhouses).

The Right to Rescue

The failure of government to protect animals has compelled some to rescue animals from factory farms and research facilities. The ethical question of the 'right to rescue' arises with animals because, like children, animals are not able to verbally ask for help.[76] In law, there is no *general* obligation to rescue, but in some cases, the law does afford well-intentioned rescuers with criminal and/or civil immunity under so-called Good Samaritan laws.

As of early 2022, at least 31 states in the United States have enacted laws that afford immunity to someone who rescues a distressed animal from a hot vehicle (or have enacted laws that prohibit animals from being left in vehicles under dangerous conditions).[77] The laws are modeled after laws that afford immunity to someone who breaks the window of a hot car to save a child. The risk to dogs in hot cars is no different from the risk to pigs, cows, and chickens in hot trailers, but laws fail to recognize the

[75] What Animal Law can Learn from Environmental Law, at xxv.

[76] Animals do seek help from humans, like the elephant who sought help from a wildlife refuge after being shot by poachers, but humans often fail to recognize it. *See,* e.g., Schelling, Ameena, "Desperate Elephants Shot With Poison Arrows Travel To Humans For Help", *The Dodo*, September 17, 2015.

[77] Some state laws only provide immunity to first responders or animal control but at least 14 states (California, Florida, Connecticut, Colorado, Arizona, Indiana, Kansas, Louisiana, Ohio, Massachusetts, Oregon, Tennessee, Vermont, and Wisconsin) allow anyone to rescue an animal in distress. *See*, Wisch, Rebecca F., "Table of State Laws that Protect Animals Left in Parked Vehicles", *Michigan State University, Animal Legal & Historical Center*, 2022.

similarity. Farm animals are more vulnerable due to the complete lack of transparency, but laws do not protect these animals.

There are strong policy grounds for extending the protection of "Good Samaritan" laws to animal rescues, including: insufficient governmental resources and oversight of industries that trade and profit on animals; inadequate legal protection for animals; failure to enforce existing laws; risks posed to public health; and the lack of transparency by industries. Imagine a case where an individual, compelled by moral conscience to "look closely and without blinking into the faces of the forgotten, the frightened, and the unforgiven",[78] rescues a dying calf from an industrial farm's "kill pile", pays for emergency veterinary care for the animal, and finds the animal a permanent home at a sanctuary. If "Good Samaritan" laws applied, the individual would be immune from criminal and civil liability for his or her actions. What happens instead is that the rescuer will be charged with crimes, such as trespass and felony theft, and the dying animal will be ordered returned to the kill pile.

In contrast to "Good Samaritan" laws, some laws impose affirmative duties to act with reasonable care (with liability for failure to do so). This legal duty to rescue can be required by statute and has been imposed by courts where a person creates a hazardous situation,[79] or if there is a special relationship (e.g., employer's duty to employees; common carrier's duty to passengers; innkeeper's duty to guests; storekeeper's duty to customers; spouse's duty to a spouse; jailer's duty to inmates; and teacher or school official's duty to students[80]). The federal Child Abuse Prevention and Treatment Act requires each state to have procedures in place that require certain individuals (e.g., teachers, health-care workers, and child care providers) to report known or *suspected* instances of child abuse and neglect.[81] Federal law also requires individuals in federal settings to report *suspected* child abuse, with criminal penalties for failing to do so.[82] All states have some form of legal duty that requires certain individuals to report cases of

[78] Neil Abramson, *Just Life: A Novel*, New York, Center Street (Reprint Ed), April 4, 2017. ISBN-13: 978-1455591068.

[79] For an analysis of this duty, *see* Bayles, Michael and Chapman, Bruce, "Ethical Issues in the Law of Tort", *New York, Springer-Verlag*, at 20–21. ISBN 978-90-277-1639.2.

[80] W. Prosser & W. Keeton, The Law of Torts, §56, at 376–77 (5th ed. 1984).

[81] Child Abuse Prevention and Treatment Act, 42 U.S.C. §5106(a)(b)(2)(B)(i).

[82] Victims of Child Abuse Act of 1990, 42 U.S.C. §13031.

abuse or neglect of children[83] and the elderly.[84] The policy behind affirmative duties is clear: children and the elderly are vulnerable, with limited ability to protect themselves; so suspected abuse and neglect should be investigated. The same is true for animals.

The lack of accountability by industries, the secrecy that prevents public scrutiny, the lack of government oversight, and the lack of adequate laws each warrant the imposition of a legal duty on anyone who keeps animals to act reasonable and to report any abuse or neglect (or suspected abuse or neglect). The duty to act reasonably and to report suspected neglect or abuse should apply to anyone with animals in their care, whether it is on factory farms, in research facilities or in any other places where animals are held, including the infamous Meat Animal Research Center in the United States.[85]

In addition to extending 'Good Samaritan' laws and affirmative legal duties to protect animals, there should be a general legal right to rescue animals in distress. The current legal climate, however, has extreme bias against anyone who rescues an animal. In one case that made headlines, the rescue of two sick and malnourished piglets from a Utah Smithfield Foods farm resulted in a multi-year, multi-state investigation involving the FBI, raids of animal sanctuaries, and DNA analysis obtained by slicing off part of a sick piglet's ear.[86] The millions spent to hunt down the piglets and to prosecute the case was a stunning development given that the prosecutors deemed the value of the two piglets to be only $84.40. The jury agreed and acquitted the individuals, who had been charged with felony burglary and theft.[87] It was reported at the time that the FBI assigned

[83] The Federal Child Abuse and Prevention and Treatment Act (CAPTA) requires each state to adopt procedures that require certain individuals to report instances of child neglect or abuse. 42 U.S.C. §5106a(b)(2)(B)(i).

[84] *See generally*, "Citations to State Adult Protective Services Laws and Long-Term Care Ombudsman Laws", *American Bar Association Commission on Law and Aging*, April 2020, at https://www.americanbar.org/content/dam/aba/administrative/law_aging/2020-aps-ia-ltcop-statutes-citations.pdf

[85] *See* Chapter V for more on this research facility.

[86] *See*, e.g., Jacobs, Andrew, "Animal Rights Activists Are Acquitted in Smithfield Piglet Case", *New York Times*, October 18, 2022; *see also*, Moyer, Justin Wm., "FBI raids animal shelters, searching for piglets rescued from factory farm, activists say", *Washington Post*, September 14, 2017.

[87] Bolotnikova, Marina, "Activists Acquitted in Trial for Taking Piglets from Smithfield Foods", *The Intercept*, October 8, 2022.

around eight agents[88] to what was in reality a petty theft case that should have been handled at the local level. Instead, the FBI allowed itself to became the strong-arm of animal agriculture, wasting limited resources to appease an industry that prioritizes profits over people and animals.

The Smithfield case stands in stark contrast to the thousands of non-violent misdemeanor offenses that, on policy grounds, are not prosecuted in the United States.[89] Fair and just laws would impose obligations on the owners of, and workers at, industrial farms to aid malnourished, sick and dying animals. Current laws, however, treat abuse and neglect on factory farms as "common agricultural practices" that are excluded as cruelty under state anti-cruelty laws. It is disturbing to see government resources used to prosecute animal rescues to such a tremendous degree, but not used to prosecute animal cruelty on factory farms. This rescue appears to have received more scrutiny than one of the most horrific crimes against women. The resources used to hunt down the rescued piglets, including the costs of DNA technology, could have been used to test one of the hundreds of thousands of untested rape kits in police departments and crime lab storage facilities across the United States.[90]

This rescue underscores the bias against animal rescues in the United States. Rescue a stressed bison calf struggling to cross a river and park rangers will euthanize the animal.[91] Save a moose calf from a potential black bear attack and you will be fined and lose your job.[92] Feed lettuce to starving manatees in Florida and you will be charged.[93] Animal rescues involve some level of personal risk, but so do many other legal activities.[94] Individuals who rescue an animal in distress, and do so in a reasonable manner, should be shielded from criminal and civil liability, but laws protect industries.

[88] Ibid.

[89] Merrefield, Clark, "Choosing not to prosecute low-level crimes may reduce future crime, research times", *Association of Prosecuting Attorneys*, February 14, 2023.

[90] *See*, "What is the Backlog?", *End the Backlog*, n.d., at www.endthebacklog.org/what-is-the-backlog/

[91] Nichols, Jake, "Yellowstone Bison Calf Euthanized After Tourist Tries To 'Rescue' It", *Cowboy State Daily*, May 23, 2023.

[92] McEntyre, Nicholas, "Canadian man fired from job after saving baby moose from bear: I couldn't just leave her", *New York Post*, July 16, 2023.

[93] *See*, "Living with Florida Manatees", Florida Fish and Wildlife Conservation Commission, at https://myfwc.com/conservation/you-conserve/wildlife/manatee/#

[94] Many dangerous activities, such as bungee jumping, amusement park rides, motorcycle riding, and mountain climbing, are all legal.

Ag-Gag Laws

The horrors of factory farming are hidden from the public for a reason: industries want the unfettered ability to commodify animals in a manner that would never be accepted by the public. This policy of keeping consumers in the dark, together with misleading advertising that further obscures how animals are actually treated, has given rise to activists who want to educate the public about the realities of life on these farms. Without that knowledge, the public becomes an unwitting participant in animal cruelty to the extent that people support industries involved with factory farming.

The entire foundation of industrialized agriculture is based on institutionalized cruelty[95] that prioritizes profits and efficiency over the welfare of animals and engages in practices that, if done to a companion animal, would violate anti-cruelty laws. Modern animal agriculture involves machines of torture that disregard the sentience of animals. The suffering of animals who are treated as mere widgets for profitability is precisely what activists want to expose.

In response to the efforts of activists to expose cruelty, "Ag-Gag" (or anti-whistleblower) laws, which criminalize the recording, documentation and reporting of animal abuse in factory farms, have been enacted.[96] These laws violate the First Amendment free speech rights under the United States Constitution and they are being struck down when challenged. To date, Ag-Gag laws in Idaho,[97] Iowa (with laws struck down as

[95] Institutionalized cruelty includes non-anesthetized cruel practices such as tail docking, dehorning, hot-iron branding, castration, debeaking, and extreme confinement, all of which are standard practice on factory farms.

[96] Some state laws criminalize obtaining access to animals by "false pretenses", such as securing employment to document animal cruelty. *See,* e.g., Ala. Code 1975 § 13A-11-153(3) (2002).

[97] Idaho § 18-7042 (2014), struck down as unconstitutional in 2015. On appeal, the Ninth Circuit struck down a majority of Idaho's law on First Amendment grounds. *See generally*, Berry, Harrison, "Ninth Circuit Appeals Court Strikes Down Key Provisions of Ag-Gag Law", *Idaho Press*, July 16, 2020.

unconstitutional three times),[98] Kansas,[99] North Carolina,[100] Utah,[101] and Wyoming[102] have been struck down by courts as unconstitutional.

As of the end of 2022, a handful of states have active Ag-Gag laws, including Alabama,[103] Arkansas,[104] Iowa,[105] Missouri,[106] Montana,[107] and North Dakota.[108] The laws have a chilling effect on free speech and associated rights protected by the First Amendment of the U.S. Constitution and they remain the law even though similar laws have been struck down by appellate courts as a violation of free speech rights. The Animal Enterprise Terrorism Act[109] is another overly vague and broad law that is thought to be unconstitutional on First Amendment free speech grounds.[110] It was supported by wealthy agricultural and biomedical special interest groups. This law, along with similar legislation enacted by

[98] Iowa Code § 717A.3B, struck down as unconstitutional in 2019 (on appeal). Iowa Code § 717A.3A, partially struck down as unconstitutional in 2021. Iowa Code § 727.8A, struck down as unconstitutional in 2022. For background of Iowa's repeated attempts to make the filming of farm animal cruelty illegal, *see*, Pitt, David, "Federal court finds 3rd Iowa 'ag-gag' law unconstitutional", *The Associated Press*, September 28, 2022.

[99] K.S.A.47-1825 – 1830, struck down as unconstitutional in 2021. *See generally*, Malo, Sebastien, "10th Circuit rules Kansas 'ag-gag' law unconstitutional", *Reuters*, August 19, 2021.

[100] NC Gen. Stat. Ch. § 99A-1-2, struck down as unconstitutional in 2020. On February 23, 2023, the Court of Appeals for the Fourth Circuit agreed that the law was unconstitutional as it applied to protected newsgathering activities. *See*, People for the Ethical Treatment of Animals, Inc., et al., Plaintiffs-Appellees v. North Carolina Farm Bureau Federation, Inc., Intervenor/Defendant – Appellant, and Attorney General of the State of North Carolina and Chancellor of the University of North Carolina-Chapel Hill, Defendants, U.S. Ct. of Appeals For the Fourth Circuit, No. 20-1776, filed February 23, 2023.

[101] Utah Code §76-6-112, struck down as unconstitutional in 2017.

[102] Wyo. Code §6-3-414 (criminal) and Wyo. Code § 40-27-101 (civil), struck down as unconstitutional in 2018.

[103] Ala. Code 1975 §13A-11-153 (2002).

[104] Ark. Code §16-118-113 (2017).

[105] Iowa Code §716.7A.

[106] Missouri §261.099 (2021); Missouri §578.045 (2017); Missouri §578.013 (2012).

[107] MCA §81-30-101-105 (1991).

[108] ND §12.1-21.1-01-05 (1991).

[109] 18 U.S.C. §43 (1994).

[110] *See*, "Animal Enterprise Terrorism Act (AETA)", *Civil Liberties Defense Center*, April 24, 2014.

some states,[111] has the same chilling effect on free speech. The result is a weaponization of the legal system, where unconstitutional laws are enacted (or stay on the books) as a means of silencing activists. This tactic has proven to be highly effective because it is cash-strapped nonprofits who must challenge the laws in court. Recall that in other countries, the trend is for more, not less, transparency, with video surveillance being installed in slaughterhouses. In the United States, however, special interests corrupt the political process because politicians are beholden to them for campaign funding.

The relationship between politicians and special interest groups is so close that at times there seems to be a kneejerk reaction by politicians to protect industrialized animal agriculture at the expense of their constituents. For instance, in Texas, a freelancer was flying his drone over the Trinity River when he recorded the Columbia Packing Company illegally dumping pig blood into Cedar Creek, which flows into the Trinity River. The recording was turned over to authorities and individuals were indicted for water pollution. A few years later, however, Texas enacted legislation to make it illegal to use an unmanned aircraft to capture images of privately owned real property in order to conduct surveillance.[112] In 2017, the law was amended to specifically include animal feeding operations as "critical infrastructure facilities", for which no-fly provisions apply. The law was challenged and was found to be unconstitutional on First Amendment grounds,[113] but the law is a good example of how some politicians prioritize industrial animal agriculture over the interests of both people and animals.

[111] *See*, e.g., Farm animal and field crop and research facilities protection act, Ky. Rev. Stat. Ann. §437.420 (1990); Animal Facilities Protection Act, Okla. Stat. Ann. tit. 21, §1680.1 (1991); Florida Animal Enterprise Protection Act, Fla. Stat. Ann. §828.40 (1993); Offences Against Animal Research and Animal Production Facilities, Ala. Code §13A-11-150 (1993); Farm Animal and Research Facilities, Ark. Code Ann. §5-62-201 (1991).

[112] Texas Privacy Act, H.B. No. 912, amending Subtitle B, Title 4, Government Code, by adding Chapter 423 (Use of Unmanned Aircraft).

[113] National Press Photographers Association, Texas Press Association and Joseph Pappalardo v. Steven McCraw, Director of Texas Department of Public Safety; Dwight Mathis, Chief of the Texas Highway Patrol; and Wes Mau, District Attorney of Hays County, Texas (March 28, 2022), U.S. Dist. Court for the W District of Texas, Austin Division. Case 1:19-cv-00946-RP.

Much has been written as to why anti-whistleblower and Ag-Gag laws make for bad policy. Transparency, worker protection, food safety concerns, unsafe working conditions and illegal activities are among the many reasons why free speech should always be protected, even if critical of well-connected industries. In light of allegations that nursing homes drug patients[114] and daycares drug children to make the jobs of employees easier,[115] there are sound policy reasons to permit video surveillance and recording on industrial farms, where poor hygiene practices can threaten meat contamination, risk the spread of disease and possibly give rise to new zoonotic diseases that threaten public health.

Factory farms are one of the few places where video surveillance is not used for a vulnerable population. Police body cameras protect the public, "granny cams" protect the elderly, and daycare security cameras protect young children. Extensive video monitoring is done by employers, businesses and all levels of government as a protective measure. The reasons for such fierce industry resistance to transparency are the appalling conditions under which animals are forced to live and die,[116] and the reason for Ag-Gag laws is to chill the free speech of anyone who dares to criticize them.

The Corrupting Influence of Politics

Animals face tremendous obstacles when it comes to gaining legal protection, and the entanglement of policy makers with industries is particularly challenging. Too often, politicians put their own political ambitions ahead of animals and the people they serve. To appease Iowa voters ahead of the 2016 presidential election, former New Jersey governor, Chris Christie, defied the will of nearly 90% of New Jersey voters,[117] who supported a ban

[114] *See,* e.g., Thomas, Katie, et al., "Phony Diagnoses Hide High Rates of Drugging at Nursing Home", *New York Times*, October 15, 2021.

[115] *See,* e.g., Carvajal, Jessica-Lynn, "Stafford daycare owner arrested after toddlers eat drug-laced food", *DC News Now*, April 15, 2022; Biswas, Joyeeta, "Daycare owner drugged kids, tied them into car seats: Police", *ABC News*, September 19, 2018.

[116] *See,* e.g., Jackson, David and Marx, Gary, "Whipped, kicked, beaten: Illinois workers describe abuse of hogs", *Chicago Tribune*, August 4, 2016.

[117] A Mason-Dixon Polling & Research poll showed that nearly 90% of New Jersey voters supported a ban on gestation crates. *See*, Ettinger, Jill, "Pigs Fly in New Jersey: State Passes Ban on Cruel Gestation Crates", *Organic Authority*, October 22, 2018.

on the extreme confinement of pigs.[118] Christie, pressured by Iowa governor, Terry Branstad, to veto the ban, disregarded the broad bipartisan coalition of state lawmakers who supported the animal welfare measure and vetoed the bill.[119] Naked political ambition and the corruption it breeds come at a high cost to society. Still, legal justice can be delayed but it cannot be denied. In 2023, polls revealed that 93% of New Jersey voters still supported a ban on the extreme confinement of animals.[120] In June 2023, New Jersey lawmakers again passed legislation to ban the extreme confinement of mother pigs and calves and this time it was signed into law.[121]

North Carolina politicians have also put the interest of industry groups ahead of the interests of people and animals. Despite numerous studies documenting the health risks associated with toxins that emanate from hog farms, North Carolina enacted a law[122] that makes it difficult, if not impossible, to sue hog farmers.[123] The law was passed by lawmakers in response to successful lawsuits brought by residents who were harmed by hog farm pollutants, including the toxic mixtures of animal waste, blood, insecticides, afterbirth, chemicals and other compounds that rain down in areas where people reside, attend school and worship.[124] Similar to

[118] *See*, Associated Press, "Chris Christie vetoes ban on hog gestation crates", *Des Moines Register*, November 29, 2014.

[119] Colvin, Jill, "Christie faces Iowa pressure on pig crate ban", *The San Diego Union-Tribune*, November 12, 2014.

[120] Frank, Elissa and Hackett, Brian R., "A Common-Sense Proposal to Outlaw Gestation Crates", *Insider NJ*, May 18, 2023.

[121] New Jersey Legislature (Session 2022–2023), A1970 and S.1298.

[122] North Carolina's Right to Farm Act (N.C. Gen. Stat. §106-701, 106-702 (2019)) was challenged but on December 16, 2022, the Supreme Court of North Carolina denied an appeal claiming that the state's Right to Farm Act was unconstitutional. *See generally*, Jensen, Kitt Tovar, "North Carolina Supreme Court Denies Appeal Challenging Right to Farm Act", *Iowa State University, Center for Agricultural Law and Taxation*, January 4, 2023.

[123] *See generally*, Sorg, Lisa, "Court of Appeals rules NC lawmakers were within their authority to all but outlaw hog nuisance lawsuits", *NC Policy Watch,* December 21, 2021.

[124] Large lagoons of animal waste are emptied by dispersing liquid waste into the air, which can then travel to nearby communities. *See generally*, Formuzis, Alex, "Manure in the Mist: Hog Hell Permeates Duplin County, N.C.", *Environmental Working Group,* July 11, 2016; *see also*, Yeoman, Barry, "'It smells like decomposing body': North Carolina's polluting pig farms", *The Guardian*, August 27, 2019.

residents who live near toxic tanneries in India,[125] residents in North Carolina who live in close proximity to hog farms have elevated risks of disease and death.[126] A growing body of evidence shows that toxic releases from hog farms contribute to respiratory illnesses,[127] high blood pressure,[128] reduced quality of life,[129] and mental health issues.[130] Rates of death for all studied diseases, including septicemia, kidney disease, tuberculosis, anemia, and infant mortality, are higher in communities located near large hog CAFOs.[131] The toxic pollutants from hog CAFOs, cesspools, and waste sprayers disproportionately impact low-income people and people of color, primarily African Americans who suffer from reduced lung function, respiratory conditions, and other health conditions.[132]

If the legal system reflected the high standing that society assigns to animals, they would not be treated as "property" but as individuals with legal rights and protection. Current laws, regulations, and politics are the result of industry lobbyists that disregard our empathy for animals and keep us disconnected from the animal kingdom. Politicians have allowed

[125] *See* Richard Pearshouse, Toxic Tanneries: The Health Repercussions of Bangladesh's Hazaribagh Leather. Human Rights Watch, October 2012, https://www.hrw.org/report/2012/10/09/toxic-tanneries/health-repercussions-bangladeshs-hazaribagh-leather#

[126] Kravchenko, Julia, et al., "Mortality and health Outcomes in North Carolina Communities Located in Close Proximity to Hot Concentrated Animal Feeding Operations", *N C Medical Journal*, 2018 Sep-Oct; 79(5):278–288. https://doi.org/10.18043/ncm.79.5.278. PMID: 30228132.

[127] Thorne, Peter S., "Environmental Health Impacts of Concentrated Animal Feeding Operations: Anticipating Hazards – Searching for Solutions", *Environmental Health Perspective*, Vol. 115, No. 2., February 1, 2007. https://doi.org/10.1289/ehp.8831

[128] Wing, Steve, et al., "Air pollution from industrial swine operations and blood pressure of neighboring residents", *Environmental Health Perspectives*, January 1, 2013. https://doi.org/10.1289/ehp.1205109

[129] Schiffman, Susan S., et al., "The effect of environmental odors emanating from commercial swine operations on the mood of nearby residents", *Brain Research Bulletin*, Vol. 37, Issue 4, 1995, at 369–375. ISSN 0361-9230. https://doi.org/10.1016/0361-9230(95)00015-1

[130] Horton, Rachel, et al., "Malodor as a Trigger of Stress and Negative Mood in Neighbors of Industrial Hog Operations", *American Journal of Public Health* 99, S610-S615 (November 2009). https://doi.org/10.2105/AJPH.2008.148924

[131] Duke Health News, "N.C. Residents Living Near Large Hog Farms Have Elevated Disease, Death Risks", *Duke University School of Medicine, Duke Surgery*, September 18, 2018.

[132] Wing, Steve and Johnston, Jill, "Industrial Hog Operations in North Carolina Disproportionately Impact African-Americans, Hispanics and American Indians", *The University of North Carolina at Chapel Hill, Department of Epidemiology*, August 29, 2014.

industries to hide their exploitation and abuse of animals from society, while the public is fed a steady diet of false and misleading narratives and advertisements that deceive them into believing that the animals are fully protected, safe, and content. An informed public, armed with accurate information, would be shocked. Institutionalized animal abuse or cruelty disclosed through snippets obtained by Freedom of Information Act requests or by whistleblowers consistently provokes outrage. The combination of profit-driven industries and an uninformed public has allowed the devaluation of animals to continue. Laws governing the treatment of animals should embody the values held by society. Too often, laws are the result of industry lobbying that prioritizes profits over animal welfare.

CHAPTER 6

Animal Law as an Emerging Field

In an animal cruelty case that involved the abandonment and starvation of a black Lab named Jack, a judge wrote in her decision "[t]his is murder. An animal, in this court's opinion, is no different than a child."[1] This statement reflects the growing discomfort felt by many with the "property" classification of animals in the United States. This discomfort has given rise to the emerging field of animal law.

In the last two decades, law schools have added animal law courses, seminars, and programs that examine the rights and standing of animals and the laws that protect them. As late as 2001, there were only nine animal law classes offered in the United States.[2] Today, there are more than 100 animal law courses.[3] Prestigious law schools, including Harvard Law School,[4] Stanford Law School,[5] Yale Law School,[6] New York University

[1] Hunt, Amber, "*Man Gets Jail Time for Starving Dog to Death*", *Detroit Free Press*, July 19, 2007, at B1.

[2] "Top 10 Law School Animal Law Programs", *Kaplan*, n.d., at https://www.kaptest.com/study/lsat/law-school-top-10-animal-law-programs/

[3] Ibid.

[4] Harvard Law School, Animal Law & Policy Program, at https://animal.law.harvard.edu/

[5] Stanford Law School, Animal Law, at https://law.stanford.edu/courses/animal-law/

[6] Yale Law School, The Law, Ethics & Animals Program, at https://law.yale.edu/animals

K. C. Moore, *The Case for the Legal Protection of Animals*, The Palgrave Macmillan Animal Ethics Series,
https://doi.org/10.1007/978-3-031-46065-4_6

School of Law,[7] University of Virginia School of Law,[8] University of Michigan Law,[9] University of California, Berkeley School of Law,[10] University of Pennsylvania Law School,[11] George Washington University Law[12] and others now offer animal law courses. The Center for Animal Law Studies at Lewis & Clark Law School is recognized as having the most extensive animal law program in the United States, offering a specialty in animal law as a subset of its Environmental Law Program.[13] Organizations that work to effectuate policy changes for animals, particularly those that advocate for farm animals, now have their own in-house counsel and legal department staffed from this growing number of animal law specialists.

There is a growing number of academic journals and publications that focus on animal law, including the Journal of Animal Law and Ethics (University of Pennsylvania), the Journal for Critical Animal Studies (Institute for Critical Animal Studies), Stanford Journal of Animal Law and Policy (Stanford Law School), the Journal of International Wildlife Law & Policy (Kluwer Law International) and the Animals' Advocate (Animal Legal Defense Fund). Journals foster further discussion and research and play an important role in disseminating information on animal law to the academic community and beyond. The developing body of animal law will also help educate lawmakers and judges. Recall that judges ruled that the extreme living conditions for Lolita at the Miami Seaquarium did not violate the Animal Welfare Act or the Endangered Species Act.[14]

[7] New York University School of Law, Animal Studies, at https://as.nyu.edu/departments/environment/animal-studies.html

[8] University of Virginia School of Law, Animal Law Program, at https://www.law.virginia.edu/academics/program/animal-law

[9] University of Michigan Law, Animal Law, at https://michigan.law.umich.edu/courses/animal-law

[10] University of California, Berkeley, Animal Law and Advocacy, at https://www.law.berkeley.edu/experiential/pro-bono-program/slps/current-slps-projects/animal-law-and-advocacy/

[11] University of Pennsylvania, Penn Carey Law, Animal Law Project, at https://www.law.upenn.edu/live/profiles/1117-animal-law-project-alp

[12] George Washington University Law School, Animal Law, at https://www.law.gwu.edu/animal-law

[13] Lewis & Clark Law School, Center for Animal Law Studies, at https://law.lclark.edu/centers/animal_law_studies/

[14] *See generally*, Dunagan, Christopher, "Endangered Species Act can't help Lolita, judge says in legal ruling", *Kitsap Sun*, June 8, 2016; "Appeals court rules against groups that want to free orca", *Associated Press*, June 22, 2015.

Professional bar associations for licensed attorneys in the United States have active animal law sections and committees at federal, state, and local levels. The American Bar Association (ABA), the largest voluntary association of attorneys in the world, has two active and influential animal law committees, one in the International Law Section and one in the Tort Trial and Insurance Practice Section (TIPS). The International Animal Law Committee advocates for the protection of animals worldwide,[15] while the ABA TIPS Animal Law Committee works "to address all issues concerning the intersection of animals and the law to create a paradigm shift resulting in a just world for all."[16] Both committees have sponsored and/or cosponsored highly influential ABA Resolutions, which reflect the ABA's official policy positions on issues and serve as the ABA's "focal point" for its advocacy work before Congress, the executive branch and other governmental bodies.[17]

Since 2010, the ABA House of Delegates, the policy-making body of the ABA, has adopted more than a dozen Resolutions in the area of animal law that provide the legal framework for animal laws both in the United States and worldwide. In 2023, the ABA adopted two important Resolutions. ABA Resolution 508 urges Parties to the United Nations Convention against Transnational Organized Crime to enact laws to combat wildlife crime and to improve global enforcement efforts to prevent wildlife crime.[18] ABA Resolution 509 urges Congress and the USDA provide natural disaster preparedness training and guidance to farmers to protect human health, food safety, animal welfare and the environment.[19] Thousands of animals drown in floodwaters during hurricanes, making Resolution 509 critically important. Resolutions in the past have advocated for laws to prohibit the sale and trade of shark fins,[20] to provide for

[15] *See*, ABA International Law Section, Committees and ABA Communities, International Animal Law, at https://www.americanbar.org/groups/international_law/committees/committee-descriptions-and-leadership/

[16] *See*, ABA TIPS Animal Law Committee at https://www.americanbar.org/groups/tort_trial_insurance_practice/committees/animal-law/

[17] *See*, ABA Governmental & Legislative Work, Policy Implementation at https://www.americanbar.org/advocacy/governmental_legislative_work/priorities_policy/

[18] ABA Resolution 508, adopted by the House of Delegates, February 6, 2023.

[19] ABA Resolution 509, adopted by the House of Delegates, February 6, 2023.

[20] ABA, International Law Section, Criminal Justice Section, Section of Environment, Energy, and Resources, TIPS, Washington State Bar Association, Report to the House of Delegates, Resolution 102A.

the health and well-being of military working dogs,[21] to advocate for breed-neutral pet policies and laws,[22] to promote trap-neuter-vaccinate-return programs for community cats,[23] and to outlaw the sale, breeding, and transfer of dangerous wild animals.[24] In 2021, ABA Resolution 101C was adopted, urging all nations to negotiate an international convention for the protection of animals that establishes standards of care and treatment for all animals.[25]

In 2022, the International Association of Lawyers, an international association of lawyers from 110 countries, approved the formation of an Animal Law Commission Working Group, which will afford collaboration and information sharing among attorneys worldwide. Experts in animal law worldwide, in collaboration with Global Animal Law GAL Association, also released an initiative, the UN Convention on Animal Health and Protection,[26] to establish a framework for the protection of animals at the United Nations level.

The working groups and committees at the national and international level will help ensure that laws are carefully researched and drafted for maximum impact. Proposed legislation must be vetted for constitutional and other legal concerns. This is crucial because animal welfare measures will inevitably be challenged. California's Proposition 12 (Farm Animal Confinement) and its ban on foie gras production and sale have both been the subject of relentless legal challenges.[27] Some believe that enacting "feel good" laws (such as the Animal Welfare Act) that accomplish little for animals may also undermine efforts to achieve genuine and meaningful legal reform for animals. And, brilliant minds will disagree on which laws will better protect animals. Some argue that animal welfare measures on

[21] ABA, International Law Section, Government and Public Sector Lawyers Division, TIPS, Report to the House of Delegates, Resolution 104B.

[22] ABA, TIPS, Report to the House of Delegates, Resolution 112; ABA Resolution 100, adopted by the House of Delegates, August 6–7, 2012.

[23] ABA, TIPS, Report to the House of Delegates, Resolution 102B.

[24] ABA, Resolution 105, adopted by the House of Delegates, February 9, 2015.

[25] ABA, International Law Section, TIPS, Report to the House of Delegates, Resolution 101C.

[26] "UN Convention on Animal Health and Protection (UNCAHP), First Pre-Draft of The Global Animal Law GAL Association, August 23, 2018. For additional information, *see* https://www.uncahp.org/

[27] For a history of the legal challenges against California's ban on foie gras, see "Foie Gras", *Animal Legal Defense Fund*, n.d., at https://aldf.org/issue/foie-gras/

factory farms, such as requiring more living space, undermine real legal reform for animals, because these laws allow consumers to justify their continued use of animal products. Others argue that animal welfare measures raise public awareness of the suffering of farm animals and form the foundation for more meaningful legal change.[28]

The field of animal law is a rapidly growing area that intersects with other areas of law, including environmental law (e.g., climate change; factory farm pollution); international law (e.g., wildlife trafficking); human rights law (e.g., toxic and unsafe conditions for workers); family law (e.g., custody issues; domestic violence protective orders); constitutional law (e.g., Ag-Gag laws; California's Proposition 12; ritual slaughter); criminal law (e.g., Ag-Gag laws; the right to rescue animals); consumer protection laws (e.g., humane-washing); public health law (e.g., zoonotic diseases); and entertainment law (e.g., animals in movies; captive animals). Existing legal frameworks can provide helpful foundations for new laws that protect animals (e.g., rescues from hot cars). Courts have acknowledged that the "[t]he reach of our laws has been extended to animals in areas which were once reserved only for people".[29] A growing number of domestic violence orders protect animals,[30] and legally recognized trusts can be set up to provide for the care for companion animals upon death or incapacitation of their keeper.[31] Some family courts consider the "best interest of the animal" in adjudicating matters. In 2019, California became the third state to enact legislation that permits family law judges to consider "the best interests of the animal" instead of treating him or her as "inanimate property."[32]

Animal law is in its infancy. Specialists in animal law are embarking on a path that will lead to a more globally integrated set of rules that better align with national, regional, and local laws to provide meaningful and

[28] For analysis of this "animal welfare" versus "animal rights" debate, *see* Gary L. Francione, "Animal Rights and Animal Welfare", *Rutgers Law Review* 48, no. 2 (Winter 1996): 397–470.

[29] *See,* e.g., Feger v. Warwick Animal Shelter (59 AD3d 68 [2d Dept2008]), at 72.

[30] *See,* e.g., N.Y. Fam. Ct. Act §8429(i); *see, also,* Placey v. Placey, 51 So. 2d 374 (Ala. Civ. App. 2010).

[31] *See,* e.g., New York Estates, Powers and Trusts Law, §7-8.1 (Trusts for pets).

[32] *See generally,* Babcock, Pamela, "Are pets assets or part of the family? States are passing laws that give judges a longer lease in divorce custody proceedings", *ABA Journal,* June 1, 2019.

effective rights and protections to animals. Animal law develops when we consider how fundamental legal principles and doctrines can be extended to animals. The right to 'equal protection' under the law, for instance, is a gilded bedrock of the United States legal system. Thomas Jefferson, the third President of the United States, considered equal protection under the law to be a "sacred principle" that, if violated, would amount to oppression.[33] Lewis F. Powell, Jr., associate justice of the Supreme Court from 1972–1987, thought that equal protection cannot mean one thing when applied to one person and another thing when applied to another person because "[i]f both are not accorded the same protection, then it is not equal."[34] We deny this sacred principal, however, to animals. Equal protection of the law means little for a dog suffering in a research laboratory, while his companion dog counterparts are afforded special consideration in family law courts. Equal protection of the law lacks meaning if researchers are allowed to harm and kill animals, while others are prohibited from doing so under state anti-cruelty laws. The U.S. legal system permits disparate treatment of equally sentient animals. Wild animals, including elephants, lions and giraffes, are treated differently depending on whether they are in zoos, trophy hunts or in the wild. Monkeys receive different legal protection depending on whether they are in a zoo, an entertainment venue, or a research laboratory. The public would be very unhappy to see dogs "allocated" into categories of companion animals and research subjects. Without equal protection of the law, this happens.

In industrialized animal agriculture, farmers are protected from animal cruelty charges under state statutes if the acts or omissions are deemed "common," "customary," or "generally accepted" farming practices.[35] This is true, even if the act is unconscionably cruel, such as branding, tail docking, dehorning, and debeaking.[36] The cruelties inflicted on farm animals, if done to companion animals, would violate state anti-cruelty laws. This unequal treatment of animals is a fundamental weakness in our legal

[33] Thomas Jefferson First Inaugural Address, Marcy 4, 1801.

[34] Regents of the University of California, Petitioner, v. Allan Bakke, 438 U.S. 265, June 28, 1978.

[35] Statutory language differs from state to state.

[36] For more on these practices, *see* "Inhumane Practices on Factory Farms", *Animal Welfare Institution*, n.d., at https://awionline.org/content/inhumane-practices-factory-farms

system. The U.S. Fish and Wildlife Service seemed to recognize this when it issued its Final Rule in 2015 to treat all chimpanzees as "endangered," instead of treating captive chimps as "threatened."[37] Addressing legal principals, such as 'equal protection under the law,' is necessary but it is not sufficient. Rectifying the inequities in legal systems will require that each animal be recognized as an individual with standing, rights, and protections.

[37] "Final Rule to List All Chimpanzees as Captive and Wild as Endangered, Questions and Answers", published on June 16, 2015. Prior to the Final Rule, captive chimps were listed as "threatened", but wild chimps were treated as "endangered".

CHAPTER 7

The Road to Personhood

Rights of Nature

Like animals, nature has historically been treated as "property" that is "owned", but as ecosystems are collapsing and species are being pushed to the brink of extinction, a global movement to recognize the *Rights of Nature* is challenging jurists, legislators, and scholars to re-think how legal systems should protect the environment. As early as 1972, legal scholars have urged that natural objects, such as rivers, forests, and trees, be afforded legal rights.[1] In a 1972 Supreme Court case, Justice William Douglas, in his dissenting opinion, urged the Court to recognize legal personhood for "valleys, alpine meadows, rivers, lakes, estuaries, beaches, ridges, groves of trees, swampland, or even air that feels the destructive pressures of modern technology and modern life." The river, Justice Douglas said, "is the living symbol of all the life it sustains or nourishes—fish, aquatic insects, water ouzels, otter, fisher, deer, elk, bear, and all other animals, including man, who are dependent on it or who enjoy it for its sight, its sound, or its life."[2]

[1] Stone, Christopher, "Should Trees Have Standing? – Toward Legal Rights for Natural Objects", 45 S. Cal. L. Review 450 (1972).

[2] Sierra Club v. Morton, 405 U.S. 727, 742-43 (1972).

K. C. Moore, *The Case for the Legal Protection of Animals*, The Palgrave Macmillan Animal Ethics Series,
https://doi.org/10.1007/978-3-031-46065-4_7

Some countries, including Kenya and Bolivia, recognize the right to a clean and healthy environment as a constitutionally protected human right.[3] Rights of Nature laws go further by removing the anthropocentric lens and replacing it with an eco-centric paradigm that recognizes the rights of nature *itself*, regardless of human interests. The development of Rights of Nature laws, which represents a profound shift in legal theory, has been fueled by the recognition that environmental laws have failed to prevent many planetary catastrophes. The transformative approach of viewing natural bodies, such as rivers and mountains, as living entities with certain rights, instead of resources to be exploited, represents a radical shift in legal theory.

Rights of Nature legal theory is in its infancy, but its influence is already being felt around the globe.[4] Te Urewera, a forest reserve in New Zealand, is now recognized as "a legal entity" having "all the rights, powers, duties, and liabilities of a legal person."[5] A growing number of rivers are now recognized as legal persons, including rivers in United States,[6] New

[3] *See*, e.g., The Constitution of Kenya, 2010, Art. 42, which provides that "[e]very person has the right to a clean and healthy environment" including the right "to have the environment protected for the benefit of present and future generations." Bolivia's Constitution affords each citizen "the right to a healthy, protected, and balanced environment." Bolivia Constitution, Title III, Art. 33.

[4] David A. Boyd, *The Rights of Nature: A Legal Revolution That Could Save the World*. ECW Press, 2017. ISBN-13: 978-1770412392.

[5] New Zealand Legislation, Te Urewera Act 2014, Section 3; *see also*, Tuhoe-Crown settlement – Te Urewera Act 2014, *Maori Law Review*, October 2014.

[6] In 2018 the Ponca Nation of Oklahoma adopted a Rights of Law to recognize the rights of two rivers that flow through their territory. *See*, Horinek, Casey C. and Biggs, Shannon, "Media Advisory: Ponce Tribe Recognizes the Rights of Rivers", *Movement Rights*, July 18, 2022.

Zealand,[7] Australia,[8] Columbia,[9] India,[10] and Bangladesh.[11] Efforts are underway for other rivers to be afforded legal person status, including the River Ouse in England,[12] the St. Lawrence River in Quebec, Canada,[13] and the Great Lakes in the United States.[14] Mt. Taranski, a mountain in New Zealand, has also received legal person status.[15] Worldwide, a blistering array of recommendations, proposals, and initiatives are underway at international, national, and local levels for new Rights of Nature laws to protect the planet.

[7] The Whanganui River in New Zealand is recognized as having legal personhood status in recognition of its intrinsic value. *See generally*, Perry, Nike, "New Zealand river's personhood status offers hope to Maori", *Associated Press*, August 15, 2022; *see also*, Evans, Kate, "The New Zealand river that became a legal person", *BBC*, March 20, 2020.

[8] The Birrarung (Yarra River) and its lands are recognized as a living entity but without the legal rights of a legal person. *See*, O'Donnell, Erin, "Renewing our relationship with rivers", *American Bar Association, The Young Lawyer*, 26(4), at 6–7.

[9] The Atrato River in Columbia was held by the Constitutional Court to possess rights to "protection, conservation, maintenance and … restoration". *See*, Press Release, "Colombia Constitutional Court finds Atrato River Possesses Rights", *Community Environmental Legal Defense Fund*, dated May 4, 2017. The government of Columbia and indigenous people will share the river by joint guardianship.

[10] The Ganga and Yamuna Rivers in India were also once recognized by the Uttarakhand High Court as legal persons but the Uttarakhand decisions were subsequently overturned by the Indian Supreme Court, which ruled that the rivers cannot have the same legal status as people. *See*, Safi, Michael "Ganges and Yamuna rivers granted same legal rights as human beings", *Guardian*, March 21, 2017; *see also*, "India's Ganges and Yamuna rivers are not living entities", *BBC*, July 7, 2017.

[11] The 2019 decision, which declared the Turag River and all other rivers in Bangladesh to be "living entities" with the rights of "legal persons" was upheld in 2020 by the Appellate Division of the Supreme Court. *See generally*, Margil, Mari, "Bangladesh Supreme Court Upholds Rights of Rivers", *Medium*, August 24, 2020.

[12] River Ouse is on track to be recognized as the first river in England with legal rights. *See*, Barlow, Patrick, "River Ouse could get legal protection after Lewes council motion", *The Argus*, March 3, 2023.

[13] House of Commons of Canada, 1st Session, 44th Parliament, 70–71 Elizabeth II, 2021–2022, Bill C-271, "[a]n Act to give legal capacity to the St. Lawrence River."

[14] The Great Lakes Bill of Rights, A3604. *See generally*, "NYS Assemblyman Patrick Burke Introduces Great Lakes Bill of Rights", *Patrick Burke, Assembly District 142*, March 2, 2022, at https://nyassembly.gov/mem/Pat-Burke/story/100976

[15] Mountain Taranski, a dormant volcano mountain, was the third natural body to be recognized as a person in New Zealand. The government and eight local Maori tribes share guardianship of the feature. *See*, Andrew, Candice G., "New Zealand Grants Mountains, Parks and Rivers Personhood", *Asia & The Pacific, Nature & Wildlife*, September 24, 2019.

One of the first Rights of Nature laws was enacted in the United States. In 2006, the Tamaqua Borough in Pennsylvania became the first community to provide that "Borough residents, natural communities, and ecosystems shall be considered to be 'persons' for purposes of the enforcement of civil rights of those residents, natural communities, and ecosystems."[16] Dozens of jurisdictions and communities in the United States have followed this example, with the City of Pittsburgh, Pennsylvania becoming the first major municipality to recognize the Rights of Nature, by providing that "[n]atural communities and ecosystems, including, but not limited to, wetlands, streams, rivers, aquifers, and other water systems, possess inalienable and fundamental rights to exist and flourish within the City of Pittsburgh."[17] Lake Erie is also recognized as a natural resource that has legal status "to exist, flourish and naturally evolve."[18] Rights of Nature cases are already being litigated. For instance, in Minnesota, the White Earth Band of Ojibwe tribe is suing the state for allowing an oil pipeline company to divert billions of gallons of water away from the tribe's sacred subsistence crop, wild rice.[19] The Sauk-Suiattle Indian Tribe, an Indigenous nation, has also filed a lawsuit on behalf of Tsuladx (salmon), arguing that

[16] The Borough banned toxic waste from being dumped because it would be a violation of the Rights of Nature. *See*, Tamaqua Borough, Schuylkill County, PA, Ordnance No. 612 of 2006 (An Ordnance To Protect the Health, Safety, and General Welfare of the Citizens and Environment of Tamaqua Borough by Banning Corporations from Engaging in the Land Application of Sewage Sludge; By Banning Persons from Using Corporations to Engage in Land Application of Sewage Sludge; By Providing for the Testing of Sewage Sludge Prior to Land Application in the Borough; By Removing Constitutional Powers from Corporations Within the Borough; By Recognizing and Enforcing the Rights of Residents to Defend Natural Communities and Ecosystems; and by Otherwise Adopting the Pennsylvania Regulations Concerning the Land Application of Sewage Sludge), §7.6.

[17] The ordnance also grants standing to residents of the City to enforce rights of the natural communities and ecosystems. *See*, City of Pittsburgh Ordnance supplementing the Pittsburgh Code, Title Six, Conduct, Art. 1 Regulated Rights and actions, by adding Chapter 618 entitled Marcellus Shale Natural Gas Drilling, §618.03(b).

[18] Lake Erie Bill of Rights: Establishing a Bill of Rights for Lake Erie, Which Prohibits Activities and Projects that Would Violate the Bill of Rights, at https://www.utoledo.edu/law/academics/ligl/pdf/2019/Lake-Erie-Bill-of-Rights-GLWC-2019.pdf; *see generally*, "Breaking News: Toledo Voters Enact Lake Erie Bill of Rights: Historic Vote in the U.S. Recognizes Rights of an Ecosystem", *CELDF*, February 26, 2019.

[19] Malo, Sebastien, "Minnesota hit with novel 'natural right' tribal lawsuit over Line 3", *Reuters,* August 7, 2021.

the City's construction of dams impedes Tsuladx from migrating in violation of their "inherent rights to exist, flourish, regenerate, and evolve."[20]

In 2009, Ecuador became the first country in the world to recognize the Rights of Nature in its Constitution. Article 71 reads, "Nature, or Pacha Mama, where life is reproduced and occurs, has the right to integral respect for its existence and for the maintenance and regeneration of its life cycles, structure, functions and evolutionary processes."[21] When granted rights, nature becomes something *other than* "property"—it becomes a legal entity with standing and protections. The importance of Article 71 became clear in 2021 when Ecuador's Constitutional Court found that mining activities involving the State in a protected area of forest violated the protected area's "right to exist and flourish."[22]

Rights of Nature legal theory is recognized by international organizations, including the United Nations, which views the laws as "grounded in the recognition that humankind and Nature share a fundamental, non-anthropocentric relationship given our shared existence on this planet."[23] The Intergovernmental Platform on Biodiversity and Ecosystem Services recognizes Rights of Nature as "a legal instrument that enables nature, wholly or partly, i.e. ecosystems *or species*, to have inherent rights" and that "ecosystems *and species* have legal rights to exist, thrive and regenerate" (emphasis added).[24] Rights of Nature is a growing body of law that has been recognized by high courts around the world.

In Columbia, the Amazon was recognized by the Supreme Court as a "subject of rights," with rights to protection, conservation, maintenance, and restoration.[25] In India, the High Court of Madras recognized "the Constitutional legal rights of the 'Mother Earth'" as a "legal being" that

[20] Sauk-Suiattle Indian Tribe v. City of Seattle, Civil Complaint for Declaratory Judgment, Case No. SAU-CIV-01/22-001.

[21] Ecuador Constitution, Art. 71.

[22] Surma, Katie, "Ecuador's High Court Affirms Constitutional Protections for the Rights of Nature in a Landmark Decision", *Inside Climate News*, December 3, 2021.

[23] "Rights of Nature Law and Policy", *United Nations Harmony with Nature*, n.d., at http://www.harmonywithnatureun.org/rightsOfNaturePolicies/

[24] Policy Instrument, "Rights of Nature", *IPBES*, n.d., at https://www.ipbes.net/policy-support/tools-instruments/rights-nature-ron#

[25] Colombian Supreme Court Recognizes Rights of the Amazon River Ecosystem", *International Union for Conservation of Nature*, April 20, 2018, at https://www.iucn.org/news/world-commission-environmental-law/201804/colombian-supreme-court-recognizes-rights-amazon-river-ecosystem

is “equivalent to the rights of human beings.”[26] In recent years, Panama has enacted a Rights of Nature law, which affords nature the “right to exist, persist and regenerate its life cycles”, the “right to conserve its biodiversity,” and the “right to be restored after it has been directly or indirectly affected by any human activity.”[27] Notably, Panama’s law extends “to all living beings, elements and ecosystems” that comprise nature, and expressly provides that nature’s “living beings must be protected by law, independently from their utilitarian value to human beings.”[28] Spain granted legal personhood the Mar Menor lagoon and its basin, the first natural body to be granted legal rights in Europe.[29] Uganda became the first country in Africa to legislatively recognize the Rights of Nature, including “the right to exist, persist, maintain and regenerate its vital cycles, structure, functions and its processes in evolution.”[30] Mexico City revised its Constitution to require secondary laws with “the broadest protection of the rights of nature made up of all its ecosystems *and species* as a collective entity subject to rights” (emphasis added).[31] Rights of Nature laws are under development in the European Union.[32] UN

[26] Periyakaruppan v. The Principal Secretary to Government, Revenue Dept., the Additional Chief Secretary and Comm of Revenue Admin, Madurai Bench of Madras High Court (April 19, 2022). W.P. (MD) Nos. 18636 of 2013 and 3070 of 2020, and W.M.P. (MD) No. 2614 of 2020. §§21-23.

[27] Panama Law No. 287, Ch. II (Rights of Nature), Art. 10, 12 and 14; *see generally*, Surma, Katie, “Panama Enacts a Rights of Nature Law, Guaranteeing the Natural World’s ‘Right to Exist, Persist and Regenerate’”, *Inside Climate News,* February 25, 2022.

[28] Panama Law No. 287, Ch. II (Rights of Nature), Art. 10 and 12.

[29] Law 19/2022, of September 30, for the recognition of legal personality of the Mar Menor lagoon and its basin, published in “BOE” no. 237, of October 3, 2022, at 135131–135135; *see generally*, Mateo, Blanca Soro, “The Mar Menor Lagoon Enjoys Legal Standing: and how, what?”, *Verfassungs Blog on Matters Constitutional*, October 14, 2022. https://doi.org/10.17176/20221014-230645-0

[30] The National Environment Act, 2019 of Uganda, §4 (Rights of nature), providing that “[n]ature has the right to exist, persist, maintain and regenerate its vital cycles, structures, functions and its processes in evolution.”

[31] Mexico City Constitution, Art. 13(A)(3).

[32] Carducci, Michele, et al., “Towards an EU Charter of Fundamental Rights of Nature”, *Study for The European Economic and Social Committee*, December 13, 2019. ISBN: 978-92-830-4971-5. https://doi.org/10.2864/25113; *see also,* Darpo, Jan, “Can Nature Get it Right? A Study on Rights of Nature in the European Context” (March 2021), a study commissioned by the European Parliament’s Policy Department for Citizens’ Rights and Constitutional Affairs to analyze Rights of Nature from a legal and scientific viewpoint.

Secretary-General, Antonio Guterres, declared 2021 to be "the year to reconcile humanity with nature."[33]

Rights of Nature reforms are often accompanied with provisions that permit any person or organization to enforce the rights on behalf of nature.[34] This makes sense because nature cannot enforce its own rights, and, neither can animals. Rights of Nature laws recognize the crucial role that ecosystems play on the planet, but then again, so does the animal kingdom. Since animals are an inextricable, critical part of nature, it follows that wildlife should at minimum be afforded the same rights as nature. The Constitutional Court in Ecuador agreed.

In 2022, Ecuador's Constitutional Court reviewed a case that originated from a habeas corpus action in favor of a tiny chorongo monkey named Estrellita, who had lived in a human home since infancy for 18 years with a woman perceived by Estrellita to be her mother. Following an anonymous citizen complaint, the Ministry of Environment seized Estrellita, placing her in temporary custody at a wildlife conservation center. Sadly, Estrellita died 23 days later.[35] In recognizing that nature is comprised of "an interrelated, interdependent and indivisible setoff biotic and abiotic elements (ecosystems)" the Court determined that Estrellita was legally protected under the Rights of Nature provision in the Constitution.[36] The Court acknowledged that although nature is the subject of rights, "it shares such quality with all its members, elements and factors."[37] It further recognized that animals are "living beings with an intrinsic value that makes them holders of rights."[38] The Court cited court decisions from other countries, including a Colombia Constitutional Court case, which held that "animals are protected not only in terms of their ecosystematic

[33] "Antonio Guterres: 2021 Is the Year to Reconcile Humanity with Nature", *United Nations Climate Change*, January 11, 2021, at https://unfccc.int/news/antonio-guterres-2021-is-the-year-to-reconcile-humanity-with-nature

[34] Article 71 of Ecuador's Constitution provides that "every person, community, people or nationality may demand of the public authority the satisfaction of the rights of nature."

[35] While Estrellita's caregiver blamed the government for her death, the Court noted the necropsy report in its ruling, which cited nutritional deficiencies, stress, confinement, and unfavorable environmental conditions and mistreatment over the years that contributed to diseased lungs and malfunctioning kidneys that triggered a cardiorespiratory arrest that caused her death.

[36] Constitutional Court of Ecuador, Final Judgment: Rights of Nature and Animals as Subject of Rights, "Estrellita Monkey" Case No. 253-20-JH/22. January 27, 2022.

[37] "Estrellita Monkey" Case at §66.

[38] "Estrellita Monkey" Case at §77.

contribution, but also as sentient beings, individually concerned."[39] The Court also cited an Islamabad High Court case, holding that "it is also a natural right of every animal to be respected because it is a living being, possessing the precious gift of 'life'. Humans cannot arrogate to themselves a right or prerogative of enslaving or subjugating an animal because the latter has been born free for some specific purposes."[40] Consistent with Rights of Nature doctrine, the Court stated that "the rights of a wild animal [like Estrellita] must be protected objectively, taking its life, freedom and integrity as their own inherent rights, and not based on the claims, desires or intentions of third parties."[41]

In 2010, Bolivia enacted the Universal Declaration of the Rights of Mother Earth (Ley de Derechos da la Madre Tierra), which defines Mother Earth as "the dynamic living system formed by the indivisible community of all life systems and *living beings* whom are interrelated, interdependent, and complementary, which share a common destiny" (emphasis added).[42] This important law recognizes rights to life, diversity of life, water, clean air and contamination-free living, as well as rights to restoration if any life systems are impacted by direct or indirect human activities.[43]

Some scholars argue that even if a Rights of Nature law does not expressly include animals, there is an implicit acknowledgment that animals possess rights.[44] "Nature" is commonly understood to include "the physical world and everything in it (such as plants, animals, mountains, oceans, stars, etc.) that is not made by people."[45] Recognizing Rights of Nature as a means of protecting the environment is an exercise in futility unless the rights of its component parts are also recognized. Analyzing Rights of Nature without taking into account the life that lives therein is like considering the health of a forest without looking at its trees, or evaluating the health of a human body without considering its heart and lungs.

[39] "Estrellita Monkey" Case at §79, citing Constitutional Court of Colombia. Final judgment SU016/20.

[40] "Estrellita Monkey" Case, Footnote 125, citing Islamabad High Court from 2020, Resolution on. 1155/2019, page 60.

[41] "Estrellita Monkey" Case at §173.

[42] Bolivia Ley de Derechos da la Madre Tierra [Law of the Rights of Mother Earth], Art. 3.

[43] Bolivia Ley de Derechos da la Madre Tierra [Law of the Rights of Mother Earth], Art. 9.

[44] Stilt, Kristen, "Rights of Nature, Rights of Animals", 134 Harv. L. Rev. F. 276, March 20, 2021.

[45] Merriam-Webster, Definition of "Nature".

All life on earth is interconnected and interdependent, and animals play vital, indeed essential, roles in the web of life,[46] including, for instance, their role in pollination. Virtually all flowering plants in tropical rainforests are pollinated by animals, and 75% of global food crops are completely or partially pollinated by insects and other animals.[47] The loss of species can have cascading and detrimental effects on ecosystems, as seen when grey wolves were hunted to near extinction in Yellowstone National Park.[48] Rights of Nature laws must always include under their umbrella of protection the rights of individual animals, and not just species, because the average population abundance of species has plummeted.[49] Rights of Nature laws that fail to protect animals who reside within the protected natural feature presents an incomplete and flawed approach to environmental protection. Moreover, the intrinsic value of sentient beings must be taken into account *beyond* just their role in nature. Laws must consider sentience.

Animal Sentience

In recent decades, the science of animal cognition and intelligence has grown exponentially and has dramatically changed how many perceive animals. While much remains to be studied, research in the area of animal intelligence demonstrates that animals are highly intelligent beings, with consciousness and complex cognitive abilities.[50] This is true even though scientists tend to use metrics applicable to humans when studying the intelligence of other species. In that regard, animal intelligence is likely far

[46] For more on the importance of "keystone species", *see* McKeever, Any, "Why some animals are more important to ecosystems than others", *National Geographic*, May 19, 2020.

[47] Cho, Renee, "Why Endangered Species Matter", *Columbia Climate School: Climate, Earth, and Society (State of the Planet)*, March 26, 2019.

[48] For a history of grey wolves and their impact on Yellowstone's ecosystem, *see*, Glavas, Marissa, et al., "Restoration of Ecosystem Interactions in Yellowstone National Park, USA, With Re-Introduction of Grey Wolves", *The University of British Columbia: Open Case Studies*, at https://cases.open.ubc.ca/w17t2cons200-18/

[49] Living Planet Report 2022, *WWF*, at 4.

[50] *See* e.g., What a Fish Knows; *see also*, Grandin, Temple and Johnson, Catherine. *Animals in Translation: Using the Mysteries of Autism to Decode Animal Behavior*. Harcourt, 1st Ed. (January 2, 2006). ISBN-13: 978-0156031442. *See also*, Waal, Frans de., *Are we Smart Enough to Know How Smart Animals Are?*, W. W. Norton & Company; Illustrated Ed. (April 4, 2017). ISBN-13: 978-0393353662. *See also*, Gould James L. and Gould, Carol G., *Animal Architects: Building and the Evolution of Intelligence*. Basic Books; Reprint Ed. (March 6, 2012). ISBN-13: 978-0465028382.

greater than we think given our tendency to view intelligence through an anthropocentric lens that compares the abilities of animals against that of humans (e.g., teaching sign language to chimps; training pigs to use video games). Hanabiko "Koko" (1971–2018), a female western lowland gorilla born at the San Francisco Zoo, mastered the ability to communicate with humans using sign language and understood approximately 2000 English words.[51] The communication between dolphins is so complicated though that scientists struggle to understand it.[52] Comparing animal intelligence directly to human intelligence, such as studies on orangutans which show that they use tools, educate one another, plan ahead, and engage in deception,[53] overlooks the vast abilities and behaviors found in the animal kingdom. No studies measure the intelligence of humans by testing them against the capabilities of dolphins,[54] the memories of elephants[55] or the self-control of crows.[56] We flippantly use "bird brain" as a criticism, but the intelligence of crows rivals that of children under the age of seven.[57] We have convinced ourselves, through our narrow world view, that we are far more intelligent than other species, yet we are unable to provide adequate food, water, and housing for millions, we have caused untold suffering and death through endless wars, and our leaders threaten to use weapons that can destroy the world. Humanity could benefit from a strong dose of humility.

[51] *See generally*, Main, Douglas, "Whu Koko the Gorilla Mattered", *National Geographic*, June 21, 2018.

[52] *See generally*, "Dolphin Communication", Dolphin Research Center, at https://dolphins.org/communication

[53] Recio, Belinda. *Inside Animal Hearts and Minds, Bears that Count, Goats that Surf, And Other True Stories of Animal Intelligence and Emotion*. Skyhorse Publishing (2017) at p. 62. ISBN-13: 978-1510718944.

[54] *See generally*, Casey, Susan, *Voices in the Ocean: A Journey into the Wild ad Haunting World of Dolphins*, Knopf Doubleday Publishing Group (2016). ISBN-13: 978-0345804846.

[55] *See generally*, Krisch, Joshua A., "Do elephants really 'never forget'?", *Live Science*, January 29, 2023.

[56] Hillemann, Friederick, et al., "Waiting for better, not for more: corvids respond to quality in two delay maintenance tasks", *Animal Behavior*, 90, 1–10 (2014). https://doi.org/10.1016/j.anbehav.2014.01.007

[57] Logan, Corina J., et al., "Modifications to the Aesop's Fable Paradigm Change New Caledonian Crow Performances", *PLoS ONE*, 9(7) (2014). https://doi.org/10.1371/journal.pone.0103049

There is also near universal agreement in the scientific community that humans are not alone in our capacity to experience the world feelingly. A systematic review of scientific literature on animal sentience, including more than 2500 peer-reviewed papers, found overwhelming evidence of animal sentience.[58] In 2012, a prestigious group of international scientists, including cognitive neuroscientists, neuroanatomists, neurophysiologists and neuropharmacologists proclaimed, in *The Cambridge Declaration on Consciousness*, that scientifically, nonhuman animals are "conscious" beings, declaring that, "the weight of evidence indicates that humans are not unique in possessing the neurological substrates that generate consciousness. Nonhuman animals, including all mammals and birds, and many other creatures, including octopuses, also possess these neurological substrates."[59] The Declaration confirmed that animals experience the world not unlike ourselves.[60]

There is no universal definition for animal sentience. The scientific community views sentience as the capacity of animals to have feelings,[61] while the Sentience Institute defines animal sentience as "the capacity to have positive and negative experiences, usually thought of as happiness and suffering."[62] Others define it to mean thoughts, feelings, and individual personalities.[63] Tanzania has one of the better definitions for "sentient" in its Animal Welfare Act, defining it as the "capacity of an animal to be aware of sensations, emotions, feeling pain, suffering and enjoying

[58] Proctor, Helen S., et al., "Searching for Animal Sentience: A Systematic Review of the Scientific Literature", Animals, 3(3), 882–906 (2013). https://doi.org/10.3390/ani3030882

[59] *The Cambridge Declaration on Consciousness* was written by Philip Low and edited by Jaak Panksepp, Diana Reiss, David Edelman, Bruno Van Swinderen, Philip Low, and Christof Koch. The Declaration was publicly proclaimed in Cambridge, UK, on July 7, 2012, at the Francis Crick Memorial Conference on Consciousness in Human and non-Human Animals, at Churchill College, University of Cambridge, by Low, Edelman and Koch.

[60] "Fear is a universal emotion in the animal kingdom." *See*, Grandin, Temple, "Assessment of Stress During Handling and Transport", *Journal of Animal Science*, Vol. 75, 249–257 (1997). It's reasonable to think that animals experience other emotions as well.

[61] Broom, Donald M., *'Considering Animals' Feelings: Precis of Sentience and animal welfare (Broom 2014)" Animal Sentience*, 5(1) (2016). https://doi.org/10.51291/2377-7478.1015

[62] Anthis, Jacy R., "What is sentience", *Sentience Institute*, June 21, 2018.

[63] *See*, "Animal Sentience", *World Animal Protection*, n.d., at https://www.worldanimalprotection.org/our-work/animal-sentience

their species specific needs."[64] In general terms, sentience is thought to mean the capacity to experience feelings and emotions, such as fear, joy, frustration, pleasure, pain, suffering, anxiety, stress, depression, grief and empathy, even though it remains "poorly defined and understood by the scientific community, let alone by law people."[65] Some judges are helping. In one Argentinian case, a judge proclaimed that,

> [a]nimals are sentient beings insomuch as they understand basic emotions. Experts agree unanimously about the genetic proximity of chimpanzees with human beings and they add that chimpanzees have the capacity to reason, they are intelligent, are conscientious of themselves, they have cultural diversity, expressions of mental games, they manifest grief, use and construction of tools to access food or to solve simple problems of daily life, abstraction capacity, skills to handle symbols in communication, conscience to express emotions such as happiness, frustration, desires or deceit, planned organization for intraspecific battles and ambush for hunting, they have metacognitive abilities, they have a moral, psychic, and physical status, they have their own culture, they have affectionate feelings (they caress and groom each other), they are capable of lying, they have symbols for human language and use tools.[66]

The New York Supreme Court has recognized that "[u]nquestionably, nonhuman animals are sentient beings."[67]

Surveys show that the public understands animal sentience. In one poll, 91.7% of adults in the United States agreed that animals "have roughly the same capacity to experience pain as humans."[68] The ability of animals to experience feelings and emotions brings to the forefront the moral conflict: if it is accepted that animals feel pain and suffer in ways not unlike humans, humanity needs to come to terms with how our own actions contribute to their suffering. The need to avoid accountability is a powerful human instinct, but this becomes much more difficult to sustain as our understanding of the inner lives of animals grows. There is growing

[64] Animal Welfare Act, No. 19 of 2008 (Tanzania), §3 (definition of "sentient").

[65] Cornish, Amelia, et al., "Demographics Regarding Belief in Non-Human Animal Sentience and Emotional Empathy with Animals: A Pilot Study among Attendees of an Animal Welfare Symposium", *Animals*, 8(10), 174 (2018). https://doi.org/10.3390/ani8100174

[66] Tercer Juzgado de Garantias de Mendoza, "Presented by A.F.A.D.A. About The Chimpanzee 'Cecilia' – Non Human Individual", File No. P-72.254/15, November 3, 2016.

[67] In the Matter of Nonhuman Rights Project, Inc. & c., v. James J. Breheny, & c., et al., No. 52, State of New York Court of Appeals, June 14, 2022.

[68] Ladak, Ali and Anthis, Jacy R., "Animals, Food, and Technology (AFT) Survey: 2020 Update", *Sentience Institute*, March 17, 2021.

recognition that humanity and the animal kingdom are equals in the ability to suffer. Both people and animals suffer from hunger when food is scarce. Both suffer physically and psychologically when homeless. Both can be trafficked (i.e., human trafficking and wildlife trafficking). Both feel pain when abused. When it comes to the treatment of animals by industries, however, there is a pandemic of deniability.

In recent decades, an increasing number of laws have been passed in recognition of how animals experience the world. Nations are not just recognizing the emotional lives of animals. They are enshrining animal sentience into their laws and implicitly acknowledging that humans share many universal emotions with the animal kingdom: How will I feed my young? How secure is our home? What dangers threaten us? The recognition of sentience in animals is a titanic change on the legal landscape because it opens the discussion on why we impose such great suffering on animals. The case for affording animals moral consideration under the law has never been greater, as a number of countries have agreed.

International norms regarding how animals should be viewed and treated are rapidly changing. Strategic partners of the United States, including countries in key alliances, are updating antiquated laws to recognize the sentient nature of animals. More than 40 nations (or states or territories therein) have recognized (explicitly or implicitly, and to varying degrees) animal sentience, including: Australia (Australian Capital Territory),[69] Austria,[70] Belgium (Brussels),[71] Bulgaria, [72] Canada

[69] The Australian Capital Territory's (ACT) Animal Welfare Act of 1992 was amended by the Animal Welfare Legislation Amendment Bill passed on September 26, 2019, which recognizes animals as sentient beings. *See*, "Animal Welfare Legislative Amendment: Proposed changes to the Animal Welfare Act 1992", *ACT Government*, n.d., at https://yoursayconversations.act.gov.au/animal-welfare-bill-amendments

[70] Federal Act on the Protection of Animals (Animal Protection Act) of Austria, §§5(1) and 13, recognizing the need to protect the well-being of animals as fellow creatures, to prohibit suffering or exposure to heavy fear, and to ensure their physiologic and ethologic needs are met, including species specific social contacts. Civil Code of Austria, §285a, states that "Animals are not things; they are protected by special laws."

[71] The Brussels Parliament recognizes an animal as "a living being endowed with sensitivity, interests of its own and dignity, that benefits from special protection." *See*, Law Relating to the Protection and Welfare of Animals 2018 (Brussels), Art. 1; *see also*, Vincent, Christopher, "Brussels parliament adopts crucial animal rights bill", *Brussels Times*, November 23, 2018.

[72] Treaty on the Functioning of the European Union, expressly recognizing animals as sentient beings in Art. 13 of Title II, providing that member states "shall, since animals are sentient beings," give due regard to the welfare of animals when formulating public policies, including policies in agriculture and scientific research.

(Quebec),[73] Chile,[74] Columbia,[75] Croatia,[76] Cyprus,[77] Czech Republic,[78] Denmark,[79] Estonia,[80] Finland,[81] France,[82] Germany,[83] Greece,[84]

[73] Code Civil of Quebec, §898.1 provides that "Animals are not things. They are sentient beings and have biological needs."

[74] Ley N 20.380 – Ley Sobre Proteccion de animals (Law 20,380 on the Protection of Animals of 2009), recognizing animals as living beings and sensitive that are part of nature and that can suffer (Art. 2–3).

[75] Columbia Ley No. 1774 de 2016 (Law No. 1774 of 2016), stating that "animals as sentient beings are not things."

[76] Animal Protection Act (Croatia), OG 102/2017 (18.10.2017), recognizing that animals can suffer and experience fear (Art. 5(1)) and stress (Art. 54(3)) and requiring that "Animals bred and used for production purposes may only be kept if their biological needs" are met and their "physiological functions and species-specific behaviors" are not impeded (Art. 39(1)).

[77] Treaty on the Functioning of the European Union, Art. 13; Cyprus Law for the Protection, Health and Welfare of Animals, 46 (1) 1994, requiring animals to "be handled in a way that suits best their physiological and ethological needs" (§4(1)). The law appears to apply to only pets, captive animals and animals under human control or supervision (§3(2)).

[78] Treaty on the Functioning of the European Union, Art. 13; Act of the Czech National Council of 15 April 1992 on the Protection of Animals Against Cruelty (246/1992 Coll.), as amended, recognizing animals as "living beings capable of experiencing pain and suffering."

[79] Animal Welfare Act, Act No. 133 of 25 February 2020, recognizing "animals as living and sentient beings" in §1; *see also*, Denmark Act on the Protection of Animals No. 20 of 11th January 2018, recognizing that animals are "living beings" who must be protected against suffering and distress.

[80] Treaty on the Functioning of the European Union, Art. 13.

[81] Treaty on the Functioning of the European Union, Art. 13; Finland Animal Welfare Act (247/1006, as amended up to 1430/2006), requiring that the "physiological and behavior needs of the animals must be taken into account" and prohibiting "undue distress" on animals (§3(1)).

[82] Civil Code, art. 515–14 (Fr), provides that "Animals are living beings gifted with sentience. Subject to the laws that protect the animals, they are subjected to the regime of goods." *See also*, "France: Animals Granted New Legal Status", *U.S. Library of Congress*, April 25, 2014.

[83] German Constitution, Art. 20-A; see also, Civil Code, Art. 90-A, providing that "Animals are not things. They are protected by special statutes."

[84] Treaty on the Functioning of the European Union, Art. 13.

Hungary,[85] Iceland,[86] Indonesia,[87] Ireland,[88] Italy,[89] Latvia,[90] Lebanon,[91] Lithuania,[92] Luxembourg,[93] Malta,[94] Mexico (state level),[95] New Zealand,[96]

[85] Treaty on the Functioning of the European Union, Art. 13; Hungary Act XXVIII of 1998 law on the protection and welfare of animals; *see*, Zoltan, Toth J., "The Regulation of Animal Protection in Hungary", *Jogelmeleti Szemle / Journal of Legal Theory*, 4, at 166–175, noting that law recognizes "animals as living creatures capable of feelings and suffering" and protects "avoidable physical and mental harm."

[86] Iceland Act on animal welfare, 2013 No 55, 8 April, as amended, recognizing animals as sentient beings and the need "to allow animals to express their natural behaviour to the fullest." (§1).

[87] Husbandry and Animal Health, Art. 1(42) of Law No. 18 of 2009, recognizing that animal welfare includes "all matters relating to animal physical and mental conditions based on the natural behavior of [the] animal."

[88] Treaty on the Functioning of the European Union, Art. 13; Animal Health and Welfare Act 2013, No. 15 of 2013, recognizing that "unnecessary suffering" can be physical or mental (Pt. 1, §2).

[89] Treaty on the Functioning of the European Union, Art. 13.

[90] Ibid.

[91] The new law implicitly recognizes the sentient nature of animals by requiring animals where possible to express "their natural behaviors" and to interact with their own species or compatible species (§3.2). The law also prohibits the infliction "distress, pain or suffering" to animals (§§4.1 and 16). The law does not appear to apply to all animals. *See*, Lebanon Animal Protection and Welfare Law, translated by Animals Lebanon at http://www.animalslebanon.org/pdf/Animal_Protection_and_Welfare_Law.pdf

[92] Treaty on the Functioning of the European Union, Art. 13; Law on Welfare and Protection of Animals (Gyvūnų Gerovės ir Apsaugos Įstatymas) No XI-2271, Valstybės Žinios, 20 October 2012 No 122–6216 (LT) (2012), Art 1(a).

[93] Acknowledging that science now recognizes that animals experience feelings, Luxembourg updated its animal welfare laws in 2018 to provide that "animals are no longer regarded as objects, but as living beings" and to "guarantee their dignity, safety and well-being." *See*, "Animal protection in Luxembourg", *The Luxembourg Government*, at https://gouvernement.lu/en/dossiers/2018/tierschutz.html

[94] Treaty on the Functioning of the European Union, Art. 13.

[95] *See*, e.g., The Constitution of Mexico City (updated 2017), recognizing animals as sentient beings; *see also*, The Animal Protection Act of 2001 of Aguascalientes (reformed in 2019), recognizing that animals can feel and suffer psychologically.

[96] Animal Welfare Act 1999 (NZ), No. 142, reforming the law "to recognize that animals are sentient"; *see also*, "New Zealand: Animal Welfare Legislation Recognizes Animals as Sentient, Bans Cosmetic Testing", *U.S. Library of Congress*, May 19, 2015.

Netherlands,[97] Norway,[98] Philippines,[99] Poland,[100] Portugal,[101] Romania,[102] Slovakia,[103] Slovenia,[104] Spain,[105] Sweden,[106] Switzerland,[107] Tanzania,[108]

[97] The Animals Act of 2021, Art. 1.3, recognizing the intrinsic value of animals as sentient beings.

[98] Norway Animal Welfare Act (Dyrevelferdsloven) (NO), recognizing that "[a]nimals have an intrinsic value which is irrespective of the usable value they may have for men" and must be protected from "unnecessary stress and strains." (§3).

[99] Philippines Animal Welfare Act of 1998, as amended, pertaining to "the physical and psychological well-being of animals" and to assure their "freedom from fear, distress, harassment, and unnecessary discomfort and pain, and allowing animals to express normal behavior." (*see* §1).

[100] Poland Animal Protection Act, OJ No. 111, Item 724(1997); No. 106, Item 688 (1998), recognizing an animal "as a live creature, capable of suffering, [and] is not a thing."

[101] The Portuguese Civil Code was amended by Law n. 8/2017 of March 3, 2017. *See generally*, Mendonca, Helena C., "Recognizing Sentience in the Portuguese Civil Code", *Derecho Animal Forum of Animal Law Studies*, 8(2), 1 (2017), at https://www.researchgate.net/publication/323171810_Recognising_sentience_in_the_Portuguese_Civil_Code

[102] Law 205/2004 on the protection of animals, as amended and supplemented, Art. 12(2) and Art. 14, recognizing that animals can suffer psychologically.

[103] In 2018 Slovakia amended the definition of "animals" in its Civil Code to afford animals special value and status as living creatures with their own senses and ability to perceive the world. *See*, Spectator Staff, "Animals get the status of living creatures in Slovakia", *The Slovak Spectator*, May 20, 2018.

[104] Slovenian Animal Protection Act of 1999, as amended in 2013, in 2018 and in 2020, to, inter alia, set forth "the responsibility of humans to protect animals as sentient beings."

[105] Spain's Civil Code was amended in December 2021 by Law 17/2021 of December 15, 2021 and provides that animals are no longer considered as things but are sentient beings and family members. *See*, "Spain: New Law Providing for Increased Protection for Animals Adopted", *U.S. Library of Congress*. *See generally*, Gimenez-Candela, Marita, "The legal status of animals in the Civil Code: The long-awaited de-objectification of animals", ***dA.*** *Derecho Animal (Forum of Animal Law Studies)*, 12/2 (2021). https://doi.org/10.5565/rev/da.582; *see also*, "Spain: New Law Providing for Increased Protection of Animals Adopted", *Library of Congress*, n.d., at https://www.loc.gov/item/global-legal-monitor/2022-01-17/spain-new-law-providing-for-increased-protection-of-animals-adopted/

[106] Animal Welfare Act (2018:1192), June 20, 2018. (Sweden), recognizing the need to "promote good animal well-being and respect for animals" (Ch. 1, §1) where "they are able to perform behaviours for which they are strongly motivated for and that are important for their well-being" (Ch. 2, §2(2)).

[107] Animal Welfare Act of 16 December 2005 (Switzerland), Art. 1 (purpose is "to protect the dignity and welfare of animals") and 3 (defines "dignity" as the "inherent worth of an animal" and prohibits unnecessary "pain, suffering or harm" or "anxiety or humiliation").

[108] Animal Welfare Act, No. 19 of 2008 (Tanzania), §4(b)(i), recognizing that "an animal is a sentient being". The law does not appear to cover all animals because §4 is "[w]ith a view to giving effect to the fundamental principles of National Livestock Policy and Animal Welfare."

Turkey[109] and the U.K.[110] The law in the Czech Republic, which is representative of the growing legal recognition of animal sentience, states that animals "are living beings and are capable of experiencing various degrees of pain and suffering, and hence they deserve attention, care and protection by man."[111] The United Nations has also recognized the "strong body of science supporting animal welfare."[112]

Affording legal recognition to the sentient nature of animals changes the lens through which animals are viewed and protected. In 2019, Columbia became the second Latin American country (after Costa Rica) to ban recreational hunting when a court ruled that hunting for sport is "incompatible" with the country's constitutional mandate to protect the environment.[113] In explaining the ruling, Magistrate Antonio Jose Lizaraza said that "[t]he purpose behind killing an animal for fun or for obtaining food is different; in the end you see compassion, respect and care ... Animals are not things, they are beings with feelings".[114] In the U.K., the Animal Sentience Committee was set up to oversee governmental policy to ensure adequate animal welfare provisions.[115]

Other countries recognize that animal welfare protections should include both the physical and mental welfare of animals[116] or acknowledge that animals can experience fear and stress and can suffer.[117] Laws recognize that sentience is the bond that connects humanity with the animal kingdom, as reflected by the text of Austria's law, which aims to protect the well-being of animals "based on man's special responsibility for the

[109] Animal Protection Law (Turkey), No. 5199 (2004), Art. 1 (prohibiting "the infliction of pain, suffering and torture") and Art. 14, prohibiting "physical and psychological pain".

[110] Animal Welfare (Sentience) Act of 2022, §§1-2, recognizing animals as sentient beings.

[111] Czech Republic, Act on the Protection of Animals Against Cruelty, Act No. 246/1992 Coll. (May 29, 1992), as amended.

[112] UNEP, EA.5/Res. 1, Nairobi (hybrid), 22 and 23 February 2021 and 28 February – 2 March 2022.

[113] Harindranath, Arjun, "Constitutional Court bans recreational hunting", *The Bogota Post,* February 9, 2019; *see also*, "Colombia to ban sport hunting", *Phys Org.*, February 7, 2019, at https://phys.org/news/2019-02-colombia-sport.html

[114] Id.

[115] Animal Welfare Sentience Act 2022 (GB), §§1–2.

[116] *See*, e.g., Nepal's Animal Welfare Directive, 2073 (2016 A.D.), at §3(k). Animal welfare also includes "[f]reedom from fear and distress" and "freedom to express normal patterns of behavior." (§4(1)).

[117] *See,* e.g., Law on Animal Welfare (Serbia), Official Gazette of the Republic of Serbia, No. 41/2009, Art. 2, recognizing that "animals can sense pain, suffering, fear and stress".

animal as a fellow-creature."[118] Other countries, such as Scotland, are taking steps to consider possible legal reforms to further protect sentient animals.[119] Rapidly changing laws are the result of scientific evidence that leaves little doubt that animals are emotional beings.

When animal welfare reform was introduced in Luxembourg, the Minister of Agriculture explained that, "animal welfare legislation requires profound reform because of what scientific advances had revealed about animals, and because of changes in how animals are viewed by human society."[120] In announcing the legal change, the Luxembourg Government Council stated that animals are feeling, "gifted non-human living beings."[121] The Minister of Agriculture emphasized that attitudes toward animals have changed greatly since the prior law.[122] When the Australian Capital Territory became the first jurisdiction in Australia to recognize animals as sentient beings, City Services Minister, Chris Steel, said that science tells us that "animals are sentient, and they feel emotion and pain", and "[m]odern animal welfare is about considering how an animal is coping both mentally and physically with the conditions in which it lives."[123] The town council in Trigueros del Valle, Spain voted to recognize dogs and cats as "non-human residents," affording them equal rights to co-exist alongside humans and recognizing the equality and dignity of all residents, both human and nonhuman.[124] Petro Perez Espinosa, the town's mayor, explained that, "[d]ogs and cats have been living among us for more than 1,000 years. And the mayor must represent not just the human

[118] Federal Act on the Protection of Animals (Animal Protection Act) of Austria, §1.

[119] In Scotland, the Scottish Animal Welfare Commission was established to advise the Scottish Government on how to recognize animal sentience in its animal welfare laws. *See*, "Scottish Animal Welfare Commission: statement on animal sentience", *Scottish Government, Publication – Advice and guidance,* February 10, 2021. The Commission defines "animal sentience" as "the ability to have physical and emotional experiences, which matter to the animal, and which can be positive or negative."

[120] "Luxembourg 10th European Country to Ban Fur Farming", *Fur Free Alliance*, June 15, 2018.

[121] Ibid.

[122] "The Minister of Agriculture answers your questions: Issue 1", *Le Gouvernement Du Grand-Duche De Luxembourg*, Discover the Law, at https://deiereschutzgesetz.lu/faqs/

[123] ACT Government Media Release, "Bill passed to strengthen animal welfare standards", September 26, 2019, quoting Minister for City Services Chris Steel.

[124] Dawber, Alistair, "Human rights for cats and dogs: Spanish town council votes overwhelmingly in favour of defining pets as 'non-human residents'", *Independent,* July 22, 2015.

residents but must also be here for the others."[125] Recognizing sentience has profound ethical and philosophical implications, but recognition alone is not sufficient. Laws must follow that respect such sentience.

In countries where animal sentience has not been enshrined into law, courts are recognizing the negative impact that certain human actions can have on animals. In Argentina, a Judge ruled that a chimpanzee named Cecilia, who had spent decades in a barren concrete enclosure without companionship at the Mendoza Zoo, was a sentient being with the "fundamental right to be born, live, grow, and die in the environment that is their own according to their species."[126] The judge also requested that lawmakers provide the "necessary legal tools to bring an end to the grave situation of captivity that sees the zoo animals living in unsuitable conditions."[127] In 2015, an Argentinian court declared in a landmark ruling that an orangutan named Sandra, held captive at the Buenos Aires Zoo for two decades, was a sentient being entitled to certain rights, such as life, liberty, and freedom from harm.[128] In 2022, a court in Buenos Aires, Argentina, declared that a cougar was the "subject of rights" who must be "granted its total freedom, free of any legal measure or restriction."[129] In Israel, a Jerusalem Court judge blocked construction of a new neighborhood adjacent to the Biblical Zoo, in 2017, because animals have the "right to a life of minimal suffering", which he considered "more important than real estate gains."[130] In Italy, individuals at an animal research facility were criminally charged with animal abuse for disrespecting the

[125] Snowdon, Kathryn, "Animals in Spanish Town of Trigueros Del Valle Given Same Rights as Humans", *The Huffington Post UK*, July 23, 2015.

[126] Messenger, Stephen, "Judge Declares Chimp Has Rights And Must be Freed From Zoo", *The Dodo*, November 4, 2016; *see also*, "In Historic Ruling, Judge Rules That Chimps Have Rights! Frees One From Zoo! Jane Goodall Gets Hug", *Daily Kos*, September 2, 2017.

[127] Id.

[128] Court of the Administrative Litigation, Taxation and Consumer Affairs, Court No. 4, Case file A2174-2015/0, "Association of civil servants and attorneys for animal rights and others versus the Government of the City of Buenos Aires concerning refuge", resolved October 21, 2015; *see generally*, Roman, Valeria, "Argentina Grants an Orangutan Human-Like Rights", *Scientific American*, January 9, 2015; *see also*, Gimenez, Emiliano. "Argentine orangutan granted unprecedented legal rights", *CNN*, January 4, 2015.

[129] Court of First Instance in Criminal, Juvenile, Felony and Misdemeanor Matters No. 3, Case No. 149744/2022-0, "Ledesma, Diego Alberto Chamber 1 – Animal Protection Act, Abuse or Acts of Cruelty", decided July 6, 2022.

[130] Eisenbud, Daniel, "Judge blocks new neighborhood next to Biblical Zoo over animal welfare", *The Jerusalem Post*, April 24, 2017; *see also*, TOI Staff, "Court scraps plan for new neighborhood next to Jerusalem zoo", *The Times of Israel*, April 22, 2017.

dogs' ethology by never allowing the dogs outside and not having a common area for socialization.[131] The Italian Supreme Court later upheld the animal cruelty convictions.[132]

In 2017, Italy's Supreme Court ruled that keeping crustaceans, such as lobsters, on ice in restaurant kitchens is a crime of mistreatment (i.e., animal cruelty) because it causes unjustifiable suffering before death.[133] In 2018, Switzerland banned the boiling of conscious lobsters based on studies that suggest that lobsters are sentient creatures who can experience pain.[134] A recent U.K. report concluded that all cephalopod molluscs and decapod crustaceans, including octopuses, lobsters and crabs, are sentient for purposes of UK law.[135] These reforms are establishing the groundwork for legislation worldwide.

Internationally, experts are advocating for a higher ethical and legal status for animals. Experts in the fields of animal behavior, conservation and philosophy are advocating for A Declaration of Rights for Cetaceans that recognizes the intelligence of dolphins and whales.[136] Dolphins are highly intelligent animals who have developed the ability to use "echolocation" (sonar), which allows them to "see" using sound.[137] Dolphins have been observed to be clever problem-solvers who demonstrate self-awareness and display emotions, such as grief and joy.[138] India's Ministry of Environment and Forests agrees that research has established that cetaceans are such

[131] Margottini, Laura, "Jail sentences for staff of Italian dog breeding facility", *Science*, January 26, 2015.

[132] Ibid.

[133] Campanaro, Carla, "Crustaceans as sentient beings and their mistreatment. Sentence n. 30,177/2017 of the Third Criminal Section of Italian Supreme Court", *Derecho Animal Forum of Animal Law Studies*, August 2017. https://doi.org/10.5565/rev/da.56. ISSN 2462-7518; *see also*, Reuters Staff, "Italian court says lobsters must not catch cold before cooking", *Reuters*, June 16, 2017.

[134] *See generally*, Street, Francesca, "Switzerland bans boiling lobsters alive", *CNN*, January 12, 2018; *see also*, Karen Weintraub, "The Swiss Consider the Lobster. It Feels Pain, They Decide," *New York Times*, January 12, 2018.

[135] Birch, Jonathan, et al., "Review of the Evidence of Sentience in Cephalopod Molluscs and Decapod Crustaceans", *London School of Economics and Political Science*, November 2021.

[136] "Declaration of Rights for Cetaceans: Whales and Dolphins", dated May 22, 2010, at https://www.cetaceanrights.org/

[137] *See generally*, Wei, Chong, et al., "Possible limitations on dolphin echolocation: a simulation study based on a cross-model matching experiment", *Scientific Reports*, 11, 6689 (2021). https://doi.org/10.1038/s441598-021-85063-2

[138] "How Intelligent are Whales and Dolphins", *Whale and Dolphin Conservation, Inc.*, n.d., at https://us.whales.org/whales-dolphins/how-intelligent-are-whales-and-dolphins/

highly intelligent and sensitive creatures that they should be recognized as 'non-human persons' with their own specific rights.[139]

The body of scientific research that confirms the emotional and feeling world of animals is growing. Elephants are known to gather and mourn the death of another elephant.[140] Rats have been found to forego tempting treats in order to assist another rat in a trap.[141] Dogs have been known to save newborn babies.[142] We are likely only at the beginning of the scientific journey that will reveal the full extent of emotional and intelligent life in the animal kingdom.[143] The study of animal communication is also growing, and we are only beginning to understand the ways in which animals communicate. We certainly share much more with the animal kingdom than previously thought. Legal systems that treat animals as "property" fail to recognize the rapidly developing science that time and again confirms the extraordinary intelligence and capabilities of other species.

The United States is out of step with the growing number of countries that recognize animal sentience. Major organizations, such as the American Veterinary Medical Association and the Canadian Veterinary Medical Association, recognize that animals are capable of experiencing positive and negative physical and emotional states, including pleasure, comfort, pain, fear and frustration.[144] Encouragingly, there are positive developments at the state and local level. Oregon formally recognizes that "[a]nimals are sentient beings capable of experiencing pain, stress and fear."[145] Oregon's Supreme Court had previously recognized that animals

[139] Coelho, Saroja, "Dolphin protection", *DW Made for minds*, May 24, 2013.

[140] Robinson, Julian, "Final farewell of the herd: 400 elephants gather to pay last respects to their leader after he is killed by a rival, and even caress his corpse to say goodbye", *Daily Mail*, September 18, 2018.

[141] Greenfieldboyce, Nell, "Cagebreak! Rats Will Work to Free a Trapped Pal", *NPR*, December 8, 2011.

[142] *See,* e.g., Shoaib, Alia, "A stray dog rescued an abandoned newborn baby girl that was left to die in a trash bag, a report says", *Insider*, July 22, 2023.

[143] Recent studies suggest that even fish may have the capacity for mirror self-recognition, which has implications for self-awareness. *See* e.g., Kohda, Masanori, et al., "Cleaner fish recognize self in a mirror via self-face recognition like humans", *PNAS,* February 6, 2023. https://doi.org/10.1073/pnas.2208420120. *See also*, "This fish knows its own face in a mirror", *Nature*, 614,393 (2023). https://doi.org/10.1038/d41586-023-00352-2

[144] American Veterinary Medical Association, "Joint AVMA-FVE-CVMA statement on the roles of veterinarians" in promoting animal welfare", n.d., at www.avma.org/resources-tools/avma-policies/joint-avma-fve-cvma-roles-veterinarians-promoting-animal-welfare

[145] Oregon Rev. Stat §167.305 (2021), finding that "[a]nimals are sentient beings capable of experiencing pain, stress and fear".

can be "victims" for statutory purposes,[146] notwithstanding their classification as "property" for state law purposes and the fact that property cannot have "victim" status. Alaska broke further legal ground when it became the first state to enact a law that requires the "well-being" of animal companions to be taken into consideration in divorce proceedings.[147] Legislation has been introduced in New York City to recognize "that animals are sentient beings entitled to respect and consideration".[148] These reforms reflect growing public awareness in the United States that animals are emotional beings. Few Americans would disagree that kicking a dog is morally wrong, yet kicking an animal raised for food is generally tolerated by the legal system. Animals raised for food feel pain and experience fear as much as companion animals do, but industries drape institutionalized cruelty with the cloth of normalcy and contain it behind closed doors, where it remains off the radar of the public and lawmakers. Enshrining animal sentience into law would not only bring laws in the United States in alignment with developing international norms, it would bring to the forefront the disparate treatment of equally sentient species. English philosopher, Jeremy Bentham, understood that, in time, laws would afford animals the appropriate protection, predicting that "[t]he time will come when humanity will extend its mantle over everything which breathes."[149]

Legal Personhood

The greatest legal challenge that animals face today is overcoming their classification as "property" under the law. The classification is important because only legal persons can have rights. In the United States, legal persons include people (a natural person) and nonhuman entities (e.g.,

[146] The defendant, who was charged with the neglect of 20 horses, argued that the horses could not be victims for purposes of sentencing because horses were not legal persons. The court disagreed. *See*, State of Oregon v. Arnold Weldon NIX, 334 P.3d 437 (Or. 2014), holding that animals can be victims for purposes of ORS 161.067(2).

[147] Laws of Alaska (2016), An Act Relating to cruelty to animals; relating to the seizure of animals; relating to the destruction of animals; relating to the costs of care of animals that have been seized; relating to the inclusion of animals in protective orders and crimes and arrests for violating those protective orders; and relating to the ownership of animals upon divorce or dissolution of marriage, §§19-20. CSHB 147 (JUD).

[148] New York City Council Resolution 260, introduced by council member Carlina Rivera.

[149] Bentham, 282-83n.

partnerships and corporations). Some may question why "rights" should be afforded to animals when animal welfare laws exist. Similar questions were raised by anti-suffragists in the early twentieth century, who argued against affording rights to women on matters involving property, money and voting. Recognizing the rights of animals would provide "a sphere of action protected from intrusion of others."[150] Recognizing animals as legal persons under the law, either by legislation or court decisions, would ensure that the rights of animals under existing laws (e.g., Animal Welfare Act; anti-cruelty statutes) and under future laws are recognized, even as the legal system continues to evolve.[151]

Some international courts and jurisdictions view animals as worthy of a better legal classification, such as "living beings" or "legal persons." In the Netherlands, the civil code states that, "[a]nimals are not things."[152] In 2018, Luxembourg declared that, "animals are no longer considered as a thing, but as gifted non-human living beings with sensitivity and holders of certain rights."[153] In 2021, Turkey strengthened its laws to recognize animals as "living creatures" instead of "products."[154] The spokesperson for Turkey's ruling Justice and Development Party declared the law to be "more appropriate to our values, contemporary values and the demands of citizens and non-governmental organizations."[155] Switzerland recognizes

[150] In the Matter of Nonhuman Rights Project, Inc. & c., v. James J. Breheny, & c., et al., No. 52, State of New York Court of Appeals, June 14, 2022, dissenting Judge Wilson at 13.

[151] Common law is a body of laws (i.e., case law) developed by courts that is based on legal precedents (i.e., prior history of judicial decisions), as informed by evolving constitutional interpretations. For instance, the Supreme Court ruled in 2015 that same-sex couples have the fundament right to marry on the same terms as opposite-sex couples under the Equal Protection and Due Process Clauses of the U.S. Constitution. *See*, Obergefell v. Hodges, 576 U.S. 644 (2015).

[152] Dutch Civil Code, Title 3.1, Art. 3:2a (Animals).

[153] "Luxembourg 10th European Country to Ban Fur Farming", *Fur Free Alliance*, June 15, 2018.

[154] "Turkish parliament approves long-awaited animal rights bill", *Daily Sabah*, July 9, 2021, quoting Mahir Unal, deputy parliamentary group chair of the Justice and Development Party.

[155] Ankara, "Parliament to adopt animal protection law: AKP spokesperson." June 8, 2021.

the "dignity" of animals in its constitution and in its Animal Protection Act and it has not viewed animals as objects under the law since 2003.[156]

Two High Courts in India, the Uttarakhand High Court and the High Court of Punjab & Haryana at Chandigarh, have declared the entire animal kingdom, including avian and aquatic species, to be "legal entities having a distinct persona with corresponding rights, duties and liabilities of a living person."[157] In his decision, Justice Rajiv Sharma proclaimed that "[w]e have to show compassion towards all living creatures. Animals may be mute but we as a society have to speak on their behalf."[158] India's Supreme Court has recognized that the constitution protects both humans and other species, including animal life, noting that, "[e]very species has a right to life and security, subject to the law of the land." With respect to animal life, the high court declared that, "'life' means something more than mere survival or existence or instrumental value for human-beings"; rather, it means the right "to lead a life with some intrinsic worth, honour and dignity."[159]

In 2020, the Islamabad High Court of Pakistan affirmed "without any hesitation" the rights of nonhuman animals and ordered the release of Kaavan, an Asian elephant held in solitary confinement at the Marghazar Zoo to a sanctuary.[160] The court acknowledged the cruelty inflicted on Kaavan that subjected him "to unimaginable pain and suffering for the past three decades" and ruled that Kaavan must be relocated "to an

[156] Michel, Margot and Kayasseh, Eveline S., "The Legal Situation of Animals in Switzerland: Two Steps Forward, One Step Back – Many Steps to Go", *Journal of Animal Law*, Vol. VII (2011).

[157] Citizens were also declared to be "persons in loco parentis as the human face for the welfare/protection of animals." *See*, Narayan Dutt Bhatt v. Union of India and Others. Writ Petition (PIL) No. 43 of 2014, Uttarakhand High Court; *see also*, Karnail Singh and others vs State of Haryana, High Court of Punjab & Haryana at Chandigarh, CRR-533-2013 (May 31, 2019), at p. 104; *see generally*, Press Release, "India Court Declares Legal Rights of Entire Animal Kingdom", *Community Environmental Legal Defense Fund,* dated July 6, 2018.

[158] Karnail Singh and others vs State of Haryana, High Court of Punjab & Haryana at Chandigarh, CRR-533-2013 (May 31, 2019), at §78.

[159] The case also acknowledges that species may be deprived of life "out of human necessity." *See*, Animal Welfare Board Of India v. A. Nagaraja & Ors, The Supreme Court of India, Civil Appellate Jurisdiction, Civil Appeal No. 5387 of 2014 (@ Special Leave Petition (Civil) No. 11686 of 2007), at ¶ 62 (May 7, 2014).

[160] Judgment Sheet, In The Islamabad High Court, Islamabad (Judicial Department), *Islamabad Wildlife Management Board through its Chairman* Versus *Metropolitan Corporation Islamabad through its Mayors & 4 other*, W.P. No. 1155/2019, April 25, 2020.

appropriate elephant sanctuary, in or outside the country."[161] In the opinion, Justice Athar Minallah asked, "Do the animals have legal rights?", answering that "The answer to this question, without any hesitation, is in the affirmative."[162] There is clear evolution in legal systems to recognize the rights of animals.

In Argentina[163] and Columbia,[164] courts have recognized the right of habeas corpus to free animals in captivity, which requires that an animal be recognized as a legal person under the law. In Argentina, a court recognized a chimpanzee named Cecilia as a "nonhuman legal person," with rights to freedom of movement and a decent life, and ordered her transfer to a sanctuary.[165] Like many captive animals, Cecilia lived in isolation in deplorable conditions: a small barren concrete cage exposed to the elements with sad drawings of trees and bushes on the cement walls. In noting the 99.4% genetic identity with humans, the judge said "[t]o classify animals as things is not a correct standard. The essential nature of things is to be inanimate objects in contrast with a living being."[166] In ruling in favor of Cecilia's rights, the judge reminded us that "societies evolve in their moral conducts, thoughts, and values, and also in its legislations" and said that "it is not Cecilia who will owe us; it is us who will have to thank her for giving us the opportunity to grow as a group and to feel a little more human."[167]

In Colombia, a court granted habeas corpus to Chucho, an Andean spectacled bear, who had been transferred to a zoo after living 18 years on the more "free" Rio Blanco Reserve .[168] In ordering the release of Chucho from the zoo to "an area that better suits his habitat" and ideally back to

[161] Id., at 62.

[162] Id., at 59.

[163] Tercer Juzgado de Garantias de Mendoza, November 3, 2016,, "Presented by A.F.A.D.A. About The Chimpanzee 'Cecilia' – Non Human Individual", File No. P-72.254/15, November 3, 2016.

[164] Republic of Colombia Supreme Court (Civil Cassation Chamber), AHC4806–2017 (Establishment N 17001-22-13-000-2017-00468-02) (Habeas corpus filed by Luis Domingo Gomez Maldonado on behalf of Chucho), July 26, 2017.

[165] Tercer Juzgado de Garantias de Mendoza, "Presented by A.F.A.D.A. About The Chimpanzee 'Cecilia' – Non Human Individual", File No. P-72.254/15, November 3, 2016.

[166] Id.

[167] Id.

[168] Habeas corpus is a writ that is filed with a court to secure the release of an individual who has been arrested or detained (unless there are lawful grounds for detention).

the Rio Blanco Reserve, the Court said that "[s]ince nonhuman animals are sentient beings capable of suffering, they must be holders of rights", including the right to freedom and the right "to live a natural life, to prosper with the least possible pain ...in a responsibly preserved habitat in the biotic chain."[169] The judge explained that the point of recognizing Chucho's rights is "to include within the chain of life a universal morality, a public ecological global order and, in virtue of the interdependency and interaction that prevail between humans and nature, conferring to animals the safeguard they deserve against the irrational efforts of contemporary mankind to destroy our habitat."[170]

Except for a few dissenting judges, courts in the United States have not been as forward thinking in applying habeas corpus to captive animals. The Nonhuman Rights Project, founded by Steven M. Weiss, Esq., is the only civil rights organization in the United States that is dedicated to securing fundamental legal rights for nonhuman animals, including the right to liberty and the right to bodily integrity.[171] In landmark lawsuits, the Nonhuman Rights Project has argued that chimpanzees and elephants should be recognized as legal persons who are entitled to habeas corpus proceedings. The organization filed a writ of habeas corpus on behalf of Happy, an elephant held captive at the Bronx Zoo,[172] arguing for her release and transfer to a much more suitable elephant sanctuary. The case went all the way to the highest court in New York. While the court recognized that Happy is an "autonomous and extraordinarily cognitively complex being," it denied Happy legal recognition under the law.[173] The case demonstrates why recognized legal personhood and rights are necessary. Even though the zoo was in compliance with federal and state statutes governing elephant care, experts provided clear evidence that conditions

[169] Republic of Colombia Supreme Court (Civil Cassation Chamber), AHC4806-2017 (Establishment N 17001-22-13-000-2017-00468-02) (Habeas corpus filed by Luis Domingo Gomez Maldonado on behalf of Chucho), July 26, 2017.

[170] Republic of Colombia Supreme Court (Civil Cassation Chamber), AHC4806–2017 (Establishment N 17001-22-13-000-2017-00468-02) (Habeas corpus filed by Luis Domingo Gomez Maldonado on behalf of Chucho), July 26, 2017, at 2.4.4.

[171] *See*, "A unique and vital mission", *Nonhuman Rights Project*, at https://www.nonhumanrights.org/

[172] Happy was captured as a baby, likely in Thailand. For more on Happy's background, *see* "First elephant to pass mirror self-recognition test; held alone at Bronx Zoo", *Nonhuman Rights Project*, n.d., at https://www.nonhumanrights.org/client-happy/#

[173] In the Matter of Nonhuman Rights Project, Inc. & c., v. James J. Breheny, & c., et al., No. 52, State of New York Court of Appeals, June 14, 2022, dissenting Judge Wilson at 3.

at the zoo were inadequate for Happy. The examination of the scientific evidence and the specific circumstances of highly intelligent and sentient captive animals by a court would be a much fairer and more just result.

The grounds for the court's decision were rejected by dissenting Judge Wilson, who pointed out that the writ has been used historically to free slaves, who were treated as "chattel" under the law, and to free women and children, who lacked any legal status.[174] Judge Wilson admonished the majority, arguing that "as with our society's changed understanding of the rights of enslaved persons, women and children, our understanding of the cognitive and emotional makeup, needs and capabilities of elephants is far different than it was in bygone times."[175] With respect to the majority's reluctance to take up such a "novel" habeas corpus case, Judge Wilson responded that "a novel habeas case freed an enslaved person; a novel habeas case removed a woman from the subjugation of her husband; a novel habeas corpus removed a child from her father's presumptive dominion." Habeas corpus wasused in direct conflict with the Supreme Court's decision in Dred Scottv. Stanford[176] to free enslaved individuals.[177] In Judge Wilson's view, habeas corpus is "a tool for society to challenge confinement, construed broadly, and can document and raise awareness of injustices that may warrant legislative, policy, or social solutions", including the "strictly property-based view of animals", which he noted has been "greatly eroded" over the past two centuries.[178] The majority seemed more concerned with the implications that the case would have for other animals (the "slippery slope" concern),[179] rather than focusing on the specific rights of Happy. Similar "slippery slope" concerns were voiced by anti-suffragists in arguing against recognizing women's rights.[180]

The property classification of animals is uncomfortable for other jurists in the United States, and courts have struggled with this classification. In an animal neglect case involving a dog named Juno, who was found in "near-emaciated condition" and "eating at random things in the yard",[181]

[174] Id. at 4.

[175] Id. at 5.

[176] Dred Scott v. Stanford, 60 U.S. 393 (1856).

[177] Id. at 10 and 24-25.

[178] Id. at 36-37.

[179] Id. at 14.

[180] Willingham, A.J., "The most ridiculous historical arguments denying women the right to vote", *CNN*, August 26, 2021.

[181] State v. Newcomb, 375 P.3d 434 (Or. 2016).

the Supreme Court of Oregon acknowledged that a dog is personal property under Oregon law, but drew sharp distinctions: (i) Oregon law "limits ownership and possessory rights [for dogs] in ways that it does not for inanimate property"; (ii) Juno is "not an inanimate object or other insentient physical item of some kind"; and (iii) Oregon's laws recognize that animals "are sentient beings capable of experiencing pain, stress and fear."[182] The court said, "[a]s we continue to learn more about the interrelated nature of all life, the day may come when humans perceive less separation between themselves and other living beings than the law now reflects. However, we do not need a mirror to the past or a telescope to the future to recognize that the legal status of animals has changed and is changing still."[183]

Other courts in the United States have considered the welfare of an animal in custody despites,[184] have declared that "a pet is not just a thing but occupies a special place somewhere in between a person and a personal piece of property",[185] have stated that "modern courts have recognized that pets do not fit neatly within traditional property law principles",[186] and have bluntly stated that "we are uncomfortable with the law's cold characterization of a dog as mere 'property'".[187] One scholar advocates for a fourth category of property, "living property," whereby some animals will have more protective legal rights, with legal duties owed by humans to "living property" that can be enforced by a court.[188] This new property status would afford animals certain rights, such as (1) the right not to be harmed, (2) the right to have living space, (3) the right to be cared for, and (4) the right not to be held for or used for prohibited uses,[189] but the ethical and practical implications of the law treating animals as "property" would remain.

Affording legal personhood status to animals will require either a legislative change (most likely to occur at the state level) or a court decision.

[182] Id.

[183] Id.

[184] *See*, e.g., Champagne v. Higgins (R.I. Superior Court, December 16, 2016).

[185] Corso v. Crawford Dog and Cat Hospital, Inc. (97 Misc. 2d 530 [Civ Ct, Queens County 1979]) at 531.

[186] Morgan v. Kroupa, 167 Vt. 99, 702 A2d 630 [1997]).

[187] Rabideau v. City of Racine (243 Wis2d 486, 491, 627 NW2d, 795, 798 [2001]).

[188] Favre, David., "*Living Property, A New Status for Animals Within the Legal System*". Marquette Law Review, Vol. 93, Issue 3 (2010).

[189] Id., at 1062.

Congress often passes broad, general laws, while courts determine how the law should apply in specific situations. In our common law legal system,[190] the doctrine of stare decisis[191] obligates courts to follow precedents (i.e., prior judicial rulings on the same subject) to ensure predictability and certainty in the law. Just because a law is supported by precedent, however, does not make it just. Throughout history, all three branches of the government have denied people their freedom and fundamental rights. Congress passed the Naturalization Act of 1790, which denied U.S. citizenship to slaves, free blacks and Asians, and later passed the Indian Removal Act of 1830, which legalized the removal of Native Americans to the west. President Franklin Roosevelt signed an Executive Order that permitted the internment of Japanese Americans during World War II. The Supreme Court ruled that people of African descent could not be citizens of the United States,[192] and later upheld the constitutionality of Jim Crow racial segregation laws.[193] It was not until 58 years later that the Supreme Court overturned its decision that upheld racial segregation. In the 1954 case of Brown v. Board of Education, the Court held that the "separate but equal" practice violated the Equal Protection Clause of the Fourteenth Amendment of the Constitution based on studies showing the stigmatizing effects that racial discrimination can have.[194] In doing so, the Court rejected factual assumptions underlying the Court's prior decision in Plessy v. Ferguson, which upheld the constitutionality of "separate but equal" public accommodations.[195] Where the understanding of the facts of a case changes, courts have overturned precedent. Scientific advances have fundamentally changed how we view animals. The "property" classification is based on antiquated views that animals lack sentience or awareness, and this has been proven to be inconsistent with science.

[190] The common law system is different from a civil law system, whereby very specific laws are passed and applied by courts.

[191] Stare decisis means "to stand on a decision," the legal doctrine that precedents should be followed.

[192] Dred Scott v. Sandford, 60 U.S. 393 (1856).

[193] Plessy v. Ferguson, 163 U.S. 537 (1896).

[194] Brown v. Board of Education, 347 U.S.483 (1954). The court found that segregating children based on race had a detrimental psychological impact on black children, citing "modern authority" to overturn the "separate but equal" doctrine.

[195] Plessy v. Ferguson, 163 U.S. 537, 542, 550-52 (1896).

Common law must be able to evolve to accommodate changing societal values, including changing opinions on the proper legal treatment of animals. Common law is thought to be rooted in the customs and morals of a society, but it does allow for some flexibility in that existing precedents can be challenged and replaced by new precedents as justice or a changing society requires. Whether a court adheres to a precedent "should depend heavily upon its continuing practicality and the demands of justice, rather than upon its mere tradition."[196] Courts should not follow the doctrine of stare decisis if it is "out of step with the times and the reasonable expectations of members of society."[197] A court should not consider itself bound by stare decisis "when persuaded by the 'lessons of experience and the force of better reasoning'."[198] Whether a court follows precedent "should depend upon its continuing practicality and the demands of justice."[199] Scholars have long argued that precedents that prove to be wrong should be overruled.[200] The Supreme Court of the United States has acknowledged that there are instances when precedents should be changed if society's understanding of the facts underlying a legal issue has changed.[201] Our understanding of the emotional and intelligent lives of animals has profoundly changed in recent decades, as science continues to confirm that animals share many qualities previously thought to be exclusive to humans. Throughout history, courts have re-visited precedents, and forward looking judges have set new courses where justice demands, as it now does with animals. The obsolete legal walls that we have constructed to divide humans from the animal kingdom are not just unfair and unjust,

[196] Buckley v. City of New York, 56 N.Y.2d 300, 305 (1982).

[197] People v. Hobson, 39 N.Y.2d 479, 489 (1976).

[198] People v. Bing, 76 N.Y.2d 331, 338 (1990);

[199] Buckley v. City of New York, 56 N.Y.2d 300, 305 (1982).

[200] *See,* e.g., William O. Douglas, "Stare Decisis", *Columbia Law Review*, Vol 49(6) (1949). https://doi.org/10.2307/1119147. ("A judge looking at a constitutional decision may have compulsions to revere past history and accept what was once written. But he remembers above all else that it is the Constitution which he swore to support and defend, not the gloss which his predecessors may have put on it.").

[201] *See,* e.g., Patterson v. McLean Credit Union, 491 U.S. 164, 172 (1989) ("Our precedents are not sacrosanct, for we have overruled prior decisions where the necessity and propriety of doing so has been established."); *see also*, Smith v. Allwright, 321 U.S. 649, 665 (1944) ("when convinced of former error, this Court has never felt constrained to follow precedents. In constitutional questions, where correction depends upon amendment and not upon legislative action this Court throughout its history has freely exercised its power to reexamine the basis of its constitutional decisions").

they are counter to the natural progression of recognizing the dignity and rights of all life, and often contrary to our own interests.

Courts in the United States are guided by the "evolving standards of decency that mark the progress of a maturing society."[202] In that regard, courts take into account the legal views expressed by other nations to support their decisions.[203] Reliance on foreign precedents is not new. Supreme Court Justice, Joseph Story, relied on English law in American patent cases more than 200 years ago,[204] and the Supreme Court cited the "overwhelming weight of international opinion" in deciding a death penalty case and did not hesitate to point out that the United States was an outlier on the issue.[205] The Supreme Court has also cited decisions by the European Court of Human Rights in striking down a Texas law that criminalized sexual relations between two individuals of the same sex.[206] The Supreme Court has also cited an Amicus Curiae brief from the European Union for the determination that "within the world community, the imposition of the death penalty for crimes committed by mentally retarded offenders is overwhelmingly disapproved."[207] Other common law countries, such as Great Britain, Canada, India, Israel, New Zealand and South Africa, consider foreign precedent when analyzing national laws or adjudicating a case.[208]

Former justices of the Supreme Court have confirmed that foreign laws are taken into account in decisions. Justice Stephen Breyer (1994–2022), acknowledged that the laws of other nations have a bearing on United States law, citing the "forces of globalism, internationalism, and interdependence among nations recently" that require "[l]awyers, legislators, and judges to … look beyond their own shores to answer questions of local

[202] Trop v. Dulles, 356 U.S. 86 (1958).

[203] *See*, e.g., Thompson v. Oklahoma, 487 U.S. 815, 830 & footnotes 31 and 34 (1988) (recognizing that laws, judicial practice, and statistics of other countries can be used as guidelines in a court's decision making); *see also*, William Wayne Thompson v. Oklahoma, 487 U.S. 815 (1988).

[204] *See*, e.g., Evans v. Eaton, 20 U.S. 356 (1822).

[205] The court noted that the U.S. "is the only country in the world that continues to give official sanction to the juvenile [death] penalty." *See*, Roper v. Simmons, 543 U.S. 551, 575 (2005).

[206] Lawrence v. Texas, 539 U.S. 558 (2003).

[207] Atkins v. Virginia, 536 U.S. 304 (2002).

[208] Roudik, Peter, "The Impact of Foreign Law on Domestic Judgments: Comparative Summary", *Library of Congress Legal Reports*, March 2020.

law."[209] Justice Sandra Day O'Connor (1981–2006) believed that "[i]n the next century, we are going to want to draw upon judgments from other jurisdictions. We are going to be more inclined to look at the decisions of [the] European court—and perhaps use them and cite them."[210] Justice Antonin Scalia (1986–2016) acknowledged that "[t]he reality is that I use foreign law more than anyone on the Court."[211] Former Justice Ruth Bader Ginsburg (1993–2020) confirmed that, "our island or lone ranger mentality is beginning to change" with Supreme Court Justices "becoming more open to comparative and international law perspectives."[212] Justice Ginsburg told American lawyers and judges that, "your perspective on constitutional law should encompass the world" because "[w]e are losers if we do not both share our experiences with and learn from others."[213]

At the heart of these statements is the acknowledgment that, in cases involving deep moral considerations, it is appropriate to look beyond the borders of the United States to the laws of other nations.

When legal scholars and judges do look abroad, they will see that the international legal landscape has dramatically changed, with a growing number of nations recognizing animal dignity and legal rights. Worldwide, courts have decried how humans treat animals, resulting in evolving legal norms and jurisprudence. One Colombian court stressed that "insofar as they are part of nature, nonhuman sentient beings contribute to the ecological balance that enables the survival of mankind" and that we must recognize and assign "rights and legal identity to nonhuman animals, so that we might put an end … to the irrational destruction of our planet and

[209] Breyer, Stephen, "America's Courts Can't Ignore the World", *The Atlantic*, October 2018.

[210] New York University, "European Court Members and U.S. Supreme Justices", *News Wise*, April 11, 2000, quoting Justice Sandra Day O'Connor.

[211] Antonin Scalia. Keynote Address at the American Enterprise Institute Conference: Outsourcing of American Law, February 21, 2006. Video at https://www.c-span.org/video/?191294-3/role-international-law. However, Justice Scalia has rejected the argument that U.S. law should conform to foreign laws. *See*, Roper v. Simmons, 543 U.S. 551, 622-28 (2005) (Scalia dissenting in part on the majority's reliance on foreign practices).

[212] Markels, James N., "Justice Ginsburg's Foreign Law", *America's Future*, August 11, 2003.

[213] Id.

of nature that shamefully and tragically afflicts the present generation."[214] The emerging laws and decisions aim to protect animals from the misery and suffering imposed by mankind. In recognizing the natural rights of animals, nations are recognizing their right to be free, their right to engage in natural behaviors, their right to enjoy their own habitats, and their right to bodily integrity.

Arguments against recognizing legal rights of animals are flawed (e.g., animals lack sentience; there are no food or clothing alternatives) or fail to justify our continued exploitation of sentient animals (e.g., it would inconvenience humans; it will cost money). Ultimately, the greatest impact of affording animals legal rights would be a personal one. It would force each of us to consider why humanity inflicts such tremendous suffering on animals and how our own actions contribute to that suffering. It may call into question beliefs that we have held our entire life, and it will certainly cause us to re-examine our actions. As theologian and philosopher, Albert Schweitzer (1875–1965), said: "[w]e must fight against the spirit of unconscious cruelty with which we treat the animals. Animals suffer as much as we do. True humanity does not allow us to impose such sufferings on them. It is our duty to make the whole world recognize it." Animals are not products, commodities, or goods. As biologist Marc Bekoff describes, they are "splendid beings in their own right, who have evolved alongside us as co-inheritors of all the beauty and abundance of life on this planet."[215] Justice demands that they be recognized under scientifically informed laws and one day they will be. As this book goes to print, the first city in the United States, Ojai, California, has recognized certain legal rights of elephants held in captivity.[216]

[214] Republic of Colombia Supreme Court (Civil Cassation Chamber), AHC4806-2017 (Establishment N 17001-22-13-000-2017-00468-02) (Habeas corpus filed by Luis Domingo Gomez Maldonado on behalf of Chucho), July 26, 2017.

[215] Marc Bekoff, *Animals Matter: A Biologist Explains Why We Should Treat Animals with Compassion and Respect"*, Boston, Shambhala Publications, 2007. ISBN: 978-1-59030-522-5.

[216] An Ordinance of the City Council of the City of Ojai, California, adding Article 10 – Right to Bodily Liberty for Elephants to Chapter 4 –- Animals of Title 5 – Sanitation and Health of the Ojai Municipal Code (September 26, 2023).

CHAPTER 8

Concluding Remarks

There is nothing more powerful than an idea whose time has come.
—Victor Hugo

The past few decades have been a watershed moment for the legal status of animals. New laws are being enacted by nations around the globe in response to humanity's growing understanding of the interconnectedness of our world and the animal kingdom. These reforms are building the foundation for more promising change. As this book has described, there are many grounds upon which the case for the legal protection of animals can be made. The strongest argument is that laws should recognize and respect the innate rights of any intelligent, social, or sentient being. Just as certain human rights are universal, regardless of nationality, ethnicity, sex, color, religion or any other status, certain rights are also fundamental for animals, including the right to bodily integrity and the right to be free. This is true regardless of species, status in society, or any other construct we choose to impose on the animal kingdom. These rights exist, even if current laws fail to recognize them, and even if laws sanction the violation of these rights.

Humanity's shameful treatment of animals has been criticized throughout time. One Argentinian judge decried that "animals are involuntary

K. C. Moore, *The Case for the Legal Protection of Animals*, The Palgrave Macmillan Animal Ethics Series,
https://doi.org/10.1007/978-3-031-46065-4_8

actors in the theater of human law" and ruled that animals are "non human legal persons" with inalienable rights to live in their habitat and to be free.[1] This perspective is fueling the movement to reform laws that so callously disregard the suffering of animals. Humanity values freedom as a core value and science now tells us that this value is not unique to humans. All living beings yearn for freedom, yet our laws allow the confinement, abuse, torture, killing, and commodification of all other species. The extent to which we exploit and kill animals is so pervasive that it touches nearly every industry on earth. Powerful industries and well-funded corporate interests support politicians and decision-makers, who in turn support powerful industries and corporate interests, creating a vicious circle of corruption that has had profound consequences for humanity. Industries that exploit animals cite religion, tradition, culture, livelihoods and values to justify their cruel practices. They spend billions of marketing dollars in an effort to sanitize their treatment of animals. They spread misinformation. They donate to politicians who support laws, rules and policies that fight reforms and criminalize whistleblowing. They warn of the dire consequences of affording animals rights, but an awakening public is increasingly seeing through the smokescreen. A better informed public is learning to disregard humane-washing and to forego products that are bad for consumers, the environment, and animals. Behaviors that, in past years, would not have raised an eyebrow, such as elephant rides and animal "tricks", now draw sharp public criticism.

Scientific advances are compelling grounds for building legal systems that recognize each animal's intrinsic value and for laws that empower and protect all animals. Science has confirmed, without any doubt, that animals are sentient beings. Science tells us that each animal is an individual, with his or her own personality and emotional traits that are formed from his or her own life experiences, intellect, and abilities. Science supports what many already understand … that each animal deserves just laws that respect his or her innate rights. Recognizing legal rights for just a limited group of animals, such as companion animals, would be like recognizing human rights for just a limited group of people. Finnish legal scholars have adopted guiding principles for animal law, including the *Principal of Precaution*, which would require that all animals be considered as sentient absent

[1]Tercer Juzgado de Garantias de Mendoza, "Presented by A.F.A.D.A. About The Chimpanzee 'Cecilia' – Non Human Individual", File No. P-72.254/15, November 3, 2016.

evidence to the contrary.[2] This principal demands that legal systems respect all animals as unique beings, each worthy of legal rights and protections, not because of any purported commercial value, but because they each have value and worth in their own right.

In truth, every legal system on earth fails animals, some more than others. We see battered bodies and broken spirits in every country. The screams and cries are heard from every nation. They are screams and cries for justice, but without meaningful laws, there can be no justice for animals. Recent reforms are just the beginning of what will, in time, be a more inclusive and equitable legal system. The tree of justice will, one day, provide legal protection for all animals, and the fruits of that tree will, someday, be shared with every sentient being.

Human rights and animal rights are deeply connected, each championing the respect and dignity of the individual and each reinforcing the other. It is no coincidence that in areas where animals are abused, humans are abused as well. Laws must be passed that both lift up and empower people and their communities if we are to lift up and empower animals. We see this clearly with wildlife trafficking, which victimizes the poorest, most desperate people and the most vulnerable animals. Poachers risk their lives because they are fighting extreme poverty.[3] The billions of dollars that are made from wildlife trafficking do not benefit low-level poachers or their communities. Instead, profits are used by international criminal networks to fund other illegal enterprises that cause further havoc for humanity. To help reduce the lure of illicit trafficking, the United Nations has called on Member States to assist local communities around the world in finding alternate ways to make a living.[4] A more enlightened society would protect its weakest, whether it be human or animal. It would also build opportunities in impoverished communities for the benefit of both people and animals and for generations to come.

Legal systems are increasingly viewing humans and animals as co-inhabitants of our great earth, with shared desires and destinies. Implicit in recent legal reforms is an acknowledgment that our interests are aligned with animals, and the profound realization that we all face the same

[2] Wahlberg, Birgitta, "Animal Law in General and Animal Rights in Particular", *Scandinavian Studies in Law*, vol. 67, at 13–34, at https://scandinavianlaw.se/pdf/67-1.pdf

[3] *See*, "Impact of Extreme Poverty on Elephants and Rhinos", *The Borgen Project*, n.d., at https://borgenproject.org/extreme-poverty-on-elephants-and-rhinos/

[4] United Nations General Assembly Resolution 75/311.

planetary emergencies, including climate change, loss of biodiversity and species extinctions. These global threats are a threat to all life on the planet. Loss of biodiversity is unchallenged and accelerating, climate change is fueling destructive weather events, and our planet and its inhabitants are in crisis, but it does not have to be this way. We can save ourselves and future generations to come but this will require that we recognize the fragility of our planet and accept that our future is interconnected and interdependent with the natural world. This will require that we examine our outdated laws that are leading to such catastrophic consequences.

In *A New Earth,* Eckhart Tolle wrote of a growing awareness of social justice, fairness, and equality, where discrimination against our fellow humans and the stifling grip of patriarchy are, for an increasing number of us, becoming vestiges of the past. Tolle described an increasing recognition of our interconnectedness with animals and the planet, which is giving rise to compassion and empathy toward others.[5] It is this awareness of "oneness" that is inspiring legal scholars from all over the world to change how we treat animals. It is this understanding of our connection with all life on the planet, and the challenges that all life on the planet face, that led to a 2022 United Nations Resolution, recognizing that the health and welfare of humans are connected to the health and wellbeing of animals.[6]

Perhaps this growing empathy is due to our close proximity, historically, to the era when some people were considered "property." Or, perhaps it is owing to the scientific advances that show how much we share with the social and emotional lives of animals. We now understand that violence associated with animal cruelty destroys families, just as the violence associated with industrialized animal agriculture harms workers and destabilizes communities. The primary goal of any legal system should be to prevent cruelty and suffering; but to prevent cruelty and suffering, we must reform existing laws that are having such catastrophic consequences for humanity.

As Colombia's Supreme Court observed, animals "have been submitted to the assaults of the conquering and arbitrary man" for too long.[7] The

[5] Eckhart Tolle, *A New Earth: Awakening to your Life's Purpose",* New York, New York, Penguin Books (Reprint Ed), January 30, 2008, at xv. ISBN-13: 978-0452289963.

[6] UNEP, EA.5/Res. 1, Nairobi (hybrid), 22 and 23 February 2021 and 28 February – 2 March 2022.

[7] Republic of Colombia Supreme Court (Civil Cassation Chamber), AHC4806–2017 (Establishment N 17001-22-13-000-2017-00468-02) (Habeas corpus filed by Luis Domingo Gomez Maldonado on behalf of Chucho), July 26, 2017, at 2.4.4.

worst of humanity is in plain view for the world to see: the plundering of natural resources; the destruction of delicate habitats and ecosystems; the disruption of migration and wildlife routes; the waste of precious water resources; and the slaughter of sentient creatures, all without any consideration of the consequences of our actions. We can do better. As Pope Francis said, while humans can exhibit the worst behaviors, they have the ability to rise above their own interests and to choose what is good.[8] Prioritizing meaningful laws to protect the splendid fabric of the planet's ecosystems is good. Enacting strong and effective laws to protect biodiversity and all of the earth's inhabitants is good. Repairing humanity's broken relationship with animals is good.

Despite the impressive number of positive changes on the legal front, legal reform can at times seem achingly slow but there is reason for optimism. The pace of reforms has picked up in recent decades. The global movement to end animal exploitation and suffering is gaining traction faster than prior rights movements.[9] Changing societal attitudes toward animals are driving legal reforms across the globe. Animals have three enemies: those who are cruel, those who are ignorant, and those who are indifferent, and laws are being enacted to address each one of these. Significantly, ground-breaking legal reforms are recognizing that animals should be protected as sentient beings.

The legal system in the United States must evolve and keep pace with the exciting developments around the globe. The goal must be to welcome all animals under the umbrella of protection of the legal system in a meaningful and substantive way. The legal system in the United States will, one day, recognize basic, fundamental rights for all animals. By grace and humility, may that day come soon, for ours is a shared destiny.

[8] *See*, Encyclical Letter *Laudato Si'* of the Holy Father Francis On Care For Our Common Home, §205.

[9] This is in part due to social media. For more on the impact of social media, see chapter 3.

Index[1]

[1] Note: Page numbers followed by 'n' refer to notes.

K. C. Moore, *The Case for the Legal Protection of Animals*, The Palgrave Macmillan Animal Ethics Series,
https://doi.org/10.1007/978-3-031-46065-4

V

SPRINGER NATURE

GPSR Compliance

The European Union's (EU) General Product Safety Regulation (GPSR) is a set of rules that requires consumer products to be safe and our obligations to ensure this.

If you have any concerns about our products, you can contact us on ProductSafety@springernature.com

In case Publisher is established outside the EU, the EU authorized representative is:

Springer Nature Customer Service Center GmbH
Europaplatz 3
69115 Heidelberg, Germany

The manufacturer's authorised representative in the EU is Springer
Nature Customer Service Centre GmbH, Europaplatz 3, 69115 Heidelberg,
Germany. If you have any concerns regarding our products, please
contact ProductSafety@springernature.com

Printed and bound by CPI Group (UK) Ltd, Croydon, CR0 4YY
01/10/2026
02225894-0014